THE MUSICAL PLAYGROUND

The Musical Playground

GLOBAL TRADITION AND CHANGE IN CHILDREN'S SONGS AND GAMES

Kathryn Marsh

OXFORD
UNIVERSITY PRESS
2008

OXFORD
UNIVERSITY PRESS

Oxford University Press, Inc., publishes works that further
Oxford University's objective of excellence
in research, scholarship, and education.

Oxford   New York
Auckland   Cape Town   Dar es Salaam   Hong Kong   Karachi
Kuala Lumpur   Madrid   Melbourne   Mexico City   Nairobi
New Delhi   Shanghai   Taipei   Toronto

With offices in
Argentina   Austria   Brazil   Chile   Czech Republic   France   Greece
Guatemala   Hungary   Italy   Japan   Poland   Portugal   Singapore
South Korea   Switzerland   Thailand   Turkey   Ukraine   Vietnam

Published by Oxford University Press, Inc.
198 Madison Avenue, New York, New York 10016

www.oup.com

Oxford is a registered trademark of Oxford University Press

Library of Congress Cataloging-in-Publication Data
Marsh, Kathryn McLeod.
The musical playground : global tradition and change in
children's songs and games / Kathryn Marsh
      p.   cm.
Includes bibliographical references and index.
ISBN 978-0-19-530897-6; 978-0-19-530898-3 (pbk.)
1. Musical ability in children. 2. Games with music—Analysis,
appreciation.   I. Title.
ML83.M37 2008
398.8—dc22   2008033906

Recorded video tracks (marked in text with) and appendices 5–10 are available online at
www.oup.com/us/themusicalplayground. Access with username Music3 and password Book3234.

To Beryl and Harry who started me on my journey

and Phil, Owen, and Sascha who accompanied me

➤➤ ACKNOWLEDGMENTS ◀◀

This book is based on forms of musical play collected from many children in schools in Sydney and central Australia, Norway, the United Kingdom, the United States, and Korea. For ethical reasons I am unable to name the schools or individual members of the school communities. However, I wish to acknowledge the enormous generosity of these children in sharing their games and game practices with me and to thank the principals and staff of the schools for the warmth of their welcome and support of the project from inception to publication.

My cross-cultural investigation of children's musical play would not have been possible without the ongoing assistance of a collaborative team of colleagues who made initial contact with schools or cultural groups and provided local knowledge of children's play and cultural practices both during my time in the schools and in the following years as I endeavored to organize and make sense of the enormous amount of material I had collected. My uncertainties were assuaged by daily discussion over a meal, sometimes in the comfort of my collaborators' homes, which provided a place to relax and debrief after the rigors of field activity. To Patricia Shehan Campbell, Mavis Curtis, Elizabeth Grugeon, Young-Youn Kim, Thor Gunnar Norås, and Cecilia Riddell I owe an enormous debt of gratitude. I am also appreciative of the advice, practical assistance and friendship offered by Kjersti Schibevaag, Per-Egil Vang, Torgunn Pedersen, Torunn Molde, Terje Murberg, Andrea Emberly and Chee-Hoo Lum.

My thanks are also extended to the Papulu Apparr-kari Aboriginal Language and Culture Centre at Tennant Creek for facilitating my work in central Australia and to R. N Plummer, D. D. J. Frank, K. F. Nappanangka, D. N. Dawson, L. Dixon, and E. Dixon for sharing their knowledge. Thanks also go to R. N. Plummer and Jane Simpson for Warumungu translations and advice regarding Aboriginal cultural practices. Other translations of games and related discussion were undertaken by Thor Gunnar Norås (Norwegian), Jooyeon Song and Young-Youn Kim (Korean), Mohammed Rashid (Punjabi), Noorjahan Begum (Bangla), and Clarita Derwent (Spanish).

The book has only come to fruition through the tireless work of my research assistant, Corin Bone, whose intelligence, perceptiveness, aural acuity, and ability to tame numerous computer programs has resulted in additional insights, impeccable musical transcriptions, video clips, and a vast range of databases that have allowed easy access to all the field material. Corin, I couldn't have done it without you.

In writing this book, I was fortunate to have the assistance of the editorial team at Oxford University Press. In particular, the initial guidance, responsiveness and tactful advice of Norm Hirschy helped to shape the manuscript as it moved toward completion. I also wish to acknowledge the personal support given to me during the writing process by friends and colleagues at the University of Sydney. Thanks to Linda Barwick for her continued encouragement and friendship, which extended to reading parts of the manuscript. Other colleagues who read the manuscript include Peter Dunbar-Hall and Michael Webb. They not only provided helpful comments but also tolerated my constant obsession with the book, especially in the final stages of its preparation. I am also grateful to Margo Adelson for meticulously proofreading the manuscript and to Margaret Barrett, editor of *Research Studies in Music Education*, for permitting the inclusion in the book of some textual material from my article published in the journal in 1995.

Financial support for the research was provided by a Discovery Grant from the Australian Research Council, in addition to research grants from the Australian Institute of Aboriginal and Torres Strait Islander Studies and the University of Sydney. A writing fellowship from the Research Institute for Humanities and Social Sciences at the University of Sydney assisted me to bring the book to completion.

My family has played a continuous role in the emergence of this book. I would like to thank my father and mother, Harry and Beryl Marsh for their consistent belief in me and their tireless support of my musical and academic endeavours. I also owe unending gratitude to my husband, Phil Nanlohy, without whose ongoing emotional and practical support I could not have undertaken and completed this project, and to my sons, Owen and Sascha, who, from their early childhood when I began this project, to adulthood as I finish it, continue to exemplify the importance of play and creativity in the lives of children.

⇥ CONTENTS ⇤

CONTENTS

(Appendices 5-10 are available online at www.oup.com/us/themusicalplayground.)

→ I ←
Children's Musical Play and Creativity
Adult Views

CHAPTER I

Conceptions of Children's Musical Play

Almost two decades ago I was teaching in a children's music summer school in the Australian capital city of Canberra, about three hundred kilometers distant from my usual location in Sydney. As part of the day's activities I had decided to teach a singing game, "Sar Macka Dora," that had been collected in a Sydney playground, a game that I thought would be unknown to the local children. It transpired that I was completely mistaken in this assumption. Instead of being a novelty, the game was well known by most of the children. However, the versions that they then taught me were quite different from the one that I had taught them. From the class group of seventeen children, many of whom came from different parts of the city, I recorded thirteen variants of the game, all with identifiable similarities, but with clear differences in text, music, and movement.

These multiple variants fascinated me. How, I wondered, had the game traversed the distance from Sydney to Canberra, and why was there such a variety of individual versions within a relatively small community? My quest to find the answers to these questions began in 1990 with a lengthy investigation in a Sydney school and has continued ever since. I did not realize at the time that my ongoing curiosity would lead me to explore children's musical play not only locally but in school playgrounds in many parts of the world, including Australia, the United Kingdom, Europe, the United States, and Korea.

As I begin this account of the musical play of school-aged children, a myriad of vivid images range through my mind. A group of Latino girls and boys dance around in a circle in a leafy school playground in Seattle, singing a taunting song to a "wolf" who must respond to their sung questions before racing out to catch them. In Los Angeles two African American girls perform a lively stepping routine with a chant directing their intricate body percussion patterns. In a different hemisphere a group of boys and girls in an Australian city sit in a loose circle outside the classroom passing a clap around to a rhythmic chant while waiting for their teacher to take them into class. Two Aboriginal girls in central Australia experiment with hand-clapping patterns to make a game from the sports chants they have just heard at the school sports carnival. A preadolescent boy in an expansive Norwegian school playground leaves the game of football he has been playing to join a group of girls and boys jumping a lengthy rope to a chanted count. Some girls in an English playground devise dance routines to current popular songs. Further north, in another English school, two girls, one of Pakistani and one of Bangladeshi heritage, re-enact a song and dance sequence from a Bollywood movie. Inside the rectangular playground of a large Korean school, boys and girls form two lines, chanting calls and responses before engaging in a tug of war to pull each other over a central line drawn on the gravel surface.

The musical play of children at school thus encompasses many different forms. All of these forms are owned, spontaneously performed, and orally transmitted by children and usually involve text, movement, and rhythmic elements. In this way they differ from other genres of children's playlore that feature only text (such as jokes, taunts, and riddles) or movement (such as chasing games and marbles). They may be associated with an ongoing oral tradition or derive from performance styles experienced by children within their current environment, as with the sporting cheers and dance routines that accompany popular music, in addition to more impulsive and unstructured musical utterances (Campbell, 1998).

This chapter provides a rationale for the study of children's musical play as a phenomenon and outlines a number of pertinent issues. To provide a context for this investigation, I discuss the relationship of children's playground singing games to current music education practices and review studies of children's playlore as they relate to educational and ethnomusicological thought. The chapter thus considers adult views of children's musical play and the historical and philosophical influences on their formation.

Rationale for the Study of Children's Musical Play

Forms of children's musical play, in particular, playground singing games and chants, have been influential in the formulation of twentieth-century music education practices. As a teacher I had utilized children's playground games as raw material for developing musical skills and knowledge in the classroom, but I had not really delved into the characteristics of the games I had used. How and why did children play these games when left to their own devices? What did these games mean to them? In particular, I felt that I needed to extend my understanding of contemporary features of the music, text, and movement, and their interrelationship. While a variety of performance opportunities incorporating playground games were devised for classroom use, my attention was now drawn to children's performance practices in the playground, including the context of performance, as important factors in determining the sociomusical characteristics of these genres of musical play.

The investigation of children's musical play in the settings in which it naturally occurs has also enabled me to observe transmission practices, that is, ways in which children teach and learn the material themselves. Clearly, such observations have important implications for music education practice. In the United States, Riddell (1990), Harwood (1992, 1993a, 1993b, 1994a, 1994b, 1996, 1998a, 1998b), and Campbell (1998) have identified major differences between teaching and learning practices in the playground and those in the classroom and advocate the application of children's observed playground behaviors to facilitate the teaching and learning of music in the classroom.

Transmission practices are also pertinent to current concerns in ethnomusicology, particularly those relating to modes of oral transmission and characteristics of orally transmitted genres whereby textual, musical, and/or kinesthetic materials are both conserved and changed in performance. An examination of practices of innovation, that is, adaptation or composition of new text, music, movement, or rules in performances of children's playground singing games has much to contribute to this field of inquiry, in addition to current concerns in music education, where the nature of children's compositional and improvisatory processes is the subject of considerable conjecture.

Children's aural environments have fundamentally changed in the late twentieth and early twenty-first century. In many countries, aspects of migration and globalization have resulted in a diversity of ethnic groups being represented within the population. Technology also has an almost unlimited capacity to broaden children's auditory field. As is clearly evident, the influence of the media reaches daily into children's lives (Campbell, 1998; Marsh, 1999, 2001, 2006; Gaunt, 2006). Transmission and innovation in children's musical play thus occur in relation to a wide variety of influences, both from within and outside of what might be perceived as "children's culture."

For many years the reputed pernicious effect of the media on children's play has been a theme of the popular press, as will be discussed in detail in chapter 7. The influence of material acquired from adult sources (media, parents, teachers) that is adopted or adapted by children to become part of the canon of playground songs for varying periods of time is therefore an important focus of attention in determining the accuracy of adults' preconceptions regarding an imagined decline in children's "traditional" play. The effects of immigration on the repertoire and practices of children in their musical play also serve to delineate the features of children's musical lives as they occur in a contemporary environment.

This book, then, is concerned with issues of transmission, innovation, and performance practice, which are relevant both to music education and to ethnomusicology. In the following sections of this chapter, I discuss the philosophical and methodological frameworks of previous music education and ethnomusicological studies and understandings of children's musical play. This discussion reveals a number of parallels between conceptions of children's musical play from both educational and ethnomusicological perspectives. These parallels include an evolutionary/developmental paradigm and the generalization of "universals" from particular situations or limited samples of musical products.

Music Education Conceptions of Children's Musical Play

Children's musical games form the foundations of two principal methodologies of twentieth-century Western music education: those expounded by the German composer Carl Orff and the Hungarian composer and ethnomusicologist Zoltán Kodály. Though these methodologies were formalized by associates of Orff and Kodály, rather than by the composers themselves, both provided philosophical frameworks and pedagogical materials that became exemplars for music education practice. The ensuing methodologies, termed "Orff-Schulwerk" and the "Kodály method," respectively, have been widely disseminated and implemented in many countries. They have had a strong international influence on music education programs designed for children in primary or elementary school settings.

Orff-Schulwerk and Kodály Methodology

The philosophical and methodological tenets of Orff-Schulwerk were laid in the 1920s during Orff's work with adult students of gymnastics and dance at the *Güntherschule* in Germany and were modified in the late 1940s when Orff responded to requests for musical materials appropriate for teaching children (Carder, 1990; Choksy, Abramson, Gillespie, & Woods, 1986; Landis & Carder, 1972). Orff aimed to develop the musical potential of children by providing them with musical materials that bore a strong resemblance to their own musical vocabulary, as demonstrated in their play. In Orff-Schulwerk he conceived a "child-centered" play-based way of encouraging learning: "Since the beginning of time children have not liked to study. They would rather play, and if you have their interest at heart you will let them learn while they play and then eventually they will find that what they have mastered is child's play" (Orff, cited in Davey, 1982, p. 23).

Pedagogical materials used as the starting point in the Orff teaching process were partially derived from Orff's observations of central European folk music, particularly the musical games that children played. The introduction of rhythmic and melodic elements of music in a classroom context was made in accordance with adult perceptions of the characteristics of Bavarian children's games. The perceived sequence was from simple (that is, more "childlike" or "primitive") to complex (equated with adult Western art music). This assumption regarding both cultural and developmental evolution was characteristic of the widespread beliefs of the time, as will be further discussed in this chapter.

The term that Orff gave to music at its historical and developmental origins was "elemental" music. He defined this as:

> Never music alone, but music connected with movement, dance and speech—not to be listened to, meaningful only in active participation. Elemental music is pre-intellectual, it lacks great form, it contents itself with simple sequential structures, ostinatos, and miniature rondos. It is earthy, natural, almost a physical activity. It can be learned and enjoyed by anyone. It is fitting for children. (Orff, 1963/1990, p. 142)

"Elemental" was synonymous with "primitive," the child's musical development being seen to parallel the perceived historical development of music from the "primitive" characteristics of Western medieval and non-Western musical traditions to the more "sophisticated" characteristics of post-Renaissance European art music. In this evolutionary approach, speech rhymes with rhythmic body percussion accompaniments are extended through the use of the "elemental" falling minor third motif (the ostensibly universal melodic interval used by children at play[1]) to pentatonic, modal, and finally diatonic melodic models.

Rhythmic and formal complexity is increased in the same way, for example, beginning with simple rhythmic units in duple meter said to be "derived from children's rhymes, songs and names" (Keetman, 1974, p. 17) and extending in the later stages to the performance and manipulation of material utilizing asymmetrical meters and metrical change (Marsh, 1974). As is evident in Orff's definition of "elemental" music, reiterative formal structures develop from the use of ostinato and echo techniques into simple canons and rondos. Exemplars in material intended for the most advanced students include the chaconne and recitative (Orff & Keetman, n.d.).

The pentatonic scale,[2] which is used extensively in Orff-Schulwerk practice, was favored because it enabled children to improvise music that was "always free from dissonance" (Keetman, 1974, p. 18). In conjunction with the use of specially constructed xylophones and metallophones, the pentatonic scale creates a musical environment that, Orff maintained, allowed children greater freedom in which to improvise: "In this realm (the pentatonic scale) that corresponds to his mentality the child can most easily find individual possibilities for expression, without being exposed to the danger of leaning upon the over strong examples of other music" (Orff, cited in Keetman, 1974, p. 18).

Orff's assumptions regarding the simplicity of children's musical play and its isolation from "over strong examples of other music" merit further investigation. While the notion of developmental appropriateness has had a significant influence on educational thought in the later stages of the twentieth century (Bredekamp, 1987), the validity of creating for educational purposes an overly limited musical environment (equated both with the limited musical and conceptual abilities of children and with musical primitivism) is open to question.

Orff's postulations in this regard were symptomatic of prevailing ideologies of the time, for example the "child as primitive" recapitulation theory of G. S. Hall (1920) where child development was seen to recapitulate historical development (Rubin, 1982; Takhvar, 1988). The roots of these ideas can be found in cultural evolutionary theories of the late nineteenth century, articulated by Herbert Spencer who "endeavored to establish the evolution of the intellect and to link it with the development of mankind from savagery to civilization," a concept that was further embellished by Charles Darwin (Zumwalt, 1999).

In the 1920s Edward Tyler applied this theoretical perspective to children's folklore, maintaining that it represented remnants of "early stages in the history of childlike tribes of mankind" (Tyler, cited in Zumwalt, 1999). There was additional support for these views from some ethnomusicologists. Sachs, for example, stated: "It is [an] exciting experience to learn that the earliest known stage of music reappears in the babble songs of small children in European countries. For once the ontogenetic law is fully confirmed: the individual summarizes the evolution of mankind" (Sachs, cited in Nettl, 1956, p. 87).

These beliefs were also evident in the words of Orff's contemporaries in music education in other continents. For example, Satis Coleman, renowned for developing innovative music education programs for children in New York from the 1920s to 1940s (Cox, 2006; Volk, 1996), wrote in 1922:

I saw my little pupils going back for their first music not to the Greeks, but much, much further back, even to primitive man and the early savages ... Being little savages, they can understand savage music. I shall find the child's own savage level, and lift him gradually up to higher forms. ... The natural evolution of music shall be my guide in leading the child from the simple to the complex. (Coleman, 1922, p. 29)

Kodály also adhered to musical evolutionism, believing that "the individual child reenacts the musical development of the race, from primitive musical responses to a highly developed level of musicianship" (Landis and Carder, 1990, p. 56). Kodály advocated beginning music education during what he perceived to be the child's most receptive period, between the ages of three and seven, to facilitate musical development in children (Kraus, 1967/1990, p. 79).[3] The initial pedagogical materials devised by Kodály were therefore developmentally based, with a prime consideration being their ease of use by young children.

Kodály used the "songs and singing games of [Hungarian] village children" (Farkas, 1990, p. 103) as the basis of his pedagogy, again partly because of its apparent relative simplicity, in addition to its ready appeal to children: "This is the music that belongs to children; it is their own. It rarely goes beyond the range of the children's own voices, and it is never too difficult for them, so they participate with great energy" (Farkas, 1990, pp. 103–4). Like Orff, Kodály saw a relationship between song and movement in children's songs and singing games: "The instinctive, natural speech of the child is song, and the younger the child, the more he desires to express himself in movement" (Kodály, cited by Kraus, 1967/1990, p. 80).

The use of play songs was also seen to create a link between the classroom and the playground that would encourage children to practice musical materials learned in a classroom context in their own time: "The simple song does not hinder the action of play, rather the opposite; it makes play more attractive, more interesting. The limited time available for musical education of the child can thus be extended on the playground without diminishing the time for other activities" (Kodály, cited by Kraus, 1967/1990, pp. 79–80).

Kodály's analysis of Hungarian children's songs and singing games revealed anhemitonic melodies comprising three to five tones (Farkas, 1990, p. 104). Kodály postulated that pentatonic melodies were developmentally more suitable for young children: "It is through them that children can achieve correct intonation soonest, for they do not have to bother with semitones. Even for children of eight–nine years of age, semitones and the diatonic scale are difficult, not to mention the chromatic semitones. This latter is difficult even at secondary school" (Kodály, cited in Choksy, 1981, p. 9).

Similarly, young children's movements were seen to be metrically simple. Duple meter, whether simple or compound, was believed to be the basis of children's play movements, a belief that, as Kodály methodology has been transplanted to other cultural contexts, has been reiterated: "Triple meter is extremely uncommon as a natural expression among young children in English-speaking cultures. Based on child-developmental patterns, the earliest rhythmic teaching material in a Kodály approach is duple. Triple meters are included later, when a firm foundation in duple has been established" (Choksy et al., 1986, p. 73).

The pedagogical tenets of Kodály methodology must also be viewed in relation to its links with Kodály's belief in musical nationalism. Political and economic dominance by the Hapsburg Empire had resulted in the subordination of Hungarian music to Austrian and Germanic musical styles in Hungarian concert halls and educational establishments. Kodály and his compatriot, Béla Bartók, sought to validate the use of stylistic characteristics of Hungarian folk music in Hungarian art music. They undertook an extensive ethnomusicological collection of Hungarian folk music in order to do so (Choksy, 1981, pp. 3–4).

The inculcation of a national musical heritage in children was, thus, a guiding principle of Kodály methodology. Kodály maintained that "as a child possesses a mother-tongue—the language spoken in his home—he also possesses a musical mother-tongue in the folk music of that language. It is through this musical mother-tongue that the skills and concepts necessary to musical literacy should be taught" (Kodály, cited in Choksy, 1981, p. 7).

The repertoire used in Kodály methodology therefore progresses from nursery songs and singing games to folk songs from the child's culture, "then through international folk song which is a bridge to art form and the classics of composed music" (Landis and Carder, 1990, p. 69). Kodály required that "only music of unquestioned quality be used . . . Of foreign music: only masterpieces!" (Kodály, cited in Choksy, 1981, p. 8). This emphasis on quality music has meant that some Kodály practitioners have avoided using popular music in the classroom.

Kodály pedagogical materials develop in melodic complexity in a similar sequence to Orff materials, using first a falling minor third, expanded by the addition of whole tones to a pentatonic scale succeeded by diatonic, modal, and chromatic tonalities. Rhythmic complexity is also introduced gradually through structured materials, but the sequence is preferably guided through the regularity of the appearance of particular rhythmic patterns in the chosen repertoire (Choksy et al., 1986).

Both Orff and Kodály saw music education as the right of all children but their educational philosophies differed in emphasis. While a major aim of Orff-Schulwerk is the development of personal expression through improvisation (Addison, 1988; Campbell & Scott-Kassner, 1995), the Kodály approach focuses on the development of musical literacy. Symbolization of sound is preceded by sung performance and reinforced kinesthetically through movement games and hand signs associated with tonic solfa. Tonic solfa and variants of French time names[4] are used as mnemonic devices to promote auditory memory of melodic and rhythmic patterns (Bridges, 1984/1992).

Since their inception, Orff and Kodály methodologies have been disseminated throughout Europe, the United Kingdom, the United States, Canada, South America, Australia, the Middle East, and parts of Asia (Hochschule für Musik und Darstellende Kunst Mozarteum in Salzburg, 1972; Keller, 1970). As Orff-Schulwerk and Kodály method have been widely adopted, practitioners in different countries have sought to make the methodology relevant to their own classrooms by incorporating more culturally appropriate songs into the teaching repertoire.[5] Small changes in methodology have occurred in order to accommodate linguistic and melodic differences in folk-based material. For example, the order of introduction of some melodic intervals has been changed to reflect the frequency of their occurrence in American folk songs (Choksy, 1981) and compound duple meter is introduced earlier in Anglophone materials because of its more frequent incidence in English poetic forms (Choksy et al., 1986).

In many countries, aspects of the two methodologies have been synthesized in classroom practice. For example, solfa syllables and rhythmic mnemonics, in addition to graphic representation, are used by some Orff-Schulwerk practitioners to develop notational skills in students, following activities involving imitation and exploration of musical sounds and movement. Later improvisation incorporates this notational knowledge (Campbell & Scott-Kassner, 1995; Choksy et al., 1986).

However, the underlying philosophical and methodological tenets of Orff-Schulwerk and Kodály method have not been questioned by their practitioners, despite major changes in educational philosophy and ethnomusicological thought. The "child as primitive" paradigm was subject to criticism even as the methodologies were developing: Herzog, for example, observed that: "analogies between the child and the 'primitive' have become *cliches* of ill repute" (1947, p. 11). As Zumwalt (1999) states, "It is past time to recognize that children are not simple, nor are societies simple. The child is a complex individual, not a simple adult, or a link to the savage past" (p. 29). The whole notion of musical primitivism as applied to non-Western music has been discredited because it is rooted in the erroneous assumption that Western music has supposedly evolved from "primitive" prototypes. That non-Western musics also possess "sophisticated" musical traits has been clearly demonstrated by many ethnomusicological studies of music that has been viewed superficially as "primitive" or simple (Seeger, 1991). Yet, while the complexities of non-Western musics are acknowledged by listeners from outside of these cultures, and children are no longer regarded as primitive adults, traces of the assumptions regarding children's musical play remain embedded in common Schulwerk and Kodály practices.

What has evolved, then, are two pedagogical frameworks based on perceptions of the natural attributes of children's play. The assumed "playlike" features of children's musical play include simplicity of form, rhythm, and melody and use of movement as an expression of enjoyment and spontaneity. Translated into pedagogical equivalents, "playlikeness" is equated with simple repetitive structures, materials with a restricted rhythmic and tonal palette, and use of movement to develop musical understanding. Although adherents of either methodology often focus on the differences in their implementation (Bridges, 1984/1992), a number of common elements are clearly evident. Both have a foundation in children's traditional musical play as observed in central Europe at the time of their genesis. On the basis of these observations, both methodologies make assumptions about the relative simplicity of children's musical play. These assumptions then contribute to the creation of a developmental program of music education that uses highly structured musical and kinesthetic materials. Probably because the necessity for simple musical beginnings with young children is articulated so clearly in the Orff and Kodály literature, simple musical materials tend to be overemphasized in classroom practice, regardless of the complexity of many of the Orff and Kodály materials devised for older children. Perhaps most importantly, the proliferation of both approaches has resulted in locally based conceptions of children's musical play being generalized to a much larger educational context.

Critiques of "Playlike" Pedagogical Practices

Since these "playlike" methodologies were initiated, major changes have occurred in the musical environment to which children are exposed, with considerable implications for educational experiences: "As music is transformed by technology and by the blending of cultural traditions from near and far, children are offered a wide array of expressions from which to choose for listening and performing" (Campbell and Scott-Kassner, 1995, p. 12).

For several decades there have been critiques of music educational pedagogies for failing to take account of the complexity of children's auditory environment. McAllester (1966) and Michel (1976) have drawn music educators' attention to the lack of correspondence between music children hear through the media and the limited musical materials provided for composition and performance in the classroom. Michel's (1976) study of children in East Germany revealed that a large percentage of the song material that young children remembered was derived from radio and television, "which allows them the reception, reproduction and recognition of far more ambitious music than is expected of them frequently at school today" (p. 104). Michel discounted the evolutionary developmental paradigm, finding that preschool children were able to develop perceptual and singing abilities in relation to major, minor, and modal material and did not demonstrate a particular affinity with the interval of a falling minor third or the pentatonic scale.

When compared with the attributes of children's own music-making, the dichotomy between pedagogical materials and children's musical environment seems more clearly apparent. Following an intensive study of young children's improvised songs, Davies (1986) commented on the adequacy of contemporary classroom methodology to meet children's creative potential:

> A restricted framework, within which the child concentrates on a limited vocabulary until he can handle it confidently, may well prove helpful for some children. But . . . prescribing limits and attempting to intervene in the child's own musical activity may inhibit unnecessarily. . . . It seems likely that providing a rich and varied diet of music to sing, play and listen to is itself the most important contribution which the teacher can make to the development of compositional skills in young children. (p. 282)

In recent decades, some studies have collected and analyzed children's playground singing games and other forms of children's musical play in order to establish their relationship to the repertoire and learning processes commonly used in American music education (Campbell, 1991, 1998; Harwood, 1992, 1993a, 1993b, 1994a, 1994b, 1996, 1998a, 1998b; Riddell, 1990). Campbell's (1991, 1998) results indicate that playground songs are usually more rhythmically complex than songs found in pedagogical materials. She cites the frequent use of syncopation and some polymetric relationships between vocal and movement aspects of children's musical play, performed by children of varying ages.

Riddell's study supports this view of rhythmic complexity and attributes the occurrence of syncopation in newer rhymes to their derivation from new styles of popular music. She concludes that contemporary performances of children's singing games are "not necessarily childlike" as they owe their characteristics to adult-generated musical styles (1990, p. 336). Similarly, her melodic analysis reveals a preponderance of diatonically based melodies, some of which derive directly from popular music models. The influence of popular music and the media on text and melody in playground singing games is also clearly demonstrated by Harwood (1994b), Campbell (1998), and Prim (1989), whose study of Portuguese children's games provides additional evidence of polymetric modes of performance.

The Yugoslavian ethnomusicologist Elly Basic (1986) has criticized the pedagogical uses of children's playlore and the misconception that children's folkloric material is intrinsically simple. She claims that, in taking the "musical richness of rhythmic structures and the dynamism of open forms" of children's playlore and simplifying them for classroom consumption, educators are perpetrating the "systematic impoverishment of the children's musical creative imagination" (1986, p. 131).

Basic's claims are supported by Merrill-Mirsky (1988) who, in her study of children's playground games in Los Angeles, states: "The great difficulty here is the fine line between encouraging children's experience and mutilating it by making it conform to educational goals and practices" (p. 54). Merrill-Mirsky also cites the extensive studies of children's playground games by the German music educator and musicologist Segler, who calls German school songs "purified and tedious" in contrast to their playground equivalents (Merrill-Mirsky, 1988, p. 51). Harwood, too, abhors the educational tendency to "gentrify" playground singing games for classroom use (1994a). She continues: "The notion that there is one kind of music in real life and another in schools has been one of the most pernicious lessons of a hidden but all too common curriculum in music education" (Harwood, 1996, p. 19). Such sentiments are expanded by Campbell (1998) who makes a plea to "bring instruction in line with who the children musically are" (p. 196) and outlines a range of strategies through which this might be achieved.

Basic (1986) also questions the developmental approach of music pedagogies and adheres to the principle that an adult's conception of the progression from easy to difficult may be quite different from what a child experiences. Her contention in this regard is supported by Blacking's (1967/1995) study of Venda children's songs in South Africa. Blacking reports that "children's songs are not always easier than adult songs, and children do not necessarily learn the simple songs first" (p. 29). More difficult songs may be learnt first by Venda children simply because they have been heard more frequently. As Harwood (1992) observes, "handclap games contain some fairly sophisticated textual, musical and motor elements, in combinations that are not easily mastered" (p. 25). She maintains that they master this difficult repertoire through reiterated observation of and participation in performances of games in their entirety, "rather than breaking difficult pieces into manageable parts" (1993b, p. 8).

It is clear from the critiques cited that the evolutionary paradigm that underlies some contemporary approaches to music education cannot continue to be justified when the attributes of children's contemporary music-making are considered. Since I began my tentative explorations in 1990 it has been my intention to utilize ethnomusicological methods to further investigate this apparent mismatch between pedagogy and the characteristics, practices, and processes inherent in children's musical play. My study of this phenomenon has been framed by an awareness not only of current ethnomusicological methodologies but also of the philosophy and methodologies which have influenced past ethnomusicological studies of children's play. These are discussed in the next section.

Ethnomusicological Conceptions of Musical Play

The evolutionary paradigm found in music pedagogies formulated in the early twentieth century is also evident in early ethnomusicological studies of children's music that were undertaken to identify universals or vestiges of archaic forms of music. Herzog's (1947) study is characteristic of this. Herzog saw European children's songs as representing a repository for archaic European folk melodies that, following diffusion, could also be found in the music of Central and Western Asia, the Baltic states, and the Middle East.

Brailoiu (1954) conducted one of the earliest cross-cultural studies of children's musical play in order to try to establish universal elements of "childlikeness" in music. From an analysis of children's songs and rhymes from Europe, parts of West Africa, Russia, Canada, Japan, and Formosa, Brailoiu postulated that the "childish rhythm" had "only one essential structure": a binary rhythm equal to the value of eight quavers (1954, pp. 4, 21). Brailoiu does not elaborate on his methodology, but his analysis appears to be based on notated "documents" (p. 3) rather than examples collected by Brailoiu in the field. There is therefore no contextualization of the examples used and the analysis relates only to the text rhythm, with no consideration being given to the rhythmic characteristics of any associated movements or the relationship between these elements. Although it was clear from his analysis that the "universal" rhythmic framework was "constantly disguised by the resources of . . . variation" (p. 4), he adhered to reductionist theory. He also discounted children's repertoire which is "[i]n Western Europe at least . . . contaminated by the usual music of the media" (p. 1), reflecting the views of much research of the time into "traditional" music that an original "pure" form is contaminated rather than used as a resource for innovation.[6]

However, Merrill-Mirsky (1988), using a large body of singing game material collected through ethnographic fieldwork in multiethnic settings, has disputed Brailoiu's claim that children's rhythms are universal, stating: "Perhaps the existence of children's music is a universal in itself, but to identify rhythmic usage as a universal is to ignore the importance of and persistence of cultural traditions in the child's environment" (p. 219). By taking account of the triple and twelve-beat movement patterns that are an integral part of the performance of many collected singing games, Merrill-Mirsky also disproves Brailoiu's contention that children's rhythms are always binary, with identical placement of accents.

Blacking (1967/1995, 1985) also disputes that there is a universal rhythm in children's songs and, indeed, contends that perceived universal features are meaningless. In contrast to Brailoiu, Blacking has attempted to study the unique attributes of Venda children's songs in the context of Venda culture. He describes the rhythmic and melodic features of Venda children's songs as being compressed or simplified forms of adult Venda music, stating:

> Even if an objective classification of Venda musical patterns showed them to be similar to other musical traditions, it is most unlikely that they would both have been generated by the same cultural factors. Their musical similarity would be purely coincidental. Even cases where a style of music has apparently been diffused must be treated with caution, because similar patterns of sound may have been adopted for different reasons, or have acquired different meanings. (1967/1995, p. 195)

Blacking has eschewed the standardized forms of melodic and tonal analysis of the time as Eurocentric and, instead, espouses the "cultural analysis of music" (1967/1995, pp. 191ff.).

Blacking's study, like that of Brailoiu, has influenced the work of a number of other researchers using ethnomusicological methods to investigate the characteristics of children's games. In Australia, Brunton (1976) and Hall (1984) relate the musical properties of the play rhymes to their function. Generally, rhymes that have as their function the regulation of rhythmic actions are perceived by Brunton to have a melody that is subservient to rhythm, with the melody often being abandoned if the actions are used. Similarly, these rhymes are seen to exhibit less complex, more even and repetitious rhythmic patterns and faster tempi with duple meter prevailing. Both comment on the lessening importance of the semantic element of rhymes when employed with movement games. This finding is supported by the Opies (1988) and Harwood (1987) but not by the work of Campbell (1991).

The focus on "universal" core rhythms and intervals is discounted by recent comparative studies of children's musical play. In perhaps the most comprehensive ethnomusicological study to date, Segler (1992) collected and analyzed children's playground games across Europe and the United Kingdom. His carefully documented collection is notable for the multiple variants of different games, illustrating children's propensity to create their own localized versions with varying attributes. Norwegian musicologist Bjørkvold's (1989/1992) study of preschool children's spontaneous musical play in Oslo, St Petersburg, and Los Angeles found significant local differences in the characteristics of the play songs. For example the falling minor third calling formula was not found in the Russian play songs. He concluded that "[i]t is the predisposition to adapt for their own purposes the songs with which they are familiar that is universal, not the specific songs that have become common property through the influence of the mass media" (p. 116).

The search for universals in studies of musical play appears to derive from ethnomusicological concerns of an earlier era. More recent ethnomusicological studies attempt instead to contextualize the study of music and to view music as a changing rather than a static phenomenon. For example, Addo's (1995) analyses of Ghanaian children's singing games focus on the socio-musical meaning of the games for Ghanaian children and are linked with enculturation processes contextualized within Ghanaian society. Music, movement, and textual characteristics of the games are seen to reflect, to varying degrees, their genesis in general Ghanaian patterns of speech, music, and movement, or to relate to the legacy of colonialism in Ghana.

Gaunt's (1997, 2006) study of African American girls' play also entails a cultural analysis of musical genres. She argues that these games represent both forms of enculturation and embodiments of their players' identities as female African Americans, drawing on and contributing to the dynamic body of African American musical traditions. The investigation of children's dance, music, and song in Bali by McIntosh (2006) explores the relationship between local culture and global influences in shaping and changing children's formal and informal performance practices.

Merrill-Mirsky, outlining the "ethnomusicological standpoint" of her study, describes this as being an "emphasis on the cultural context in which the material exists. Musical style, transmission, acculturation, and change thus feature prominently in an ethnomusicological approach" (1988, p. 2). Nettl (1992), in his outline of recent directions in ethnomusicology, identifies an increased interest in the study of the processes inherent in musical change as a dominant concern in ethnomusicological research of the previous two decades. In particular, Nettl states that ethnomusicologists are "concerned with seeing how ... music changes, by what mechanisms and with what regularities" (1992, p. 381).

The apparently contradictory aspects of stability and change have also been the focus of folklore research; researchers in the field of children's playlore have devoted considerable attention to this phenomenon (Factor, 1988; Knapp and Knapp, 1976; McDowell, 1999; Merrill-Mirsky, 1988; Opie and Opie, 1988; Riddell, 1990; Turner, 1969; Turner, Factor, and Lowenstein, 1982). Stability is required for enculturation, the process by which definitive aspects of playlore are instilled in the children who perform it. In this process, children act as arbiters of appropriate practice, ensuring the maintenance of tradition (Riddell, 1990). Playground games, for example, may be preserved for an extensive period of time, in some cases over several centuries.

These games, however, are not usually preserved intact. While identifiable aspects of the games, such as sections of text or movement patterns, remain in use, others change. Thus, a game that may be identified by its textual elements in earlier collections is unlikely to be identical to that performed by children in other times and locations, although researchers may draw parallels and identify them as the same entity (see, for example, Opie and Opie, 1959, p. vi). This change frequently occurs both as the result of deliberate processes of innovation and through the processes of transmission.

However, to view stability and change in musical forms as dichotomous is problematic. Waterman (1993) defines cultural continuity not as "stasis, but as a recursive process" in which the "reproduction of individual representations of culture patterns is grounded in a flow of activity continually shaped by actors' interpretations of and reactions to constraints and incentives encountered in the world" (p. 51). The reproduction of a structure thus becomes its transformation, with tradition providing "expressive principles, and aesthetic values by means of which performances are both fashioned and made sensible" (Coplan, 1993, p. 40).

Waterman (1993) also disputes that musical products can be seen as separate from the processes involved in their fashioning. In Waterman's view it is impossible to adequately describe processes of musical continuity and change, without dealing with "relationships among patterns of musical sound and performance behavior, cultural symbolism and value, social transaction and ideology, and the material forces that encourage or constrain particular forms of expression" (1993, p. 50). In developing an understanding of children's musical play, it is important, then, to investigate the processes of continuity and change that operate within a 'traditional' orally transmitted musical genre.

Children's Play and Folklore

While aspects of change are discussed in some well-known studies of children's playlore, the pedagogical imperative seems to have been the motivating factor for some other investigations. Howard, an American scholar whose work in

1954 and 1955 was the first attempt to document Australian children's playlore in a systematic way, states: "Among elementary classroom teachers and their children I found much lively interest in recording play lore. Among Australian academicians (with important exceptions) I found that folklore has little or no prestige yet" (Howard, 1959/1976a, p. 86).

The publications of Factor (1980, 1983, 1984, 1985, 1986a, 1986b, 1988) and Grugeon (1988, 1993, 2000, 2001, 2005) have resulted from their work as literature educators. Ethnographic studies have been undertaken by educator and folklorist Howard (1955, 1959/1976a, 1960/1976b), physical educators Lindsay and Palmer (1981), and psychologist Russell (1986, Perkins & Russell, 1993). Like a number of previously discussed music education researchers, Lindsay and Palmer (1981) conclude that, compared to their curricular counterparts, playground games are much more imaginative and involve the development and practice of a much greater variety of skills.

Russell (1986) demonstrates ways in which an understanding of children's playground games can be used to enhance environments for play (Perkins and Russell, 1993). Her studies indicate that a more complete understanding of the processes at work in children's play can come only through lengthy and detailed observation of play in context and through discussion with the children themselves. She reports misunderstandings of the characteristics and patterns of children's play by teachers and researchers who have not taken the time to do this.

Most studies of children's playlore are geographically specific in reference (for example, Abrahams, 1969; Addo, 1995; Blacking 1967/1995; Brady, 1974, 1975; Campbell, 1991, 1998; Cooke, 1980; Fujita, 1989; Harwood, 1987, 1992, 1993a, 1993b, 1994a, 1994b, 1998a, 1998b; Jones and Hawes, 1972/1987; Merrill-Mirsky, 1988; McIntosh, 2006; Prim, 1989; Riddell, 1990; Stoeltje, 1978; Sutton-Smith, 1951/1976, 1959/1972, 1976). Few researchers have undertaken cross-cultural studies of children's playlore (Kartomi, 1980, 1981; Romet, 1980; Russell, 1986). Merrill-Mirsky's cross-cultural study of playground singing games in Los Angeles offers evidence of cross-cultural differences and patterns of exchange between groups of different ethnicities.

More recently, Doekes (1992a, 1992b, 1992c; Doekes & van Doorn-Last, 1993) has discussed the influence of migration and the school environment on the intercultural transmission of playground singing games. While her study is centered on the Netherlands, she cites examples of songs that include English text transmitted by children from Surinam and Morocco. Drawing on the work of Segler (1992), she also cites variant forms of these and other games, particularly those utilizing nonsense texts, which have been collected in a number of European countries. She draws attention to some cross-cultural similarities in the relationship of musical and textual elements to movement patterns and also to similar social functions of game rules.

As in ethnomusicological studies, universal functions of children's playlore have been identified by some highly regarded researchers in the field of children's traditional play (Opie, 1994; Opie & Opie 1959/1977, 1979, 1985/1988). Conversely, the work of the Knapps (1976) and Sutton-Smith (1951/1976, 1959/1972, 1972, 1976, 1980, 1982; Sutton-Smith & Rosenberg, 1972, Sutton-Smith, Mechling, Johnson & McMahon, 1999) in the United States contextualizes children's playlore and discusses its function in terms of social, linguistic, and psychological parameters.

However, the analyses of Factor, the Knapps, and the Opies are largely text-dependent. Although the Opies include a small number of musical transcriptions of singing games in one of their publications (Opie & Opie, 1988), the discussion of derivations and variation is based on text only, limiting its usefulness for socio-musical interpretation.[7] The Opies also focus on the historical antecedents of current singing games, with echoes of the "child as primitive" paradigm evident in their analysis.

It can be seen, then, that a number of philosophical and methodological limitations have permeated many studies of children's playlore within educational, ethnomusicological, and other disciplines. These limitations include a dependence on decontextualized, "product-based" analysis. In some instances the "play product" is denuded of even more characteristics and is analyzed in text form only. Additional limitations include the paradigmatic insistence on developmental and/or musical evolutionism and the search for underlying "universals." These "universals" are often derived from the generalization of patterns seen in the play of children from a single context.

In his perceptive essay on children's playlore, Turner (Turner, Factor, & Lowenstein, 1978) makes a plea for comprehensive study of children's play that treats the children's play world with respect and acknowledges the limits of adult understanding. He cites an eleven-year-old boy's idea that, while adults think they can understand the world of children, this world is surrounded by walls "twenty feet high" and adults "have only ten feet ladders" (p. 163).

In endeavoring to climb over the wall into the world of children's musical play, I have spent many years in school playgrounds, engaging with children in many different cultural contexts. In this way I have tried to gain a more complete understanding of the socio-musical characteristics of children's playground games and the processes involved in their preservation and change. By observing, recording, and analyzing multiple game performances and variations within and between performances over a number of years, and by applying contextual information to this field material, it seemed possible to gain a clearer understanding of these characteristics and of processes of conservation and innovation enacted by children.

Steps in the Ladder

In this chapter, I have drawn attention to the bounded nature of many adult constructs of children's musical play. Adult constructs of children's musical creativity may also be bounded. In the following chapter, I investigate the largely pedagogical literature on children's musical creativity as a precursor to developing an understanding of creativity in children's musical play in the playground. Theories of oral transmission and their relationship to children's creativity are also explored in chapter 2. These two chapters outline theoretical frameworks for the study of children's musical play in order to position my own exploration.

In the second section of the book, "Into the Field," I move the focus from theory toward the world of the playground. Chapter 3, "Investigating Musical Play," discusses the field collection practices adopted for the study and the scope of field data collected. Philosophical, ethical, and practical issues that frame collection practices are considered. In this chapter, I address ways in which the role of the researcher and particular problems associated with the specific contexts of this study have resulted in the evolution of a reflexive field methodology, in collaboration both with the children in the playground and my co-researchers, who have provided local, culturally specific knowledge in unfamiliar environments.

The socio-cultural contexts of children's playground singing games in the multiple research sites are examined in greater detail in chapter 4. School organization and characteristics of the school community, particularly in regard to ethnicity, are outlined. A description of relevant policies and practices and the social and physical characteristics of the playground environment at the schools in Australia, Norway, the United Kingdom, the United States, and Korea provide a framework for considering the transmission processes that are examined in the following section, "Transmission Processes in the Playground."

This section, consisting of three chapters, examines the influences on the transmission and generation of playground singing games in all of the field schools, particularly the influence of social grouping, contexts of play, age, gender, ethnicity, audiovisual and written media, and the classroom. The role of these influences in shaping and changing tradition and the relationship between transmission and generation in musical play are considered and children's own teaching and learning processes, as exemplified by transmission practices, are described.

The nexus between transmission and creativity in musical play is further examined in the next section, "Composition in Performance." Chapter 8 uses case studies of particular groups of children to investigate the compositional strategies enacted by playground performers in the context of their musical play. These strategies are compared with innovative processes found in other orally transmitted performance genres and then used to challenge a number of the assumptions and models pertaining to children's musical creativity discussed in chapter 2. In chapter 9, creative strategies and forms of variation are outlined through a detailed musical analysis of one singing game genre, "Sar macka dora", which was found in almost all the field schools. Chapter 10 explores the idiosyncratic stylistic characteristics of children's musical play and their relationship to the cultural contexts in which it is enacted.

The final section, "Conclusions and Pedagogical Implications," compares the repertoire, compositional strategies, modes of teaching and learning, and social grouping found in playground practice and classroom practice. Both pedagogical and ethnomusicological implications are drawn from the results of my playground investigations.

Throughout the text, I refer to recorded examples of children's musical play that are either transcribed or included in the accompanying digital video materials. In this way, it is hoped that the reader can also be drawn with me, even for a few moments, into the world of the playground. Video examples of illustrative game performances from international field sites are located on the companion Web site: www.oup.com/us/themusicalplayground and are denoted by the icon:

 VIDEO SAMPLE.

CHAPTER 2

Children's Musical Creativity
and Oral Transmission

The playground world has not figured largely in studies of children's musical creativity, which have emanated largely from pedagogical concerns. However, an understanding of children's abilities to manipulate and change musical materials in the context of their play also serves to illuminate conceptions of children's innovative processes in a pedagogical context. The notion of children's play with sound is integral not only to Orff-Schulwerk but also to other pedagogical approaches, which incorporate the activity of creating music as both an adjunct to the development of musical understandings and skills and as a vehicle for self-expression. The philosophies of Dalcroze (Choksy et al., 1986; Landis & Carder, 1990), Schafer (1965, 1967, 1969, 1975), the English school of the 1960s and 1970s led by Paynter (Paynter & Aston, 1970; Paynter, 1972, 1978a, 1978b), the Comprehensive Musicianship approach and the Manhattanville Music Curriculum Project in the United States (Campbell & Scott-Kassner, 1995; Choksy et al., 1986) have all extolled the value of developing children's musical creativity through compositional and improvisational experiences in the classroom.

This pedagogical emphasis on creative musical activity has been accompanied by a burgeoning interest in children's innate musical creativity and ways in which understandings of it can best be applied in the classroom. In recent years, studies of children's musical creativity have proliferated, but few have related to children's musical play. In this chapter I review a range of studies and emergent theories of musical creativity.

In the latter part of this chapter I also examine theories of creativity pertaining to the process of oral transmission whereby "traditional" material is changed as it is learnt and performed. Ideas relating to "composition in performance" (Lord, 1995, p. 11) as it occurs both within and beyond the playground are outlined. Issues that emerge from this review will later be discussed in relation to children's playground creativity in chapter 8.

Universal Models of Children's Musical Creativity

Some of the most influential studies of children's musical creativity have endeavored to provide models that predominantly focus on children's composition or improvisation. The models they present are seen to apply to all forms of children's composition or improvisation, in much the same way as early ethnomusicological studies of children's music propounded the idea that general structural elements underlie all children's songs, and studies of children's playlore focused on universal characteristics.

A well-known model of children's composition is the spiral of compositional development proposed by Swanwick and Tillman (Swanwick & Tillman, 1986; Swanwick, 1988, 1991, 1996), based on the analysis of compositional exercises, recorded under experimental conditions, of children aged from three to fifteen years. The model postulates that children's compositional processes change as they grow older, with children passing progressively through four compositional stages demonstrating engagement with Materials, Expression, Form, and Value, respectively. Each of these stages is seen to correspond with the Piagetian stages of Mastery, Imitation, Imaginative Play, and Metacognition.

According to the model, each stage is characterized by two developmental modes of composition. Initially, in the Materials stage, children's compositions in the sensory mode (from birth to three years) demonstrate unstructured and unpredictable exploration of sounds, particularly in relation to timbre and dynamic change, and rarely exhibit a steady beat. In the following manipulative mode (characteristic of children of four to five years), children are gaining greater control over sound sources and can more readily produce a regular beat, though their interest is still directed toward producing varied timbral effects (Swanwick & Tillman, 1986, p. 332).

A concern for personal expressiveness appears in children from four to six years of age. In this mode, there is spontaneity, uncoordinated musical gestures, and still little structural control. In the following *Vernacular* mode, children take on some conventions of musical vocabulary absorbed through their musical experiences inside and outside of school. Characteristics of this mode (which may be demonstrated by children from the age of five but is more clearly established in seven to eight-year-olds) include melodic and rhythmic patterning, repetition, and regular phrase lengths, in addition to an emerging consciousness of meter (Swanwick & Tillman, 1986).

In the *Speculative* mode, which becomes apparent in the composition of children from ten years of age, children deliberately deviate from musical conventions and thus tend to exhibit less control of beat or phrase lengths. These "structural surprises . . . become more firmly integrated into a particular style" (Swanwick & Tillman, 1986, p. 333) in the *Idiomatic* mode which is entered from the age of thirteen. In this mode there is a strong attempt to imitate adult musical conventions, particularly those of popular music (Swanwick & Tillman, 1986).

Swanwick and Tillman's final metacognitive stage, Value, is, according to the spiral model, observable in the compositions of children from fifteen on (Swanwick & Tillman, 1986, p. 300, Swanwick, 1988, p. 73). In this stage, the *Symbolic* mode is characterized by the ability to reflect upon the compositional experience and, in the ultimate *Systematic* mode, there is a consciousness of the underlying principles of composition and the capacity to use and develop musical systems (Swanwick & Tillman, 1986; Swanwick, 1988).

Swanwick states that children do not "merely pass through one of these modes but carry them forward . . . into the next" so that older children may revert to an earlier mode of compositional development if, for example, they are faced with unfamiliar musical materials (1988, pp. 63–64). While the sequence is seen to be age-related, Swanwick and Tillman assume that children's progress through the sequence may be influenced by their degree of exposure to musical experiences, particularly those involving composition (1986, p. 338). Swanwick's later (1991) study in Cyprus appeared to validate this assumption, with older children demonstrating the characteristics of earlier modes of compositional development, presumably because they had had fewer opportunities to compose in the classroom.

Although the Swanwick and Tillman model provides one approach to viewing children's composition, generalization of the model to all children's compositional endeavors should perhaps be given more careful consideration in the light of more recent studies. While retaining a developmental approach, Swanwick has since stated that "it is important to remember that we were not assessing children but 'placing' their compositions. A study of the same child over time will doubtless show compositions occurring in different 'layers' (also a less misleading word than stage or phase)" (1996, p. 26).

A developmental paradigm has also been adopted by Kratus (1991) in his exposition on students' improvisation. He proposes seven levels of improvisational development, apparently not aligned with particular ages, although the final level is characteristic of accomplished adult musicians. In Kratus' first level, Exploration "The student tries out different sounds and combinations of sounds in a loosely structured context." Level 2, Process-Oriented Improvisation, is characterized by the production of "more cohesive patterns." Students gradually become more aware of musical products and structures as they proceed through the various levels of this model until the fully developed musician emerges to "transcend recognized improvisation styles" and so create his or her own style in level 7, Personal Improvisation (Kratus, 1991, pp. 38–39).

Despite some clear parallels between the Swanwick and Tillman model and that of Kratus, they differ in one important respect. While Swanwick and Tillman do not distinguish between composition and improvisation (1986, p. 311), Kratus places a value judgment on the production aspect of improvisation, so that product-oriented improvisation (level 3) is seen as evidence of greater skill development than process-oriented improvisation.

A perceived dichotomy between composition as process and composition as product is central to Kratus' other studies of children's composition: "Composition as product" is defined by Kratus as "a fixed, replicable series of sounds," designed to be "shared with others" (1994, p. 129); Kratus defines "composition as process" as "the fluid thoughts and actions of the composer in generating the product," which include "generating new musical ideas, developing ideas, testing ideas, and judging ideas" (p. 129). He goes on to state, "Compositional processes are not meant to be replicated or shared with others. The process of composition as something separated in time from the performance of the product is one of the primary distinctions between composition and improvisation" (p. 129).

This separation of musical process and product and the insistence on composition as a solitary, rather than social, process seems misplaced, particularly when considered in relation to Waterman's (1993) views of the links between musical generation and performance, "patterns of social interaction" (p. 53), and the social and "material forces that encourage or constrain particular forms of expression" (p. 50), as discussed in the previous chapter. It is also out of step with the findings of other researchers in the field of children's composition, in which children's ability to compose collaboratively has been observed and endorsed as a way of extending creative outcomes (Borstad, 1990; Burnard, 2002; Davidson, 1990; Kanellopoulos, 1999; Kaschub, 1997; MacDonald & Meill, 2000; Wiggins, 1994, 1999).

The emphasis on replicability as evidence of compositional intention and, by implication, higher compositional skill, is also problematic (Kratus, 1989). Kratus sees the production of a final replicable product as the endpoint of a linear process that children undergo when they compose. This process is divided into four kinds of behaviors: *Exploration* (in which new sounds are explored), *Development* (in which "the music sounds similar to, yet different from, music played earlier"), *Repetition*, and *Silence* (the latter being employed at any time in the process) (1989, p. 9). Kratus found that the younger children in his experimental study spent a greater percentage of time on exploration, while older children spent a larger percentage of time on development and repetition. Not surprisingly, children who spent more time on repetition were more likely to be able to replicate their final product, though Kratus attributes this to "product orientation" rather than to practice.

Holistic Conception

Kratus' findings must be considered in relation to his study's experimental design. In contrasting the results of her ethnographic study of children's group composition in the classroom with those of Kratus, Wiggins (1994, 2003) notes that children participating in familiar creative activities in familiar settings do not appear to engage in exploratory behavior. Moreover, she states, "The data discussed here suggest that what might seem to be random exploration in a laboratory setting might be better described in this [naturalistic] setting as the seeds of a more holistic plan" (1994, p. 248).

Wiggins's (1994, 2003) study of fifth grade children concluded that the children had a holistic conception of their composition from the outset and that "students' invention of motivic material is intentional and purposeful, often emanating from a preconceived notion of what they want the music to sound like" (2003, p. 148). When working in groups, they tended to begin with a group discussion of overall structural aspects of the composition, then worked separately on individual development of motivic material before finally collaborating to refine and rehearse the composition. Similarly, in naturalistic research by Barrett (1996) with children aged from five to twelve, all children were seen to show an understanding of structure and form in their compositions. This did not appear to be age related, nor did it seem to reflect prior musical training.

Davies (1994), studying the invented songs of young individual children, came to the similar conclusion that the children had "super-ordinate plans—pre-conscious representations that find expression in coherent forms" (p. 127). Borstad's (1990) study of first grade children's improvisations also indicates that children conceive of their music in a holistic way. Both Davies and Borstad are impressed by young children's apparently well-developed understandings of musical structures, a sentiment also expressed by Serafine (1988) (though not specifically in relation to composition): "What is amazing about the acquisition of music by the young is . . . that they know subtler things which no-one has told them about: what counts as order in music, what features of it should be attended to, what makes melodies similar and different, what properly makes a tune end, and so forth" (p. 5).

Task Definition

Another issue in which researchers' opinions conflict considerably is that of compositional task definition. For example, Kratus suggests that "limiting the number of melodic options for novice composers may focus their attention on development and repetition faster by reducing the amount of exploration necessary" (1994, pp. 134–35). This is in direct contrast to the approach suggested by Davidson (1990), who indicates that unnecessary limitation of classroom compositional tasks results in limited compositional outcomes. This is supported by Loane (1984) and by DeLorenzo's (1989) study of sixth-grade students' composition. DeLorenzo concludes:

> That a student became highly involved in a creative project while others remained on the outskirts of the creative activity may have much to do with the student's perception of choice in the problem structure and his or her capacity to shape musical events. The more control one perceives in shaping musical events, the more likely the created product truly represents one's expressive intent. The perceived relevance of the task, as it relates to the student's personal definition of music, may also have influenced individual involvement. (1989, pp. 196–97)

While Kaschub (1997) cautions against overly broad and poorly defined compositional tasks that may lead to confusion on the part of children, other writers (Glover, 2000; Hickey, 2003; Sundin, 1998) express concern about constraints imposed by both teachers and researchers: "children work hard to make the world meaningful, including the world of music. Perhaps they cannot make such meaning out of creativity studies conducted in non-natural settings with highly specific tasks which severely limit their own imagination and also their choices" (Sundin, 1998, p. 53).

Reflexivity

In addition to task definition, the time required to facilitate children's creative decision-making is also a focus of attention. Davidson (1990) views time for reflection on compositional outcomes and consequent reworking of material as an important component of compositional activity in the classroom. Balkin (1990) sees reflection as integral to the creative process: "The creative person must continually rethink, reconsider, replace, refine, redo, reaffirm, reprocess, rewrite, and reconceptualize" (p. 32).

Webster (1995) includes reflection as a prominent element in his model of the creative process. He defines the creative process as involving the ability to "think in sound" and sees his model as equally applicable to composition, improvisation, performance, and listening (1995, p. 27). Building on the creativity work of Wallas (cited in Hickey, 2003), Webster conceives of the creative process in music as an essentially recursive one. At the beginning of the process, the *Preparation* stage, musical ideas are generated or heard. "Influenced by a host of variables (both personal and environmental), the creator generates these musical ideas as a basis for creative work" (Webster, 1995, p. 29). In the second stage, *Incubation,* the divergent thought of the first stage gives way to reflection, which might involve removal from the task, consultation between group members or, in the case of improvisation, "might be the time that the performer is not actively improvising and is listening to or accompanying others" (p. 29). From this point:

> Active return to the creative thinking process might lead back to the divergency of the preparation stage or ahead to the period of illumination and verification. This last major stage is where much time is spent developing musical ideas, doing so in a more linear and convergent fashion . . .This may lead to the final product, return to a more reflective state, or simply move toward a new cycle of divergency. (1995, p. 29)

In a more complex model of creative thinking in music, Webster (2003) outlines the movement between divergent and convergent thinking that he sees as central to the thinking process that converts *Product Intentions* into *Creative Product.* He elaborates on the personal and environmental "Enabling Conditions" (motivation, subconscious imagery, environment, personality) and "Enabling Skills" (aptitudes, craftsmanship, aesthetic sensitivity, conceptual understanding) that influence the creative act. Like Davidson (1990), he stresses the need for sufficient time to be allowed for creative thinking, particularly revision, to occur.

Cognitive Skills in Composition and Improvisation

It can be seen that Webster's model encompasses both compositional and improvisational activity. The desire to separate these two forms of creative endeavor in music and to attribute different thought processes to them has given rise to a number of studies. Sloboda (1985) sees composers as possessing a greater structural consciousness (or "superordinate plan," p. 103) and ability to select and revise material than improvisers. This is because of the limited time available for decision-making in improvisation (due to the perceived simultaneity of planning and performance).

However, Pressing (1988) suggests that, precisely because of the limited time, improvisers develop higher-order cognitive skills and aggregative memory constituents in which "very complicated interconnected knowledge structures may develop" (p. 166). He states:

> All motor organizational functions can be handled automatically (without conscious attention) and the performer [improviser] attends almost exclusively to a higher level of emergent expressive control parameters . . . such as form, timbre, texture, articulation, gesture, activity level, pitch relationships, motoric "feel," expressive design, emotion, note placement, and dynamics. (p. 139)

Campbell (1991) concurs with this view of cognitive complexity in the improvisational process:

> It requires a thorough knowledge of the melodic and rhythmic codes . . . that define a style and a grounding in how this vocabulary of music fits within the structure of a work. It demands a powerful ear and an aural and kinetic memory for patterns . . . . It necessitates extensive listening and performance experience to develop familiarity with a musical style, confidence in the performance of standard works within the idiom, and an independence of spirit that will allow the individual to experiment with new arrangements of representative melodies, rhythms, and textural elements within the style. (pp. 22–23)

This view is informed by the author's extensive ethnographic and ethno-musicological research. It is evident that studies that have involved the collection of rich descriptive data (such as those of Barrett, 1996, 2003; Borstad, 1990; Burnard, 1999, 2002, 2006; Christensen, 1992; Davies, 1986, 1994; DeLorenzo, 1989; Glover, 2000; Kanellopoulos, 1999; Loane, 1984; Pond, 1980/1992; Stauffer, 2001, 2002; Sundin, 1998; Wiggins, 1994, 1999, 2003, and Young, 2003) are more likely to acknowledge the greater complexity of the cognitive and metacognitive processes involved in children's creative activity, whether composition or improvisation, and to emphasize the proclivity of even quite young children to shape sounds quite consciously into formal structures.[1]

Structures and Processes

The nature of these structures and the processes through which they are formed is quite variable and dependant on a range of factors. For example, in examining the musical play of very young children in early childhood settings, Young (2003) draws attention to the inextricable link between music-making and movement. The children in Young's study created "special patterns arising from the placing of their playing movements in relation to the instrument structure" (2003, p. 52), then consciously extended them using "sequences of exact or transformed repetitions" (p. 52). Children developed patterns through processes of repeating, clustering, or chaining. Working with a much older group of middle-school children (twelve year olds), Burnard (1999) also found that kinesthetic patterns associated with previous performative experiences on particular instruments formed a "well-spring of existing ideas" (p. 171) that influenced improvisational and compositional forms.

Stauffer (2001, 2002) and Folkestad (1998) have explored the processes and structures involved in children's and adolescents' computer compositions. Folkestad has identified horizontal or vertical approaches to structuring compositions, whereby adolescents either conceive of fully worked "chunks" or work horizontally through a composition then gradually flesh out the "arrangement" (instrumentation). Stauffer notes that both the compositional structures and processes of children in her study were influenced by the digital medium in use, by time in which to interact with musical material within this medium, and by external experiences, including instrumental tuition and performance and musical styles absorbed from the media.

Intentionality

When investigating the processes of children's musical creativity, it is clear that a special effort is required to understand children's intentions in their compositional endeavors. From observations of and discussions with children in a school setting and examination of their compositions, Glover (2000) lists a range of musical purposes which children in her study articulate in their creative music making. These include the improvisatory "just playing"; "making some music" (where ownership and production are part of the intent); imitating music making which a child has observed; "making a 'song'" (a deliberate structure which may be a song in the standard sense or an instrumental piece); making preconceived patterns and structures; developing a musical idea or motive into a whole piece; developing an expressive idea into a piece; "making music for a specific function" (for example dancing or marching); creating programmatic music; and structuring music around the musical interaction with others (pp. 28–30).

Kanellopoulos (1999), who explored the latter idea with eight-year-old Greek children, views "shared intentionality" (p. 184) as a characteristic of group improvisation. Shared intentionality is demonstrated by the children "rendering a piece [of improvised music] a concrete entity with specific boundaries, using particular sounds and combinations of sounds" (p. 184) which are agreed upon by the group.

Social Interaction

Sometimes children's intentions are made most clearly evident in their interactions with others in a group. Burnard (2002), discussing the free improvisation of a group of twelve-year-olds states that "what improvisation came to mean to each child was not generated within one mind but, rather, constructed between people. The children's understanding of group improvisation was jointly negotiated and constructed as provisional, and frequently contested" (p. 168). Burnard found that children's contributions to the group improvisations gradually aligned themselves as they listened and responded to each other and reached a shared and negotiated realization of intent. Children took on various roles as leader or supporter but these roles could change in subsequent improvisations and were in a constant state of flux, with children on occasion "dissolving the role of leadership through interacting freely and exploring some interesting ametrical musical exchanges. The direction of play appeared to shift between taking control and allowing freedom" (p. 164). Burnard also noted that the social bonding within the group experience enabled children to take risks with music-making within a supportive situation.

The enhancement of children's composition through social interaction has also been the focus of a study by MacDonald and Meill (2000), who investigated the different processes and compositional outcomes produced by pairs of friends as opposed to non-friends. They found that compositional activities initiated by friends contained more musical and verbal transactions that resulted in the extending of musical ideas. Consequently, their compositions appeared to be of a higher standard (as judged by an experienced teacher). Kaschub (1997) endorses the notion that collaboration leads not only to more highly developed compositions but also to the development of creative and critical thinking: "Collaborative efforts allow students to challenge each other's ideas and to experiment with compositional decisions which may be questioned or criticized by their peers. It is through these types of exchanges that students are challenged to think creatively and critically about their compositions and about the compositions of others" (p. 27). This observation is supported by Wiggins (1999), who further outlines the benefits for individual children composing within groups of varying sizes:

> Work within the groups seems to promote and nurture independent musical thinking by creating a rich and safe environment within

which students seem to feel at ease generating original musical ideas. As they work, students draw upon or intentionally oppose ideas of others within the group . . . . In these settings, students received immediate feedback, which may cause them to restate, justify, defend or alter their ideas. Experiencing the ideas of others has the potential to generate within the individual a sense of possibilities, thereby motivating and empowering the individual to explore higher levels of complexity during subsequent attempts at creating. (p. 86)

In generating group compositions, children draw upon shared musical understanding that reflects both previous compositional and classroom experiences and experiences external to the classroom. Their shared vision of the appropriate musical idiom and activity also "reflects cultural influences, including influences of the media and the music of the children's world" (Wiggins, 1999, p. 85).

Social Situatedness

As is evident in the preceding comment by Wiggins, recent research into children's musical creativity has firmly situated creative activity within a social and cultural milieu (Barrett, 2003; Burnard, 2006; Glover, 2000; Stauffer, 2002; Sundin, 1998; Wiggins, 2003). As Glover (2000) noted, children "find purposes for composing that reflect both their inner sense of music's possibilities and the ways in which music is woven expressively and functionally into community life. Their composing has musical intention and cultural currency" (p. 2). She states that, while there are developmental factors that affect children's formulation of compositions, experiential factors are more influential. She illustrates this with children's song-making, discussing the fact that children understand song structures and functions, for example, because they have encountered and used songs on a recurrent basis from a very early age.

Affirming the importance of social and cultural factors, Burnard (2006) maintains that creativity is not age-dependent but, instead, develops in response to contextual and environmental influences. She proposes that rather than there being a single overarching form of development of creativity, it is shaped by exposure to the expectations and possibilities of the social and auditory environment. She concludes that: "By conceptualising children both as individual actors and as social beings we may come to focus on musical creativity as cultural action, which is present and ongoing in the daily interactions of any community as something socially constructed and socially mediated" (Burnard, 2006, p. 370).

Sundin (1998) also discusses the intersection of the individual and social worlds of children in their creative activity, citing influences such as gender, social class, and school atmosphere as important. He notes that children may exhibit two contrasting manifestations of musicality: that which is spontaneous and creative, and that which is designed to meet the expectations of the adult world.

Like Burnard, Glover (2000) indicates that the complexity of societal influences blurs ideas of musical creativity:

> Unparalled global evolution in cross-cultural perceptions of music have (sic) resulted in populations whose musical culture is more complex in mix, fusion and access to different world musics than ever before. In such a climate, any fixed notion of what composing is has been thoroughly deconstructed as it becomes clear that the processes of making music are as diverse as the musics themselves. (p. 3)

In view of this, a number of researchers call into question the notion that any single model of children's musical creativity can be applicable to all children in all contexts (Burnard, 2006). Loane (1984) draws attention to the subjective nature of any research into children's musical thinking: "because verbal thinking must fall short of the musical thinking it studies, each of us will inevitably find different aspects of our pupils' work to comment on, and each of us will develop his or her own 'ways of thinking' accordingly" (p. 230). One must therefore question whether any one model can adequately represent children's musical creativity as it is enacted in multiple situations in a variety of societal settings.

This book attempts to develop one "way of thinking" about children's musical creativity as it is exemplified by the generation and transmission of music observed among children engaged in musical play in naturalistic settings. The results of my cross-cultural research are related to the issues emerging from the foregoing review of the literature on children's musical creativity. These include the applicability of current models of creativity; the type and complexity of children's compositional thought processes; the relationship of these to improvisational activity; processes involved in collaborative improvisation; and the social contexts in which creative activity takes place.

Creativity in children's "traditional" forms of musical play occurs in interactive situations as part of an oral tradition. Children's playground singing games are transmitted predominantly, though not exclusively, through oral means, from child to child. Changes that occur through transmission processes affect the three integral elements of this genre of children's musical play: music, text, and movement. Theories of creativity pertaining to oral transmission, therefore, must also be explored when considering conceptions of children's creativity. Most of the work on oral transmission theory has been formulated with reference to adult traditions of performance. In the following section these theories are examined and their more recent application to instances of children's musical play and folklore is discussed.

Theories of Oral Transmission: Past and Present

Theories of oral transmission and performance are concerned with the ways in which oral forms are both produced and reproduced in performance, having been transmitted from one performer to another or from one performance to another. Characteristics of orally transmitted forms of performance have been discussed by Lord (1960, 1995), Treitler (1974, 1986), Ong (1982), Edwards and Sienkewicz (1990), and Rubin (1995), among many others.

Initial work in this field was conducted in relation to the epics of Homer by Parry (cited in Edwards and Sienkowicz, 1990; Lord, 1960; Ong, 1982; Rubin, 1995; Treitler, 1974). Parry concluded that these works had not been composed in written form, but were the remnants of an oral tradition. They were composed orally by combining culturally predetermined formulae, a formula being defined as "a group of words which is regularly employed under the same metrical conditions to express a given essential idea" (Lord, 1960, p. 30), that is, a standardized pattern of sounds that has an implicit meaning for those within the culture. Ong (1982) sees such formulae as mnemonic devices, the repetition of which is necessary for the maintenance of knowledge in oral cultures.

Parry's theories were applied by Lord to the study of a living oral tradition, that of epic performance by *guslars*[2] in the former Yugoslavia. While Lord retained Parry's definition of the formula as text-bound, it is clear from Lord's descriptions of the transmission process that recurrent melodic patterning (which might be construed as melodic formulae) is also a feature of this form of performance that is learnt by apprentice performers (Lord, 1960).

In generalizing these findings to the study of oral composition in plainchant, Treitler (1974) extended the concept of a formulaic system into the melodic domain, to include "the singer's assimilated sense of the pattern of a melodic phrase" (p. 359). According to Treitler, the processes of oral transmission and composition are interconnected: "[The performer] learns one melody and he imitates its pattern in inventing another like it. At some point his inventions do not refer back to the model of concrete melodies but are based on his internalised sense of pattern" (1974, p. 360). These internalized patterns comprise a "generative matrix" which, when used by successive performers over a succession of performances, results in many variants (Treitler, 1986, p. 46).

Also inherent in oral composition is the notion of "composition in performance" (Lord, 1995, p. 11). Edwards and Sienkowicz describe oral composition as "an act of recreation in which performers, skilled in thinking on their feet, draw on traditional tools rather than rote memorisation. These tools include the shared expectation of the overall pattern of the performance; the use of formulae and repeated themes; of special language, music and metre" (1990, p. 13). These "structural props" (Edwards and Sienkowicz, 1990, p. 13) enable performers to simultaneously create and perform. Their use serves to differentiate oral composition from "impromptu, extempore creation," as the performer's command of formulae, acquired through frequent use and practice, is integral to accomplished oral performance (Lord, 1995, p. 11). Performance can therefore be seen as "the enabling event, tradition as the enabling referent" (Foley, 1995, p. 27).

Edwards and Sienkowicz expound further on both the acquisition of traditional tools of oral composition and their use by talented performers:

> they nourish their talents by listening, observing and internalizing the requirements of the performance, sometimes practising in private, sometimes trying out their skills in competition with others. They model themselves on other good performers, inheriting a corpus of themes, conventions and formulae which link them with an uninterrupted oral tradition. Their accomplishments as performers, however, depend not only on their ability to learn or memorize what has gone before: they must be able to manipulate the structures to their advantage, improvising, embellishing and extending. (1990, p. 35)

Also central to an understanding of "composition in performance" is the interaction between performer and audience (Edwards and Sienkowicz, 1990, p. 218). Ong (1982, pp. 41–42) partly attributes the performers' deliberate innovation to the need to engage the audience. He sees originality as relating not to the introduction of new materials, but to the ways in which the traditional materials are used to fit a new situation (p. 60). According to Edwards and Sienkowicz (1990), however, the nexus between composition and performance results not only in original deployment of formulae, but also in new references to contemporary material, persons, issues, and events, which change with the circumstances of each performance: "Performance is thus dynamic, never static, and changes from one occasion to the next" (Edwards and Sienkowicz, 1990, p. 218).

A more contentious element of these theories is that, although oral performances are dynamic, the modes of thought that characterize oral composition and performance are seen as unchanging and able to be generalized to members of any culture that is "untouched by literacy" (Ong, 1982, p. 6). For example, it is postulated that these thought processes result in forms which are always additive, aggregative, and, consequently, repetitious, with content focused on present, concrete realities rather than the abstract (Ong, 1982, pp. 31–77).

In dismissing this paradigm as an oversimplification, Feld (1986) states:

> If "orality" was in fact such a determinant or limiting condition on mental processes as revealed in musical form, we would expect far less variety in the music of small-scale societies, and far less variety in its forms of composition and transmission than has already been documented. . . . [T]he notions of the oral psyche . . . or "orality" as a "state of mind" are most misleading and dangerous in the way they dismiss rather than address the meanings, uses, and creative inventions that characterize music in societies of oral tradition. (p. 25)

Niles (1999) adds that "[n]o one model of oral composition can have universal validity, but dynamism is always the rule" (p. 58). Questioning the supremacy of a single oral-formulaic process, Finnegan (1992) indicates that, although commonly occurring, it is not necessarily the only compositional process in use in oral transmission.

Oral Transmission and Children's Lore

As indicated by Finnegan's admonition above, the discussion of transmission and oral composition processes has more recently extended upon the oral-formulaic theories of Parry and Lord. Applying psychological methods and constructs to the study of memory in oral traditions, Rubin (1995) has postulated that semantic meaning, imagery, and patterns of sound (rhyme, alliteration, assonance, meter, and rhythm) operate to cue memory and to provide constraints on the level of variation that can be created. All of these elements combine to form schemas or generative rules. Rubin sees formulae as the products of (or solutions to) combined constraints. In applying his ideas to the study of one genre of children's musical play, counting-out rhymes, he identifies multiple constraints, particularly relating to patterns of sound (for example, rhyme and meter), which lead to their relative stability: "Why are counting-out rhymes so stable? Because the children who use them are sensitive to the constraints of the genre, as expressed in the individual pieces, and once the constraints are followed, there is little that can vary" (1995, p. 252).

Harwood (1998b) supports this view of immutable constraints on creativity in her study of African American girls' playground singing games. Although she acknowledges improvisation in individual play, she maintains that "the repertoire they share as a group—their traditional music lore—contains relatively little scope for individual innovation" (p. 113). She attributes this both to the formulaic nature of the performances and to social constraints that focus on correct forms and the maintenance of authenticity: "Against this backdrop, where everyone is a critic, where performing the correct way is the only socially acceptable way, and where correctness means faithful adherence to the existing tradition, it is little wonder that improvisation, in the sense of individual melodic, rhythmic, or textual embellishments of the "right" tune, does not flourish" (1998b, p. 115). However, Harwood does outline a range of prescribed forms of improvisation within certain social situations or play genres which enable some or all players (more frequently the most adept) to create variations within stipulated guidelines, noting that there is a balance between "children's fiercely conservative impulse" and "the attraction they have for innovation and novelty" (1998b, p. 115).

In contrast, McDowell (1999) indicates that children's interest in novelty fuels creativity within their folklore, stating that "children frequently first exhaust the store of traditional items, and then move on to novel items, spontaneously composed on the model of familiar traditional items" (p. 57). Fascinated by "the almost amoebic ability of children to incorporate extraneous materials into their expressive competencies" (p. 53), McDowell outlines a process by which children transmit their folklore. In this process of encoding, reception, decoding, and re-encoding of folkloric "messages" (pp. 52–59), children create the material within defined formulaic structures, then pass it on to another child or group of children who receive and assimilate it within their own frameworks "in association with familiar archetypes" and individual "aesthetic proclivities" (p. 56). Within the "creative, generative dimensions of this message processing stage . . . these assimilative processes refurbish the materials received," including those originally derived from adult and popular culture sources, "endowing them with their inimitable fidelity to the outlook and expressive preferences of the communities in which they circulate" (p. 57).

The process continues with further possible re-encoding and decoding involving spontaneous creation: "The exuberant and unbounded give-and-take of children's play ensures the continuous reworking of traditional materials" (p. 57). Rather than being overwhelmed by constraints, in McDowell's view "the child emerges as the genius of composition, a complex cerebral and sentient locus of serious effort at self-expression and communication" (p. 62).

In examining why there might be such a discrepancy in views of "composition in performance" within genres of children's musical play, it is useful to consider that processes are not universal and may be influenced by a range of situational issues, as with the various pedagogical theories pertaining to children's composition. McDowell cites various factors contributing to relative stability or instability of folkore, including mood, the type of folklore genre, and the "rhetorical purposes of the performers" (1999, p. 59).

Finnegan (1986) stresses the continued need for contextual study:

> there is no *one* way in which oral elements in verbal art are necessarily expressed and formulated. . . . 'Orality' or 'oral tradition' can be realised in manifold different forms which cannot be predicted *a priori* but must be discovered through detailed investigation and in full appreciation of the variety and complexity inherent in oral, as in written, modes of expression and communication. (p.76)

In view of this critique, I have attempted to provide a detailed, contextualized account of transmission processes and the factors that affect oral transmission, creation, and performance of musical play forms by children in a range of schools in international locations. The length and regularity of my contact with the performers at one school (as outlined in the following chapter) has enabled me to trace these processes and their outcomes over six years, revisiting particular performers and discovering new influences on playground performance as they have emerged. However, as context is crucial in determining patterns of behavior, processes of transmission observed in this school are further examined in relation to other cultural environments. The following chapter discusses the ways in which my investigation of transmission processes and other aspects of children's musical play developed in response to the different contexts in which it was conducted and the perceived needs and responses of the children and adults with whom I engaged.

INTO THE FIELD

CHAPTER 3

Investigating Musical Play

Ethics and Pragmatics

I n the following outline of my fieldwork methods, I have deliberately adopted a discursive approach in an attempt to convey the fact that my methodology, in addition to the theoretical outcomes of the investigation, has been grounded in the nature of the material to be studied. While initial protocols were developed in response both to the nature of my enquiry and to perceived limitations of earlier studies of children's traditional play, my methodological approaches evolved over time, as understandings of the nature of the material grew and constraints on the development of these understandings became apparent. As Shelemay (1997) observes, ethnography entails "a reality of sharing and interaction, one predicated on negotiated relationships" (p. 202). The growth of my relationships with the children with whom I interacted in a variety of settings and with adult research partners who contributed to my understanding of children's practices in these diverse localities also affected my research processes and outcomes over the lengthy period in which I was engaged in this endeavor.

In developing my research methods, I was initially confronted by a number of philosophical issues and practical constraints. These issues, elaborated below, had considerable bearing on the collection methods I employed and on my methods of analysis.

Philosophical Issues

Contextualization

The first issue concerns the understanding that children's culture, while drawing upon adult society, has its own integrity. It is therefore necessary to view the material collected within the subculture of children in terms of the attributes that are important to children, rather than the qualities that adults perceive as "useful." In Grugeon's critique of the Opies' substantial body of work on singing games and other forms of children's playlore (Opie and Opie, 1959, 1969, 1985), she expresses the need to fully contextualize the collected material in order to derive meaning from it:

> The Opies had left me none the wiser about the relationship between the singer and the song. Their concentration on texts left no room for reflection about the reasons for the continued transmission of this culture by children. . . . Somehow the Opies in their search for literary gems seem to ignore the evidence under their eyes. . . . What is absent from their collection is any account of the way these rhymes are part of small girls' culture. (1988, pp. 13–15)

Grugeon is particularly critical of the Opies' evident distaste for what Bauman terms "the seamy underside of childhood" (1982, p. 175) and their tendency to disregard the more "disreputable" material (Grugeon, 1988, pp. 14–15). In contrast, Bauman argues for truly ethnographic studies of children's folklore, which entail: "investigating their folklore as a cultural system in its own terms, attending to the ways and contexts in which it is used by them in the conduct of peer group social life, neglecting nothing that is meaningful to them—decorous or indecorous, sense or nonsense— . . . [regardless of whether] it is meaningful to adult sensibilities" (1982, p. 175).

Factor, an influential researcher in the field of children's folklore, deplores the "widespread acceptance . . . of a pragmatic and utilitarian ideology which emphasises the 'product' and evaluates the worth of a human action or idea by the profitability of its outcome" (1988, p. 31). Bauman labels the results of this instrumentalist approach as "adultocentrism" (1982, p. 174), in which children are regarded as "proto-adults . . . as yet unfinished bearers of adult culture" (1982, p. 173). It has therefore been necessary for researchers to break through what Sutton-Smith (1970) refers to as the "triviality barrier" (where all nonproductive play is seen as trivial) and to study "the patterns and functions of [children's] folklore as situated communication, rendered meaningful in terms of endogenously determined contexts of use" (Bauman, 1982, p. 174).

In attempting to apply this maxim to the study of children's musical play, I was met with some particular methodological problems. By far the most accurate assessment of "endogenously determined contexts of use" is provided by the participants. However, it would seem that an adult, by nature of her adultness, or "otherness," cannot be a participant observer. As Fine (1999) states, "Adults are always salient in children's societies by virtue of the authority that is implicit in their status, and all data collected from children by adults must be examined for effects arising from their presence" (p. 130).

Children's interactions may be altered even when the researcher views the children's performances from the point of a nonparticipant observer, as both the context and nature of the performance may be changed by the performers to meet the perceived requirements of the observer and to maintain the privacy of the participants. Because of researcher effect, Hammersley and Atkinson (1995) contest the notion of researcher as nonparticipant observer. They maintain that, through acting (however unobtrusively) on the field in which research is undertaken, the ethnographer must be a participant in the field and thus, by definition, a participant observer, albeit a participant with a range of different roles. In research with children, Fine categorizes these roles as "supervisor, leader, observer, and friend" (1999, p. 128), each of which involves varying levels of authority and consequent differences in rapport, trust, and access to information.

Distortions of children's performances and subsequent interpretation may be magnified by the need to observe elicited, rather than completely natural performances. The spontaneous and fleeting nature of naturally occurring instances of children's musical play do not easily allow for the predictable and replicable recording situation required for transcription and musical analysis. Problems with elicited performances have been discussed by Brunton (1976), whose recordings were of individual children selected by adults, in a non-naturalistic setting. Not only did this limit the amount of information regarding the performance practice and context of children's games, but their spontaneity was also affected. Brunton described the initial discomfort and embarrassment children displayed when revealing their songs and rhymes (particularly those considered to be "improper") to the researcher and commented on the positive effects of interviewing two or more informants together. Harwood (1987), in her study of the memorized song repertoire of schoolchildren, also reported the increased spontaneity of responses when recording groups of friends rather than individual children.

In order to observe the "conduct of peer group social life" discussed above by Bauman and to lessen any diffidence in children's response, I aimed to record children performing games in friendship groupings in a naturalistic playground setting. I initially collected material by observing and recording children at Springfield Public School in Sydney, Australia, over a period of six years, from December 1990 to November 1996. Fieldwork was initiated during two weeks in December 1990. For reasons discussed later in the chapter formal fieldwork was conducted for periods of four weeks during November and December of both 1993 and 1994, supplemented by informal observation throughout the period from 1991 to 1995. In addition, short periods were devoted to recording specific game performances in April and December 1995, and September and November 1996.

In 1990 my initial contact with children at the school was in response to information from teachers regarding the location of game sites and the children known to perform the games. This information was limited by the teachers' general lack of knowledge of the games' existence. All but a few teachers claimed that traditional games had virtually disappeared from the playground in this school. This "invisibility" to adults, partly due to the games' perceived lack of functional use, as previously discussed, has been reported by a number of other researchers into children's playground games (Bishop & Curtis, 2001; Grugeon, 1988; Opie & Opie, 1985; Perkins & Russell, 1993). However, as my presence in the school continued, teachers became more aware of the occurrence of musical play, and both the staff and I observed more game sites and participants.

During the two-week collection period in 1990, I observed children playing singing games in the playground and when "lining up" before entering the classroom. I approached groups of children I had observed playing in the playground and recorded them in naturalistic settings, using, simultaneously, a handheld video camera and fixed audio recorder.[1] However, I quickly encountered some of the difficulties that had led other researchers to elicit game performances. Although all the equipment was portable, it was sometimes impossible to set up both the video and audio equipment in time to record a game as it was observed in the playground. Similarly, games in their natural context could be interrupted by the arrival of a teacher or interference by other children.

Recordings of such "flawed" performances can still reveal much about playground interactions and provide valuable contextual information (Bauman, 1982, p. 177). However, musicological analysis of the games requires audible, as well as visible recordings. The high level of extraneous sounds in the playground rendered the musical characteristics of the games inaudible at times.

To counter these recording problems, I experimented with several strategies. First I began eliciting game performances in their natural context: after a short period of observing the performers engaged in playing the games in the playground I would approach them and ask if I could film their games. They were then asked if they knew other games, and I would continue filming until their repertoire was exhausted (rarely), their interest flagged, or external events, such as the end of the lunch period, intervened. To alleviate sound problems, recording sessions of their extended repertoire were often conducted with the players inside an empty classroom, or in the relatively quiet playground after classes had resumed.

As most of the children were eager to be recorded, many approached me again on subsequent days and recording sessions were conducted in an empty classroom. Children also reported other friends or groups known to perform the games and would often bring them to me for recording. In these instances, recording was usually initiated in an empty room and was followed by a visit to the area in which the children normally played, to gain some understanding of the context.

Although adult interest is sometimes a stimulus for performance, as Bauman (1982) and Russell (1986) attest, any researcher must be aware of the implications of inducing a performance, however natural the setting may appear to be. An example of the distortion that can result occurred during my 1990 fieldwork at Springfield. I was surprised and somewhat excited when two boys volunteered to perform some clapping games, assumed by many researchers to be "owned" and performed only by girls (Knapp and Knapp, 1976, Merrill-Mirsky, 1988, Grugeon, 1988). Subsequent interviews some months later revealed that it was the presence of a video camera that had been the stimulus for their involvement and that these boys did not normally perform clapping games (although other boys did). Similarly, Russell (1986) reports ephemeral realignments of friendship groups in order to perform for her and so claim her attention.

Recordings were always initiated during recess and lunch times. Occasionally, recording sessions continued into class teaching periods, but, with one exception, all recording sessions were conducted with small groups of children in the absence of teachers. On the one occasion when I was invited by a teacher to record the games in a classroom, the teacher's presence considerably affected the performance practice. All of the children were initially required to demonstrate the games, regardless of their interest or the regularity of their playground participation in them. As the teacher was implementing a nonsexist policy with her class, the children were required to sit in a circle with boys interspersed between girls. Once these restrictions were lifted, particularly after the teacher left the room, the boys' participation ceased and game interactions between small groups and pairs of interested girls resumed a greater degree of spontaneity. As a result of this experience, I resolved to avoid doing any further recording under teacher supervision.

During the first recording period in 1990, interviews regarding performance practices were conducted with children, using unstructured interview techniques. While some of these interviews immediately followed recording sessions, others were sometimes done on subsequent days, after I had reviewed my field notes. In the initial stages of fieldwork, elicited interviews were not recorded audiovisually, but in field notes, along with the results of brief interviews with teachers concerning phenomena observed in the playground or background information about game performers. This practice was modified in subsequent collection periods, for reasons discussed below.

Appropriation

A second area of philosophical concern is the encroachment by adults on the private world of children and their resulting disenfranchisement. The unequal power relationships of adult researcher and the children being studied are revealed in Sutton-Smith's assertion: "Unfortunately, even children in all their spontaneity do not offer themselves with naive realism to ethnographic grasp. They are more often possessed by us through our contemporary and sometimes contemptible obsessions about childhood" (1982, p. 32).

Although most recent researchers into children's playground singing games are cognizant of the need to establish a rapport with their child informants, some have failed to recognize the implications of the inherent power relationship created by their role as former teachers of these informants.

It is also evident that children, "a powerless and officially inaudible group" (Factor, 1988, p. 32), have, in some cases, been refused access to their playlore once it has come into the possession of adults. In a notorious instance of this, the first major Australian publication of children's playlore texts, *Cinderella Dressed in Yella* (Turner, 1969) was banned from the shelves of children's libraries in Australia because of the scatological nature of some of the contents. Throughout the world, collections of children's playground games are published for use by teachers but, as Hall (1984) and Fine (1999) point out, children who have contributed to the publications are rarely acknowledged, nor do they receive the royalties.

The appropriation and commodification of "original creative product by primary tradition bearers" (p. 239) that has occurred with "World Music" has been discussed at length by Feld (1994a, 1994b). What is clear from this discussion is that, in the contemporary environment, the interaction between powerful and powerless groups is complex and multi-faceted, with appropriation and re-appropriation leading to the generation of new cultural products for both groups. My qualms about appropriating playground games from children were somewhat diminished by my gradual realization, as field collection proceeded, that children constantly draw on adult material when creating and varying these games, and that game material published by adults in forms accessible to children (for example, Factor, 1983, 1985, 1986; Russell, 1990) is also a popular source of ideas and models for their creative activity. It became apparent, too, that children have developed a range of strategies for regaining control of their own play, such as modifying their song material once it is known to adults and thus invalidating adult ownership.

Nevertheless, I was conscious that, in trying to enter the world of children, I would need to offer something of value to the children I was recording. It would also be necessary to establish myself in a role that would engender feelings of mutual trust, rather than obtain mere physical proximity: "The free peer group activity of children is by its very nature a privileged realm in which adults are alien intruders, especially so insofar as much of the children's folklore repertoire violates what children understand to be adult standards of decorum" (Bauman, 1982, p. 178).

To the children I defined myself as someone interested in their games, a collector who wished to film their games and disseminate them to other adults, including teachers who could use the games with other groups of children. Their response was one of great generosity. One group of eight-year-old children told me they would like to share their games with other children who might not have their own repertoire and would consequently be bored. For each group of children I was also providing adult attention and interest, and to some extent, adult validation of their pursuits. The lure of the video camera was also not to be underestimated.

Children's participation was by choice, although that choice was obviously mediated by many factors, including curiosity, peer pressure, and the desire to gain the approval of an adult. With the exception of some brief contextualizing footage of children in lines and in the playground, usually filmed at a distance, children's permission was always sought prior to filming and participants joined and left the play sites at will.

Recording of Multiple Performance Elements

The rationale for the use of audiovisual technology for recording purposes, briefly referred to in the preceding discussion of field techniques, requires further elaboration. As most researchers into children's playlore have come from disciplines other than music, the greatest body of collected material has been documented in the form of text only. The primary focus of much of the previously published material on this subject has been textual analysis, with the interpretation of social function centered on text meaning.

However, it is evident from ethnomusicological and anthropological studies of singing games and other performance genres involving combinations of music, movement, and text (Addo, 1995; Beresin, 1999; Campbell,

1998; Clunies Ross and Wild, 1984; Ellis, 1985; Gaunt, 2006; Kaeppler, 1972) that analyzing the text in isolation from the other elements of the performance, as well as from the performance's context, leads to an incomplete and often erroneous interpretation of meaning. In some cases this indicates either that the semantic content of the text is of secondary importance, or that the performers have provided the researcher with a "false front" or superficial meaning which diverts the attention of an "outsider" from the "real" meaning of the performance.[2]

Finnegan (1986) also discusses the inadequacy of text-based analysis to encompass the important performance elements of orally transmitted musical forms, including "style of delivery (tempo, mood, dynamics, or tone . . .), . . . audience involvement and response, [and] verbal interplay." Where music is removed from "the act of performance with its richness of specific occasion or succession of variations," what remains is "a seriously incomplete account of most oral . . . performances as they are actually experienced by performers and listeners" (p. 74).

As I was interested in the processes of transmission and variation in children's musical play, and the factors that affect them, I sought to document as many details as possible of the performance practice of multiple performers. Audio recording of performing groups provided me with information regarding many nuances of performance. For example, disagreements between individual participants' contributions in relation to the melody were clearly evident. When several versions of a game and associated performers' comments were audio recorded, it was possible not only to begin to analyze variant forms but also to discern some aspects of the performance that were particularly important to the performers, for example, tempo and group size.

By video recording playground singing games,[3] however, it was possible to document a much broader range of performance parameters. Video recording of multiple performances enabled me to document the context of the games, performers' interactions and comments, the relationship between sound and movement, and discrepancies between individual performers within a group, thus helping to delineate patterns of ownership, leadership, and levels of competence. Discrepancies between different performances indicated many additional things potentially of value to the music educator, such as compositional techniques, preferred tessitura, the role of tempo, and intervallic and rhythmic features that might be relatively easy or difficult to perform, as well as "the range of cognitive and communicative skills implicated in the performance of the genre" (Bauman, 1982, p. 178).

I therefore endeavored to collect, in a playground context, a large sample of group performances, using synchronized audio and video recordings, with additional documentation provided by field notes. The dual mode of recording provided two complementary sources of information to enable more complete transcriptions and minimize the loss of data through equipment failure. A total of 618 performances of playground singing games by 139 children,[4] aged from five to twelve years, was recorded during the first period of fieldwork from 1990 to 1996 at Springfield. In order to study variation practices in detail, I restricted recording primarily to one playground game genre, the clapping game, which contained the elements of text, music, and movement. Performances of additional genres were recorded incidentally. From recorded performances, eighty-four different game types were identified. For ethical reasons, pseudonyms were created for all performers and other informants. In creating pseudonyms, I endeavored to retain some sense of the character of the original name, for example, with regard to ethnicity.

In transcribing the material, I adopted a descriptive method of notation (Ellingson, 1992) in which the formal elements of text, music, and movement are given equal attention. Variations between multiple performances or between the contributions of individual participants have also been transcribed. For a full discussion of transcription methods and conventions used see appendix 2.

The fieldwork at Springfield provided an immense amount of material for analysis. It was also evident that a longitudinal study in one school would provide more information regarding patterns of variation and transmission within and between groups of performers over time than a number of short-term studies in different schools. However, my study and those of Campbell (1991, 1998), Merrill-Mirsky (1988), Riddell (1990), Addo (1995) and Harwood (1992, 1994) were each context-specific. While previous cross-cultural musicological studies existed (for example that of Segler, 1992), they were limited to the study of the musical characteristics of European games. As time wore on and I had increasing encounters with colleagues from other localities and disciplines who shared their experiences of research in this field, I felt a need to investigate how children from other socio-musical contexts, speaking a variety of languages, including English, engage in musical play within the confines of school life. In 2001 I embarked on a cross-cultural study of children's musical play in a range of international locations. In the following section I outline my reasons for selecting the initial field site in Sydney and the sites for the subsequent international study.

Selection of Research Sites

The choice of my initial site, Springfield Primary School, was governed firstly by the need to find a playground with a multiethnic population, as the impact of immigration on the transmission and performance of playground games in Australia was one focus of my interest. Additionally, there were practical considerations. I required a primary school in which I could have access to students and would be assured of a reasonable degree of co-operation from the school staff.

I had worked at Springfield Primary School, a local multiethnic school, first as a classroom teacher and then as an ESL (English as a Second Language) and music teacher from 1979 to 1982 and again for a short period in 1984. I knew several staff members, either from when I had worked at the school or because they had been involved in state teacher training courses I had run. However, enough years had elapsed since I had taught in the school that the children did not have an image of me as a teacher.

As a trained teacher and previous staff member, I was regarded as a trusted colleague and there were no legal sanctions on my unsupervised contact with children. Access to students and the staff's general co-operation with my requests were therefore assured to some degree. The timing of the collection periods, in the weeks immediately preceding the end of the school year, also maximized my access to students. This period is traditionally a time when classroom programs are more relaxed and less bound by internal school requirements, so teachers happily acceded to any requests I made for children to continue recording sessions during class time.

The field sites selected for fieldwork from 2001 to 2004 represented a broad range of geographical locations with differing social and cultural characteristics. Because of my desire to collect in-depth, locally specific data from a wide geographical and cultural sphere, I needed to utilize the skills and knowledge of research collaborators who had a long-term engagement and research connections with particular communities. The specific research sites were therefore, to some extent, determined by the willingness of colleagues from the disciplines of music education, ethnomusicology, and folklore studies, to undertake collaborative fieldwork within the communities with which they were most familiar and to help me analyze the collected material.

Several schools in rural and remote environments in central Australia were also chosen. Since these field sites offered a complete contrast to the original inner city Sydney school, they functioned as Australian "control" cases. These schools were selected for variety in the extent to which Aboriginal and non-Aboriginal children were represented in the population; in the languages spoken at home and in the school; in school size and facilities; and in the population's relative ease of access to media sources. The major site, "Telford Spring," was also chosen because of my previously established relationship with members of the Aboriginal community associated with the Papulu Apparr-kari Aboriginal Language and Culture Centre, through ongoing work on Warumungu culture by affiliated linguists and ethnomusicologists. This association enabled me to obtain the appropriate permission for fieldwork from the Aboriginal communities and created some points of initial personal contact with adult Aboriginal community language translators and informants.

Other sites were chosen in the localities of Bedford and Keighley in the United Kingdom. These areas were selected because of the representation of different immigrant communities in the population and because of variations in size of the settlement, in addition to existing links between research collaborators (Elizabeth Grugeon in Bedford and Mavis Curtis in Keighley) and the relevant communities. Both collaborators had been collecting examples of children's play in these areas for several decades and could therefore provide an informed perspective on current practices.

In Stavanger, on the west coast of Norway, ongoing documentation of children's traditional play had been occurring for many years under the auspices of Thor Gunnar Norås and the Norsk Dokumentasjonssenter for Barnekultur i Stavanger (Norwegian Documentation Center for Children's Culture in Stavanger). As a field site, Stavanger offered the opportunity to engage in a continuing collection project involving European children who were linguistically and culturally different from children in the Australian and English field sites. Because of the continued collection of field recordings over time, this site also provided a unique opportunity to analyze children's play in Stavanger diachronically through examination of archival recordings.

Fieldwork in the United States took place in the western seaboard cities of Seattle and Los Angeles. This field collection built on the musical play materials previously collected and discussed by Patricia Shehan Campbell (1998) and Cecilia Riddell (1990). These cities were located within the dominant American culture, with English as the lingua franca, but, like Sydney, had very culturally diverse populations.

Two primary schools in the city of Busan, South Korea provided a monocultural East Asian field site, contrasting culturally and linguistically with all other locations. Field collection at this site was conducted with Young-Youn Kim who, as a Korean resident of this area and collector of traditional Korean children's songs, had the linguistic and cultural knowledge to interpret game practices and children's perspectives on them.

The research from 2001 to 2004 therefore constituted a multiple case study, each field site comprising a case with its own particularities. Demographic characteristics of each site and periods of fieldwork are shown in table 3.1. To maintain the confidentiality of participants, schools have been identified by pseudonyms throughout the text.

A detailed description of each site and its geographical and social contexts is outlined in chapter 4.

Table 3.1. Field Sites, 1990–2004

School	Location and Year	Students	Characteristics	Ethnic/Language Groups
Springfield Primary School	Sydney, Australia 1990, 1991, 1993, 1994, 1995, 1996	700 students aged 5–12	Inner suburban school	Multiethnic: 41 different ethnic groups
Telford Spring Primary School	Northern Territory, Australia 2001, 2002	300 students aged 5–12	School in town of 3,000	Anglo Australian, Aboriginal (Warumungu, Warlpiri), small number Thai, Filipino, Greek, Papua New Guinean.
Auston Community Education Centre	Northern Territory, Australia 2001, 2002	120 students aged 4–16	School in remote town of 500	Aboriginal (Jingili, Mudburra)
Bradford Well School	Northern Territory, Australia 2002	25 students aged 4–17	School in Aboriginal homelands settlement	Aboriginal (Jingili, Mudburra)
Maringa Primary School	Northern Territory, Australia 2002	17 students aged 5–13	School in Aboriginal homelands settlement	Aboriginal (Alyawarre, Kaytetye, Warumungu, Warlpiri)
Bysiden Skole	Stavanger, Norway 2002	370 students aged 6–13	Urban school	Majority Norwegian, small number Somalian, Eritrean, Ghanaian, Bosnian
Strandli Skole	Ryfylke, Norway 2002	190 students aged 6–15	Rural school	Majority Norwegian
Summerglen Lower School	Bedford, southeastern England 2002	347 students aged 4–9	Urban school	Anglo, Afro-Caribbean, Indian, Italian
Ellington Primary School	Keighley, West Yorkshire, England 2002	420 students aged 4–11	Predominantly "Asian" suburb	Pakistani, Bangladeshi, small number Anglo
St. Augustine's Primary School	Keighley, West Yorkshire, England 2002	420 students aged 4–11	Catholic school	Majority Anglo, some Pakistani, Irish, Polish, Spanish
Birch Vale Elementary School	Seattle, U.S. 2004	325 students aged 5–12	Outer urban school, economically disadvantaged area	Anglo, Hispanic, African American, Samoan, Hawaian, Thai, Filipino, Vietnamese, Native American

(continued)

Table 3.1. *(continued)*

School	Location and Year	Students	Characteristics	Ethnic/Language Groups
Nora Conn School	Los Angeles, U.S. 2004	500 students aged 5–12	Alternative school	Anglo, Hispanic, African American, Indonesian, Japanese, Filipino
Pada ch'odung hakkyo [Elementary School]	Busan, South Korea 2004	1241 students aged 5–12	Urban school	Korean
San ch'odung hakkyo [Elementary School]	Busan, South Korea 2004	960 students aged 5–12	Suburban school	Korean

Roles and Relationships

Although I have outlined one conception of my role as a researcher above, it is necessary to elaborate on the changing nature of this role over time. These changes occurred during both the initial period of research from 1990 to 1996 and the subsequent study, as I worked collaboratively with other researchers. In this section I discuss my changing roles at Springfield Primary School. The effects of these changes on my methodological practices are reviewed below, followed by a discussion of changing roles and methods in later research periods.

During the course of my initial fieldwork period in 1990, as a result of my former contacts with staff in the school, I was invited to fill a staff vacancy in the following year. Consequently, I joined the staff as a part-time teacher of English as a Second Language (ESL) in 1991. Ironically, though I seemingly had greater access, this position actually created a greater distance between myself and the children in the school, both in terms of time and role. Whereas I had been regarded as an interested adult observer, I was now a teacher with an entirely different power relationship with the children. My position as "other" was thus considerably magnified. The recess and lunch times I had devoted to field collection were now taken up either by my own need for a respite from teaching or by supervisory activity in the playground in which I was required to exercise a "duty of care."

The impact of these strictures on my research is reflected in the fact that I engaged in only one brief recording session during this period of employment at the school. The nature of my relationship with the children at this time is clearly recorded on the video of this session. Not only is the children's diffidence very evident, but their careful preparation for the occasion is also clear. As I did not have my video camera with me each day, I had arranged to record these children after seeing them at play on the previous day. Their politeness in the recording is accentuated by their having dressed for the recording session in their best clothes.

It was with some relief, then, that I left the school staff to take up a university lecturing position in July 1991. For a number of reasons, I did not resume field recording in the school until November 1993. During this period of formal absence, though, I had taken up a new role in the school community, that of parent. As Springfield Primary School was the local school, my elder son entered Kindergarten in February 1993 and was joined by his younger brother in 1995.

My viewpoint and access to children in the school were widened by this new role. As I took my son to school, I was able to informally observe children at play for a short time almost every morning of the school week and was well informed about incidental occurrences that might affect life in the playground. After I resumed filming later in the year my son also became an avid informant, telling me about new performers or games he had seen or in which he had participated. He was frequently able to provide me with contextualizing details, for example, relating to friendship groupings or sites of play. Although I occasionally conducted some music sessions with my son's classes, as part of a parent participation program, my role as "Owen and Sascha's mum" tended to screen my former identity as teacher.

In other ways, my parental role enlarged my sources of information. A significant number of the children whom I recorded, particularly in 1994 and 1995, had attended preschool with my son or had developed friendships with him in school. In some cases, I had observed aspects of their development, sometimes from infancy, and had witnessed their social interactions over a number of years. I was also well acquainted with their parents, from whom I was able to glean further information, for example, about friendship affiliations. When my younger son entered the school as a student, he joined his older brother's friendship group and I was able to closely observe social interactions and forms of teaching-learning behavior between children of different age groups.   ·

My informal observations also allowed me to discover new games or markedly different variants of games as they emerged in the playground. It was such an observation that led to my specific recording of new games in 1995 and 1996. Regular contact with school personnel also facilitated the organization of additional recording sessions, which helped to clarify analytical questions. For example, information on classroom teaching practices relating to the game genre *Sar macka dora*, which was chosen for detailed analysis, was augmented in April 1995 by recording two music lessons the specialist music teacher in the school conducted with two classes of children in their first year at the school.

Evolution of a Reflexive Field Methodology

The changing nature of my interactions with the children at Springfield Primary School over the years of fieldwork there can be illustrated by contrasting two recording sessions involving scatological material. My "outsider" status at the beginning of my investigation is indicated by the discussion in 1990 of the meaning of the game "Michael Jackson," in which the text (reproduced below) was accompanied by several movements that were seemingly of a sexually explicit nature:

> My name is Michael Jackson
> Girlfriend, Madonna,
> Kissing in the garden
> (kiss) (kiss) (ugh) (ugh)   [Kissing motions and pelvic thrusts]
> Out comes the baby,
> Out comes the boy.
> All the girls "Boo Hoo"
> Sexy!   [Girls lift up skirts]

This game had been recorded by a group of children from Years 2 and 3 toward the end of the collection period in 1990,[5] and an interview was elicited from some of the performers the following day. When Sofia volunteered that the song was about "having sex and having a baby," the other members of the group vigorously denied the sexual reference. Carrie maintained that they didn't think about the meaning, that what was important was that the words rhymed and the game was fun.

While this reported aspect of game practice might have been true, especially for a group of younger children, these apparently guarded answers to my questions contrasted markedly with the response of a large group of Year 2 children when I replayed my recordings of the games to them at the end of the collection period in 1990. In addition to re-enacting the games as they watched, the children freely discussed aspects of the games among themselves and laughed heartily at parts that they considered humorous or rude, joining in with the games as they watched. As a result, I decided to institute a much more reflexive form of recording and interviewing, which would allow children to simultaneously demonstrate and comment on games and in which the momentum of the games and associated group interactions would encourage comments

57

among the child participants, rather than just the "correct" answers to my questions.

In subsequent periods of fieldwork, recording sessions, though initiated in the same ways and locations as those in 1990, entailed continuous video and audio recording both of performances and of the interview questions, which were incidentally interspersed between performances in response to each performance. Usually this resulted in the recording session becoming less formal as it proceeded, although the camera sometimes magnified the "performance" orientation of children's presentation of their games, with several groups of children framing their performances with introductions to a "show."

A measure of the success of this changed fieldwork strategy may be found in the following exchange between members of a group of Year 3 children recorded in 1994:[6]

> k: Last year, Andrea and Nancy and Lucy, when I was filming you, you were talking about how you made up new things sometimes. Do any of you still make up new ones?
>
> NANCY: I made up one but it's a bit rude.
>
> k: It's a bit rude, is it?
>
> MIRIAM: What one?
>
> [Whispered exchange between Nancy and Miriam]
>
> MIRIAM: Oh yeah. It's very, very rude. It's too rude. It's too rude to put on tape.
>
> k: Oh. Do you want to film it or not?
>
> ALL: [Excitedly] Yeah. Yeah. Alright.
>
> [All jump up to get into formation for the game]
>
> MIRIAM: [To Nancy] Hey, can we do it all together, 'cause we know it.
>
> NANCY: [As they get into formation] It's very rude.

[Andrea gives instructions to the others and the performance of "My Mother, Your Mother" ensues immediately. The text includes the words "penis" and "boobies" (a colloquial term for breasts). Another "rude" version is offered immediately afterward.]

As the exchange above suggests, my rapport with the game participants also increased when I re-established contact with groups of children I had recorded in previous years each time I engaged in a new period of field recording. This had the added advantage of ensuring that variation techniques and patterns of transmission between and within groups were mapped over the whole collection period from 1990 to 1996. This strategy was used whenever possible. However, the reestablishment of contact was not consistently pursued with all groups during each recording period as it depended on children's interest and availability. Some children had left the school in the intervening periods or could not be readily located. Others no longer played the games regularly or were too involved in other activities to be recorded again.

During each new period of field recording, I also tried to give groups of children the opportunity to comment on the performance practices of group members by replaying recordings of their previous performances, sometimes from several years before. This allowed children to reflect on their own play in former years and on the changes in their play practices. In addition, valuable comments were sometimes obtained from new group members who had joined the friendship group some time after the recording had been made, (having often come from another school) and who could therefore offer both an "insider's" and "outsider's" point of view.

This strategy of enabling children to review their own and others' material, combined with the comments garnered from interviews in the context of performances, helped to gradually build up a picture of performance, variation, and transmission practices which incorporated their own perspectives and knowledge. In this way, I hoped to give children some control over the outcomes of this research.

The multiple roles of the researcher that I have outlined gave me multiple points of access and positioned me in a variety of ways, both in relation to the children and staff in the school. This multi-positioning perhaps enabled me, as a single participant observer in the field, to represent multiple viewpoints, or, in the words of Galton and Delamont (when describing collaboration between several researchers within one field), to speak "with forked tongue" (1985, p. 163). While this metaphor implies a form of prevarication, it is my aim to validate my findings through the use of many voices, as outlined by Delamont (1992). Although the textual authority in this account is mine, by transcribing the children's voices both within and between performances, and adding these voices to the account, I am endeavoring to achieve, in some sense, the "polyvocality" advocated by Clifford (1986, p. 15).

The widening of my viewpoint was, in some respects, analogous to the changes in my recording practices. Feld describes microphones and cameras as "reductive technological devices that imitate human sensory apparatus by performing specific ranges of limited functions from which perceivers then recreate fuller perceptual cues" (1994b, p. 282). In my initial fieldwork recordings of 1990, I limited the voices of the performers to the performance itself and used a narrow camera angle that focused attention on specific hand and foot movements of individual players. From this material it was impossible to recreate a full sense of the interactions between the children and the context of the performance. The wider camera angle used for video recordings in subsequent years documented these aspects of the performance with much greater clarity and the addition of children's comments through continuous recording considerably increased the complexity and inclusiveness of the data for analysis.

Reciprocity and the Widening Viewpoint

Both my role and views of what I was aiming to achieve changed further as I left the relative comfort and familiarity of my local area and began to work in very contrasting environments within settings in which my cultural and linguistic knowledge was much less secure. I was also mindful of the message of Nyomi (2001), reflected in the recent work of many ethnomusicologists, that researchers from affluent Western societies have an ethical obligation to work collaboratively with members of less economically powerful communities to provide a public voice for the culture-bearers of their traditions and to facilitate a reciprocal exchange of knowledge. This collaborative relationship should assist in the preservation and dissemination of cultural traditions within these communities for their own benefit. I therefore aimed to provide information of value for members of the communities in which I worked.

In my first forays into unfamiliar fields, the remote communities around "Telford Spring" in central Australia, I intended the collected game material and information pertaining to game traditions to be used by the local Aboriginal Language and Culture Centre to assist with language and cultural maintenance programs in the schools and by teachers to create culturally appropriate music and language programs. I hoped that my investigation might also show ways in which Aboriginal and non-Aboriginal children negotiate cultural difference in playground settings, so that such techniques might possibly be applied within the classroom and wider community in these localities.

A conflict between "the interests of science and the interests of those studied" (Hammersley and Atkinson, 1995, p. 275) is one of many dilemmas ethnographers confront in the field. As I became more familiar with the school situations in which I was conducting my study, it was clear that my carefully developed research aims were not necessarily congruent with the more immediate daily preoccupations of teachers working in the schools. In Telford Spring and Auston the staff were helpful but puzzled by my interest in the games, partly, I think, because of the peripheral place they occupied in the daily educational requirements of the school. Although there was a wide range of playground singing games in evidence at Telford Spring, their place in the life of the school seemed less central than it had been in Sydney.

I began to question the importance of my research, particularly when faced with the hierarchy of educational needs at Auston School, where the primary focus was, of necessity, literacy, encouragement of regular patterns of school attendance, and maintenance of nutrition. Several children shared their games with me but were not interested in doing so on an extended basis, unlike the children in Sydney and at Telford Spring. It seemed that I was imposing research needs that were entirely inappropriate to this context, where other issues were of much greater importance to the children, the teaching staff, and the Aboriginal community.

Perhaps I was reacting to the common feelings of marginality experienced by ethnographers in the field (Hammersley & Atkinson, 1995). In Sydney I had been able to contextualize observed behaviors and information derived from interviews within a well-known framework of school life and as a known identity. In contrast, my initial fieldwork period at Telford Spring and Auston (three weeks) was relatively brief, and gave me little time to fully develop an understanding of patterns of school and playground behavior and complex systems of social interaction. I seemed to be overwhelmed by the "crisis of representation" involving "questions concerning cultural authority, representation, power and agency" which have engaged ethnomusicologists since the closing decades of the twentieth century (Barz, 1997, p. 206). As Barz states: "It is little wonder that the contemporary ethnomusicologist agonizes when putting pen to paper, doubts the validity of research agenda, questions all forms of authority and representation, and chases shadows in the field" (1997, p. 206).

Faced with the immediacy of fieldwork and little time in which to reflect, I decided to widen my focus and try to record what was offered that was seemingly meaningful to the children, school staff, and members of the wider Aboriginal community, regardless of whether it apparently fitted my previous research agenda or not. This strategy seemed to have some immediately positive effects. For example, while I was at Auston, I recorded a disco evening held at the school. The children, staff, and Aboriginal language workers viewed my video recording of the school disco with enthusiasm on the following day and a copy was requested for school use. I therefore began to be regarded as someone who could usefully contribute to the school, which increased my rapport with members of the school community. The recording and subsequent interviews relating to it also gave me much greater insight into the musical preferences of the children, their kinesthetic and vocal responses to various popular musical genres and to factors which influence the transmission of music among the local population. I began to realize that broadening my focus to encompass a wider range of musical behaviors of children in the playground and its environs could reveal a much richer view of children's musical lives, as so deftly demonstrated by Campbell (1998).

With a similar rationale, I recorded and transcribed songs in Warumungu language based on European models, which had been devised by my main adult informant and translator in Telford Spring for the purpose of teaching Warumungu to children. Although children did not generate them, they were important to my informant, who felt greatly validated by their appearance in publication-ready form when I presented them to her on a second visit to Telford Spring the following year. Recordings and transcriptions of these songs were also given to the school to use in language maintenance programs. From an ethnomusicological point of view, these songs provided examples of the way in which rhythmic features of the original European models were changed when translated into Warumungu, a consideration of some importance in the investigation of intercultural transmission processes.

As the stories told by Aboriginal elders of their childhood play become even more important once they are no longer around to tell them, it was essential that they be preserved for familial and wider cultural use. All recorded adult materials were returned to Aboriginal informants in a form that could be used and shared, and archival copies were given to the language and culture center for further use or publication. I gave photos and videos to some of the children on my return visit in 2003, to their evident delight, and full sets of photos and videos of school events such as assemblies and sports carnivals were presented to the schools.

I was much more comfortable with the broadened scope of research in 2002. Recordings made at "Bradford Well" documented language learning through songs and the creation and practice of a song based on an Aboriginal Dreaming story in a collaborative process between two adult Mudburra speakers and children attending the school. For the school children, staff, and community language workers, the recording provided a soundtrack to a video that they were submitting to a competition in the state capital city. From a research point of view, the recording showed a unique form of co-construction and culture-specific processes of teaching and learning which could inform my understandings of creating, learning, and teaching in musical play in this context.

This widening viewpoint and concern for forms of reciprocation continued as I began to work with my international research collaborators. Many had undertaken previous research from different perspectives, which I needed to recognize and accommodate within my own approaches. While this was not always easy, and there were times when we had to "agree to differ," these fresh insights increased my understanding of possible interpretations of field experiences in ways that were immeasurably beneficial.

This was especially the case when a language with which I was not proficient was entailed. I had been working for years in the field as a sole adult, trying to maintain a non-authoritarian persona. I was concerned when I entered the field in my first school in Norway that my rapport with children might be affected by the presence of an additional adult. As many of the older children spoke some English, I endeavored to make my way around the playground myself. Any thought of relative unobtrusiveness was dispelled by the nature of my initial day in the "Bysiden" playground. In an effort to ensure that there would be plenty to record, the school had organized a mass demonstration of "traditional" play during the recess period. Not only did this result in an overwhelming assault on the senses, but I found that I was also a subject of scrutiny by the local press, being filmed and interviewed along with the children, a somewhat unnerving experience for an ethnographer who was trying to blend in as much as possible.

Although I was initially quite perplexed by this, the result was my exposure to a plethora of games, and quite intense interest on the part of many children, in response to the excitement of viewing themselves on national television news. As the normal school pattern resumed on subsequent days, I was easily able to approach groups of children to record what I had seen them playing during the mass breakout of play, as well as games which were occurring "naturally." It is quite likely that the frequency of the occurrence of musical play was increased by the knowledge of my interest and ever-present video camera, but, as I wandered out onto the playground at irregular intervals and saw play in progress, there was obviously a core of ongoing musical play in the playground. That I had an effect on the field in which I was participating was most clearly evident from the composition of a special clapping game of which I was the subject, devised and performed for me in both Norwegian and English by two of my most prolific ten-year-old informants, Charlotte and Ine:

Kathryn Kathryn Kathryn Kathryn
We love you here in the school
And we hope you will be there longer
Tra la la la la la la
And we hope you will be there longer
Tra la la la la la la

In this playground I managed to communicate by having the more proficient English speakers, selected by their playmates from among the children, translate my questions and requests. I utilized my standard procedures of filming as I came across games, then eliciting recordings both in situ and in quieter locations inside. Undoubtedly my interchanges were affected by my lack of facility with Norwegian and the children's varying abilities to communicate in English; in retrospect I am not sure my decision to fend for myself in the playground was wise. However, I was concerned to avoid the mediation of children's spontaneous responses through additional adult preconceptions if at all possible.

To counter my imperfect knowledge of Norwegian language, play, and culture, I discussed recordings and playground activities each day with my research collaborator, Thor Norås, whose comments on events were informed by his extensive knowledge of the games. His preference for standard forms of the games was sometimes at odds with my interest in variability. Nevertheless, my understanding was considerably enriched by his experience and his translations of interchanges between children on the recordings. This was especially valuable when I had used my very faltering Norwegian with younger children who were unable to speak English. My interpretation of many social aspects of school life was also informed not only by the children and Thor, but by the school principal and several staff members who became companions both in and out of school hours.

As had become my standard practice at Springfield and in central Australia, I replayed video recordings of games to the groups of children who had agreed to be filmed and discussed them further during these sessions, learning much through this process. As usual, the children were delighted to view themselves and to receive copies of the videos of their group at play for their own use (though one group of twelve-year-old girls requested judicious editing of the video to eliminate expressed preferences for a particular boy revealed during the performance of a game). I prepared edited materials and photos for the school to illustrate a talk on children's play that the staff had requested. During this presentation I showed some examples of games I had collected in Sydney and was gratified the next day to find that they had already been put to use as classroom activities by one teacher, who invited me into her class to see the children performing them. Once again, "researcher effect" was clearly evident.

At my next school, in Bedford, in the United Kingdom. I maintained my usual role as solo ethnographer. Once again, the knowledge of my research collaborator, Elizabeth Grugeon, was indispensable. She had arranged for my visit to the school, based on reports of her teacher-education students that there was a prolific play culture in evidence there. She watched my field recordings on a regular basis, providing me with background information and points of comparison from her own fieldwork in previous years. As with Thor's contribution, this acted as a second form of description and analysis, the polyvocality of Clifford (1986) emerging in the voices not only of knowledgeable children but of informed and erudite adults familiar with the field.

Mavis Curtis, my collaborator in Keighley, United Kingdom, was eager to participate in a new round of fieldwork to see how the games had changed over a period of ten years since her first collections in these schools. Fieldwork therefore became an overt team effort, and we used the opportunity to double our observations and discussions with children in the playground. We frequently split up and ventured into different parts of the playground to work with various groups of children. This was particularly useful at "St. Augustine's" where there were quite separate playgrounds for children of differing ages. As Mavis was relying on field notes rather than recordings, she would point out groups of children who had provided material of particular interest so that I could observe and video their play and comments. We would often confer over a snatched lunch in the school staffroom, discussing what we had found most intriguing and planning strategies for the next round of observations and recordings. This collegiality was a great support and also meant that there were dual sources of information. Indistinct texts of recorded games could be checked against field notes (written by both of us), and the veracity of the field notes could be checked against the recordings. As a form of "investigator triangulation" (Cohen, Manion, & Morrison, 2000, p. 114), the coexistence of the two ethnographers in the field was very productive, as much because of, as despite some differences in theoretical perspectives.

I adopted a similar strategy with Cecilia Riddell in Los Angeles two years later, though the period of fieldwork had emerged fortuitously and was only conducted over two days. In Seattle I reverted to my solo status, after an initial introductory visit to the school in the company of Patricia Shehan Campbell, who had arranged the field school for me and who shared her insights with me each evening as we discussed the day's events in the field. In addition to a highly informed perspective, Pat also provided collegiality and companionship that supported me through the sometimes arduously intensive days of field documentation and reflection.

In Korea, where little English was spoken and I spoke almost no Korean, I was most dependent on the regular assistance of co-researcher Young-Youn Kim, who accompanied me into the schools on most days, staying with me to translate during interviews and to pose additional questions of interest. As well as interpreting what was occurring during recording sessions, she also helped me to navigate my way through a range of social interactions with members of staff in contexts that were culturally far removed from my previous experience. In addition to the customary photos of children playing that I provided for every school, I exchanged culturally appropriate gifts and spent time as a guest of the principals during lunchtimes, as this was expected of me, though my preferred focus was the playground. On days when Young-Youn was not available I ventured into the playground armed with a few carefully rehearsed questions and phrases of request in Korean, but blundered both socially and linguistically, though I still managed to record some field material of value. Left to my own devices in the Korean schools I was most conscious of the difficulty of deciding what was valuable to view and record during the precious short recess times and more than once failed to record potentially interesting activities such as dance routines, because I didn't have the communicative ability to initiate quick changes to recording sessions.

Beyond the field, my research collaborators continued their valuable partnerships, with Thor translating Norwegian game performances and providing commentaries on my initial analysis. Thor made additional visits to Bysiden school to interview children when I had particular questions that required clarification and he made several recordings of games or contextual activities for some time following my fieldwork there. Thor and Young-Youn labeled all the games whose names I had not adequately recorded and Young-Youn arranged for translations of all the Korean games by a postgraduate student who was able to add other comments to the analysis. The analysis process was therefore many layered and reflected the perspectives of multiple commentators.

Reciprocity took different forms. As mentioned previously, for children I provided adult attention and endorsement of their interests and, when practicable, photos and videos of their play.[7] Schools were provided with photos of the children at play and verbal reports of issues relating to play that might be of benefit in planning play policies and playground environments. Occasionally I presented the schools with teaching materials or information on education in Australia in which they expressed an interest. Because of concerns for children's ownership and privacy, particularly where they had performed scatological material or expressed subversive views, I did not leave video or audio recordings with school staff. However, in the interest of contributing to bodies of local field-recorded materials, I made copies of all field recordings and analyses for the research collaborators, who were free to use them for their own continuing research within ethical guidelines. For them, the field materials provided new insights and understandings of play within familiar environments, documenting new or surprising developments in contemporary musical play that contributed to knowledge in a variety of disciplines.

A Final Analysis

The later project produced a large corpus of material: more than seventy hours of recordings, including 1,554 additional separate recordings of children's musical games, representing 333 different genres of games and other forms of musical play collected from 436 children. The process of analyzing all of the field materials collected since 2001 took several years. All interview and game performance data were coded and qualitatively analysed using annotated indices to identify major features of the games and emergent themes, in relation to teaching and learning processes; degree of cross-cultural transmission; factors affecting language use; and effects of audiovisual media on games. With the exception of the Korean recordings, which required special assistance from Young-Youn Kim, I undertook this initial coding either during or closely following each period of fieldwork so that I retained some sense of the immediacy of the experience within the analysis. Field notes supported this process.

Text transcriptions and translations were made of games in Warumungu and Mudburra (recorded in central Australia, 2001–02) Norwegian and Eritrean languages[8] (recorded in Norway, 2002), games in Bangla and Punjabi (recorded in the U.K., 2002), games in Spanish (recorded in Seattle, 2004) and Korean games (recorded 2004). Translators who were fluent in the languages made these transcriptions and translations and often provided additional commentary. A comprehensive database of game genres cross-referenced to field video and audio recordings was created. Selected playground game recordings, including multiple performances of specific genres, were transcribed using descriptive transcription methods to facilitate variant analysis in terms of text rhythm, text setting, movement patterns, melodic contour, and the interrelationship of these elements (see appendix 2 for transcription methods). Although I had transcribed the Springfield recordings myself, selected game performances of later recordings were transcribed by my research assistant,[9] using the methods I had originally employed, but I transcribed interview material in order to illustrate and elaborate on emergent themes.

Whether the success of this enterprise can be determined solely in relation to its productivity is, of course, questionable. The relatively short terms in the field during later years might well be considered inadequate to construct the understandings characteristic of ethnography, which typically documents encounters occurring over protracted periods of time, as with my study of children at Springfield. However, my sustained relationships with my research collaborators enabled me to continue to interrogate the material in conjunction with those who were thoroughly familiar with the milieu of recorded playground life well beyond the field experience. Although these ongoing dialogues with the data were filtered through adult perceptions, they nevertheless allowed the continued development of interpretations of the children's words and actions (and sometimes entailed a return by research collaborators to further discuss material with the children). My understanding could also be said to have grown in an aggregative manner over the whole course of my fieldwork and analysis from 1990 to 2006.

In this account, I have attempted to describe the development of a reflexive methodology that would enable me to collect and document, as accurately as possible, the practices associated with the children's musical play within a wide range of schools over a period of nearly fifteen years. The difficulties inherent in this process have resulted in a number of limitations that have been outlined. In spite of these limitations, however, the rich source of material shared by the children has allowed me to gain considerable insight into the teaching and learning, generation, variation, and transmission processes used by children in these schools in relation to the forms of musical play that are an integral part of their culture. The following chapter describes the varying contexts of play, exploring issues that influence these processes.

CHAPTER 4

The Playing Fields

I n this chapter I provide a detailed description of the schools in which my fieldwork was conducted, examining the socio-cultural characteristics and institutional framework of the school communities and the teaching policies and practices that are seen to frame or influence playground play. The conditions under which children's musical play is performed are discussed as a preface to a more extensive exploration in the following chapters of the situational factors that influence game transmission and performance. As my investigation of the first school, from 1990 to 1996, was much lengthier and more intensive than that of subsequent schools, a greater proportion of this chapter is devoted to it than to subsequent sites. However, I have endeavored to provide a comprehensive picture of school life in each of the localities to which I was given access and which have informed my views of play.

Australian Schools

Springfield Public School, Sydney

The school in which I conducted my initial and longest period of fieldwork is located in Springfield, an inner suburb of Sydney, the largest city in Australia. With a current population of more than four million people, Sydney, on the east coast of the state of New South Wales (NSW), is the site of original European settlement in Australia in 1788. Its deep-water harbor provided the initial impetus for settlement and facilitated its development as a prosperous farming community, center of government and growth into a major commercial city during the nineteenth and twentieth centuries.

As discussed in the previous chapter, the school was chosen for this study partly because of the multicultural community that it serves. The extent of cultural and linguistic diversity in Australian school populations varies according to locality. For the majority of Australian schoolchildren, however, a culturally diverse environment is more typical than a monocultural one, since Australia was largely populated through successive waves of immigration. The ethnic and cultural diversity of the Australian population particularly increased in the 50 years following World War II, with Australian immigrants being drawn from over 100 birthplace groups (Collins, 1991). In 1994, 44.1 percent of school students in the Sydney region of which Springfield Public School is a part had language backgrounds other than English[1] (Information Technology Directorate, 1994).

In the decade prior to the fieldwork, which took place from 1990 to 1996, Springfield had undergone considerable urban renewal. Although some low-cost housing remained, occupied predominantly by immigrant families, an increasing proportion of the area had been "gentrified" and was occupied by the families of predominantly Anglo-Australian professionals. The school community was therefore mixed in class and ethnicity. During the period of fieldwork the largest group of children with language backgrounds other than English were newly arrived Chinese Australians, with Cantonese and Mandarin being the principal non-English languages spoken. The influx of ethnic Chinese migrants into the school during this period reflects a demographic trend in migration patterns in Sydney during the 1990s (Australian Bureau of Statistics, 1993). However, there was a high level of linguistic and cultural diversity within the school population during the period of fieldwork, with children of 41 different ethnic and linguistic backgrounds from East and Southeast Asia, the Indian subcontinent, the Middle East, Europe, the Pacific, West Africa, and South America. The significance of this diversity for the transmission and performance of playground singing games is discussed in chapter 5.

SPRINGFIELD PUBLIC SCHOOL'S PROGRAMS AND ORGANIZATION

Springfield Public School is one of the state-funded public primary (elementary) schools, under the jurisdiction of the New South Wales Department of School Education, and caters for children aged five to twelve. As in the majority of state primary schools in NSW, children at Springfield are grouped in classes on the basis of age. There are seven age levels or grades (designated "years" in this system) from kindergarten to Year 6. Each class, averaging 30 children, is usually taught by a single classroom teacher. At Springfield during the fieldwork period there were two or three classes for each grade, with a small number of "composite" classes formed across two or three grades. Thus, although the normal pattern of age grouping in school classes was homogeneous, each year there were several classes with heterogeneous age groupings, a factor that appeared to affect social grouping and the resulting transmission of games in the playground, as discussed in chapter 5. At Springfield, friendship groupings were also influenced by the practice of reorganizing and mixing class cohorts at the beginning of each year.

The size of the school's population has continually fluctuated since the school was established in 1883. During the period in which the major part of the fieldwork was conducted, for example, the number of children enrolled in the school grew to 666 and there were 23 classes formed in the school. In 1995 there were fourteen primary classes from Years 3 to 6 (that is, for children aged eight to twelve) and nine "Infants" classes from kindergarten to Year 2 (that is, for children aged five to eight).

Four of the classes in Years 5 and 6 were opportunity classes for intellectually gifted children drawn from a large number of schools in the inner western area of Sydney. Each year, 60 children were selected to join these classes, designated "OC." There was therefore a new intake of approximately 90 kindergarten children and 60 Year 5 children at the beginning of each school year in February, in addition to the less predictable ongoing enrollment of new arrivals to the school throughout the year.

The many children for whom English was a second language received learning support from the school's three specialist English as a Second Language (ESL) teachers. All new arrivals were placed in classes according to age, but those with language backgrounds other than English were met by an ESL teacher who, in conjunction with classroom teachers, arranged for peer support by a "buddy" with the same first language. The ESL teachers cooperatively planned and taught with the classroom teachers, working for at least half of each day in a team-teaching situation within the ordinary classroom.

In addition, ESL teachers withdrew some English language learners from the classroom for short periods of more intensive small-group activities. Newly arrived English language learners (particularly ethnic Chinese) were often grouped with other children of the same language background and ethnicity, with whom they established friendships that were sustained in the classroom and on the playground. Within the "Infants" classrooms, however, the majority of teachers made an effort to mix children of different ethnicities when grouping them for learning activities. Most Infants classroom teachers also tried to create a classroom climate in which cultural difference was acknowledged and accepted.

There was a varying degree of acceptance of the use of children's first languages in the classroom. Many parents discouraged their children's use of their first language at school, in the belief that it would hinder their development of proficiency in English. Newly arrived primary-aged children were usually more confident in their use of their first language but were not consistently encouraged by primary teachers to use it in the classroom. In these instances, the ESL withdrawal classes provided a situation in which children could use their first language with a greater degree of comfort.

As a result, while newly arrived children, especially those in kindergarten, initially tended to establish friendships with same-language peers, friendship groupings usually became more eclectic over a period of time. By Year 2, many children were actively initiating and maintaining friendships with children from other ethnic and linguistic backgrounds. This was reflected in the multi-ethnic composition of 26 of the 34 friendship groups whose games were recorded during the period of fieldwork at Springfield.

To some extent, the school's Student Welfare Policy complemented practices relating to multicultural education at Springfield. Among the aims of the policy was for the children to develop "an ability to communicate effectively; . . . a sense of personal dignity and worth; a sense of cultural identity; a feeling of belonging to a wider community; a caring attitude towards others; and an ability to form satisfying and stable relationships" (Springfield Public School, n.d., p. 2).

Within this framework, there were two programs that seemed to influence the formation of relationships between children of different ages in the playground. The first of these, labeled "Pairing and Sharing," had been operating for at least a decade. It involved the pairing of an Infants class with a Primary class on a weekly basis for curriculum activities that were determined by the teachers of both classes. For these activities, each child in the Infants class was paired with an older child in the Primary class. The pairs of children then worked co-operatively to complete a set task, with the older child encouraged to assist the younger one. The purpose of the program was in part to promote co-operation, a sense of "family," the care of younger children on the playground, and self-confidence on the part of older and younger children (Springfield Public School, n.d., pp. 10–11).

The Peer Support Program entailed small groups of children of mixed ages, who met weekly to work cooperatively within a classroom environment on activities planned by the children but supervised by a classroom teacher. The aims of this program, which commenced in 1993, were "to have small groups of students interact in a K-6 'structured' setting, to improve communication, self-esteem/confidence, co-operation and general behavior. And to encourage teachers to make more use of co-operative groups in their classroom as well" (Springfield Public School, n.d., p. 9).

These programs had obvious implications for playground interactions. Heterogeneous age groupings were encouraged and could be continued in the playground. For example, of the 34 friendship groups that I recorded in the playground, six were composed of children of differing ages. Similarly, the classroom supported an ethic of cooperation and the development of cooperative skills that were also manifested in the playground.

Springfield Public School also had an extensive music program, which might be seen to have an impact on the musical play of the children. Unusually for state primary schools in NSW, the school employed a full-time specialist music teacher and drama teacher. Each class had approximately one hour of classroom music delivered by the specialist teacher each week. Children could also elect to participate in one of several school bands, orchestra, or choir. It is notable, however, that the musical material taught in the music program was often much less complex conceptually than that enacted in the musical play of children in the playground.

THE PLAYGROUND

The school grounds, which occupy one and a half blocks, are bounded by streets on three sides and a laneway on the fourth. Although two of the school buildings date from the nineteenth century, they had been completely remodeled in 1979 and new Infants and administration blocks had been built. Since the refurbishment, the Primary classes had occupied the old buildings (one with two storeys and the other single storey). For the main part, infants and primary departments were separated physically for the majority of class time.

As in many inner city schools in Sydney, the playground area at Springfield was fairly limited for a school population of this size. Playground areas had either a grass or asphalt surface. Shade was provided by trees positioned around the perimeter of playing spaces. The grass in the area adjacent to the Infants building was frequently depleted by constant use and this area was usually placed "out of bounds" for play during several months each year. The Infants courtyard, the carpark, and the space between the two primary buildings were also prohibited areas for play during recess but often functioned as play areas before school and during assembly times. A limited amount of wooden or metal seating was placed in the playground, mostly in close proximity to the buildings. As in the majority of Australian schools, children brought their own lunch to school or purchased it from the local shop or (in later years) the canteen. The seating provided a place for children to eat lunch, though children assembled on these seats also engaged in play activities.

Singing games were among the many games children played in the playground before school, during morning recess, and at lunchtime, when, dressed in school uniforms, they congregated in various parts of the playground. The uniform was a practical combination of white polo shirt and blue shorts or simple blue and white shift in summer, and blue tracksuit for both boys and girls in winter. Because of the sunny climate, blue hats were compulsory and a "no hat, no play" policy was enforced during break times.[2]

Many forms of play were in evidence at Springfield, including various kinds of football, cricket, basketball, handball, chasing, and pretend play. Playground singing games, particularly clapping games, were generally performed by pairs or small groups of friends from the same school grade, though some friendship or play groups could involve children of different ages, as previously described. This also occurred when children had older or younger siblings attending the school. Often younger children would be included in play activities of their older siblings (and friendship group), particularly when the age difference was less than two years.

Friendships initiated outside the school, for example, between neighbors or children attending before- and after-school care centers, were often maintained in the playground. This also helped to support the heterogeneity of friendship groups, both in terms of age and ethnicity. Children from different ethnic groups played together from kindergarten onward, although, as mentioned, newly arrived learners of English sometimes grouped together initially. Friendship groups were usually gender based, but there were times when boys and girls played together, as is further explored in chapter 5.

Although Springfield staff members were generally conscious of the cyclical appearance of skipping games, marbles, and hopscotch, it is notable that many teachers in the school were unaware of the presence of clapping games and other forms of musical play in the playground. Initially, when I questioned staff, I met with a similar response to that encountered by Opie and Opie at the beginning of their study in the 1950s: that "children no longer cherished their traditional lore" (1959, p. v) and, therefore, that these games had virtually disappeared from the playground at Springfield.

This is evidence, not so much of teachers' failing powers of observation, as of the "triviality barrier" discussed in chapter 3 (Sutton-Smith, 1970, p. 1). This form of play occupies small spaces, involves small groups of children and no equipment, and is ephemeral. It is also regarded as nonproductive and lacks the official sanction of competitive games such as cricket and basketball. These factors combine to render many kinds of traditional play, including clapping games, invisible to teachers. In turn, this invisibility has meant that teachers tend to be unaware of the characteristics of these games. As a consequence, they are often unaware of the potential of these games for enabling the crossing of social boundaries. Equally, they are unaware of the real complexity of the skills children use in the performance, variation, and transmission of the games. This lack of recognition of the presence and importance of the games was a pattern that was repeated in many, though not all, of the field locations in which I found myself over 15 years of research.

Telford Spring Primary School

Several years intervened before I commenced my cross-cultural investigation of children's musical play. My starting point was still within Australia, but in an entirely different geographical and cultural context from that of urban Springfield. In June 2001 and 2002 I spent several weeks in central Australia engaging with children and adults in some remote settlements in the arid grasslands of the Barkly Tablelands in the Northern Territory. The field sites included schools in two small towns, "Telford Spring" and "Auston," in addition to schools in two Aboriginal Homelands communities. As outlined in chapter 3, the schools were selected because of a previously established relationship with Aboriginal people at Telford Spring and the contextual variety of the other sites. Telford Spring, with a population of 3,500 people, is the sixth largest settlement in the Northern Territory, the most remote and sparsely populated state of Australia. The town, at the edge of the Tanami Desert, is located on the Stuart Highway, which links Alice Springs, the nearest city 511 kilometers to the south, with the city of Darwin, approximately 1,000 kilometers to the north of Telford Spring. Built near the site of an overland telegraph station on land traditionally owned by the Warumungu Aboriginal people, the town developed as a result of white pastoral and mining interests, although tourism is now a significant industry.

Following the establishment of cattle stations in the late nineteenth century, the Warumungu people were displaced from parts of their land and moved onto Aboriginal reserves. The discovery of gold (and subsequently copper) in the 1930s led to the influx of non-Indigenous inhabitants. Because of water shortages and the competing demands of the pastoral and mining interests, the Warumungu and some neighboring Warlpiri people were moved first to Phillip Creek and then south to settle at Warrabri (now Alekarenge) on the traditional land of the Alyawarre and Kaytetye people. The decline in Aboriginal employment on cattle stations and the gradual removal of restrictions on Aboriginal employment in the town in the 1960s led to increasing settlement of Aboriginal people from several language groups (largely Warumungu, Warlpiri, Wambaya, and Alyawarre) in camps on the town periphery and in houses within the town (Lea, 1989; Nash, 1984). As the level of self-determination for Aboriginal people has improved and a range of government offices has been established in the town, Telford Spring has taken on the role of a service provider for non-Indigenous and Aboriginal people, those both living in the town and traveling between the town and other locations, including other towns and outstations on Aboriginal land. In 2001, Indigenous people made up more than a third of the Telford Spring population, and about a fifth of the population spoke a language other than English at home.

At the time of my field visits, Telford Spring Primary School was a school of approximately 300 students aged from five to twelve years, with equal numbers of non-Aboriginal students and Aboriginal students (mainly from Warumungu and Warlpiri language backgrounds). The non-Aboriginal population of the school was predominantly Anglo-Australian, though there were a small number of children from Thai, Filipino, Greek, Papua New Guinean, and other non-Anglo backgrounds. With the exception of the Aboriginal education assistants, most members of the teaching staff were non-Aboriginal.

Because of the moderate size of the school population, a considerable proportion of classes contained children of two age groups. A special class with children from several age groups had also been created for Aboriginal children newly arrived from outstations and cattle stations who needed intensive assistance with English and acculturation into school life. In all other classes there were both Aboriginal and non-Aboriginal children. Friendships thus occurred across racial and age boundaries, but familial and kinship ties strongly influenced patterns of friendship and play affiliations, as did geographical proximity to other children in the home environment, whether in the town or town camps.

The school was well resourced and had large and pleasantly landscaped playground areas with modern play equipment and two large sports fields (the North and South "ovals") fitted out for football, basketball, and other ball games at either end of the school grounds. The ubiquitous red earth of the district was well covered by grass in the majority of the play areas. Because of the intense heat during most of the year, especially in the summer months, the bright pink school buildings all had verandahs and were connected by covered walkways. Additional shelter from the sun was provided by open pavilions and shade covers constructed over some of the fixed play equipment. As in many Australian primary schools, hats or caps were a standard part of the school uniform. The uniform was a bright and serviceable red and blue polo shirt but many children wore casual clothes suited to the climate. The heat was a contributing factor in the design of the school day, which began at 8:00 a.m. and finished at 2:30 p.m. with relatively short lunch and break times. In summer, when temperatures can reach well over 40 degrees Celsius, the children often do not play outside. Even in June (winter in Australia), when my visits to the school took place, the daytime temperature in Telford Spring rose to 28 degrees on some days.

The playground was divided into several areas, defined according to function or the age groups for which they were designated. The early childhood playground and the North oval were used by children from transition (kindergarten) to grade 3 and children from the Aboriginal class. In addition to an expansive area of grass, the early childhood playground had climbing equipment in the shape of a flying saucer with a sandpit providing soft fall underneath. A covered weathershed contained small bikes and toys for younger children. Children played a plethora of games, from the elimination games "Duck Duck Goose Goose" and "What's the Time Mr. Wolf," to clapping games, sand play, climbing and chasing games on the North oval.

In the central playground there were swings and several large climbing frames, one with a covered slide, on which children described playing a game called "tunnel block" with obvious relish. The fixed play equipment was always covered with children engaged in boisterous and athletic activity. Adjacent to this playground was "the quiet area" in which running and noise were prohibited. This area was landscaped with some large trees, tropical plants, a fishpond, an earthen mound, and several sets of tables and benches. Children engaged in pretend play around the trees that were the focus of quite complex counting out and fantasy activities involving the exposed tree roots and branches. They also played card and board games on the tables, and clapping games were often to be observed in the covered verandas which bordered this area, particularly when children were waiting in lines to re-enter the classrooms at the end of break times.

The South oval was frequented only by older children, who used the area for a range of ball games (football, softball, basketball, and netball) and games involving chasing, such as Red Rover and tag. Except for netball (played by girls), these games were popular with both boys and girls. Other small play spaces with additional play equipment lay between or adjacent to buildings. The vibrancy of the playground environment was enhanced by a number of large murals depicting Aboriginal art or scenes of significance, such as the Devil's Marbles, a geological attraction 80 kilometers south of the town.

Auston Community Education Center

I drove in the opposite direction nearly 300 kilometers north of Telford Spring, through a landscape dotted with scrub and rocky outcrops, to reach the much smaller town of Auston, with a population of around 500. The land on which Auston was built was originally owned by the Jingili people but became a nucleus of three major stock routes following the development of the pastoral industry in the area. The town was built in conjunction with an army depot during World War II and today provides services for nearby cattle stations and travelers traversing the Barkly region of the Northern Territory. It is located on a remote section of the Stuart Highway, the only other principal town of the region, Katherine, being more than 450 kilometers further north. It is on the climatic boundary between the arid grassland to the south and the tropical north, so the vegetation is more lushly tropical than that found in Telford Spring.

As with Telford Spring, white land use in the region has resulted in dispossession and changing patterns of Aboriginal settlement, so that both Mudburra and Jingili people now inhabit Auston and the surrounding area. The majority of the population is housed in two Aboriginal camps at either end of the town. Town facilities comprise two petrol stations that also sell provisions, a clinic, a police station, a small hotel and caravan park and the school.

Auston's school, for children from preschool to secondary school ages, is classed as a community education center. Almost all of the students are Aboriginal children of Jingili and Mudburra language backgrounds. At the time of the field visits there were about 120 students enrolled in the school, though only half of this number attended school regularly. Although the staffing changed between my two visits, there were two Aboriginal and three non-Aboriginal teachers in the school, and each of the classes (except the post-primary class) had an Aboriginal teaching assistant. Unfortunately, both the school and the community had undergone considerable upheaval between 2001 and 2002 and what was a settled environment in 2001 was much less cohesive the following year. Such situations are not unusual in remote schools where teachers are frequently brought in from metropolitan environments in other states and therefore may be unfamiliar with the cultural, linguistic, and learning needs of their students. Communal and familial rivalries can also lead to difficulties within schools.

In both Telford Spring and Auston the traditional languages spoken by Aboriginal people are in decline. School lessons are conducted in English and most of the children of school age speak Aboriginal English (a dialect of English) or, at Auston, Kriol, originally a pidgin language that developed as a result of colonization of Aboriginal lands further north, which has now become a lingua franca among a growing number of Aboriginal people in northern Australia (Walsh & Yallop, 1993). The removal of Aboriginal people from their tribal lands, which have both economic and religious significance, has resulted in social, cultural, economic, and spiritual dispossession. While aspects of traditional Aboriginal culture remain, for example complex kinship systems and forms of related social obligation, language and belief systems are gradually being subsumed by the dominant European culture. As in many isolated rural locations in Australia, high levels of unemployment, poverty, poor health, substance abuse, and domestic violence present challenges for these communities. Aboriginal families in both of these towns travel frequently (to meet family, social and ceremonial obligations, or to go hunting or visit outstations on tribal lands), which, in addition to previously described social problems, results in poor school attendance rates by many Aboriginal children. For many remote schools, attendance, nutrition, and the development of English literacy skills are critical issues.

Such social conditions have an inevitable effect on children's behavior in the playground. Children's play affiliations at Auston were usually kinship based, although friendships were forged with new children in the playground, including those who had traveled vast distances. The very few non-Aboriginal children appeared to experience some difficulty in being fully accepted by the other children but nevertheless developed friendships and participated in a range of play activities.

Though much smaller than Telford Spring Primary School, the school at Auston was well-established in terms of buildings and equipment and had a huge playground, also with ornate new fixed play equipment, and football, volleyball, and basketball areas. The older boys spent a large amount of time playing football while older girls gravitated toward volleyball. Younger children engaged in various ball games, both standard (such as volleyball) and invented. Again, games of skill involving counting out, and elaborate rituals were imaginatively embellished by the children. The climbing frame, slide, and swings tended to attract younger children. Children wore brightly colored sports clothes that allowed freedom of movement, and the influence of American hip-hop culture was evident in the clothes of the older boys, despite the remoteness of the location.

This was the only school in all of my field sites in which I found it very difficult to locate clapping games. Apparently only two small familial groups and one or two of their playmates from other states played them. It appeared that these games were played more at home where there were few toys and not in the school environment where there was play equipment to divert and engage.

Bradford Well School

Twenty-five kilometers north of Auston was the tiny Bradford Well School, located next to a lagoon just off the Stuart Highway. Because of the ready source of water, Bradford Well was the true junction of the major stock routes that initiated white settlement at Auston. As with Auston, white pastoral tenure displaced the land use by the local Jingili and Mudburra people, and a large cattle station still abuts the school grounds. The school's students are children of Jingili and Mudburra language backgrounds from preschool to post-primary ages from the nearby Aboriginal homelands settlement of approximately 100 people. At the time of the field visits there were about 25 students aged 4–17 in the school. There were two teachers, one Aboriginal (from the local community) and one non-Aboriginal, and an Aboriginal teaching assistant. A peripatetic teacher and temporary volunteer tutor expanded the teaching resources.

There was a strong disposition both within the community and the school to preserve traditional culture and language. The school featured a language maintenance program involving elders from the community and their extended family, some of whom were talented musicians who some years previously had formed a band specializing in country, gospel, and rock music. They used music extensively for teaching language (mainly Mudburra), translating songs from English to Mudburra, and creating songs from Dreaming stories (the Dreaming being the beginning of time, which is central to the Aboriginal belief system). The program and its teachers were accorded respect by the Aboriginal children who (with the exception of the non-Aboriginal teacher's son) made up the entire student population.

The school consisted of two buildings that housed classrooms, library, kitchen, administrative offices, an ablution block, and storeroom. The older building had an extended open covered area where much teaching and play took place. The newer buildings were all demountable, with verandahs that the children put to good use in their play. Colorful murals adorned the walls, one depicting hands of friendship to which passing travelers were encouraged to add. The extensive school grounds were pleasantly landscaped, with trees and tropical shrubs, and well equipped with play materials, from basketball hoops and football goals to toys for make-believe play. The children were comfortably dressed in casual clothes, with shoes an optional extra.

The large playground adjoining the buildings was used particularly by the older boys for football, basketball, and softball. By far the most popular form of play at Bradford Well was pretend play, either in the "shop" set up on the verandah, in the "house" in the covered area, or with toy spades, cars, and trucks in the sandpit next to the newer classroom. Both girls and boys engaged for lengthy periods of time in emulating various domestic scenes, wheeling "babies" along to the shop to witness their transactions. In the sandpit children took their trucks on hunting expeditions or used spades to dig roads for the CDEP program.[3] A number of girls played clapping games which they had learnt from friends and relatives in the homelands settlement or on trips to Darwin, the principal city of the Northern Territory, many hundreds of kilometers north.

Maringa Primary School

It was not until 2002 that I had the opportunity to visit the other Aboriginal homelands school, at "Maringa." Maringa lies 80 kilometers south of Telford Spring on Aboriginal land that had been returned to the traditional owners in

1992 after they purchased the cattle station on the land. The school services both the Maringa community and another outstation in the area. In 2002 Maringa school had 17 children aged 5 to 13 from Alyawarre, Kaytetye, Warumungu, and Warlpiri language backgrounds. As they came from four different language backgrounds, the lingua franca among children in the classroom and playground was Kriol, although teaching was in English, and Aboriginal languages were spoken in the home. There were strong kinship links between most of the children, both within and between language groups, and the children referred to each other using both their European names and skin names (kinship terms). The school had a non-Aboriginal teacher and three Aboriginal teaching assistants from the community. The teacher frequently consulted with and deferred to the teaching assistants on cultural matters and it was clear that community consultation was integral to the daily operation of the school.

The school day at Maringa was short, finishing at 1:00, with a brief break mid-morning for a snack and play. Children did not have lunch at the school as a number of them had to travel for an extended period of time to and from school. The shorter day facilitated more regular attendance.

The school's focus on developing English literacy was clearly evident in the single classroom. Its walls were festooned with colorful displays documenting the children's recent activities, favorite films and TV programs, bush tucker (food found in the bush), the latter labeled with their Aboriginal names, and completed work. Specially constructed big books contained favorite nursery rhymes to which even older children would repeatedly return, to the extent that they created clapping games to their texts. The teacher also had a regular classroom music program and children had learnt many (Anglo) songs and enjoyed performing percussion accompaniments to them. Again, the girls used some of the classroom songs as raw material for clapping games. These games were all performed in English, though children quickly switched to Kriol or Aboriginal English to communicate with each other between performances. The children, dressed in casual sports clothes, were engaged with classroom activities and materials that included resources for pretend play. Inter-age play was consistent, with kinship being the dominant influence on play groupings.

I was only in the school for one day so was unable to gain a picture of the daily life of the school over a longer period of time, nor of the normal ebb and flow of play activities. Outside, the playground was dusty and bare, the red earth framed by the single school building constructed of sturdy concrete blocks with windows covered in heavy security mesh. A water tank and shed defined the boundary of the play area, which appeared to have little equipment except for a basketball hoop, in contrast to the well-equipped interior of the classroom. Nevertheless, the children were actively engaged in play during my short period of observation. The isolation of this school was more marked than that of any other that I visited (though this school, being close to the Stuart Highway, was not nearly as remote as many others in the Northern Territory). Apart from the small cluster of community houses nearby, the view of spinifex grass tufts and occasional low trees stretched unbroken in all directions. Links with Telford Spring (which had jurisdiction of Maringa school) seemed distant indeed.

Norwegian Schools

Bysiden Skole

There could hardly have been a greater contrast between Maringa and my next field site, Bysiden Skole, located in Stavanger, a port city on the southwest coast of Norway. Because of the deep harbor that is the focal point of the city, Stavanger has been a center of various forms of trade since medieval times. During the nineteenth and early twentieth centuries, Stavanger was a major fishing port and herring canneries were the mainstay of the town's economy, but the industry had significantly declined by the middle of the twentieth century. Since the 1970s, the North Sea oil industry has revitalized Stavanger, creating a stimulus for massive growth. The oil industry has attracted workers from many parts of the world, so that what was a predominantly monocultural town has become a multicultural city within a relatively short period. In 2001 approximately 10 percent of the population of 109,000 had parents who were both born in other countries. In recent years Stavanger's location in the western fjord area and its accessibility by air, ferry, and road have also created an expanding tourist trade (Aga & Næss, 2001; Statistics Norway, 2004).

In Norway, primary (elementary) school education extends from the ages of six (grade 1) to thirteen (grade 7). Bysiden Skole is one of a number of primary schools in suburban Stavanger and surrounding areas. Situated in a pleasant tree-lined suburb several kilometres from the city center, it caters for a predominantly middle class population, although there is some socio-economic variability in the school community.

I visited Bysiden School in autumn 2002 and spent about three weeks immersed in playground life. At the time of the field visit, the school comprised a two-storey brick structure hidden from view of the street by the small wooden houses characteristic of the area, and a larger junior secondary school adjacent to the site. Built in 1966, the administrative center, older children's classrooms, assembly hall, and music room were housed in one block, and classes for younger children were located in a separate block. In the main block, several sections of the upper storeys were supported by pillars, which created a sheltering overhang that the children put to good use in their recreational time.

The playground was attractive and extensive, with a number of areas facilitating different forms of play. The largest of these areas, next to the school building, was a flat graveled space in which children of both sexes played games such as football (soccer), basketball, jump rope, and, occasionally, ring games. When not participating in these games, which required more space, older children tended to gravitate toward a small grassy hill bordered by trees where they congregated in groups to play with *Pokemon* cards, climb trees, or just "hang out" and talk. Younger children were more often to be found in a wooded section of the playground adjacent to well-constructed fixed play equipment. The slightly concealed nature of this locale made it ideal for pretend play. The area underneath the overhanging storeys of the school building afforded shelter and a more intimate space for playing clapping games, line games, and elastics which were more frequently (but not entirely) the domain of girls.

What was evident in both this playground and that at "Strandli" school was that there was a much greater emphasis on freedom and unregulated play than is sometimes found in other countries, where concerns for children's safety place considerable constraints on the types and locations of playground play. Although teachers undertook supervision in the playground, they also often participated actively in the play, for example, turning skipping ropes for groups of children. Both the principal and long-standing members of the school staff and executive had an interest in children's traditional forms of play and were promoting it in a number of ways, including teaching games from their own childhood which had gone out of fashion in the playground.

Another aspect of the school's philosophy and organization had a considerable effect on the play environment in the Bysiden playground. Several years before the field visit the staff of the school had initiated a classroom program focusing on small group co-operative learning to encourage independence and flexibility. As children were working individually and in small groups, whole class sessions were of limited duration and the timetable of each class was determined by the teacher. Different classes therefore had breaks at varying times so that at any given time a single class might appear on the playground. There was only one morning recess of about thirty minutes that was common to all classes. This meant that, although there were fewer opportunities for play between children of disparate age groups, there was also more space for play and ongoing playground activity throughout the day.

Perhaps as a result of the pedagogical emphasis on developing independence and flexibility in the classroom, children at Bysiden displayed a high level of self-sufficiency and co-operation in the playground. This cooperation was evident in relationships both between children and between children and teachers. For example, children playing competitive games with *Pokemon* cards readily gave friends some of their own cards so that they could participate in the games. Although various forms of joking and taunting were still part of the playground repertoire, I did not witness any obvious disputes or discipline problems during my time in the playground. Similarly, there was no visible exercising of overt authority on the part of teachers; any discussion of behavior was kept at a discreet and nonconfrontational level.

Children recognized the different competencies of their peers and were used to drawing on these individual competencies within a group context. The clearest example of this occurred in my own interactions with groups of children. Since my ability to communicate in Norwegian was very limited, I endeavored to speak English with children, whenever possible.[4] Children would immediately put forward the most proficient English speaker in their friendship group to facilitate my discussions with the group. I was often dependent on the group 'interpreter' for translating my questions and my requests to demonstrate various games and aspects of play.

The majority of children in the school were of Norwegian background. However, there were a small number of children of different ethnicities, some of whom had recently migrated and others who had been born in Norway. Approximately fifteen ethnic groups were represented in the school population, including Turkish, Serbian, Bosnian, Eritrean, Somalian, and Ghanaian. The school had participated in several initiatives to engender intercultural understanding within the school community and was nominated as "a school that has particular expertise in intercultural relations and migration" (Comenius 3 Network, 2002). A Turkish teaching assistant was employed by the school to support children of Turkish background, and a multicultural mothers' group had been established in previous years to help integrate children of varying ethnicities into the school. Nevertheless, the dominant language in the playground was the *Bokmål* form of Norwegian that is spoken and taught in the majority of Norwegian schools (The Royal Ministry of Education, Research and Church Affairs, 1999). Although some classes had been involved in investigating the birthplaces of classmates and their parents, there seemed to be more of a focus on assimilation into the Norwegian culture rather than on delineation of cultural diversity within the school.

For the majority of my time at Bysiden, the weather was unusually warm and dry. Children were thus free to play without interruption, though I was told that they were so used to the more usual drizzle and rain that they would play regardless of inclement conditions. Both boys and girls wore jeans, comfortable pants or shorts with t-shirts, decorative tops (girls) and, when the weather finally changed, sweatshirts and hooded parkas. Sneakers or sandals completed the casual attire. Two Somalian sisters wore headscarves and skirts over their long pants but were able to participate in active forms of play without restraint. The children's clothing in many ways embodied the lack of restriction found in the playground.

Strandli Skole

Although the focus of my Norwegian fieldwork was on Bysiden School, I briefly visited a number of other schools in the vicinity of Stavanger. The trip to "Strandli" was memorable for the extreme beauty of the country through which I traveled. Though Strandli is located in the Ryfylke province only about fifty kilometers northeast of Stavanger, the journey by ferry and bus took some time. The ferry wended its way between small towns and villages on the sides of the fjords through which we passed. Alighting at one of these towns, my colleague Thor and I boarded a bus which wound its way up steep hills and through magnificently lush farming country, arriving at Strandli, perched on the edge of a broad stretch of water (the junction of four fjords) and surrounded in all directions by mountains. Formerly a shipbuilding town in the nineteenth century, Strandli is now the administrative center for one of the eight communes in the Ryfylke region (Høibo & Tjeltveit, 1992).

Strandli's primary school was situated amongst rolling hills slightly outside of the town. The school has a much smaller population than Bysiden—fewer than 200 children at the time of my visit, with only one class per grade. Despite this, the school grounds were huge, affording children seemingly endless opportunities for play of various kinds. There were play areas assigned to older and younger age groups, the younger children playing on the upper levels of the playground and the older children in the more expansive lower spaces. As with Bysiden School, the largest flat areas were covered by gravel, a surface that is clearly durable and practical in the wet climate of this region of Norway. On the lower level there were swings, a volleyball net, fixed play equipment, and a homemade skate park with a range of ramps and other challenges for skateboard and bike riders. Children of both sexes played together, participating in volleyball, football, and a boisterous ring game that resulted in some spectacular collisions as participants chased each other around the circle. At my request, groups of older children demonstrated with some dexterity clapping games that were clearly known to both boys and girls, though they stated that they did not often play them at their age.

A staff member confirmed that children of both sexes customarily played together at school. Until the previous year, the school had also housed junior high school classes, and it was interesting to note that once students reached this age, the play of boys and girls was segregated by the students.

The graveled spaces were surrounded by extensive grassed areas dotted with trees, shrubs, and hedges. Children rolled down grassy slopes, chased each other, and played hide and seek and other traditional line games in the shelter of the trees. A ship structure and several cubbies under construction as a learning project afforded further opportunities for climbing and pretend play. As at Bysiden the school provided skipping ropes that were used mainly by younger children during my visit. Some younger children also played clapping games, but my lack of facility with Norwegian and the limited time I spent in the playground precluded much discussion of them with the children.

Clearly play was a valued part of the primary school experience in this part of Norway. Nevertheless, I was told on a number of occasions that there was a current debate in Norwegian society about whether children have too much play. To some extent this seemed to be linked with a concern to maximize the effectiveness of the formal curriculum by ensuring that school time was used efficiently. In the previous decade the starting age for primary schooling had been lowered from seven to six years of age. The age range for formal schooling was one of a number of contrasts with the school system in England, where my next field investigations took place.

English Schools

Summerglen Lower School, Bedford

The city of Bedford, located fifty miles north of London in the southeast of England, provided my first experience of English school life. Bedford has developed from a prosperous medieval market town, one of a number of towns, villages, and small hamlets on the banks of the River Ouse. With population growth over the years, many of these smaller hamlets have merged, although there are still many small rural villages in the vicinity. In 2001, the national census listed the population of the Borough of Bedford as 147,911 people, including 78,991 in the main part of Bedford, 19,433 in the adjacent town of Kempston, and the remainder in the rural areas. The town experienced some industrialization during the nineteenth century and has maintained both population growth and an air of prosperity into the twenty-first century, partly because its transport links allow easy commuting to other urban centers such as Luton, Milton Keynes, Cambridge, and London.

While there is a thriving business community, light manufacturing, and retail industry within Bedford and nearby towns, the area is still surrounded by farmland. During the 1950s, a recruitment drive by the local brickworks attracted a large number of immigrant workers from southern Italy. As a result, approximately 10 percent of the population of Bedford is of Italian descent. Migration from South Asia, Eastern Europe, Greece, Cyprus, the Middle East,

Africa, and the Caribbean has added to the ethnic diversity of Bedford and surrounding areas.

This ethnic diversity was reflected in the population of "Summerglen" Lower School, which I visited over two weeks in October 2002. Although the majority of children were of Anglo background, a significant minority were of Indian descent. During my visit I observed and interacted with children of Anglo-Caribbean, African, Italian, and Croatian ethnicities. Most of these children were born in England to families who had lived there for two or three generations. However, the small number of children from Eastern Europe had arrived in recent years.

The school was located in one of the adjacent towns that are part of the Bedford conurbation, in an area that is slightly less prosperous than the main city. The local housing near the school appeared to be a mixture of privately owned and council houses, mostly semi-detached and built in the second half of the twentieth century, and the small row of local shops was rather dilapidated. Nevertheless, the single-storey brick school (opened in 1969) was well maintained and attractively landscaped, with an indoor pool for swimming classes concealed from view.

Bedfordshire is one of the education authorities in Britain that maintains a three-tier school system, with Lower schools for children from four to nine years of age, Middle school (nine to thirteen years), and then Upper school for their final years of schooling. The first year of school is designated as Nursery and is usually conducted as half-day schooling. At Summerglen, as in many schools, the nursery class was partially separated from the main school in terms of scheduling and nominal play times, with children playing in a separate fenced-in area at different times than the older children. Thus, the children with whom I interacted in the main playground at Summerglen were in the five to nine years age range.

The playground at Summerglen School was very large, with a lower grassy rectangular field that afforded ample space for ambling, running, football, and clapping and ring games, all of which I witnessed during break times. Football goal posts were fixed at either end. The field was separated from the other section of the playground and the school buildings by a small hill dotted with trees.

The upper playground, covered in asphalt, was also quite spacious, and children seemed to spend the greater proportion of their recreation time there. Like the field, it was bordered by neat hedges, with some shrubs softening the façade of the school buildings. Doors from classrooms and a main internal thoroughfare opened directly onto this playground. A large open area was marked out for various games, including netball. At the far end of the playground was a set of fixed play equipment ("the bars") behind a small brick structure comprising a wall with a square hole, a stepped platform, and brick seats. This structure was the focus of a great deal of imaginative play, particularly by younger children, who regularly climbed and crawled over and through its different spaces and levels. On several occasions I watched as groups of children pretended variously to be parents, dogs, or other imagined beings in its vicinity. It was with some regret, then, that I found that parents regarded this structure as a safety hazard (because of the potential for children to climb the wall and fall onto the hard surface of the playground) and there were plans for it to be demolished. Another wall on the edge of the playground was a favorite location for rituals associated with chasing games.

Children had a fifteen-minute morning break from classes and a lunch break lasting just over an hour. Younger children (in Years 1 and 2) had an additional fifteen-minute afternoon break. Children spent about half of the lunch break eating in the hall that doubled as a dining room. Children either ate the lunch provided by the school kitchen or brought their own lunch from home. During both the eating time and the playtime that followed, children were supervised by a group of women employed specifically for this purpose. At lunch a range of special play equipment was brought into the upper playground by the lunchtime supervisors in an effort to provide a focus for children's play. Equipment included small bats and balls, miniature plastic hockey sticks, ropes, and hoops. These appeared to be more popular with younger children, who tended to use them in nonstandard ways. Only the hockey sticks seemed to be used in the intended manner.

In their creative use of play equipment the Summerglen children seemed to be regaining command of their play in an environment which was much more overtly controlled by adults than that of the Norwegian playgrounds. Children were frequently given directions by teachers or the lunchtime supervisors, who intervened whenever there was any perceived possibility of harm. The end of playtime was signaled by a whistle, and children were required to stop playing and move silently to line up ready to proceed into the building.

This presented such a striking contrast to what I had observed in Norway that I was initially baffled by what seemed like unnecessary restrictions. However, I realized after some time that the discipline imposed on the playground and the emphasis on safety was symptomatic of the larger concern with child protection that had permeated British school life in the aftermath of the 1996 Dunblane massacre, in which a gunman had killed sixteen children in a Scottish primary school. Recommendations of the inquiry that followed the incident included increasing security measures in schools. Thus Summerglen, like other English primary schools that I visited, had external doors that locked from the outside and strict procedures for visitors to the school. These included checking of identity by an administrative assistant, entry to the school through locked security doors, and the wearing of an identity badge at all times. Child protection concerns had been further exacerbated by the abduction and murder of two young girls by the caretaker of their primary school in the neighboring County of Cambridgeshire only two months before my fieldwork at Summerglen. Debate about child protection issues was a constant theme in the media for the latter months of 2002. Concern for children's wellbeing formed an integral part of the approach to children's recreational time at school.

Another obvious difference between Norwegian and English schools was in the clothing worn by the children. At Summerglen, as in all English schools, children are expected to wear a school uniform. The cold weather uniform at Summerglen was both colorful and comfortable, entailing a red sweatshirt, white shirt, and full-length black or grey trousers for boys and girls. Though some girls wore a grey skirt that was also a uniform option, most chose the trousers that enabled untrammeled movement. Black leather shoes completed their outfits. As the weather became colder, many children appeared in the playground in heavy coats or parkas, creating much more variety in colour and type of attire. It seemed that the children found ways to inject individuality into their environment, despite any constraints imposed by adults.

There was a view expressed by one teacher that children need to be taught games in order to play, a view that I have heard echoed in conversations with numerous teachers in different schools internationally. It was very clear from the thriving play culture in this school that children's play forms proliferated, regardless of adult restrictions.

Keighley Schools, West Yorkshire

My culminating experiences of school life in England occurred in a very different environment from that of Summerglen. I spent the month of November 2002 at two primary schools in Keighley in the north of England, five hours' drive north of Bedford along the major motorway, the M1. Keighley is a West Yorkshire town of about seventy-six thousand people, located twelve miles northwest of the city of Bradford. Situated in the Aire and Worth river valleys within the Pennine range, Keighley is surrounded by hills and wild moors intersected by streams, a landscape made famous in the novels of the Brontë sisters who lived in the nearby village of Haworth.

The beauty of the natural environment contrasts markedly with much of the built environment, a legacy of the industrial revolution, when the fabrication of textiles, which had begun as a cottage industry in the district in medieval times, grew into a major manufacturing industry. As Keighley occupied a gap in the Pennine hills, it formed an ideal nucleus for roads, railway, and the canal system and therefore a focal point for the transport of industrial products. In the nineteenth century, woollen mills and the manufacture of machinery for the textile industry replaced cotton mills in the Keighley district. The area is still dominated by the factory buildings and rows of terraced cottages that housed mill workers that were constructed during that era.

Bradford and Keighley formed the center of the woollen textile industry in Britain for more than a century and share many of the same demographic features. In the first half of the nineteenth century the population of Keighley grew from six thousand to more than sixty thousand during which time Irish immigration into the area was prevalent. Another wave of immigration, mainly of displaced persons from Eastern Europe, followed the Second World War. From the 1950s the textile industry began to decline and factories were required to operate on continuous twenty-four-hour cycles to remain economically viable. This need coincided with large-scale migration of men from south Asia,[5] most notably from the Mirpur region of Pakistan (which borders Kashmir) and the Silhet region of what is now Bangladesh. The Pakistani and Bangladeshi workers engaged in unskilled shift work in the factories often returning to their homelands for long periods. It was not until the 1970s that they began to bring family members to settle in the area. Currently people of Pakistani and Bangladeshi descent comprise about 10 percent and 1 percent of the population respectively. Because of racial prejudice, economic necessity, and the wish to live in close proximity to familial and cultural support networks, the south Asian immigrants and their descendants tend to live in discrete ethnically homogeneous communities within Keighley.

The demise of the textile and manufacturing industries in the late twentieth century has meant that many families in these communities are socioeconomically disadvantaged. Because of the intensive work practices in which they were engaged, men were unable to learn English with any proficiency or develop the skills necessary to work in the service industries that have largely replaced manufacturing. Traditional cultural practices have precluded women joining the workforce, and the custom of returning to rural Pakistan to marry means that many women brought into the community have limited English and poor literacy. Marriage within familial groups drawn from a limited geographical region has also resulted in a high level of genetic disability. Unemployment within the Pakistani community in this region is therefore three times that of the white community (Commission for Racial Equality, 2002; Curtis, 2000; Singh, 1994).

Ellington Primary School

"Ellington" Primary School is located within one of the Asian enclaves in Keighley. Of the 466 children registered as attending the school in the year prior to the field visit, 345 were of Pakistani descent, 107 of Bangladeshi descent, and 14 were listed as "white." The majority of the children spoke Punjabi as their first language, with the children of Bangladeshi descent speaking Bangla (Bengali) as their first language. A limited number of children spoke Gujerati. Most children did not speak English when they first came to school. The 2001 school inspection report stated that the children's spoken and written English skills were well below the national average.[6] The children spoke an idiosyncratic form of English that combined elements of the local Yorkshire accent with Punjabi or Bangla inflections. Long absences from school, during which children accompanied their families on holidays to Pakistan or Bangladesh, affected their fluency in English and academic achievement but also assisted the maintenance of their first language and the acquisition of culturally specific forms of play.

The school focused on catering for the needs of these children. Colorful multilingual signs welcomed children and their families to the school, and posters and notes to parents were also multilingual. A significant number of staff members (including all the lunchtime supervisors) were of Asian descent and bilingual, speaking Punjabi, Bangla, or Urdu. This provided support for children with English as their second language, particularly in the nursery, reception class, and lower grades, and enabled direct communication between parents and the school. Vegetarian and Halal meals were available for school lunches, and there were several assemblies during the week to enable the practice and exploration of different faiths. The school prospectus emphasized the support of bilingualism, tolerance of cultural and religious diversity, and anti-racist behavior. There was a feeling of genuine warmth among many of the children and staff. The interior environment of the school buildings (rebuilt in 1989 but recently extended and refurbished) was brightly decorated with children's work and the open plan design created a feeling of space, light, and comfort.

In contrast, the area surrounding the school was lined with cramped rows of Edwardian terrace houses, with no gardens and tiny backyards. The streets were narrow, but the rather grim stone of the houses was offset by colorful rows of washing, hung on lines stretched across the backyards from house to house. The school playground was bounded on one side by these houses, with a factory building on another, and a park with attractive expanses of grass and trees on the furthest side. The school building, opening directly onto the playground, formed the final side of the rectangular playground space.

For a school of this size, the playground was relatively small, so most organized sports took place in other locations. Because of concerns about safety, the gate to the adjacent park was locked during the school day, although the school prospectus mentioned that the park was sometimes used for outdoor activities. Children therefore had at their disposal a single gradually sloping asphalt space in which to play during the morning break and lunch times. Despite the lack of space, there was a plethora of play activity. Boys engaged in chasing, cricket, and football, while girls spent more time playing clapping games, elastics, and practicing dance routines derived from both English popular music television programs and Bollywood movies.

The school had only recently converted from the lower school model to a primary school for children from four to eleven years of age. Nevertheless, there was a great deal of inter-age play, with younger siblings of both sexes being drawn into the games of their older sisters. This was possibly a result both of familial routines within extended families and school policy, which encouraged older children to take responsibility for looking after younger children at school dinner times. There was a general feeling of acceptance, and the many children with some form of disability (almost a third of the school population) were readily included in play activities both by children and teachers. I witnessed one of the teachers playing a clapping game with a girl with Down's syndrome, who joined in slowly but confidently. Like Summerglen, Ellington Primary School provided some skipping ropes and balls for play and there was fixed play equipment for climbing activities.

Although the majority of children were practicing Muslims, girls were just as active as boys, and their school uniform allowed freedom of movement; for most girls, it consisted of a grey salwar kameez (long tunic over long trousers) with a choice of bright blue, turquoise, or maroon sweatshirt or cardigan. Boys wore sweatshirts in the same colors and grey trousers. During most of the time I was at the school it was Ramadan, the Muslim fasting month. A number of the girls wore headscarves to indicate their dedication to the fast, but, again, for most of them it did not preclude their participation in games. Many children were in the habit of going home for lunch, which they continued throughout Ramadan (despite the fast). This sometimes made it difficult to make contact with particular children during different play times in the day.

Another factor that caused some difficulty in observing play was the weather. As it was late autumn in the north of England the playground was often cold and wet and the frequent rain, wind, and mist kept children in their classrooms during some break times. The wet playground surface was covered in fallen leaves and children were required to bring both "outdoor" and "indoor" shoes to school. For this reason, a greater amount of time was spent in recording elicited play activities indoors at this school. This enabled my colleague Mavis and me to observe the counting-out and other games learnt in the parents' countries of origin. These were games that were usually played on the ground so could not be played in the slushy playground at this time of the year.

St. Augustine's Primary School

I spent the latter part of my time in Keighley at St. Augustine's Primary School, a Catholic school for children from four to eleven years of age. The school had been established on the site in 1857 but both the facilities and the student intake had changed over time. At the time of the field visits, there were 420 children in the school, with about 75 percent being Anglo and approximately sixty children having Pakistani backgrounds. A small number of children had European or Irish backgrounds. Despite the difference in religion, many Pakistani parents in the area chose to send their children to a Catholic school because of the perceived advantages of a religious education and expectations of better discipline and pastoral care. As the diversity of the school population has increased, the school has had a greater proportion of children with English as their second language and literacy difficulties. The school maintained a strong Catholic ethos but had established some connections with local Muslim entities and made some provisions for a multifaith community. However, there appeared to be fewer strategies to bridge the cultural divide between the home and the school than those in evidence at Ellington Primary. For example, there was an emphasis on the teaching of European languages at the school, rather than any focus on bilingualism, and there were fewer bilingual staff.

Located amidst rows of neat terrace cottages, the school building was an imposing three-storey nineteenth-century stone structure that covered a large proportion of the site. It had a rather overpowering effect on the playground, with three asphalt play areas being tucked around its mass. A small back playground was used by children in the early years of school. On the other side of the building was a lower playground for children in third and fourth grade and, connected by a ramp, an upper playground for use by the older children. This playground was relatively open, with surrounding houses and trees clearly visible. However, the lower playground was surrounded by the high walls of the school on two sides and high brick walls on the others. The dour effect was increased by a sign stating, "No unauthorised playing of games" on one wall of the school.

Nevertheless, there was a vibrant play culture in this school as in all of the others and the principal and many of the staff were interested in our study. They had obtained a grant to improve the playground and were keen to plan an environment to facilitate play. The principal expressed the view that children's play should not be ordered by adults, as children had so little control over other aspects of their lives and should have the freedom to direct their own play.

In the various playgrounds children ran and played enthusiastically. There appeared to be more gendered play in this school, with many boys engaging in ball games, including football, played between two goal posts painted onto the walls. Although there was a lack of space, children cooperatively respected the areas set aside for ball games. The girls played clapping and ring games in addition to string games taught at home. Although the children played together happily in interethnic groups, there was greater reluctance to show games deriving from parents' countries of origin or even from other schools where play practices were different. Several girls had come in from schools in other villages or towns and were diffident about revealing games that deviated from the standard forms played in the school. A number of girls of Pakistani descent demonstrated Pakistani games such as "Zig Zag Zoo" and string games taught by family members. They told us that they played these at home but not usually at school.

The uniform was more strictly adhered to at St. Augustine's and more girls wore skirts and tights, despite the cold, though some wore long trousers like the boys. All the children wore the maroon sweatshirt emblazoned with the school insignia but, again, there was some diversity introduced by the warm outer coats and jackets that many children wore. Our time in this school was relatively short—only a few days. Access had been more difficult to obtain because of concerns about videoing the children and child protection issues outlined earlier. Even in this short time, however, we were able to gain some insight into the intensity of the play culture in this environment.

Schools in the United States

Birch Vale Elementary School, Seattle

The major field site in the United States, which I visited in April 2004, was in Seattle, a city of approximately 573,000 people in Washington State on the Pacific Northwest Coast. Surrounded by coastal waterways, lakes, and mountains, Seattle was originally home to the Duwamish people but, in the nineteenth century, grew from a small trading settlement serving fur and logging industries to a large town providing goods and services for the Alaskan gold rushes. The city is now the hub of several major manufacturing and high-tech industries, including Boeing and Microsoft. It is a major U.S. port and entry point for immigration, particularly from Asia. The 2000 census noted that nearly 17 percent of Seattle's population was born overseas, the major countries of origin being the Philippines, Vietnam, China, Mexico, Korea, Japan, Ethiopia and Etritrea, Germany, the United Kingdom, Cambodia, Laos, India, Thailand, and Russia. There are also growing communities of Pacific Islander and South American immigrants.

94

Birch Vale Elementary School is located in a lower socio-economic area at the edge of the city. The school community is ethnically diverse, with relatively large groups of Latino, African American, and Asian American (Thai, Filipino, Vietnamese) children and a small number of Samoan, Hawaiian, and Native American families. At the time of the field visit there were 325 students aged five to twelve years at the school, 28 percent of whom were Anglo American. There were two intensive English as a Second Language classes for children who had been in the United States less than one year. A significant proportion of the children in the area came from single parent or blended families. Many parents were unemployed and received economic or housing assistance, and three quarters of the children were eligible for free or reduced price meals at school. In school programs there was a major focus on developing literacy and on providing an enriched learning environment. For a large number of children the school provided a level of stability that was not found in their home life, and school lessons also concentrated on developing self-esteem and self-discipline within a supportive framework. Both the principal and teaching staff provided a considerable degree of pastoral care for the children. There were specialist music and physical education teachers and a recreation coordinator who organized formal play activities in the playground during the break periods.

The area in which the school was located was quite densely wooded, with small neat houses and gardens set among trees along an adjacent road that climbed up a gentle hill. The main school building was at the top of the hill. Built in 1948, this was predominantly a single-storey brick building with a basement housing the lunchroom and several classrooms. Classrooms and hallways were colorfully decorated with posters, signs, and labeled children's work. There were two aging demountable buildings, one directly behind the main building and the other, the music classroom, at the bottom of the hill. The playground was mainly contained within the area around and between the two demountable buildings.

During the fieldwork period, new school premises were being built on the site, so the playground area was diminished to less than half of its previous size. It was bare of grass and covered by a layer of dry bark mulch in most places, though a large area sloping down from the middle building had been worn down to dusty earth and gravel. A concrete path meandered down from the top to the bottom of the hill. In one corner of the lower playground a new and ornate set of fixed metal climbing equipment with two slides was in constant use, particularly by younger children. Next to this, several tetherball poles also attracted attention. Two basketball hoops were also in this area but did not seem to be in regular use. The hilly topography resulted in natural divisions in the locations of different types of play, with organized forms of play such as football at the top of the hill, pretend play along the boundaries of the playground, jump rope on the path, and tetherball in a lower corner. Clapping games, cheers, and other forms of musical play permeated the entire playground.

Probably because of the reduced size of the playground, break times for younger and older children were staggered so that at any given break time there were children from kindergarten to grade 3 followed by children from grades 4 to 6 in the playground. This limited the amount of inter-age play between younger and older children. The break times were also quite short: fifteen minutes at mid-morning, mid-afternoon, and after eating at lunchtime. While this made the recording of play organizationally difficult, it did not seem to reduce the intensity of the play in which children engaged. They played with gusto, even when the wind blew the woodchips around in dusty spirals. The weather was unusually fine and warm for Seattle in April and early May and the children made the most of uninterrupted playtime.

There were clear demarcations along gender lines in some forms of play. Girls gravitated toward tetherball, jump rope, clapping games, cheers, and dance routines, while the boys played football and chasing tag games. The climbing equipment, equally popular with boys and girls, was rostered for use by different grades on different days. Younger children of both sexes made great use of the woodchip mulch for building cubbies, "houses," and "forts" against the perimeter fence. Older children, particularly girls, spent considerable time walking around and chatting in small groups. The recreation coordinator kept a constant stream of organized activities going in the upper playground. These activities, including football and running races, were equally appealing to boys and girls, probably because the coordinator had a wonderful rapport with the children.

Although there were instances of taunting and rivalry between different groups, there was generally a relaxed atmosphere in the playground. Children and teachers alike wore comfortable casual clothes and footwear and there was little intervention by the teachers in the children's spontaneous play. Because of the high level of ethnic diversity, children tended to play in groups of mixed ethnicity, with the exception of children in the English Language Learners classes, who carried their class groupings into their playground activity.

Nora Conn School, Los Angeles

Following my fieldwork in Seattle in 2004 I was afforded an unexpected opportunity to visit a school in Pasadena, a city that is part of the Los Angeles conurbation on California's southwest coast. Pasadena is located in the San Gabriel Valley, ten miles north of downtown Los Angeles. This area has experienced waves of settlement over the last 250 years. In the latter half of the twentieth century the population significantly grew and diversified as the construction of freeways gave commuters working in the industrial areas of Los Angeles easier access. There are therefore areas of prosperity contrasting with areas of economic disadvantage. In the 2000 census the population of Pasadena was listed as nearly 134,000. Of these the majority groups were Anglo American, Hispanic, and African American. Current demographic information from the Pasadena Unified School District indicates considerable ethnic diversity of school-aged students in the area. Of the students enrolled in Nora Conn School, approximately a third are "White," a third Hispanic, and 28 percent are African American. There are small percentages of Asian (including Filipino), Native American, and Pacific Islander students. At the time of the field visit, languages spoken at home by students who were interviewed included English, Spanish, Tagalog, Portuguese, Indonesian, and Japanese.

The school began as an alternative school in 1972, focusing on learning through exploration and creative problem-solving. Since then it has grown from a single experimental class to a school of over 500 students from kindergarten to grade 8. It incorporates both elementary and middle-school classes, though there are fewer students in the upper grades. The school moved to its current site in 1982 and now occupies the refurbished buildings of an older school that was originally established in 1941 on that site. The school buildings are single-storey brick, with colorful doors that open directly from classrooms onto the playground. Several brightly colored murals decorate the walls of buildings and walls dividing sections of the playground, which is a large flat concrete expanse. Although there are plenty of trees in the surrounding area, which has well-maintained brick and stucco bungalows, there are only a few trees offering shade within the playground. The nearby mountains frame the view on one side of the playground.

I visited the school for two hot sunny afternoons in May 2004, along with my collaborator, Cecilia Riddell, at the invitation of one of her former teacher-education students, Barbara Johnson, who ran an after-school arts program at the school. During the visit, we spent some time observing and interviewing fifth-grade children at play during the scheduled physical education session in the playground. Barbara had negotiated with the school staff for children to demonstrate clapping, jump rope, and ring games to us during this time, which they did willingly and energetically. Almost all the fifth graders who did this were girls. A number of games and ensuing discussion regarding game practices took place within the limited time available. The children wore comfortable clothing—jeans, shorts, and colored t-shirts with sneakers and socks. A few wore bright blue t-shirts with the school insignia prominently printed on the front. The school dress code prohibited sandals, clothing that was overly bare, and clothing that was gang-related, a reflection of the influence of gangs in the Los Angeles area.

Following the end of the school day, about 20 children remained at the school for the privately run after-school arts program, which provided a snack, homework, and free play time, and structured music, dance, and drama activities for children ranging in age from five to eleven years. Although most participating children attended Nora Conn School, a few came from other schools in the district. The children gathered around a sheltered seating area for their snack, then moved off into the playground to play in pairs or small groups. Children played jump rope, football, and tetherball in mixed gender groups and it was evident that this was a usual occurrence. A number of boys also joined in with the clapping games played by several girls. These games used stamping and other forms of body percussion which I had not encountered anywhere else, and some incorporated quite extensive forms of improvisation. There were quite a few pairs of siblings attending the program and children happily played both with age peers and with siblings. Although there were clearly defined friendship groups, the play groups were fluid, and interethnic play was quite characteristic.

Barbara allowed extended play for our visit while she interacted informally with a variety of children who clearly enjoyed her company. She had a particular interest in games from her own African American heritage and had taught some of them to the children, though most of the games being spontaneously played by the children had come into the playground by other means. During the two afternoons some of the children also engaged in the structured music and dance activities the program offered, so it was possible to observe their behavior both in music and movement activities structured by adults, and in their own musical play.

This level of informality between students and teachers was very different from what I found in my next field schools in Busan, Korea, which I visited only a week after leaving the United States. Korea presented the most marked cultural contrast to other field sites, and concomitant differences in school life and play practices were also very evident, though play maintained its integral role in children's lives at school.

Korean Schools

Busan, South Korea

With nearly four million people, Busan is the second largest city in South Korea, a bustling port on the southeastern coast of the Korean peninsula, directly across the Korean Strait from Japan. Its geographical position has made it a center of trade since the sixteenth century, a status it has maintained despite waves of colonization by surrounding powers and social and financial strictures resulting from various local and global conflicts. Its development as the major port in Korea dates from the late nineteenth century. Successive occupation and conflict has only served to increase its economic dominance and the size of its population, which was listed in 2005 as 3,657,840.

Busan's mild climate and coastal attributes have also led to its popularity as a resort area for Koreans. The beaches that fringe the city are focal points of a large domestic tourist industry that also draws on the mountainous hinterland for recreational activity. Like many Korean cities, Busan is typified by a large amount of high-rise development, but the water or mountains are visible from many vantage points.

Pada ch'odung hakkyo and San ch'odung hakkyo

I spent two weeks in late May and early June 2004 visiting two Busan elementary schools, "Pada" ch'odung hakkyo and "San" ch'odung hakkyo[7] in the company of my Korean research collaborator, Young-Youn Kim. Pada is located in an urban beachside area, a short distance from the beach, though the many residential buildings and small shops surrounding the school obscure the coastal view. On each visit we approached the school from one of the narrow streets by which it was bordered. It was an impressive brick edifice built in 1970, with two blocks housing classrooms, a lunchroom, and administrative and staff areas. Each block was four stories high, and a paved patio stretched along the whole length of the main block, separating it from the large rectangular playground, which was covered in tawny gravel to absorb the rain that falls during the summer monsoon season in June and July. The school buildings and a building of similar size bounded the playground on three sides, the fourth boundary being marked by a high wall and gateway onto the road. Trees softened the playground perimeter, though many had been heavily pruned and did not offer extensive shade in the heat of early summer.

There was quite a large amount of fixed play equipment, ranging from brand new brightly colored slides and climbing frames at the end of the playground near the preschool classrooms, to weathered and well-worn equipment including seesaws, climbing frames, slides, and football goals. A sandpit marked out by a border of rubber tires was located on the edge of the playground closest to the lunchroom. Of particular note were the wooden Nolttwigi, or jumping seesaws, that were constantly in use during play periods. Both boys and girls played a traditional virtuosic Nolttwigi game in which one child jumped heavily on one end of the seesaw, catapulting the child at the other end of the seesaw into the air. The Nolttwigi were always surrounded by a crowd of chil-

dren awaiting a turn or enjoying watching the game, which had become popular through its performance at a community festival. The principal had a special interest in traditional play and had encouraged its practice by students
during her tenure at the school.

In 2004 the school had a population of 1,241 children, including school
students aged from six to twelve years, in addition to children attending the
preschool classes housed within the building. There was also a small class of
children with intellectual disabilities integrated within the school. According
to the principal, the average population size of elementary schools in Busan
was one thousand children and Pada was in the middle-size range.

"San" ch'odung hakkyo was slightly smaller than Pada School, with a student population of 960 at the time of the field visit. It was located in an outer
suburban area of Busan, surrounded by mountains that were visible from all
parts of the playground. The houses in the vicinity were small, detached cottages, many with vegetable gardens, giving a much greater feeling of space to
the environment. San School consisted of a relatively new five-storey brick
building constructed in 1998, with an imposing front entrance and a set of
steps and concrete path stretching along the full length of the façade. Two
open shelters on the steps provided shade for children eating snacks or resting.
The flat rectangular playground had a similar surface to that of Pada School
but was bordered by attractive flowerbeds and larger trees. There was less fixed
play equipment, but the slides, climbing frames, and monkey bars seemed
sufficient.

The school day in Korea contains a lunchtime during which children have
a hot lunch provided by the school and some free time in which to play. At
Pada School children had lunch in a large lunchroom, a noisy hive of activity.
At San School trolleys containing the meal were wheeled around to each classroom where children ate. In both schools the recess system was different from
that in many of the schools I had visited. There were regular short ten-minute
breaks between forty-minute lessons rather than a single longer recess. This recess system seemed to result in different play patterns. As there was little time
available, many children frequently played games inside the classrooms or in
the corridors instead of going into the playground. In these confined locations
both boys and girls engaged in forms of musical play that required little space
or equipment, with forms of "Scissors Paper Rock" figuring prominently.

However, during lunch and in some short breaks children played a range
of games outside, albeit in smaller numbers. Boys at Pada and San played soccer. At each school, children of both sexes chased each other and played on the
fixed climbing equipment. "Nolttwigi" was popular at Pada, in addition to another traditional call and response tug of war game and elastics. The steps at
San School formed a focus for the creation of new games, including one called

Elevator by its creators. Several groups of girls were observed practicing song and dance routines learnt in the classroom or from television. Some clapping games appeared to be the province of girls, while others were also learnt and played by boys inside but not, typically, outside in the playground. In their colorful casual clothing (t-shirts, shorts, jeans, and long sports pants), children played freely and energetically in the playground, the classrooms, and corridors, whenever there was a hiatus in organized activity.

Conclusion

Play clearly formed an essential part of school life in all of the field locations, and musical play was a conspicuous component of playground activity. In the following three chapters I examine the influence of the children's social and cultural environments on the ways in which musical play in its various manifestations was enacted, transmitted, and changed, with examples drawn from the many different playgrounds I observed over time.

III

TRANSMISSION PROCESSES
IN THE PLAYGROUND

→ CHAPTER 5 ←

The Influence of Social Grouping

To understand the processes inherent in the performance, teaching, learning, and generation of forms of musical play, it is necessary to comprehend the social dimensions of this play. The following vignette may serve to introduce a number of important aspects of musical play which frame the behavior of the players.

At Birch Vale Elementary School, five grade 4 girls who are close friends have been playing clapping games in a range of combinations. They form a circle and begin to play "Quack Diddely Oso" (a variant of the game genre "Sar Macka Dora" where players are progressively eliminated from the group), passing a clap around the circle on the beat while chanting the song. A girl from outside their friendship group runs in to watch as the game progresses, standing so close to the players that she is almost touching them. She clearly knows the game rules well, laughing and pointing as one of the girls misses her clap and is "out." Despite her proximity and eagerness, she is not let into the circle. However, she briefly joins with the girl who has been eliminated in a two-person version of the game beside the circle as the main game continues. This is short-lived, and she goes back to watching the circle game as it proceeds. Several boys occasionally dart in close to the circle to watch but are ignored and quickly lose interest, moving off to play chasing games.

Playground singing games, particularly clapping games, are generally performed by pairs or small groups, rarely exceeding six children, though some game genres can attract a larger number of players. Usually these groups are made up of friends from the same school grade. Friendship groups may function as a whole group for game performances, with, for example, six performers participating concurrently in a performance, most frequently in ring formation but sometimes in a line arrangement. Alternatively, performances are conducted by pairs of children who are members of one friendship group, with different dyads forming for different performances. These dyads may be related to strong friendships between particular pairs of children but are more usually fluid, with different children initiating a pair formation because they are next to each other in the ring formation, because they seek the particular skills of an expert player of a nominated game, or because they have composed or practised a particular version of a game with another player.

Group performance immediately requires some modification of the oral transmission paradigms outlined in chapter 2, as these paradigms have largely been formulated in relation to the solo tradition of epic or ballad performance. Group performance must take into account the extra dimension of interaction between performers that is necessary to achieve cohesion during "composition in performance." Notions of performer—audience interaction must also be modified. Although games may attract onlookers who may take on various roles, the performers within the group also function as their own audience.

As can be seen in the Birch Vale example above, the group form of performance operates as a mechanism for social inclusion or exclusion. The "charmed circle" of ring games is imbued with particular social characteristics by Jones and Hawes (1987), who state that the ring "includes and excludes at the same time, . . . surrounds and enfolds while it walls off and repels" (p. 87). Gaunt (1997) also alludes to the "protection and concealment" (p. 15) function of the ring, enabling players to improvise freely and disclose elements of personality and personal preference within its boundaries of social safety. For Jones and Hawes the democracy of the ring structure is another inherent feature: "The strength of the ring is in its construction. Since it has neither beginning nor end, there can be no ranking of its parts—no strong or weak, big or little . . . no captains, no opposing ranks" (1987, p. 87).

There is considerable debate about the inclusive or exclusionary role of play groups in regulating oral composition and performance. Some researchers maintain that children's play is highly prescriptive and that traditional modes of performance are demanded at all times (Harwood, 1992, 1993a, 1993b, 1998a, 1998b; Riddell, 1990). According to Harwood (1992) the maintenance of tradition leads to the hierarchical status of performers, based on their competence. Differences in performance practice are not tolerated and result in the literal exclusion of the offending performers from the performing group: "In large circles, those who 'mess up' are identified and removed by the more experienced players who can, while maintaining the clap pattern themselves, monitor the performance of others in the circle" (p. 23). Players are not allowed to rejoin the performance until they can adhere to the norm.

However, a different context reveals a very different picture. The play of Venda children is described by Blacking (1985) as "an exercise of individuality in community" (p. 46), where "the collective effort produced both new cultural forms and a richer experience for the participants" (pp. 46–47). "Knowledge of the children's songs is a social asset, and in some cases a social necessity for any child who wishes to be an accepted member of his own age group" (Blacking, 1967/1995, p. 31), but variation is also valued. The introduction of new elements into familiar song texts may enable Venda children to gain prestige, and polyrhythmic performance of the games requires both "the realization and elaboration of a basic musical pattern" (Blacking, 1985, p. 45) where individual skill and group co-operation are manifest. "Pleasing others and pleasing oneself in musical performance were two interrelated aspects of the same activity" (Blacking, 1985, p. 45).

At Springfield, the cooperative dynamic necessary for game completion seemed to lead to an emphasis on inclusion, rather than exclusion. The need to be inclusive of all group members was reflected in variants that were consciously made to accommodate the differing performance practices of single members of a group. For example, in 1993 I observed one group of Year 4 girls adding a new opening formula to their performance of "Down Down Baby" because one participant preferred to begin the game with a sequence ostensibly learned from the film *Big*:

ELLA: Before that, before that it does something different.

[Game performance continuing.]

It does something different before that. [Game performance continuing.]

It does something different! [Game stops]

ALICIA: What happens then?

ELLA: It goes like this. It goes. . . .

HONG-SOO: "Roller coaster, up and down." Is it that one?

ELLA: Yeah, and then it goes "Gimme gimme Coco Pops. . . ."

HONG-SOO: Chimmy chimmy. . . .

ELLA: Chimmy chimmy pow,

Chimmy chimmy Coco Pops, Chimmy chimmy pow,

Granma granma sick in bed.

HONG-SOO: OK, you can play that.

ELLA: OK, you can help me 'cause you know it.

SADIE: OK.

This group also varied the usual practice in their performance of "Sar Macka Dora." When eliminated, each player in this group joined a subgroup, thus minimizing any feelings of exclusion for individual participants. This approach to inclusion was also observed among players of this game genre (entitled "Down in the Jungle" at this school) at St. Augustine's, West Yorkshire.

At Springfield, individuals or pairs of participants within a group of children frequently performed synchronous variants of text, music, or movements without comment or dissension, while fully aware of the differences. For example, a performance of "Susie Had a Baby" by a pair of Year 2 girls recorded in 1994 had major discrepancies in text and movements between the players that were maintained throughout the performance. When questioned, the girls attributed this to the coexistence of two different "versions."

A more sophisticated approach to the negotiation of variants was evidenced by the play of several children at the after-school center in Los Angeles in 2004. Khryslynn, a ten-year-old girl, had been demonstrating various games with her friend Pam and nine- and ten-year-old boys Ben and Patrick who had all been playing together in the playground in the break before the after-school arts activities began. When Pam went home, the three remaining children began to play "Miss Susie Had a Steamboat." The game required quite rapid rendition of words with double entendres at alternate line endings, in conjunction with a fast three-beat clapping pattern.[1] They started off briskly:

Miss Susie had a steamboat
The steamboat had a bell, ding ding
Miss Susie went to heaven
The steamboat went to
Hello operator, please give me number nine
And if you disconnect me
I'll cut off your
Behind the 'frigerator. . . .

Patrick dropped out of the game because he was having trouble with the triple clap at this pace. From the fifth line on, Khryslynn was chanting a slightly different version of the text. Initially she stopped at the first variant but then proceeded, maintaining the clapping pattern. Her solution to keeping the game going was to stop singing and listen each time the text differed, deferring to

Ben. However, toward the end of the game, Ben called, "You take over," and Khryslynn took over the text:

KHRYSLYNN: I know I know my Ma

I know I know my Pa

I know I know my sister

With the (what is it?) with the alligator bra.

BEN: I thought it was the 24 size D bra.

KHRYSLYNN: With the . . . what? [said with some surprise]

BEN: [Laughs delightedly] 24 size D.

KHRYSLYNN: With the 24-sized bra.

It is possible in the instance of the three players above that the cooperative dynamic of the after-school arts center naturally led to an easily negotiated settlement of differences. Where cooperation is actively promoted, it appears to filter through to game practice to some extent. However, the careful observation and rule-bound behavior (such as turn-taking for particular movements) that enables singing games both to be learned and successfully performed can also help children negotiate the integration of variants within a performance, as illustrated by the previous example in Los Angeles and another scene observed at Ellington School in West Yorkshire.

Three older Year 5 girls, Halima, Rukhsana, and Nasheen, had joined a group of Year 4 girls and the younger brother of one of the girls who were demonstrating and discussing game practices in a small classroom at lunchtime. They had been sitting in a circle and now started to play "Down By the River" (a form of the elimination game "Sar Macka Dora"). The version known by the Year 4 girls was:

Down by the river goes hanky panky
Where the two fat frogs go bank to banky
With a hip, hop soda pop
And this is where it stops.

The version known by the Year 5 girls (or at least Halima) had "zoom, zam" instead of "hip, hop." As in all renditions of this game, the text is performed repeatedly with one child being eliminated at the end of each iteration. In this performance there were six iterations of the text. The first time Halima sang "zoom, zam" while the Year 4 girls sang "hip, hop." Halima looked surprised as she recognized that the text was different. In the second iteration, the voice of Farah (a Year 4 girl) was dominant. Halima tentatively sang "hip, hop" slightly after the others. She tried to add another "hip, hop" but stopped when she realized that this was wrong. After this iteration she said, "We do it different." In the following iteration she sang "zoom, hop" and added the extra "hip" again. At the next elimination point, Farah pointed to Halima and said, "You do it your way." As a result, in the next iteration Halima's voice was dominant and she confidently sang "zoom, zam." Farah also modified her text to "zoom, zam." Halima said to Farah, "That's how your sister does it," with Farah responding, "Oh!" in surprise as she retired from the circle (having got out in the last round). For the final two rounds of the game Halima was still in the diminished circle, but the rest of the eliminated onlookers sang the "hip, hop" version loudly and Halima joined in this version, now enthusiastically and without the additional word. (⬤ **VIDEO SAMPLE:** See video example *Ellington Hanky.*)

Disagreements seem to be most prominent when variation interferes with the synchronization of game elements, especially movement. For example, different versions of a game at Summerglen in Bedford prompted a very different reaction from that seen in the previous examples. One lunchtime Teela had volunteered to show me "My Name is X Baby" which I had seen before in the playground. It was a game that began with the criss-crossing of hands held together in a prayer-like movement and then alternating right and left hand claps above and below a central clapping point. Teela chose Kirstie to play with her but they had repeated false starts. After about four attempts to begin the game, Teela exclaimed to Kirstie, "You're doing it wrong!" and they gave up. Teela then chose Zoey to play. This attempt was more successful, though there was still a slight discrepancy in the first clap above the central point. Teela explained to me at the end of the game that there were several ways in which the clapping pattern is formulated and that different people do it in different ways. If the two players' movements are made in different directions, the game will not work.

Nevertheless differing levels of musical and kinesthetic competence may be accommodated, with deliberate teaching strategies being employed to teach less able (particularly younger) players so that they can successfully participate in the game. These are discussed in chapter 6 in the section, "Accommodating Difference in Teaching and Learning."

This does not mean that hierarchical social structures are absent from this or other playgrounds. Patterns of dominance can be enacted in game performance in a number of ways. For example, at Birch Vale and Ellington I saw individual girls whose leadership status was undeniable, flouting or manipulating the rules of elimination games so that they always won. At Birch Vale (Seattle) the girl's playmates questioned her quite evident transgression of the rules of "Quack Diddely Oso," but she ignored their protests and stayed in position to complete the game, ousting another player from her rightful place. By contrast, at Ellington (West Yorkshire) the girl more subtly ensured that her position in the sequence of counting would result in her winning the game, an approach that I also saw at Telford Spring in central Australia. Similar instances of strategy or presumption of success by more adept or socially prominent performers have been recorded by Brady (1975), Eckhardt (1975), and Hughes (1999).

Other forms of dominant behavior resulted in quite vehement disagreements between players, as exemplified by a group of six-year-old girls at Telford Spring in central Australia in 2001. They had played several games, with the overbearing Danielle issuing a range of orders having to do with performing solo versus as a group, coordinating the three-beat clap, and adding mimetic movements to the games. Danielle's dominance was threatened by the equally determined Jessica as they played "My Mother Your Mother" in a threesome with Emma. The issue of contention was the change from trio to duo formation at particular points in the game and the resulting negotiation of the triple-clap pattern. This change in combinations of players appeared to be a form of variation with which the larger group had been experimenting.

ALL: My mother your mother lives down the street [played by three].

Eighteen nineteen Marble Street [Jessica turns and claps with Emma only].

JESSICA: [To Danielle] You don't know how to do it.

DANIELLE: Yes I do [demonstrates the triple clap].

JESSICA: Then Emma and I will do it and then when I go off . . . [indistinct].

DANIELLE: Alright, alright.

[The three start the game again.]

ALL: My mother your mother lives down the street [played by three].

Eighteen nineteen Marble Street [Jessica turns and claps with Emma only, but the movement isn't synchronized and the play stops].

JESSICA: [To Emma] You're dumb at it.

DANIELLE: I'll tell you when to stop. I'll tell you when to stop and then we'll both go [claps]. Go!

ALL: My mother your mother lives down the street.

Eighteen nineteen

DANIELLE: Stop! [She moves away as the other two continue. The game proceeds with Danielle standing up and the others clapping until the line "Boys are sexy," when Danielle's movements are different from Jessica's].

JESSICA: No, you're wrong! Danielle, you don't know how to do it.

Jessica issued further instructions about grouping. The game was then played successfully to the end, with only one intrusion by Danielle who called out to the others to hold hands as they moved from a sitting position to begin the culminating leg-crossing formula.

Such examples demonstrate the varying degrees of influence that children's levels of competence and individual personalities can bring to game performance. Children's friendships wax and wane, and children attain popularity within friendship groups to different extents. At some schools (Telford Spring, St. Augustine's, Summerglen) a few less popular or powerful children expressed reluctance to perform certain games in front of others who they felt to be censorious. At Summerglen, two rather shy marginal members of a Year 4 group were loudly told by their friends that they were wrong when they demonstrated a game variant they had made up the previous year. They told me afterward that this was a "secret game" which they only played together away from the others, clearly to avoid censure.

However, it seems that participation in the games, particularly those which flout adult conventions, is also a means of confirming group solidarity and increasing individual popularity, as a group of Year 6 girls at Springfield discussed:

K: Did you do it deliberately for people to watch? Was that important?

CLARA: Yes.

TARA: We did it for fun as well, but we did it. . . .

CLARA: More to show off.

K: To show off. You did it—like "Firecracker" was a showing-off one.

ALL: Yes.

K: Were there others that were showing-off ones?

TARA: Yeah, the one—the Madonna one where we lift up our skirts.

K: OK, so ones that had lifting up skirts, that was sort of showing-off stuff, was it?

ALL: Yes.

K: Were there any others that were a bit like that, do you think?

TARA: There's some, like with a lot of actions and stuff that you could—like "Granma Granma."

K: Yes.

TARA: Yeah. And "My Mother Your Mother Lives down the Street"—at the end we like, jump around like this [indicates leg-crossing movement] so people could watch all this jumping . . .

MATU: So then they notice you.

K: They notice you.

CLARA: They look at you and then you say, "Oh yes, I'm popular" [much laughing].

It also appears that the cooperative ethic of the games may have helped children in the Springfield playground to cross social barriers that operated in other circumstances. For example, Sheila, a fairly tenuous member of a friendship group filmed in both 1993 and 1994, was welcomed into many performances by this group, even though she was an object of some ridicule outside of the game context.

The cooperation evident in the game performance in the Springfield playground therefore seemed to increase social mobility and tolerance of diversity, both in relation to performers and performance content. This contrasted with the exclusionary behavior and conformity Harwood (1992) and Riddell (1990) observed in the United States. As can be seen from the various examples in the preceding section, however, processes of accommodation are quite fluid and vary between different groups and different localities. To understand why this might be the case, it is necessary to consider the institutional and playground contexts of the games at field schools and the consequences in terms of transmission across social boundaries.

Contexts of Play

Not surprisingly, singing game performance occurs mainly outside of class time, either before school lessons commence, from the morning arrival time until the bell rings, or during recess periods throughout the day. Singing games are among the many games children play in the playground before school, during recess, and at lunchtime.

While games such as cricket, football or soccer, basketball, handball, and various chasing games tend to occupy larger spaces in the playground, singing games, particularly clapping games, can take place in any area. Although they occur in designated "play" periods following eating times at recess and lunch, they are most often seen when children are required to wait. In this way, clapping games seem to occupy small spaces, both in terms of place and time in the lives of the children who play them.

At Springfield, performances of clapping games proliferated particularly during times when children were required to assemble in lines before entering school in the morning and at the end of recess and lunchtime, as attested by a Year 6 girl:

K: When do you usually like to do those games?

JULIE: Um . . .when we've got nothing else to do, like when we're on the floor we just, like, all my friends, we just all get together and we start playing then. Or when we're in lines waiting for the teacher to come we just start playing then.

As is evident from the above transcript, the minimal space, time, and equipment requirements mean that clapping games can be played almost any time when children are waiting and consequently bored. Many children cited bus trips (on school excursions or to sports venues) as common occasions for clapping games:

JOANNE: Like if we go somewhere on a bus Thuy and I normally play a couple of games.

At Telford Spring, a group of friends in Years 4 and 5 elaborated on the many times and places when clapping games could be used to relieve boredom:

K: You were talking about the kinds of places that you play games. . . . Can you tell me some of those places again?

STEPHANIE: In class.

GEORGIE: Yeah, in class if we get really, really bored.

SEVERAL: In free time.

K: In free time.

STEPHANIE: Excursions.

MARY ANN: Outside.

JESSICA: Sometimes we do it when we're getting ready to get into our house [sports] teams when we're just waiting when people are setting us up. We just sit there [demonstrates clapping pattern].

GEORGIE: Yeah. When they do races, sometimes if we get a bit bored watching the people we just go [demonstrates clapping].

K: And do you do it in lines?

MARY ANN: Yeah while we're waiting for the bell to go.

At the schools in Busan, Korea, multiple short (ten-minute) recess periods rather than a single longer recess meant that many children stayed in the classroom rather than going down to the playground during breaks between lessons. In the confined space of the classroom children of both sexes therefore engaged in a variety of musical play activities involving clapping or elimination, many of which included the movement and verbal formula "scissors, paper, rock," or, more accurately, "scissors rock cloth" (Gawi bawi bo). On our first visit to San School in May 2004, we peered into a classroom during recess time and were invited in. In the space of nine minutes we observed no fewer than eight different games played by pairs or small groups of both boys and girls.

Several children at Springfield reported learning or participating in clapping games while waiting for organized activities outside school hours. This might occur in before- and after-school care centers that were set up on the school premises or nearby. Instances of the learning and performance of different forms of musical play were observed in the after-school activity program at Nora Conn School in Los Angeles in 2004. Clapping games also reportedly took place during waiting periods in settings related to specialized recreational pursuits such as ballet or gymnastics lessons (Springfield). Some of the most prolific players of clapping games and cheers at Birch Vale Elementary School in Seattle stated that they learned a number of games and cheers while waiting to play at softball and baseball games.

At certain times children's use or positioning of clapping games became more specialized. For example, in 1990, a group of Year 6 boys at Springfield used a textless clapping game ("Down by the Banks") as a greeting ritual when their playmates entered the school gates at the beginning of the school day (Tony, Rafael, interview, December 5, 1990). However, the function of musical play to alleviate boredom was also described by Merrill-Mirsky (1988), who observed handclapping games in Los Angeles schools. At Springfield this appeared to be the case, regardless of age, as some Year 6 girls described to me:

> TARA: 'Cause we used to do it in lunchtime or something, like, just for fun. Like there's nothing else to do so we'd just sit down and play [makes clapping movements]. . . .
>
> K: OK. So some of you—you three: Thuy, Joanne, and Clara—are still playing the games sometimes. Is that right?
>
> THUY: Yes.
>
> K: . . . But what about you, Tara and Matu, you—would you say you never play them now, or. . . .
>
> TARA: Sometimes when we're waiting in lines we play "Sar Macka Dora."

The games are played during waiting times, partly because they require no equipment. Tasha, a ten-year-old girl at Bradford Well in central Australia told me that she would play clapping games "when we don't have anything to play with." Other Year 5 girls at Springfield gave a more detailed account:

> ANNETTE: . . . it's something you do when you're bored with no equipment except your hands. You just need your hands.

SADIE: So you don't have to go up to class and get a pencil or anything like that—you've got all your equipment here [shows hands]. . . .

ANNETTE: Yeah. In wet weather it's very useful because if you're not allowed to touch any particular things you can just get a whole group of people who are bored—the whole class—and you can just sit down and play a game.

It is evident from the previous exchange that games are most frequently played between groups of peers. When games are played in class lines, performing groups are restricted to classmates. Games played in these circumstances may involve both girls and boys, as reported by Year 5 girls at Springfield:

K: Does that ever happen—like the whole class joins in?

HONG-SOO: Yes. It happened.

ANNETTE: [Yes with] "Sar Macka Dora."

HONG-SOO: Yes, it happens in our class because now even the boys, they all play. We all sit in a kind of circle and we all start playing "Sar Macka Dora.".

Crossing the Boundaries

As can be seen in the previous statement and in some of the preceding vignettes, these games appear to enable children at some schools to cross social boundaries. In the following section I discuss evidence of game transmission across boundaries of gender, age, and ethnicity.

Transmission between Genders

Although I was never witness to a whole class spontaneously playing a single game as described by Annette and Hong-Soo, I recorded many instances of boys engaging in musical play over the lengthy period of my playground fieldwork. For example, at Springfield I saw both boys and girls from a Year 1 class playing clapping games in lines in 1990, and recorded boys and girls from two Year 2 classes playing clapping games in lines in April 1995. One of the latter performing groups was a mixed-gender group, who were playing together while waiting for their teacher. Another mixed-gender group of performers from one Year 6 class was recorded in 1990 after being observed playing the games in lines by their teacher. Five of the thirty-four performing groups recorded at Springfield Public School were of mixed gender and three were made up of boys only.

Several of the girls interviewed at Springfield reported playing the games with boys, particularly their siblings:

K: Did you learn that one from other kids as well?

CHRISTABEL: I learned it from my brother.

K: From your brother?

CHRISTABEL: Yeah.

K: How old is he? Is he in this school?

CHRISTABEL: Yeah, he's in Year 5 . . . but I learnt it when I was in kindergarten and he was in Year 2 [Christabel is in now in Year 3].

K: Oh right. So he used to play those games did he?

CHRISTABEL: Yeah.

K: Does he still play them?

CHRISTABEL: No [shakes head].

Younger male siblings were observed playing clapping and other musical games quite proficiently with their sisters and sisters' friends at Ellington Primary School in West Yorkshire. In this school, where 95 percent of children were of Punjabi or Bangladeshi descent, familial groupings seemed to extend quite naturally into the playground, though boys' major outdoor play pursuits were cricket and chasing games. Nevertheless, boys were more familiar with certain forms of musical play than others. For example, Amreen's brother Amar joined in with Amreen and her friends playing the clapping games "Down by the River" and the Punjabi "Zig Zag Zoo." He also actively took part in several counting-out games, including "Eeny Meeny Miny More," its Punjabi equivalents "Akkar Bakkar" and "Tu Khota," the Bengali "Mas Mas Amar Mas" and "Honica Bonica," learned by Amreen from her Punjabi father but said to be in English. However, he sat back and watched as the girls moved on to play the exuberant "Cat's Got the Measles," which involved leg-crossing movements rather than clapping or the finger pointing of the counting-out games.

Although several other children reported the boy-to-girl transmission described above by Christabel, girls are evidently still seen to be the major source of game knowledge, as both boys and girls at Springfield attested:

K: OK, but you learnt it from Fiona, did you?

OWEN: No, not me. I learnt it from my class people, last year. . . .

K: So who did you learn it from?

OWEN: Um, Camille . . . Alexis [both girls].

K: Did the boys do some of those as well?

TARA: Yeah. They were on there [points to video].

MATU: Yeah. Demos and Ray.

K: Did they sort of do it on a regular basis, do you think?

CLARA: Well, I think they did it to show off like we did.

TARA: We taught them most of it.

K: Yeah?

TARA: They used to say, "Oh let us," you know.

K: So they wanted to join in.

CLARA: Yeah.

At Strandli school in Norway older girls and boys were seen playing both the clapping game "Slå Makaroni" and the ring game "Slå På Ringen," in which two children chased each other in opposite directions around the circle of singers. They told me that both boys and girls regularly played these games at school but that the girls had learned them first and then taught them to the boys.

Christabel's testimony that the boys' participation decreased as they grew older was endorsed by several other older girls at Springfield. However, even in the case of the Year 6 boys recorded in 1990 who regularly played the games, a difference in girls' and boys' knowledge of the games was evident. For example, while the girls performed "Down by the Banks" with a text, the boys' performance of this game genre was textless, although it was given the same title by players of both sexes. Similarly, grade-7 boys playing jump rope games with girls at Bysiden School in Stavanger showed an equal knowledge of the rules but were less competent skipping the rope. By contrast, boys at both of the Korean schools demonstrated that they were as kinesthetically competent as the girls in many of the complex forms of musical play in which they both engaged.

The participation by boys in clapping games and other forms of musical play that I observed in the various playgrounds I visited differs markedly from reports in the literature. Knapp and Knapp stated in 1976 that "clapping is still emphatically a girls' game" (p. 144), played only by girls, although girls in the United States were increasingly participating in "boys' games." A similar situation was reported by Lindsay and Palmer (1981) in their Brisbane study and by Russell (1986) in Melbourne. Although Merrill-Mirsky (1988) found some evidence of boys playing some girls' games in Los Angeles, the incidence of boys' participation in hand-clapping games was very limited. This was also the case in the Illinois playgrounds studied by Campbell (1991), who reported that boys played the games at home rather than in the public, school environment. Grugeon (1988) also described clapping games in England as the domain of girls. Harwood (1992, 1993a, 1998) chose a girls' after-school club in Illinois as the site of her study of hand-clapping games, partly because these games were played mostly by African American girls in this location. In studies within the last two decades, only Riddell's Los Angeles work (1990) indicates that boys and girls were equally familiar with these games.

There are a number of reasons why there seem to be fewer gender differences in play in many of the field schools I visited than those reported in the literature. One important factor is the integration of girls and boys in "waiting" locations such as lines, where proximity, combined with boredom, encourages boys to learn and participate in the clapping games as an easily accessible form of entertainment. The proliferation of musical play forms that both boys and girls perform in the Busan school classrooms during the short recess times between formal class activities supports this explanation. Boys generally did not play these games outside in the Busan playgrounds but devoted themselves to more boisterous pursuits.

Another possible reason boys participated in clapping games at Springfield Public School is the school's policy of nonsexist education. Concepts of nonsexist behavior were articulated by children even in the early years of school, but were most clearly understood by older children, as demonstrated by the following discussion among Year 6 girls about a "sexist" game text:

TARA: Some are sexist, like the one that goes,

"Boys go to Jupiter to get more stupider

Girls go to Mars to get more bras." . . .

CLARA: It's sort of good to be girls and good to be boys.

K: So you wouldn't do sexist ones now? . . .

CLARA: 'Cause everybody's friends with . . . well most people are friends with everybody else. Yeah. Boys and girls are all friends but. . . .

TARA: When we were little we were all friends but. . . .

CLARA: Urr . . . boys' germs [demonstrates cringing movement]!

MATU: Yeah. When we were little we didn't care about sexism.

K: So you're conscious of that now, are you, and you try to avoid being sexist?

MATU: Yeah.

Also of significance, however, is the classroom validation of some game genres, for example, at Springfield, "Sar Macka Dora." This game had been taught regularly by both of the specialist music teachers employed at the school since 1989 and by at least one of the Year 6 classroom teachers in 1990.

The classroom was reported as the source of this game by a mixed-gender group of Year 6 children recorded in 1990 and by many other children throughout the field collection period, including Year 2 members of a male friendship group recorded in 1995: "We done it with our whole class, with Miss Fallwood." The classroom teaching of clapping games shifts the perception of them as girls' games to that of a pursuit suitable for all children, regardless of gender.

This could also have been the case to some extent at Pada School in Busan. On our initial visit to the school it was clear that children had been specially taught games to perform for us in the playground. However, there were also some games that were taught as a standard part of the "Happy Life" segment of the Korean school curriculum for grades 1 and 2. The Happy Life curriculum incorporates music, dance, painting, and physical education, which become separate subjects from grade 3 onward. Wandering around the corridors of the school, we came upon a class practicing, on successive days, two singing games with actions. One, a traditional Korean game called "Dari Segi" (Counting legs) or "Igeri Jeogeori Gakgeori" (This way, that way, many ways), was a counting-out game where legs were successively counted out then eliminated at the end of the song. The boys and girls were segregated for the performance of this game. They were also segregated on the following day when we found both boys and girls in the class loudly and exuberantly practicing "Sutccha Nori"(Playing with numbers) with a recording. As well as wordplay, this song had a complicated movement sequence involving lateral and figural movements and clapping. Both boys and girls were equally adept at these movements and the game was clearly very familiar to them. Although we didn't see this game performed in the playground, many of the movements from it appeared to be used in a game devised to the theme song from a Japanese animated television show which we later saw played with great dexterity by a group of older girls and some of the boys from their class. It would appear that in-class practice of some games in the earlier years of school both endorsed the idea of their performance by children of both genders and developed some of the kinesthetic skills that were required to perform them.

At Bysiden School in Stavanger, the staff policy of encouraging traditional forms of musical play in the playground resulted in the boys being involved in a number of games in conjunction with girls. This encouragement took a number of forms. Sometimes teachers would tacitly support play by turning a rope while children jumped. In other instances the endorsement was more active, with both the principal and other members of staff initiating ring games and inviting children of both sexes to join in with them. On one such occasion in August 2002, I observed the principal, deputy principal, music teacher (a male) and several other teachers playing the ring game "Ein-å-tyve" and gradually recruiting boys and girls into the circle. They continued for quite a long time, gradually adding more traditional games, including "Slå På Ringen" with its singing and chasing formulae. The message that musical play was acceptable for both boys and girls was quite clearly promoted.

That this message had been received seemed to be borne out by the number of times in which I saw the Bysiden boys (particularly those in older grades) spontaneously joining in with a number of traditional ring and jump-rope games in the playground. On one particularly memorable afternoon after school I witnessed some tall athletic boys abandoning an informal game of soccer to jump rope with a group of girls.

Perhaps the clearest evidence of the effect of adult-generated classroom activities on the acceptance of musical play as a valid form of cross-gender play was found at Nora Conn School in Los Angeles. The after-school arts activities center provided many formal learning experiences involving music and movement, including singing and choreographed and creative dance. All of these experiences included children of both sexes in co-operative and interactive performance. As a result, the boys and girls played together in a completely spontaneous and unselfconscious way whenever they had free time in the playground. The interaction between boys and girls extended from games such as tetherball and chasing, to jump rope, clapping games, and other genres of musical play.

In the course of two afternoons I saw many instances of boys and girls playing together. On the first afternoon a small group of girls and boys of various ages were playing jump rope, each jumper choosing which game he or she would prefer. Pam, Brendan, Mika, Patrick, and Khryslynn all took turns at jumping, choosing the games "Bluebells," "Teddy Bear," and "Ice-cream Soda," each with their idiosyncratic text and movement demands. (⬤ **VIDEO SAMPLE:** See video example *NoraC jumprope*.) The onlookers of both sexes enthusiastically recited the texts, which they obviously all knew well. Brendan and Danielle moved on to play the clapping games "Slide" and "Lemonade" and then expanded the group to play "Down by the banks" (another "Sar Macka Dora" variant) in a circle with Mika, Pam, Patrick, Khryslynn, and Keenan (Pam's brother).

The following day the African American girls Pam and Khryslynn were playing tetherball in turn with two boys, one an Anglo American and the other, Ben, of African American and Japanese descent. Ben had not been at school the previous day when I had first discovered Pam and Khryslynn playing games that I hadn't seen before: "Jigalo" and "H-E-L-L-O." When I asked if I could see these again, Ben immediately started to perform "H-E-L-L-O" with Khryslynn, after first exchanging performance ideas. The game started with the spelling out of the word "hello," each line culminating in a virtuoso display of foot stomping and ankle slapping, creating a complex polyrhythmic percussive sound in response to the text:

> H-E-L-L-O [movements]
> This is how we say hello [movements]
> Now that we've got the beat [movements]
> Listen to our magic feet [movements]
> Sound off [movements]
> Three four [movements]
> Take it down [movements]

(⬆ VIDEO SAMPLE: See video example *NoraC HELLO*.)

Both players indeed seemed to have "magic feet" and an equal level of virtuosity. Ben told me that both boys and girls played it, in addition to hand-clapping games. When I asked if he could play "Jigalo" too, he and Pam obliged. This game is nominated as a cheer by Gaunt (1997, 2006) who sees it at least partially as embodying African American female identity. Having read about this only a week before my visit to Nora Conn School, I was somewhat surprised to find a bicultural boy performing it with knowledge and competence, if not the fluidity of movement which his female partner displayed.

The integration of boys and girls as performers of clapping games in this context was evidenced not only by the boys' involvement and proficiency, but also by structural alterations that permeate the performance of certain games. The clearest example of this was the clapping game "When Miss Sue Was a Baby," which was automatically changed to reflect the gender of the player impersonating "Miss Sue," who was required to improvise a response at each stage of her or his life as articulated by the text. Thus, when the game was played by Pam, Ben, and Khryslynn (clapping) with Patrick in the middle as the protagonist, the text became (for example):

PAM, BEN, KHRYSLYNN: When Mr. Sue was a teenager a teenager a teenager

[Clapping] When Mr. Sue was a teenager

He went like this.

PATRICK: Mum, where's my underwear and my boxers? [Improvised mimetic movements]

PAM, BEN, KHRYSLYNN: When Mr. Sue was a mummy, a mummy, [self-correct] a daddy

When Mr. Sue was a daddy, he went like this.

PATRICK: Kids, go to your room now!

Although there were differences in the boys' levels of knowledge and skill related to the games, with Ben being an expert performer of many games and Patrick less so, musical play in the after-hours center at this school was as much the boys' as the girls' domain.

Another possible influence on male performance of these games is the media's portrayal of clapping routines as a signification of male friendship. In the popular movie *Big*, for example, a version of the game "Down Down Baby" was played by two boys in their early teens as a form of greeting ritual. The Year 6 boys recorded at Springfield in 1990 used the clapping routine of "Down by the Banks" in the same way, to greet friends as they arrived at school.[2] Although this group did not name *Big* as a source, it was nominated as a game source by another child in 1994.[3] The role of the media in game transmission is further discussed in chapter 7.

Some forms of musical play appear to attract boys' interest more than others. Many of the Korean games had a high level of competitiveness and physicality, which may have contributed to their attractiveness to boys. The singing game "Uri Jipe Whe Wanni" (Why do you come to my house), played by a mixed gender group in the playground at Pada School, had a tug-of-war across a line drawn in the gravel (to delineate the boundary of the "house") as an integral part. Other circle games such as "Hana Tul Set" (One two three) and "Sam Yuk Gu" (Three six nine) entailed counting out and a combination of luck, strategy, and cognitive skill as well as painfully physical punishments of hard hand-smacking or pounding on the back for the hapless person who was out. These games were played by girls and boys, either in mixed or separate sex groups inside. This is not to say that these games and others with equally strategic or physical aspects were less attractive to girls, who played them with equal frequency and verve. Their similar pleasure in such pursuits was demonstrated by their interest in the "Nol twiggi" (Jumping seesaws) at Pada, where girls and boys alike propelled themselves into the air with energy and skill. (⏺ **VIDEO SAMPLE:** See video examples *Pada Uri jipe* and *San Hana tul set*.)

At Birch Vale School in Seattle I did not observe any instances of boys playing clapping games. However, when a group of Spanish-speaking immigrant girls moved from demonstrating clapping and jump rope games to playing a Spanish singing game entitled "Lobo" (wolf) in which the "wolf" devoured those who were caught with particular ferocity, some of their male classmates joined in. Again the physicality of the game seemed to be an attractive feature for the boys.

Finally, I must acknowledge that "researcher effect" may have contributed slightly to the number of boys performing clapping games and other forms of musical play in varied school locations because of the attraction of the video camera and my continued attention to the games and their performers wherever they occurred. However, the effect of my presence and interest does not completely explain the ongoing performance of these games by boys, as reported and observed in a number of school playgrounds over fifteen years.

Transmission across Age Groups

Although the majority of friendship groups in most schools are made up of age peers—children either from the same class or other classes at the same grade level, a number of factors combine to ensure that transmission also occurs between children of different age groups. These factors will now be considered in detail. The first factor is the constitution of "composite" classes across two or more age groups, which often results in the formation of friendship groups between children of varying ages, though the variation is likely to be no more than two years. This explanation was given by a group of Year 6 girls at Springfield who in 1990 were discussing the membership of a performing group to which they belonged:

CLARA: . . . we were in Year 2 and there were girls who were a year older than us.

TARA: They were in Year 3 because it was a 2/3 class.

Proximity in waiting situations, such as lines, often leads to inter-age transmission, as it does to inter-gender transmission. However, performances by the group consisting of Year 2 and Year 3 children described above continued during free time in the playground at lunchtime, which was where they were initially viewed and recorded in 1990. The group therefore appeared to operate as a permanent friendship group during the time in which they were placed in the same class. Examples of these enduring multi-age friendships resulting from being placed in the same classroom were also found at Telford Spring, Summerglen, Birch Vale, and Maringa, though the relationships at Maringa were also kinship-based.

Probably of greater importance to the transmission process are inter-age alliances formed outside of school, which continue to operate in the playground. The most significant of these alliances are those between relatives, most usually, but not always, siblings, as discussed by Year 6 girls at Springfield:

K: I saw you one day playing with one of the little kids, one of the kindergarten kids, I think she was, or Year 1.

THUY: I think she was in Year 1.

K: Is that something that you or any of the others would do very often?

SEVERAL: Sometimes.

K: [To Thuy] So this is just a child that you know, is it?

THUY: Yeah.

K: Like a neighbor, or how do you know her?

THUY: Like, she has a cousin, a big cousin in 6OC and, like, I used to be best friends with her and she just plays with Jodie and I just play with her.

K: Oh, I see. Right. And do you still play with your younger

... brother? [Thuy had discussed this the previous year.]

[Thuy nods]

K: Yeah?

THUY: We play clapping games too.

K: So he's in, what, Year 4, is he?

CLARA: Year 3.

Several other children at this school reported playing clapping games with their siblings at home, even if they were now beyond the age of playing them regularly in the playground:

K: So most of you aren't playing them any more. Is that right?

CLARA: No, not really. I sometimes do with my sister but. . . .

K: OK. Is your sister younger or older, Clara?

CLARA: Younger.

Others reported learning the games from their siblings, particularly if the siblings were older. During the fieldwork period at Springfield, two sets of siblings were observed regularly playing together in the playground. These siblings were Blanche and Camila, whose ages differed by a year, and my sons Owen and Sascha, whose age differed by two years. In each case, either of the siblings would spontaneously invite the other, along with members of their respective friendship groups, to elicited recording sessions, a practice that occurred with siblings at nearly every school I visited.

The recordings of Sascha playing within Owen's friendship group gave me some insight into the transmission practices from older to younger children, the direction of transmission outlined by Harwood (1992), Merrill-Mirsky (1988), and Grugeon (1988). Blanche and Camila also described the ways in which they taught their younger cousin (see chapter 6) and Camila's first request for me to include her older sister in the recording sessions because "she knows all the games" indicated that the older child might be considered to have a greater repertoire.

However, Blanche and Camila's performances at school and their reported behaviour at home demonstrated the practice of co-construction of variants rather than transmission of the tradition from the older to younger sister. Composition in performance seemed to be the equal privilege of both girls, with neither being deemed to have superior knowledge. In this case, it may be that the difference in age was too small to be significant. Alternatively, as these girls were relatively prolific in terms of generating new games and new versions of games, it may be that the desire to compose in performance negated the age boundary.

In other cases the circumstantial possession of superior knowledge enabled younger children to take on the teaching role. For example, in 2002, after two Anglo Punjabi sisters at Ellington Primary School in West Yorkshire demonstrated the Punjabi game "Zig Zag Zoo," which they had learned on a holiday visit to Pakistan, the younger sister, Kaneez, aged seven, told me that her Pakistani friend had taught her the game and that she had subsequently taught the game to her nine-year-old sister Saima.

A similar example of younger-to-older transmission was provided in 2001 by three sisters at Auston Community Education Centre, in central Australia, where there was a concerted effort by members of the Aboriginal community to teach some Aboriginal language in the school. As part of a language education program, a version of the Christmas carol "The Twelve Days of Christmas" incorporating the Mudburra names for local wildlife had been taught by the "language ladies" (older Aboriginal women with a knowledge of the traditional language) to the seven-year-old sister as part of a class learning experience during the previous year. She had subsequently taught the song to her older sisters and the siblings had transformed it into a singing game with an accompanying clapping pattern. It is notable that these sisters were not Mudburra themselves, having come from a distant outback town in another state, but they had generated play material from the youngest sister's current school classroom.

Other reports of transmission between children of different ages at Springfield tend to reinforce the older-to-younger transmission thesis of Harwood (1992), Merrill-Mirsky (1988), and Grugeon (1988). Children learn games from older children when they are placed together in a play situation. Games are therefore learned from older neighbors at home and from children in the after-school care centers. Quite large age differences can apparently be accommodated in this form of play. For example, in 1996, at a local after-school care center attended by Springfield children, I observed a kindergarten and a Year 6 girl from a neighboring school performing together the complex clapping game

"Slide." Similarly, a Year 1 (six–year-old) girl recorded in 1994 nominated an American teenager who had been staying with her family as the source of her version of "Sor Macaron Son Ferio."

As can be seen, the greater amount of time for play that exists outside of the school environment clearly assists familial transmission. At Nora Conn School in Los Angeles, Mikeyla, a ten-year-old girl of mixed Latino and African American heritage, told me about having her cousins over to play at her house every day, resulting in increased learning opportunities:

> K: Do you play those kinds of hand-clapping games at home as well as at school?
>
> MIKEYLA: Yeah. My cousin, Winter, she's eight years old. . . . She taught me how to play "Lemonade." I didn't know how.
>
> K: Oh, right. So she told you . . . "Lemonade"?
>
> MIKEYLA: Yeah. She told me how to play some of the games.

Mikeyla also nominated her grandmother as a source of at least one game. At every school I visited, children reported learning games from members of their immediate or extended families, including sisters, brothers, cousins, mothers, fathers, aunts, and grandmothers. These familial sources provided a range of knowledge that formed the basis of musical play exhibited at school. Such material varied from very traditional games such as the Korean "P'urun Hanül Ŭnhasu" (Blue sky milky way, also known as Half moon song), reportedly learned by Korean girls from their mothers in both Busan and Sydney, to rap ideas borrowed from brothers and cousins and used as the starting point for raps and dance routines generated by several children at Birch Vale in Seattle.

Specific kinship relationships between Aboriginal groups in Telford Spring, in central Australia, also mean that transmission occurs between relatives of widely differing ages. Although there was some playing of clapping games observed between Aboriginal and non-Aboriginal friends at Telford Spring in 2001 and 2002, Aboriginal children in the central Australian schools frequently cited members of their extended families (most commonly sisters, "cousins," and "aunties," but also "cousin sisters," delineated by their skin names, encompassing a wide network of kinship relations), rather than friends, as the source from whom they had learned games, and as the people with whom they usually played the games.

The travel patterns of Aboriginal families further affected the transmission process through kinship affiliations. Games were reported by some Aboriginal children at Telford Spring to have been learned from cousins during family visits to distant towns, for example Borroloola, some 700 kilometers north of Telford Spring. One girl had learned games from her cousins whom she visited at Palm Island on the coast of another state 1,300 kilometers away. There was therefore a constant source of new game material provided by the long-distance travel that was a regularly occurring part of life, related to social and ceremonial obligation, visits to "country," hunting, and employment.

It would seem that inter-age play might be more transferable from one play situation to another than from a formal classroom situation to the playground. However, where children of different ages are placed together in a classroom setting for a sufficient period of time to form strong friendships (as in the case of composite classes), the friendship groupings support inter-age play in the playground. This was evidenced at the after-school arts activity center at Nora Conn School in Los Angeles, where children aged from five to twelve participated in a range of organized arts activities. As previously mentioned, friendship groups observed during free play times in 2004 incorporated boys and girls of different ages and competencies who amicably engaged in musical and other play activities together.

The children's disposition to accommodate and assist younger children with a different level of competence may also be a direct outcome of specific school practices such as the Pairing and Sharing and Peer Support programs implemented at Springfield. Strategies used in teaching younger players are outlined in chapter 6, where differences in the performance practice of younger players are also explored.

Transmission between Ethnic Groups

Another social boundary that is crossed in the performance of playground singing games is that of ethnicity. The notion of inclusion in game performance is manifested in two ways in relation to ethnic groups: multiethnic membership of friendship groups who perform games together and inter-ethnic transmission. Of these, the most obvious is the multi-ethnic membership of performing friendship groups. Of the thirty-four performing groups recorded from 1990 to 1996 at Springfield, twenty-six groups were multiethnic in composition. Formation of these groups appeared to be influenced both by the simple proximity of children of different ethnicities in the classroom and the practice of many of the teachers of children in the younger years at Springfield in creating groups of mixed ethnicity for classroom learning experiences.

Another major factor in the apparent acceptance of ethnic difference by the children at Springfield was the high degree of ethnic diversity in the school. Collins (1988) has commented on the relatively low incidence of racial tensions in Australia in the latter part of the twentieth century, stating that "the evidence suggests that the greater the ethnic diversity, the smaller the chance of racial conflict" (p. 222). At Springfield, the wide range of ethnic groups represented in the school population seemed to lessen the possible construction of non-Anglo-Australians as "other." There were so many "others" with a variety of racial, cultural, and linguistic attributes in the school, that difference was normal.

This was also the case at Nora Conn and Birch Vale schools where multiethnic friendships were also quite usual. However, children seemed less disposed to engage in interethnic transmission of games at these schools in the United States than the children I had seen at Springfield. Again, this might be partly attributable to teaching practices and policies in the different schools. At Springfield, the teaching staff, to some extent, took on the function of authoritative opinion-makers, who, especially with younger children, endorsed ethnic identity. The ESL teachers, in particular, team-teaching within mainstream classrooms, consciously modeled an acceptance of children from varied ethnic groups, both to other staff and to children. The acceptance of difference was reflected in the inter-ethnic transmission of clapping games at Springfield. Knowledge of and participation in the games assisted both Anglo-Australian children and children from language backgrounds other than English to gain social acceptance.

Despite the apparent tolerance of diversity at Springfield, transmission was mostly unidirectional, with children from other ethnic groups learning games from the dominant Anglo culture. The majority of games recorded in the playground either had texts in English or incorporated vocables, "nonsense" words with no apparent literal meaning. For children developing competence in English, the repetitive use of formulae within the game texts and the accompanying movements, which could easily be imitated without the need for verbal instructions, made the learning of games easier.

I saw the results of such a process at Birch Vale School in the play of newly arrived immigrant children from Mexico and South America. These children, aged six to nine years, from the specialized junior ELL (English Language Learners) class had been in the United States for less than a year. Though most of their games were played in Spanish, they also played the jump-rope game "Ice Cream" in the playground. This involved reciting a simple formula with a repeated word at the beginning and continued counting until the jumper tripped up and was out:

Ice cream ice cream cherry on the top
How many boyfriends do you have?
A-one, a-two, a-three, a-four. . . .

The jumping and turn-taking conventions were easily observed and imitated by the children, who performed the game competently, though counting beyond twenty in English was still difficult for some.

Irrespective of their verbal comprehension, bilingual children's participation in games appears to be enhanced by the nonsense element of many of the texts, a view supported by Doekes (1992c). The standard use of vocables or nonsense words in game texts reduces the need for players to understand the meaning of the words. This characteristic also enables non-English words to be included in game repertoire. Indeed, children attempt to legitimize nonsense words by attributing them to another language. At Springfield the popular game "Sar Macka Dora," with a text made up almost entirely of vocables, was seen to have several possible linguistic derivations:

BLANCHE: It's just an Aboriginal song and if you hit the other person's hand that means they're out.

K: Right. It's an Aboriginal song?

SEVERAL: Yeah.

K: How do you know that?

BLANCHE: Because we were taught it by our music teacher.

K: Right. And she told you it was an Aboriginal song, did she?

SU LI: Yeah.

ERMA: Not really.

BLANCHE: Yes, she did, remember?

One group of children told me that this game was different because it was in Italian. Their enthusiasm for the game was not affected by the lack of meaning in the words.

HONG-SOO: Most of us know the tune but we have absolutely no idea what country it comes from.

SUNNI: It is from Italy.

K: Where do you think it's from?

SEVERAL: Italy. It is.

K: It's from Italy. Why is it from Italy?

ANNETTE: I could probably find out the words for it.

ALICIA: Because her Dad's Italian.

SHEILA: "Sor Macka Dora"'s Italian but it might have an Australian meaning. So "Sor macka dora" might mean, "Hello, how are you" in Australian, so we might be singing a song that we don't really know but it's in Italian.

ANNETTE: It might be quite rude.

K: Does it worry you that you don't know what the words mean?

ALL: No.

HONG-SOO: Not a single bit.

It is possible that the text's lack of semantic importance has contributed to the mass dissemination of this game. Variants of this game were found over the fifteen-year period of my fieldwork in all schools except those in Korea and in the smaller Aboriginal settlements in central Australia. Segler (1992) has also reported a large number of variants occurring in many European countries. At Ellington School in West Yorkshire, which had a predominantly Punjabi-speaking population, children reversed the attribution of language of one form of this game, called "Sella Ella Oola." In this case, any text that was not understood was rationalized as being English. Thus, a ten-year old-girl told me that the text of "Sella Ella Oola," given below, was in English:

Sella ella oola quack quack quack
Say yes chigga chigga challi chap chap
Say yes chigga chigga flor, flor, flor flor flor
Say one two three four five.

A group of nine-year-olds in this school applied the same rule to another game made up almost entirely of vocables, "Honica Bonica."

Regardless of the accuracy of the performers' accounts of the origin of "Sar Macka Dora" and its variants, it is evident that the transmission of other games from minority ethnic groups to members of the dominant culture also occurs in the playground, as Year 5 girls at Springfield maintained:

ANNETTE: . . . as new people come in from different countries and if they have a handclapping game or something, they'll teach us.

HONG-SOO: And as Springfield is quite a . . . .

ALICIA: Multicultural school

HONG-SOO: Multicultural school, yeah . . . .

K: Can you give me an example of what you're talking about maybe? . . . Are there any other games from other countries that . . .?

SEVERAL: Hong-Soo knows one.

ANNETTE: There's a Korean one that I was taught by Hong-Soo but I can't remember it.

SADIE: Yes, so was I but I can't remember.

In both this recording session and another recording session in 1993, Hong-Soo talked about learning this Korean clapping game, "P'urun Hanül

Ŭnhasu," from her mother. In 1993, I recorded her trying to teach the complicated movement pattern of the game to several other members of her group, who, with the exception of the Italian-Australian Annette, were Anglo-Australian. In 1994, the friendship group had fragmented slightly, because the girls were placed in three different classes. Although they still played together in some circumstances, they tended to play in smaller clusters. Hong-Soo's new Korean-Australian friend, Sunni, who had entered Springfield school in 1994, joined in some of these activities. During the recording session in 1994, at my request Hong-Soo demonstrated the complex Korean clapping pattern with Sunni. Neither of them could sing the song with the movements. As they demonstrated, the rest of the group crowded around to watch the game carefully. Afterward, while I was discussing the game with Hong-Soo and Sunni, Sheila and Annette were spontaneously attempting to perform the Korean clapping pattern together.

To some extent inter-ethnic transmission may be attributable to children's inherent interest in novelty, as a twelve-year-old girl at Springfield who had just watched a video of some of my field recordings from 1990 and 1991 confirmed:

CLARA: I remember all of them except for that last one. . . .

K: OK. You seemed quite interested in that one. Was it because it was different, or . . .?

CLARA: Yeah. . . .

K: What was interesting about that? What attracted your attention?

CLARA: Just, I think the fact that I didn't really know it. . . .

K: Does it have that immediate attractive quality if you come in on a game like that?

CLARA: Oh, yeah. Sort of. I think you're attracted to anything you don't know. Like, somebody's doing a clapping game or something and it's one that you don't know how to do it and you hear it and you listen to the words and show it to your friends.

Nevertheless, other factors are also important in determining the degree to which inter-ethnic transmission occurs, such as the circumstances in which games are learned and the confidence and popularity of the children involved. The Korean-Australian Hong-Soo described above was a highly articulate, confident child who was able, in the context of her friendship group's play, to teach the Korean game to her friends. A similar case was presented by John, an extroverted Year 1 boy who had emigrated from Korea eight months before I encountered him, whom I observed teaching another Korean clapping game,

"Ach'im Baram," to several of his male Anglo-Australian and Fijian-Australian friends while waiting in lines in December 1994. The group of boys, including Adam and Lloyd, told me how John had first taught them the game one lunch-time when they had to remain seated on a bench for an extended period of time. They were unable to play more active games so filled the time playing the clapping game that John had experienced as a common form of recreation in Korea. Finding his friends in this situation, Adam had also learned the game and enjoyed it, even though he normally preferred to play soccer.[4] (🔊 **VIDEO SAMPLE:** See video example *SpringF Ach'im baram.*)

When questioned, John's teacher was of the opinion that John's transmission of the game was facilitated by his outgoing personality and general popularity. This view of the importance of individual popularity in the transmission of games was endorsed by Year 2 and Year 3 girls recorded in 1994, who were predicting the playground fate of a new game they had created:

K: You think that other kids will actually start to adopt this practice now, do you?

BLANCHE: Yes. 'Cause she's very popular [indicating Christabel], she's very popular [indicating Camila], and I'm very popular.

K: Oh. And does your popularity affect whether other kids do the same things?

BLANCHE: Sometimes.

K: So if you're more popular, more kids are likely to do things the same way as you do? Is that right?

[Blanche, Christabel, and Camila nod in affirmation.]

Individual self-confidence and the support provided by a strong friend-ship group may also contribute to interethnic transmission. At Bysiden School, in Stavanger, in 2002, a group consisting of three pairs of sisters of Eritrean, Somalian, and Ghanaian descent formed a close-knit play group both at home and at school. They taught each other games in their respective languages, learned originally from parents or on visits to their parents' birthplace. They were equally happy to play Norwegian games learned in the playground, as well as games derived from popular songs sung in English.

Likewise, the social safety obtained by belonging to a dominant ethnic group at Ellington School in West Yorkshire enabled children to make use of multiple musical worlds in their play. Children were observed playing Pak-istani, Bangladeshi, and English games and generating games from Bollywood Hindi movie songs and popular English songs with equal avidity and fluency. All of these games were played openly in the playground, with the game "Zig

Zag Zoo" being particularly popular. This game, played in pairs, entailed clapping the partner's hands above and below a central point until the final surprise punch:

Punjabi (Anglicized Script)	English Translation
Zig zag zoo	Zig zag zoo
Kabhi ooper	Sometimes on top
Kabhi neechey	Sometimes underneath
Kabhi oonchey	Sometimes high
Kabhi taley	Sometimes low
Kabhi mukkey	Sometimes punches

(⊙ **VIDEO SAMPLE:** See video example *Ellington ZZZ* and appendix 4 for a notated version of this game.) Many Ellington children recounted how they had learned the game either on visits to Pakistan or from various family members at home, then taught it to other friends in the playground.

This contrasted with the experiences of the Anglo Punjabi girls at St. Augustine's School in the same town. These girls also learned "Zig Zag Zoo" from family members at home but largely restricted their playing to home. Although at school there was some limited playing of the game with other Punjabi-speaking girls, generally the girls did not feel that playing Punjabi games was acceptable in the school playground. This could have partly been due to their minority status in the school population. However, it also seemed to be influenced by the ethos of the school. Whereas Ellington had a strong focus on individual identity and support of difference (particularly ethnicity), this was not the case at St. Augustine's. A girl of Spanish descent at St. Augustine's demonstrated to me a game in Spanish that she had learned from her mother but told me that she had only taught it to one friend and was not comfortable teaching it on a larger scale at school.

As in the case of inter-gender transmission, it is also possible that a teacher's validation may influence inter-ethnic transmission of the games. The game "Da Da Dexi," recorded in 1990, was added to the playground repertoire after a Greek Australian teacher at Springfield taught it to members of her class (see "Influences of the Classroom" in chapter 7). A similar example of inter-ethnic transmission from teacher to students is reported by Doekes and Van Doorn-Last (1993), who discuss the teaching of a Surinamese version of "See See My Playmate" to children in a Dutch school by their teacher, who was a Surinamese immigrant.

Game popularity also affects the degree of interethnic transmission, as three Chinese Australian girls at Springfield discussed in relation to the game

"Black and White TV", which one of the girls, Wendy, had learned on a visit to her home city of Shanghai:

> K: And have you taught that to anyone else since you've been back?
>
> WENDY: No. Never, 'cause I just remembered it just then.
>
> K: You just remembered it then? Do you think you will teach it to anyone?
>
> ALL: Yeah.
>
> K: Yeah? Do you think it would be a popular game?
>
> WENDY: Yeah. 'Cause most people they like it. Like, my friends in China, they all like that game.
>
> SU LI: Yeah. I like it too.
>
> K: You like it too, Su Li? Will you teach it to other kids, who are English speaking kids, do you think?
>
> ALL: Yes [nod in affirmative].

This game was still being played at Springfield two years later and was still being learned by other younger children. It is notable, however, that the game was always played with an English text.

The modification of text is one of several transformations made in the process of accommodating difference in the playground, a process that is looked at more closely in the following chapter, which examines the ways in which children teach and learn games and other forms of musical play in their own milieu. The multiple forms of adaptation, appropriation, and generation of new material from adult, child and mediated sources are then the focus of chapter 7, "Changing the Tradition."

➝ CHAPTER 6 ➝

Teaching and Learning in the Playground

O ne of the aspects of children's traditional forms of play that has most in-
trigued adults is the way in which a game is passed on from one child or
group of children to another. In the playground children teach and learn games
prolifically, so that games may be passed through a large population at quite
amazing velocity.

Children are quite conscious of the processes involved, as my conversation
with a group of Year 4 girls at Springfield school in 1995 attests. They were discussing the transmission of a textless clapping game for which they had no
name but which was identifiably the game "Slide," described by Riddell (1990)
and Gaunt (2006). According to these girls, it had been introduced to the
Springfield playground by Clarissa, who had entered the school earlier that
year and had learned it from friends at ballet[1]:

K: Do other people play it besides you?

SEVERAL: No.

CLARISSA: Yes. Like, quite a few people . . . like Alison and Jessica.

GLENNA: 'Cause they've sort of copied it.

CLARISSA: 'Cause they sort of learnt it off us. . . .

MARGARET: Yes, Sophie Watson—I taught Sophie Watson. She was hope-
less at the beginning. . . .

ANDREA: I think it's only our class.

K: Just kind of people in your class?

ALL: Yeah.

CLARISSA: But I've noticed other people, like Year 3 playing it in the playground.

GLENNA: And also Year 5's.

K: You've seen some Year 5's and some Year 3's playing it?

CLARISSA: Yeah, yeah.

GLENNA: So above and below our year they've sort of learnt it off us.

K: You think nobody in the school was playing it before Clarissa taught it?

GLENNA: No, no-one was. . . .

K: And . . . so how do you think the other kids have learnt it?

GLENNA: They just stare. They just go like [demonstrates stare].

CLARISSA: I think they just . . . I just think . . . I taught Margaret and then Margaret taught Emma . . . And then everyone teaches. . . .

ANDREA: Lots of people have been trying to teach me. But at the beginning all I knew was [clapping movements].

CLARISSA: Like I taught Margaret and then Margaret taught Emma.

GLENNA: And you taught me.

ANDREA: And Glenna started off by trying to teach me.

CLARISSA: Yeah, and everyone like . . . I taught it to people and then they taught it to someone else.

GLENNA: Yeah. I taught it to Sophie and Sophie taught it too. And I taught it to Josephine and stuff like that.

K: Where do you normally play it?

ANDREA: At lines or something.

CLARISSA: Yes, just when we're in lines waiting for our teacher, or something.

K: Usually in lines. And how do you think, say, the Year 3 people have learnt it then?

ANDREA: They . . . well, I've seen a couple of people when we were playing . . . when we were playing at lines before school. I've seen a couple of Year 3's looking at us.

K: OK, right. And you think they've learnt it that way?

GLENNA: Yeah.

The girls were clearly aware of the genealogy of the transmission process, the roles and competencies of different teaching and learning pairs, the sequence in which they acquired game skills, the way in which other children outside of their immediate friendship group had learned the game through observation, and the location in which transmission had primarily occurred.

Modes of Teaching and Learning

During the years in which I traversed various school playgrounds I was afforded a wealth of conversations and experiences that gave me insight into the mechanisms of transmission. This chapter illuminates these processes by describing and analyzing examples of the transmission of playground games and other forms of musical play as observed in different schools. Perhaps the most illustrative metaphor used by children to describe the process of transmission is that of "catching" the games. This is used in the sense of contagion, as described by a nine-year-old girl at Springfield:

BLANCHE: And I think it's going to be like a disease, going from one person to the other . . . It's like something that you pick up, like the measles from school.

The metaphor of catching the games pervades many of the children's descriptions of the way they teach and learn the games and is confirmed by my own observations. Within a friendship group, children "catch" the game elements from each other, often literally turning and catching hold of a partner to impart a game movement or to join in and learn a new movement, game, or game variant. Children move in close proximity to each other to facilitate the contagion. The learning process is marked by close observation, physical contact, and modeling of new game behaviors, as examples throughout this chapter demonstrate.

Another inherent aspect of the learning process is the recognition of known movement, textual, and melodic formulae, as illustrated by the following scene from Ellington School in West Yorkshire in 2002. Inside a small classroom three nine-year-old girls had been demonstrating and discussing games with me. On the previous day I had seen a group of older girls in the playground performing the game "Sella Ella Oola" (a variant of the elimination game "Sar Macka Dora"), which the younger children did not seem to know, though several of them had been watching it attentively. I had invited the players of this game inside to demonstrate it again in relative quiet. All the girls joined in together to play in a circle. Although the younger girls did not know this version of the game, one girl, Farah, immediately recognized that it had the same beat passing and elimination actions as a known game, "Hanky Panky." They were therefore able to play the game movements almost immediately, with only a few pauses as Halima and Farah (the most knowledgeable players of the two groups) gave brief instructions regarding the elimination movements.

After two renditions of the song by the older girls, Farah started to mouth the words and by the end of the game she was singing the song along with Halima. As we discussed various aspects of this game, another of the nine-year-olds sang snippets of the song. When I asked if she knew it I was told that she was just practicing this new song. The following day the nine-year-olds wanted to show me some more games, the first of which was "Sella Ella Oola." They told me that they had remembered it from the recording session the day before and had practiced it with the older girls and then each other after school. Their initial attempt at the game was faltering, with many stops, particularly by Amreen who didn't know the movements very well. However, the second time, they played the game confidently, having remembered the song almost perfectly. They told me that they liked to learn new games and this one had now entered their repertoire. (⬤ VIDEO SAMPLE: See video example *Ellington Sella ella*.)

As can be seen in the Ellington example, movement formulae usually appear to be acquired first, followed by textual and melodic formulae. This sequence of acquisition was elaborated by two sisters, Camila and Blanche, and their friends in Years 2 and 3 at Springfield:

K: How do you pick it up? Like, when you're learning it . . . ?

CAMILA: Like, you hear what their words . . . and you, like . . . we know how to do that [demonstrates three-beat clap] or you could do that [demonstrates C/O C/P clapping pattern[2]]. Then you start joining in [continues clapping] and then . . .

K: And . . . so you know some of the movements already, do you?

BLANCHE: Yes

K: Are there different movements? Do the same movements fit different games?

ALL: Yes.

CAMILA: Yeah. You just go like that [demonstrates C/O C/P pattern] and just sing and you just keep on doing that [same pattern] until it's finished.

K: OK. So you'd wait until you—what—learnt the words first, or what?

BLANCHE: Well, basically. . . .

CHRISTABEL: They're both together.

BLANCHE: Well first you learn the hand movements.

K: Yes.

BLANCHE: But the second time you'd start. . . .

CAMILA: Singing.

BLANCHE: Remembering the words.

K: Right. You'd remember the words . . . and what about the tunes that some of them have?

BLANCHE: Well basically it's like a record—like, it gets stuck de de de de de de [Blanche and Camila imitate the rotation of a record with their fingers]. It keeps going around.

The internalization of formulae was further described by Blanche:

BLANCHE: Well, my friend, she taught me the hand movements from this one and, basically, when she was doing the hand movements, she said the words, and I kind of, like, got the rhythm. Like you got the rhythm in here [indicates chest and starts rocking] and suddenly it's going all over your body and you got it in your hands [hands move up and down] and then that's—you keep doing it.

The process described by Blanche can be illustrated by the play of a group of ten-year-old girls recorded at St. Augustine's in West Yorkshire in November of 2004. Francesca had been teaching Penny a new game that she had brought from her previous school. They had tried it out a couple of times outside but now had come in out of the wet weather and demonstrated it inside. The game, "Eeny Weeny Popsqueak," had a complicated movement pattern which involved both clapping and hand-gripping on the beat at three different levels, the hands weaving above and below each other, in a similar but more extended way to "That's the Way I Like It," a game that was well-known by this group. Penny carefully watched Francesca's hand movements and matched them almost simultaneously, managing to keep up the movement without any real hesitation. Francesca waited very briefly with hands poised for Penny to match movements any time she lagged slightly behind, a form of synchronized modeling. The second time through Penny started to sing the song with Francesca, her voice very softly dropping in and out with more or less familiar text. When I asked them afterward how they learned new games, their replies again revealed that a combination of observation and kinesthetic memory was involved:

K: How do you learn it when you're learning a new one?

CLAIRE: It's like if you watch them do it. . . .

LAUREN: You just get into it. . . .

PENNY: And your hands just glide into it.

K: Your hands just sort of go into it?

FRANCESCA: Yes.

K: So you're watching what's going on. . . .

FRANCESCA: You watch it and you pick it up.

Zach, a nine-year-old boy at Birch Vale School in Seattle, provided another perspective on this phenomenon after demonstrating a lengthy and intricate sequence of dance steps that he had devised to a rap recording. Although this was not a form of traditional musical play, it was one in which he engaged regularly and with considerable skill, a genre that had its own repertoire of music-related movement formulae.

K: OK. And how do you remember all the steps? Do you do them the same way each time?

ZACH: Well, like, once you get used to doing the dances and stuff, I think it gets into your body so you can remember and know how. You know, like when I went like this [action as though pulling head up with a string] and I pull myself up and I went like this [shoulder roll] so it looks like you're rubber. It gets into your body so you do that.

K: So your body just kind of remembers what to do. Is that right?

ZACH: Yeah.

The physical manifestation of the formulae described by Blanche at Springfield (Australia), the girls at St. Augustine's (United Kingdom), and Zach in Seattle (United States) is reminiscent of Rice's (1994) description of the attributes of the first three nodes of musical cognition that he identifies in performers of Bulgarian dances. In Rice's analysis, the nodes relate to the acquisition of an understanding of beat, meter, and rhythm, respectively, which are demonstrated through movement in performance. As the nodes are associated with the structural characteristics of Bulgarian music, they would not, of course, be exactly replicated in the quite different musical structures of playground games and other forms of musical play, but what is similar is the observable physical demonstration of rhythmic and metrical aspects of the musical tradition.

These are acquired through observation, participation, and practice. Perhaps the textual formula, "Let's get the rhythm of the [different body parts]," which is used reiteratively in a popular game in many playgrounds, "Down Down Baby," takes on a new meaning when considered in this light.

The manner in which movement, textual, and musical aspects of a performance are acquired is also demonstrated by a learning episode I recorded at Springfield in 1994. On this occasion, a group of Year 6 girls had been watching my field recording of some of their members filmed in 1990. The recording showed, among other examples, three consecutive performances of the game "Michael Jackson." In the first of these performances there were many discrepancies between each player's version, and I had requested a slower performance, in the mistaken belief that this would assist the performers. The slower tempo merely caused the players to falter and then disagree, and a third performance at the "correct" tempo ensued. Because of discrepancies between players, the text of the final line was difficult to distinguish.

The Year 6 girls no longer played the game but remembered having done so. They were fascinated by it and requested repeated viewings. They saw approximately seven partial or complete performances of the game. As they observed the game, they gradually started to reconstruct a performance, which varied slightly in text and movements from the original. It was evident that the girls each learned slightly different parts of the game and co-constructed it. After collaborative reconstruction of the text and movements of the final line by Clara, Tara, and Thuy, they checked their version by observing three full video performances. Tara tended to mirror movements and text but was quietened by Clara, who preferred to observe in silence. Following this period of observation, the group performed the full game.

There is evidence here, then, that learning of the various elements of the games is aggregative, although it takes place in relation to whole performances. Which parts are most easily learnt depends on the nature of the performances being observed and practiced. In this case, the repeated movement and melodic formulae of the first two text lines ("Michael Jackson/ girlfriend Madonna") were the first to be duplicated, followed by the initiating formula ("My name is") and the conspicuous mimetic textual and movement formulae with sexual connotations (grunting and lifting of skirts) at the end of the second text line. The change of movement formula in the third line, and the indistinct rendition of the final line, caused the most difficulty in the learning process and resulted in the most variation.

What is perhaps most significant is that the elements of text, music, and movement are more likely to cause difficulties if they deviate from expectations derived from the children's understanding of the formulaic nature of the genre. It is deviations from the norm that are the most difficult to accurately reproduce. The main melodic formula, in this case, was rapidly recognized and assimilated. While it might well be predicted that children in this older age group could easily learn this simple melody (G-G-E-D), it is interesting that it was not the initial phrase that was learned first, but the first phrase of the re-iterated melodic formula, and learning of this formula was then generalized to the rest of the game.

Novel formulae, such as those at the end of the second line of the game, are also easily learnt because they pique curiosity. The combining of movement, melodic, and text formulae seemed to be accommodated by these girls, with the movement perhaps operating as a mnemonic device rather than a hindrance to accurate learning. There seemed to be a symbiotic relationship between movement, music, and text that would indicate that separating these elements into disjunct segments would hinder learning rather than assist it. At all times the learners listened to complete renditions as models for imitation, never requesting that the recording be stopped at any point within the performance.

Obviously, this example records only one instance of a learning sequence, and generalizations concerning the acquisition of game elements must be made with care, as both the content of the game and the context of teaching and learning will, necessarily, affect the outcome. In this example, the performance on audiovisual media distanced the performers from the observers. The Year 6 children were outside Jones and Hawes' "charmed circle" (1987, p. 87) of the performing group they were observing. Their learning therefore differs to some extent from what happens inside the circle of friends.

Nevertheless, there is evidence that this mode of learning from the audio-visual media is a significant factor in the transmission of games in the school, as will be discussed in the following chapter. It is also clear that learning games by watching performing groups from outside of the friendship circle and then practicing them within the social safety of the observers' own friendship groups is quite common in the playground. The boundary of the friendship group seems to be one that is more difficult to cross than other social boundaries:

BLANCHE: Well basically it's like watching a movie. You find it very interesting and then next time you say "Mum, can we watch *this* movie," whatever it is.

K: OK. And, so, do you watch the whole thing a few times before you'd join in, or. . . .

ALL: Yes.

BLANCHE: About twice. You'd watch them about twice.

K: And then you'd actually join in the group and do it, would you?

CHRISTABEL: Yes.

BLANCHE: It's kind of like it gets stuck in your mind and when you get home you try it on someone else to see if it works.

K: And do groups let you join in?

CAMILA: Sometimes.

BLANCHE: If they're kind.

CHRISTABEL: Sometimes they do.

Quite frequently, transmission seems to be enacted by a process of direct coaching within a friendship group, combined with a parallel process of observation and subsequent practice by children outside the friendship group. I came upon an example of peer group coaching and observation in the Birch Vale playground during morning recess in 2004. There was a group of fourth grade girls who were prolific performers of clapping games and cheers and were often devising new routines. Romina and Chelsea were learning "Tic Tac Toe" from Ashley (the authoritative leader of the group), who had learned it after school in the baseball dugout on the previous day. Their friends Gina and Luisa stood very close to the players, watching intently. The game had several sections. The first entailed a vertical clapping pattern, to the spoken text:

Tic tac toe,
Three in a row.

This was followed by a "Scissors-paper-rock" formula, then silent pointing by one player on the back of her partner's neck. The partner then had to select the finger that had been used for pointing. The sequence in which each of these elements was taught and learnt is documented below in table 6.1. (●VIDEO SAMPLE: See video example *BirchV Tic tac toe*.)

What is interesting here is that Ashley seemed to break up the game into sections to teach, a practice which I did not see in any other instance of playground peer teaching and learning and which was at odds with Harwood's (1992, 1998) observations of playground learning. This may have been a conscious strategy but possibly could have been necessitated by Chelsea and Romina's inability to proceed with the movements beyond the first section, causing the game to break down each time at this point before the girls returned to the beginning to try again or continued on to the next section. The other two members of this friendship group, Gina and Luisa, were engaged in observation and practice as a separate pair while the overt coaching took place.

Practice of newly acquired games or game elements most often seems to occur between pairs, as can be seen in the previous examples of teaching and learning in "Slide," "Sar Macka Dora," "Michael Jackson," and "Tic Tac Toe." This is probably because the coordination of movement formulae is much eas-

Table 6.1. Peer Coaching of *Tic Tac Toe* at Birch Vale Elementary School

Speaker	Text and Instructions	Movements
Ashley	*Tic tac toe*	Romina and Chelsea move hands in "prayer" position back and forth.
	Three in a . . .	Romina and Chelsea move their hands up and down, clapping above, below, and at a central point. The text slows down and trails off as movements falter.
Ashley	No you do this: *Tic tac toe* *Three in a row*	Ashley takes the right hand of each girl in both of her hands and manually moves the hands to clap first against their centrally held left hands, then right hands together, then above and below the central point. This is done in time with her recitation of the text.
Romina	Oh, OK.	
Ashley	*Tic tac toe* *Three in a row*	Ashley allows Romina and Chelsea to try the actions by themselves, but models the movements right next to the others' hands.
Ashley	And then you go: *Rock*	Ashley models placing the clenched right fist in her open left hand. Romina and Chelsea are still practicing the clapping pattern.
Ashley	*Rock* *Rock*	Ashley demonstrates the "rock" movement again twice. Romina and Chelsea imitate the rock movement.
Ashley	*Paper scissors* Let's do that.	Romina and Chelsea try these movements while Ashley recites the text.
Ashley	*Tic tac toe* *Three in a row*	Romina and Chelsea try the movements by themselves but become confused.
Ashley	Here, like this. No, like this.	Ashley moves between the pair and goes through the whole routine now as a performer with Chelsea while Romina watches.
Ashley	Then you just turn around. I'm gonna poke you with a finger and you have to guess which one. Yes.	Ashley turns Chelsea around by her shoulders and gives instructions. She parts Chelsea's hair at the back of her neck and places her finger on Chelsea's neck. Chelsea then turns around and chooses which finger has been used.
		Romina and Chelsea recommence the game.
Romina and Chelsea	*Tic tac toe* *Three in a row*	Romina and Chelsea perform the actions but again become confused regarding the direction of the hand movements.
		Meanwhile Gina and Luisa have started to play the game independently as a separate pair.
Ashley	*Tic tac toe* *Three in a row*	Ashley begins to model the first part of the game again as Romina and Chelsea stop.
Romina, Chelsea & Ashley	*Tic tac toe* *Three in a row*	Ashley again models the game parallel with Romina and Chelsea.
Ashley	Now turn around. [Inaudible directions for the last set of movements]	Romina and Chelsea follow through the last set of movements (finger pointing on partner's neck and choosing the finger used).
		The game is finally completed as the bell rings and they all move off.

ier between pairs than between multiple performers. In addition, the pair formation may offer a modicum of privacy to the players. In this respect, the learning process at Springfield resembles that of the Illinois girls discussed by Harwood (1992), who reports the withdrawal of children from the main group to practice in pairs prior to attempting reentry of the group performance. However, the teaching and learning of games by the girls Harwood studied differs in one major respect: that of accommodating difference in both skill and performance practice between players. In many instances of teaching and learning which I observed, both members of the performing group and the outside audience, though they might self-correct or offer suggestions for change, generally accepted differences in performance practice.

Accommodating Difference in Teaching and Learning

Harwood (1992) notes that, in Illinois, "Experienced players in the main were not patient with those unable to keep up and would not slow down the pace, nor coach a younger player" (p. 22). Unlike the girls in Harwood's (1992, 1998a) study, players of clapping games at Springfield and many other schools adjusted their performance and teaching practices in response to the needs of the performers. For example, although the maintenance of an appropriate tempo is an established characteristic of performance practice (see, for example, the previous comments on the 1990 performance of "Michael Jackson"), children frequently used a slower tempo for teaching new games or game formulae to less experienced members of their friendship group.

An example of this was observed at Summerglen School in 2002. I had been talking to a group of five-year-old girls in the playground about the games that they played. Sade, of Afro Caribbean descent, told me that she had learnt games from her older brother (now at middle school) and mainly played with her older sisters at school, as I had seen earlier in the day. However, at this point another five-year-old girl, Chloe initiated a game, "That's the Way I Like It," with Sade. Clearly Sade could play the game, with its complicated vertical movement pattern of alternatively gripped and clapped hands, with much more facility than Chloe. They started the initial formula, "ABCDEFG," flipping hands held in a prayer formation back and forth. Sade commenced the clapping pattern by clapping her own hand on "Hit it" and taking the lead, gripping Chloe's hands alternately left and right, and chanting, "That's the way uh huh uh huh" with Choe finishing the phrase, "That's the way I like it."

However, Chloe could not synchronize her hand movements and the game stopped. Chloe took over leading the movements but without success. At this point they began again, with Sade taking on a more overt teaching role.

As soon as they reached the vertical movement pattern Sade held her right hand open at the correct height and motioned with her head to Chloe. She waited until Chloe had put her right hand into hers before proceeding with the text at a very reduced tempo, putting each hand slowly into place at a pace that allowed Chloe to match each separate movement with Sade's help. This strategy worked well until they reached the verse section of the game where text must be improvised and again the regularity of the movements faltered; the girls eventually resorted to rocking their gripped hands up and down in time with the text. (**VIDEO SAMPLE:** This sequence can be seen in the video example *SummerG Peer teach.*)

Another strategy that players may adopt for teaching purposes is to adjust their own movements to allow for easier coordination. This practice was outlined at Springfield by two girls, aged seven and eight, who were discussing the teaching of the "down-up" (D/U) movement formula, which requires the right hand to clap down on another player's hand while the left hand claps upward:

CHRISTABEL: Sometimes I help my babysitters and, like, they do it the wrong way when I'm doing it that way [D/U position]. They do it the same way but. . . .

CAMILA: Because if you're doing it like that [moves in and performs D/U clap with Christabel but with the backs of her hands hitting D/U on Christabel's].

CHRISTABEL: They're doing it that way. They're doing it the same as that. So I actually change my hand [reverses hand movements] and they also change it the same way.

K: Oh. So you adjust it.

CAMILA: And so she goes like that [claps].

CHRISTABEL: And then I say, "leave it like that" and then I change mine [reverses clapping position] and then it starts getting going.

The tailoring of teaching strategies to meet specific needs is most clearly evident in the teaching of younger children, as further outlined by the sisters at Springfield:

BLANCHE: I'm teaching my younger cousin—she's five or so—and I'm teaching her to go da da da da da da [performs slow three-beat clap with one clap per sound] over and over until she gets the rhythm.

K: Right.

BLANCHE: And then I start giving her the words to it then. I think that's enough for her to practice.

K: Is she finding that easy to do or does she find that difficult?

CAMILA: Difficult.

BLANCHE: Well I basically help her. Like I help her put the hands in order [demonstrates D/U clapping movement]. And she remembered that when I've got my hands like this [D/U position], she has to go like that [opposite D/U position]. That's the bit she's not as [used] to.

K: Right. So would you move her hands to help her, or. . . ?

CAMILA: Yes.

BLANCHE: Yes. If I'm like this [D/U position] and she goes like this [identical D/U position] the same as me, I swap her hands around.

CAMILA: Sometimes. . . .

K: Oh. You just move them around for her. Right.

BLANCHE: [Nods] and then she will learn. . . .

CAMILA: Sometimes Blanche asks me to move her hands [performs three-beat clap] and then we could do it because she's—it's hard for her because . . . [she's] not five, . . . [she's] four.

K: So sometimes you would actually help by moving her hands while Blanche. . . .

CAMILA: Is telling her.

The assistance given to younger children can be quite subtle and can occur within the performance of games, as seen in another example of "That's the Way I Like It" from Summerglen School. Two different groups of girls had been inside at lunchtime demonstrating games to me. Bethany, aged nine, had stayed back with her five-year-old sister Bayley. They stood up to show me the game, quietly negotiating which of the pair would go first, as this game is characterized by turn-taking for the partly improvised verses. Bayley pointed to Bethany and said "You," so Bethany took the lead. The sequence documented in table 6.2 ensued. (● VIDEO SAMPLE: See video example *SummerG inter-age*.)

There were no instructions throughout the sequence, just modeling and gentle manipulation of hands. Bethany's role was to guide and support Bayley so that the game could progress to a successful culmination without interruption. Bayley looked to her sister for guidance but, because the game had been brought to completion without any intimations of error, Bayley could also feel a sense of achievement that helped her develop confidence.

In some situations, younger children are not only given physical assistance, but are allowed to perform movements that diverge from the performance practice of older children as they acquire an understanding of the per-

Table 6.2. Teaching and Learning between Girls of Differing Ages at Summerglen

Speaker	Text	Movements
Bethany	*Myyyy name is Bethany* *My game is tennis* *Boys aren't on my mind*	Bethany pauses with hands poised on the first syllable until Bayley matches her position. They proceed with a fast duple clap (C/O C/P) that doesn't coincide with the rhythm or tempo of the text.
Bethany	*Sooo*	Bethany pauses and readies her hand for the next section.
Bethany	*That's the way uh huh* *uh huh* *I like it uh huh uh huh*	The movement pattern for this text is: Grip R, Grip L, C/R twice above gripped left hands Grip R, Grip L, C/R twice below gripped left hands Bethany slows the tempo and gently grips Bayley's hand, moving it into position. This is done with alternate hands and positions, the hands moving up and over then below the central clapping point. For each movement Bethany puts her hand into position and waits until Bayley moves her hand close to the correct point, then gently grips Bayley's hand and moves it completely into position. This is done repeatedly so that the game progresses quite slowly but completely through the complex clapping sequence. They pause again as Bethany models the starting position for the verse. She gestures to Bayley with her head that it is Bayley's turn. Bayley nods.
Bayley	*My name is Bayley* *I . . . my game is hide* *and seek* *Boys aren't on my* *mind, so*	The duple clapping pattern C/O C/P proceeds slightly slower than before as Bayley has a more leading role. Bethany mouths the text as Bayley chants.
Bethany	*That's the way uh huh* *uh huh* *I like it uh huh uh huh*	Grip R, Grip L, C/R twice above gripped left hands Grip R, Grip L, C/R twice below gripped left hands Again Bethany uses similar strategies for the chorus, at one point gripping Bayley's hand and moving it into the right position.

formance requirements. For example, at Springfield, in six-year-old Sascha's performance of "Sar Macka Dora" with Sam, a member of his older brother's friendship group, he tended to "echo" Sam's movements for most of the game, but performed a different closing movement formula, which Sam followed. (🔊 VIDEO SAMPLE: See video example *SpringF inter-age*.)

Inherent in the staged teaching process is the understanding of a developmental sequence of movement formulae that underlies the performance practice of children at various ages, with the three-beat formula considered to be the basis of most games in many locations. This was discussed by Year 5 girls at Springfield:

HONG-SOO: Have you ever heard that clapping sort of goes with the ages, if you know what I mean? . . .

SADIE: Cinch ones when you're little and then harder ones when you get older. . . .

HONG-SOO: You lose the little ones and you take on the old ones. . . .

HONG-SOO: The clapping games are basically based on that pattern [demonstrates three-beat clapping formula].

Younger children are perceived to find duple-clapping formulae easier. Bethany, when I asked about her use of the duple-clapping pattern with Bayley in the teaching sequence described above, told me that this was "the first stage" and that she used this pattern with her sister because Bayley couldn't manage the triple-clapping pattern. Girls aged seven to nine at Springfield enlarged on this notion:

CHRISTABEL: We're used to this pattern [three-beat] but the other pattern [is] like this:

[C/O C/P].

K: Why did you choose the pattern that you chose then?

CAMILA: Because it's much more easier.

CHRISTABEL: And we're used to it.

BLANCHE: It's like the old type. See there are [kids] younger than us. . . .

K: Yes

BLANCHE: Younger than us you would go like this: [C/P C/O R/R C/O L/L C/O].[3] That's the way you could do it.

CAMILA: Yes.

BLANCHE: But the other way. . . .

K: It's for older kids is it?

BLANCHE: Yeah. But with really younger kids you could go like this: [C/O C/P].

Ashley, a very adept player at Birch Vale in Seattle, also described the different levels of difficulty:

K: OK. So how do you work out which way to do it?

ASHLEY: You can do it—well you can just do it like this [demonstrates a line of "Miss Susie Had a Steamboat" with a C/O R/R C/O L/L pattern]. Well, you can do it that way or you can do it more complicated ways.

K: Oh, OK. So what's a more complicated way?

ASHLEY: Like [demonstrates "Miss Susie Had a Steamboat" with a three-beat clap].

A Year 5 girl at Springfield ascribed the difference in difficulty to the coordination of the additional D/U movement in the three-beat formula:

ALICIA: The first pattern I ever was taught was: [demonstrates C/O C/P formula].

And then when I was taught one that went like that [demonstrates three-beat clapping formula] it took me three weeks to catch on to . . . having this [D/U] movement in there and I used to think that was really complicated.

K: So why did you consider the next clapping pattern more complicated? Why did you find that hard, Alicia?

ALICIA: Well, like, this was when I was five. I came to school and I had this friend and she taught me how to do just plain ordinary ones . . . . And then when I got into second class, it might have been first class, I think Sadie or Annette introduced me to a new one. Like, I was at home and I used to get my Mum to, like, teach me how to do it 'cause I found it really hard to coordinate just moving from such a simple two rhythm one to having an extra movement there . . . . And, like, there's an extra movement to coordinate.

My own observations supported the view that, by the age of six, children had been introduced to the three-beat clapping formula and were capable of maintaining it, although some six-year-old children still preferred to use the C/O C/P formula. For example, at Springfield in May 1994 I noticed two pairs of Year 1 girls playing "When Susie Was a Baby" in lines, using the duple-clapping formula. The girls in this friendship group seemed to still favor the duple formula when filmed at the end of the year. However, another group of Year 1 girls filmed in December 1993 used the three-beat clap with some dexterity. What was perhaps more remarkable, though, was that children as young as six years old were capable of formulaic "code switching"[4] to meet the needs of different performers, as shown by a discussion of performance practice of "Miss Brown" with two Year 1 girls:

K: When I saw you first playing it with Stephanie I noticed that you were playing it a bit differently to how you were playing it with Hope.

AMALIE: Yeah.

K: Why was that?

AMALIE: I play it like this [three-beat clap] to Stephanie and like this [C/O C/P] to Hope because she doesn't know how to do that [three-beat clap] because whenever we do that [three-beat clap] we get mixed up—well Hope does.

K: Oh OK. So how did you know that she couldn't do the one that has three claps?

STEPHANIE: She told us.

AMALIE: Yeah, like we were starting to do like that [three-beat clap] and then she told me. So we did that [C/O C/P] 'cause she wanted to.

K: Oh, right, I see. And does it matter to you which way you do it?

BOTH: No.

K: Which way do you prefer to do it, or don't you care?

[Both demonstrate three-beat clap]

AMALIE: We don't care.

STEPHANIE: We don't care.

K: OK, but if you play it with Stephanie do you always play it that way?

AMALIE: Yes.

K: And if you play it with Hope you always play it the other way?

AMALIE: Yes.

Older girls sometimes used the six-beat duple formula described previously by Blanche but seemed to abandon the C/O C/P formula. There was conflicting evidence as to whether mimetic movements were considered to be easier or more difficult, as they were recorded in performances of children from all age groups.

A developmental sequence in the acquisition of movements has also been identified in the United States by Harwood (1992) and Jones and Hawes (1987). Harwood's description of patterns of acquisition is similar to that found in Springfield, although there are differences in some details, and some of the movement formulae she describes as being performed only by older girls, such as the thirteen-beat vertical handclap formula, were performed by children from Year 2 onward at Springfield. Jones and Hawes' (1987) developmental sequence, identified in African American players, relates more to the performance of different game genres as children mature. This practice was not reflected at Springfield or most of the other schools that I visited.

Although many instances of transmission of games from girls to boys or vice versa were reported to me, I did not witness many examples of girls and boys engaged in inter-gender teaching and learning transactions. However, as more boys were visibly involved in musical play in the Busan schools, I had an opportunity to observe this phenomenon. The most extended example occurred at Pada School, where a group of grade-6 girls had spent several sessions demonstrating games to me after initially being observed playing clapping games in the playground. They had come into the music room (our agreed meeting place) to demonstrate again and a number of children had gathered to watch. These included a group of boys who joined in and played a number of games with the girls, telling me that both boys and girls usually played. I asked if the girls could play a game that they had demonstrated on a previous day, comprising a clapping pattern paired with the theme song from a television program, *Digimon Adventure*. The song was quite long and the clapping pattern, consisting of 16 movements, was very complex, as can be seen in table 6.3.

The girls grouped as if to play the game by themselves then invited the boys to play, gathering them into a circle. Three of the girls demonstrated the first two text lines with the full movement sequence. This was done twice while the boys tried to join in. The second time through the demonstration all of the boys joined in, but one boy, Su Hyo, stopped them after the first line so that he could try the pattern again. They all performed the first two lines again, a little slower and with Ji Eun (the most able female player) slightly exaggerating the movements. Two of the girls also practiced the last few movements, which Su Hyo was still finding difficult to learn. Su Hyo then tried the game movements by himself with the two girls gradually joining in again with the song and movements as if to support him. By this stage, Su Hyo was able to manage the movement sequence and Ji Eun exclaimed "OK!" delightedly, motioning that they were now ready to play the full game.

They all started the performance with the "sse sse sse" formula, the girls singing with gusto. One of the three boys also sang confidently, another less so, singing off and on. All of the children performed the movements but Su Hyo dropped in and out of the movement pattern, periodically stopping to observe, then re-entering the pattern. He remained within the circle and was easily assimilated into the game each time he resumed the pattern. By the end of the lengthy song, Su Hyo had mastered the movement sequence.

When I asked if the girls had been teaching the boys, they said that the boys "could follow." In answer to my question regarding the boys' prior knowledge of the game, I was told that one boy had played it about nine times, another twice, and Su Hyo never. When I asked if they could play the game again, they all sang it enthusiastically, negotiating the movement sequence with equal competence. Even Su Hyo was able to sing most of the song accompanied by the movements. (⏺ **VIDEO SAMPLE:** See video example *Pada Digimon*.

Table 6.3. Text and Movements of Digimon Game, Pada School, Busan

Text	Movement Sequence
Sse sse sse	Initial formula: hands shaken up and down with the 3 words.
Chajara bimil-ui yeol-swei (Find the secret key)	4 sets of 4 movements, one movement per beat. There are 8 beats in each text line.
Miro-gachi Eolkin Mohomdul (Adventures like a labyrinth)	1.1 hands out to side, index finger + thumb extended 1.2 ""Same + middle finger
Hyonsil-gwa tto-darun sesang (A world not like reality)	1.3 ""Same + whole hand 1.4 bring hands across to cross over, clap on the way
Hwansang-ui digital sesang (Fantastic digital world)	2.1–2.3 as above in crossed-over position 2.4 bring hands back to center (no clap or gesture)
P'yeol-ch'eora maum sok nalgae (Expand the wings of your heart)	3.1 RH fist on LH fist (vertically) 3.2 LH fist on RH fist
Idaero momch'ulsun ubsso (Can't stop here)	3.3 index finger + thumb of each hand at right angle, other fingers folded, diagonally insert one hand into the other R on left (into webbing between index finger and thumb)
Bitnanun himang-ul silk'o (With a bright hope)	
Odum dd'ulko nagaja (Let's go through the darkness)	3.4 same with other hand left on right
Ojj'oda hamjeong soggae bb'ajiljirado (Even [if] we fall in the traps)	4.1 C/O 4.2 C/O
Wigiui p'ado sogae gach'il-jira-do (Even [if] we're trapped in danger)	4.3 C/P 4.4 C/P
Sang-gak-han daero irugo sip'eo (Wanna make it as we thought)	Pattern repeated till end of Digimon song
Uriga ganun gu got odi-dun (Wherever we go)	
Digimon ch'ingu-dul, Let's go Let's go (Digimon friends, let's go let's go)	
Sesang-el guhaja. Let's go Let's go (Let's save the world, let's go, let's go)	
Seunglinen eonjena uri-ui geot (Victory is ours every time) Let's go, go go	

There are aspects of this teaching and learning vignette that are difficult to interpret. It is quite possible that the boys may have already known the television theme song, though the addition of the movement pattern was new. There was also evidence from discussion with the girls that the movement pattern came from another game that may have been taught to all children in the classroom in the early years of school. Both of these forms of prior knowledge may have contributed to the amazing rapidity with which Su Hyo learned the game. Certainly the recognition of known movement formulae would have assisted learning, as discussed earlier in the chapter. However, it is also possible that the performance of many games involving the kinesthetic skill and fast cognitive processing that characterized a large number of the Korean games that I saw in Busan schools enabled the boys, as well as girls, to learn complex games quickly. There appeared to be no special forms of accommodation when teaching the boys, probably because they were equally adept with many forms of musical play.

What was perhaps more significant was the demonstration of the first part of the song as the focus for learning. It would appear that the girls were segmenting the game for teaching purposes. However, they sang enough of the song to demonstrate the entire 16-beat movement pattern and it would seem that it was this pattern that was conceived of as a whole. Once this whole pattern was mastered, the game was performed in its entirety, and there was no attempt made to break up the text or melody to facilitate learning. As with examples of teaching and learning observed in other contexts involving only girls, the imparting of games occurred through a combination of modeling, parallel imitation, practice (in this case within the circle), and the inclusion of performers with different levels of initial competence who were allowed to participate or not at will.

Similarly, no specific strategies seemed to be utilized by children when teaching others with contrasting language backgrounds. While I witnessed many instances of transmission of games in English to children from language backgrounds other than English, the strategies employed in the teaching and learning of the games appeared to be identical to those used by members of any peer group, that is, modeling, observation, and practice. This was also the case when children taught games in other languages. What was significant, however, were the changes in performance practice that were negotiated in the process of interethnic transmission. In some cases, this meant that there were changes to the playground game tradition enacted either on a small scale within friendship groups or on a larger scale within a playground. The ways in which these changes were enacted are the subject of the following chapter.

↦ CHAPTER 7 ↤

Changing the Tradition

It is clear from previous descriptions of the ways in which children teach, learn, and negotiate the content of their musical games in the playground that changes of various kinds are made to game material in the process of transmission. In this chapter I examine the ways in which the singing game tradition in a range of playground localities is changed through the influences of interethnic transmission, audiovisual and written media, classroom transmission, and material from other sources external to the school. Conditions that affect these processes of transmission are also discussed.

Influences of Interethnic Transmission

The demography of the playground can greatly affect both the forms of musical play and the ways in which they are transmitted and changed. One of the most important changes in performance practice that occurs during the transmission of games from one ethnic group to another in the playground is in the use of language. The following vignette from Springfield School in Sydney illustrates one form of change.

> Three ten-year-old girls are playing around a flat rectangular structure covering a drainage area in the playground at Springfield. Born in mainland China, they have each emigrated to Australia but speak three different first languages or dialects: Cantonese, Mandarin, and

Shanghainese. One of the girls, Wendy, has learned the game "Black and white TV" on a recent holiday to Shanghai and has introduced it to her friends. They stand in different corners of the rectangle, calling out "black and white" and swinging their arms up and down on each syllable. On the final syllable they turn their palms up or down. The odd one out stays in her place while the others jump to the next position, halfway along their sides of the rectangle. The object is to catch up to the next player who is then out. When Wendy is eliminated, the other two girls change to "Scissors-Paper-Rock" for their hand movements, successively calling out "scissors, paper, rock" and moving around the rectangle until Su Li is eliminated and Amy wins the game.

A significant change in the performance of games at Springfield School was the translation of texts that were originally in other languages into English when games were transmitted to players of another ethnic or language group, as seen in the performance of "Black and White TV" described above. The title of this game referred to the elimination formula "black and white"[1] and to the rectangular shape of the ground on which the game was played, which was likened to the shape of a TV screen. The movement formulae of the game were directly transferred to Springfield, but the text was performed in English. Partly, this may have been because English was a lingua franca of the group. However, in a subsequent interview in 1996, this group maintained that they played all their games in English and did not teach other children games in Chinese languages because "they're not popular."

More accurately, this might be viewed as a reflection of their general attitude to using English, which they preferred to use at school because they perceived it as the language of the school. This, in turn, might have been due to parental attitudes. The ESL teachers interviewed in 1995 felt that Chinese Australian parents, in particular, discouraged their children from using Chinese languages at school.

However, there were other instances at Springfield of children's reluctance to use languages other than English when transmitting games. This appeared to occur more often as children grew older and perhaps was related to the primary teachers' diminishing acknowledgment of languages other than English at the school. Hong-Soo, for example, demonstrated both the movements and accompanying song of her Korean game to her friends in 1993, when she was in Year 4. In 1994, when she was in Year 5, though she was happy to teach the movements of a related Korean game, she claimed not to remember the text.

As is evident from the previous examples, attitudes at Springfield to the teaching and learning of games from other cultures were quite complex, as was the effect of the transmission of these games on the playground traditions in the school. A closer examination of Hong-Soo's transmission of the Korean game in 1993 discussed in chapter 5 suggests the complexity involved. It was quite clear that several members of the group were familiar with the clapping pattern of the game. Ella performed the game movements with Hong-Soo with some dexterity but did not perform the text. Group members observing this performance commented, "It's supposed to go a lot faster." Between and after the performances, Annette and Sadie practiced a clapping pattern that was clearly derived from the Korean movement formula, since both of them used the idiosyncratic curved trajectory culminating in a back-to-back hand-clap that was characteristic of the Korean movements. Despite this, Hong-Soo stated that she hadn't taught the game:

K: And have you ever taught it to the other kids here?

HONG-SOO: No, never.

K: Why haven't you taught them the Korean one?

HONG-SOO: Because I just think . . . because I get embarrassed. Like, I don't really like to speak Korean where there are people around who speak English.

It may have been that Hong-Soo was happy to demonstrate the textual aspects of the game within her friendship group but not outside it. The attitudes of her friends were somewhat ambivalent. During Hong-Soo's performance, Alicia asked her to sing the words in English, which Hong-Soo was unable to do. When questioned, though, Alicia professed a desire to learn songs in other languages[2]:

K: How would you feel about learning some [songs] in other languages?

ALICIA: I'd love to learn some in other languages.

The related game movements that Annette and Sadie subsequently performed were nominated by Ella as belonging to the game "See See My Playmate" (although no performances of this particular combination of text and movements were recorded by this group or any other at Springfield). It would seem, then, that movements of games from one culture are, in some circumstances, more readily transmitted into a new playground context than texts and that they may be adopted as part of the repertoire of movement formulae that can be used with other games.

Russell (1986) and Cruickshank (1991) comment on the lessening importance of text and corresponding increase in the importance of movement in the performance of playground games involving participants from a minority bilingual culture and majority Anglo Australian culture. This is attributed to the Anglo Australian children's suspicion and nonacceptance of texts in languages other than English. Clark (1981) maintains that it is only when there is a dominant minority group that transmission of non-English texts appears to take place. This theory is supported by the freedom of transmission of non-English texts at Ellington School where there was a dominant minority group, contrasting with transmission practices at the nearby St Augustine's School, as discussed in chapter 5.

It seems that in Springfield, however, a high degree of ethnic diversity within a friendship group assisted the transmission of non-English texts. An example of this at Springfield in 1993 was a multiethnic group of eight-year-old girls who had Chinese, Tongan, Rumanian, and Anglo backgrounds. Carmen, an Anglo Australian girl, had learnt a bilingual Greek and English game "Ana Thio Thio" (one two three) at her previous school, which had a large Greek Australian population, and had introduced it to her friends at Springfield, where it had become a standard part of the play repertoire of this group. When I asked Carmen for a translation into English, she and a Tongan Australian girl, Mereki, obliged. However, this demonstration resulted in a spontaneous improvisation of various versions of the game by different children in their first languages: Cantonese, Rumanian, and Tongan. In each instance the game was played by a pair of girls, one of whom spoke the language and the other to whom it was completely new. Most of the partners joined in with the movements, listening to the unfamiliar text for cues. However, two of the girls, who spoke different Chinese languages (Cantonese and Mandarin), actively co-constructed the game with Cantonese text, even though it was less familiar to one of them. All of the girls were quite open to allowing their partners to take a linguistic lead and were fascinated with the different versions that ensued.

In the example above, the freedom to perform games in unfamiliar languages may also be attributable to the "psychological safety" provided by the friendship group. Isenberg and Jalongo (1993), drawing on the creativity theories of Rogers (1954/1970), define psychological safety as being "dependent upon the existence of a low-risk environment. Children feel psychologically safe when significant others accept them as having unconditional worth, avoid external evaluation, and identify and empathize with them" (1993, p. 14). For many children in multiethnic environments, such as that at Springfield, the friendship group can be seen to provide these conditions.

Perhaps the most striking example of the psychological safety of a friendship group allowing the interethnic exchange of games to flourish was witnessed at Bysiden School in Stavanger, where three pairs of sisters of Eritrean, Somalian, and Ghanaian descent lived in close proximity to each other at home and were constant playmates both at home and at school. I observed them at play over a number of days, in the playground and in elicited recording sessions inside. They appeared to have a remarkable flexibility in terms of their assimilation of singing games. The Eritrean sisters, Feven and Jodith, had been born in Norway but had visited their parents' homeland and learnt a number of games there, which they then had played with their friends. One game was obviously very well known and all of the group members played it enthusiastically.

This game was not in their first language of Tigrigna, but in another Ethiopian language, so the sisters were unable to give it a name or identify its meaning. It had movements that were very different from any others observed in the Bysiden playground, beginning with the girls crouched down on the ground with their heads bent and arms crossed, holding hands around the circle for the first section of the game, then rising and touching heads and hips with alternate hands at an increasing tempo. It was perhaps these idiosyncratic movements that gave the game its major appeal to the group. Another favorite game of this group was "En Ten Tini," a clapping game that had been learnt by one of the Somalian sisters from another friend who was a Bosnian refugee:

> En ten tini
> Savalaka tini
> Savalaka tikka takka
> Elle melle proft
> Trift traft troft

It seemed to contain a large number of vocables,[3] with wordplay (rhyme, alliteration, and assonance) that caused considerable delight on the part of its performers and, again, contributed to its appeal.

However it appeared that the girls' strong relationship meant that any member could proffer a new game knowing that it would be accepted by the others regardless of its content. Within a twelve-minute period on one day, I recorded the sisters in various combinations playing several singing games in Norwegian, a clapping game utilizing a combination of Norwegian and English ("Åli Åli Ei"), one derived from a popular song in English ("That's the Way I Like It"), three Eritrean games, a Somalian game, and the Bosnian game "En Ten Tini." The friends' mutual trust meant that they had a great deal of freedom in which to experiment with a range of different singing games, rejecting none that were brought into their shared pool of play resources by their playmates. As a result, they had a very eclectic repertoire, seemingly creating their own micro-tradition within the larger tradition of the playground. (🅐 VIDEO SAMPLE: See video example *Bysiden Eritrean games* and notated versions in appendices 4, 5, and 10).

These micro-traditions can also be maintained when there is a critical mass of children to provide the psychological safety for children to openly perform and exchange games. At Birch Vale School in Seattle, the ELL (English Language Learners) class groups formed what Harwood (1998), drawing on the work of Lave and Wenger (1991), has termed a "community of practice" (p. 52) within the greater playground community. The members of this class were almost all Spanish-speaking, having come to the United States from Mexico or Peru within the previous year. They played together in the playground in groups of varying sizes, with many of their games being common to their countries of origin, despite minor variants. The familiarity of the games, together with the solidarity of these children as a class group, enabled them to play clapping, ring, and chasing games from their homelands in Spanish within the group. In contrast, another Spanish-speaking girl who was part of a mixed Anglo and Spanish-American friendship group, told me that she didn't ever feel that it was appropriate for her to share her Spanish games at school, even though she played them frequently at home with relatives. Similarly, the Spanish games did not appear to be transmitted from the ELL children more generally within the playground.

The contrast between the two schools in Keighley was similar. The relative isolation of Punjabi children in St. Augustine's seemed to preclude their openly performing and teaching Punjabi games and consequently influencing the playground tradition. However at Ellington, the dominant majority of Punjabi and Bengali children formed a community of practice that encompassed home and school, so that children felt confident to regularly share games brought from Pakistan or the home with friends in the playground. In turn, this changed the tradition within this playground, where games in English, Punjabi, or Bangla were equally popular, and songs from English and Bollywood popular music sources formed part of their musical play repertoire (as will be discussed further under "Influences of the Media").

In some of the instances outlined above, particular characteristics of games in other languages may have made them easier to learn and to be accepted. The Eritrean game that was a favorite among the friendship group of sisters at Bysiden not only had idiosyncratic movements but was also very textually and melodically repetitive, a feature that seemingly facilitated its acquisition (⬤ **VIDEO SAMPLE:** see video example *Bysiden Eritrean games* and notated example in appendix 5).

The six-year-old Ghanaian sister picked up several of the repeated phrases of another less familiar Eritrean game as Feven and Jodith performed it, singing along while the rest of the group observed. Similarly, the repetitive sound patterning in the Bosnian game, which was well known to all members of the group, had probably made it easier to learn.

The multilingual performances of "One Two Three" at Springfield may also have happened more naturally because the game incorporated a known movement formula and a relatively simple text formula that was easy to translate into different languages. The textual formula that was translated was a reiterated number ("one, one, one," and so on), while the other textual formula, "Give me a . . . ," was always sung in English.[4] The movement formula was a simplified form of the formula employed in many performances of another quite popular game at Springfield, "Down by the Banks."

The recognition of familiar, or common, formulae thus appeared to influence the relative acceptance of game elements from non-Anglo cultures in the Springfield playground. Some elements were retained, while variants were cooperatively negotiated. Another example of this was found in the performances of "Ach'im Baram" (cold morning wind), the Korean game played by John and discussed in chapter 5. (🔘 **VIDEO SAMPLE:** See video example *SpringF Ach'im baram.*) This game ended with the textual and movement formula of "Scissors-Paper-Rock," a game that had been played in Australian playgrounds for many years.[5] In John's performances with his six-year-old friends Adam and Lloyd, the section of the game that was familiar to the English-speaking children with whom John played was chanted in English by both players, while the unfamiliar section was sung in Korean by John.[6] Adam obviously recognized the formula, declaring that the game was "just 'Scissors-Paper-Rock.'"

At Ellington School, common formulae also led to the categorization of games as identical, even when their texts were in different languages. A number of counting-out games shared the same movement formulae and were deemed to be virtually interchangeable. In all of these games, the players sat in a circle and spread their fingers out on the floor. One player then pointed successively to each finger of all of the other players. The finger at which the point landed when the final syllable of each couplet or quatrain was sounded was eliminated (bent under the rest of the hand) and the game proceeded until all but one finger of a player had been eliminated. Game texts to which this applied, which were often alternated or played in close succession, are shown in table 7.1.

The final version, "Mas Mas Amar Mas," was presented somewhat tentatively to her Punjabi-speaking friends by a Bengali girl, Aklima. Whether this was because she had made up the text, as she later told me, because she was shy, as another member of the group attested, or whether she was reluctant to speak Bangla when the games preceding this had all been in Punjabi or English, is uncertain. What was evident, though, was that, over a five-minute period of discussion and demonstration, she gradually gained the confidence to share the game and that the others (all Punjabi-speaking) immediately joined in with the familiar movement formula. Farah, often a leader in the games, immediately began to imitate the repeated initial words, "mas mas" and Aklima's

Table 7.1. Alternative Texts of a Counting-Out Game at Ellington School (Keighley, U.K.)

Game text	Translation
Akkar bakkar pahmba poh Chori mari poorey sow. Akkar bakkar pahmba poh Assee navay poorey sow. Akkar bakkar pahmba poh Assee marey poorey sow. . . . (Punjabi)	Akkar bakkar pahmba poh (vocables) Done some stealing makes a full hundred. Akkar bakkar pahmba poh Eighty, ninety, full hundred. Akkar bakkar pahmba poh We killed a full hundred
Eeny meeny miny more Put the baby on the floor If it cries slap it twice Eeny meeny miny more. Eeny meeny miny more Put the baby on the floor If it cries kick it twice Eeny meeny miny more. (English)	

Khota, khota, khota, khota, tu khota, khota,
  khota, tu khota, main khoti, tu kala khota,
  main kali kutti, khota, khota, khota, khota,
  Donkey, tu kala khota, main kali kutti . . . .
(Punjabi)
	Donkey, donkey, donkey, donkey, you are a
	  donkey, donkey, donkey, you are a donkey, I
	  am a female donkey, you are a black donkey, I
	  am a black bitch. . . .
	Note: this game is a play on the homonyms:
	  khota, khoti, kutta and kutti, meaning don-
	  key, female donkey, dog and bitch. Some of
	  the words are identical in Bangla

Scooby dooby doo went to the loo Out came a bacha with a kala tuhu. Scooby dooby doo went to the loo Out came a bacha that was you. Scooby dooby doo went to the loo How many plop plops did you do. Scooby dooby doo went to the loo Out came a bacha with a brown tuhu. Scooby dooby doo went to the loo Out came a bacha with a green tuhu . . . . (English and Punjabi)	Bacha = child Kala = black Tuhu = bum
Mas mas amar mas Ami tumara kaytham Tumi oilay amar mas Ami tumara khalimu Ona amara dew Ona ami kaymu . . . . (Bangla)	Fish fish my fish I want to eat you You are my fish Am going to eat you Now give me Now am going to eat you . . . .

translation, "fish fish," clearly as a prelude to further performance, though the extended discussion precluded this. (⚫ **VIDEO SAMPLE:** See video example *Ellington Mas mas* and appendix 6 for a full transcription of "Mas Mas.")

There was some dissension over the performance of the "Tu Khota"text of the game because of a dispute about whether or not the text involved swearing, as Aklima maintained—partly because of a double entendre caused by the play on words (see table 7.1) but also apparently because of the slightly different meanings of some words in Bangla and Punjabi. Farah staunchly defended her use of the words as being beyond reproach, but her mischievous smile as she delivered the words and the translator's later comments clearly indicated that she regarded the words as rude.

Other changes to the tradition of playground games have been attributed in the literature to interethnic transmission. Merrill-Mirsky (1988) ascribes a greater degree of textual misunderstanding and concomitant variation to bilingual performers whose comprehension of English is still developing. This may exemplify Coffin's (1977) statement in his analysis of variation in the American traditional ballad that "Changes seem to increase in direct proportion to the amount of meaning that is lacking in the lines" (p. 5). Certainly the omissions from the text of "Marble Street" by the bilingual performer in the example in table 7.2 support this view.

It is possible, however, that children who are becoming bilingual may develop highly sophisticated listening skills that enable a more accurate oral transmission of text. For example, in the case of one performance of "Down Down Baby" recorded at Springfield in 1993, the text (rendered with an imitation of an American accent due to the song's media transmission, as described later) was misunderstood by a monolingual Anglo Australian performer and explained to her by her bilingual playmates. In this case, the presence of chil-

Table 7.2. Comparison of Recited Texts of *Marble Street* by Monolingual and Bilingual Playmates (Elicited after Performance of Game)

Carolyn (Monolingual Anglo Australian)	Jenny (Bilingual Chinese Australian)
My mother your mother lives down the street	Mother . . your . . rotten . . girl . . sexy . made out of . . . Down the street
Eighteen nineteen Marble Street	Eighteen nineteen Marble Street
And every time they had a fight	And every time had a fight
And this is what they told me.	And this is what they told me
Boys are rotten made out of cotton	Boys are rotten
Girls sexy made out of Pepsi	Girls are sexy made out of Pepsi
Insy winsy lollipop insy winsy woo	Sinny sin lollipop
Insy winsy lollipop boys love you	Sinny sinny lollipop boys love you
And that's not true.	That's not true.

dren from language backgrounds other than English helped maintain the stability of the tradition, rather than changing it.

Over the years in which I observed children in different localities playing, it seemed that children's delight in novelty led them to make creative use of their bilingualism, in situations where they felt the social support of their friendship group or larger socio-cultural environment to do so. Thus, the grade-4 girls from Ellington School discussed above devised a variant of another counting-out game, "Honica Bonica," derived from a Punjabi game but now consisting of vocables and English words:

Honica bonica
Supersonica
Honica bonica bonk

The game was shown to me by Amreen, Farah, and Amreen's brother, Amar. After the demonstration I asked them about the language used.

K: Is that in Punjabi . . . or is it in words that don't really. . . ?

AMAR: English words.

K: They're English words are they? OK. So where did you learn that one?

AMREEN: Miss, from my Dad.

K: Oh, from your Dad. OK. So this is one that's played in Pakistan?

AMREEN: Yes.

K: Right.

FARAH: Miss, the words have been changed.

K: The words have been changed have they?

FARAH: We made it into English.

AMREEN: There should be Punjabi words but I don't know what those ones are. My Mum told me what they mean in English though.

The children were plainly comfortable with the use of both English and Punjabi within the games and had also created games combining textual and movement formulae from both Punjabi and English game traditions (though clearly the text of this game also contained vocables which were construed as English). Thus a standard form of the Punjabi game, "Zig Zag Zoo," was rendered by Amreen and Farah in two successive bilingual versions that used formulae derived from the two traditions in different proportions. In the first version, Amreen and Farah began the game in English but switched to Punjabi after the first line, mainly because this was the version Farah seemed to have in mind. They therefore retained the more standard Punjabi movement formulae:

Text	Movements
Zig zag zoo	Hands in prayer formation. Flip backward and forward on beat.
We're going up	C/O, clap partner's right hand above central point.
Kabhi neechey	C/O, clap partner's right hand below central point.
Kabhi oonchey	Clap partner's hands
Kabhi taley	Clap partner's hands back to back
Kabhi mukkey[7]	Punch each other in stomach

The "English" version of the game was extended by the addition of textual and movement formulae from other English games in circulation in the final three text lines:

Text	Movements
Zig zag zoo	Hands in prayer formation. Flip backward and forward on beat.
We're going up	C/O, clap partner's right hand above central point.
We're going down	C/O, clap partner's right hand below central point.
We're going criss cross lollipop	C/O, RH across chest, LH across chest, point R finger to mouth.
Turn around	Swing body around (Farah left, Amreen right).
Touch the ground	Bend over and touch ground.

It can be seen, then, that children's personal interactions with traditions emanating from cultures other than their own cause changes to the game repertoire. These changes may just affect games played by small groups or may be on a larger scale, affecting whole subgroups or school populations. The extent to which this occurs depends on the psychological safety provided by friendship groups and other forms of social support offered by school structures. Children's recognition of common formulae and their enjoyment of novelty also contribute to this form of change. Finally, children's proclivity to innovate using the resources derived from the multiple stimuli in their auditory environment ensures that playground traditions are constantly evolving.

Influences of the Media

The role of the media as a change agent in children's playground games has been the focus of considerable attention in the public domain. The current popular debate about the negative impact of technological media on children's play (see, for example, Factor, 2001) mirrors that reported by Opie and Opie (1959) prior to their collection of games more than three decades earlier: "The generally held opinion, both inside and outside academic circles, was that children no longer cherished their traditional lore. We were told that the young had lost the power of entertaining themselves; that first the cinema, and now T.V. had become the focus of their attention; and that we had started our investigation fifty years too late" (Opie and Opie, 1959, p. v). At the end of their study, during which examples of children's playground games were collected from over five thousand children in the United Kingdom, the Opies concluded that, despite the prevailing predictions of decline, "The modern schoolchild, when out of sight and on his own, appears to be rich in language, well-versed in custom, a respecter of the details of his own code, and a practising authority on traditional self amusements" (Opie and Opie, 1959, p. ix).

Similar misconceptions regarding the demise of the games were evident among the staff of many of the schools that I visited over the period from 1990 to 2004. Quite evidently, the flourishing practice of games in the schools refutes this argument. In the following section, the children's use of media-derived forms in the composition and performance of their playground games and other forms of musical play is further discussed.

One of the most obvious examples of the influence of audiovisual media on children's play has been the provision of textual material, as documented by a number of researchers (Opie and Opie, 1959, 1988; Turner, Factor, & Lowenstein, 1982). More recently, the relationship of audiovisual media and musical play practices, involving the creative use by children of textual, musical, and movement material derived from these media, has been explored by Harwood (1994) and Gaunt (2006) in the United States; Bishop and Curtis (2006) and Grugeon (2001, 2005) in the United Kingdom; and McIntosh (2006) in Bali, in addition to my own discussion of this phenomenon (Marsh, 1997, 1999, 2001, 2003, 2006).

Harwood maintains that the intrusion of "popular culture spread through electronic sources, including Top 40 songs, TV theme songs, [and] commercial jingles" (p. 188) into the oral tradition of children's play enriches rather than destroys this tradition as children select material from the media and use it for their own purposes. This argument is taken further by Gaunt (2006), who, in keeping with my own view (Marsh, 2006), sees children's appropriation from media sources as a function of orality:

The practice of "borrowing" from one setting to another is inevitable in music, where orality is still the dominant form of transmission. The lyrics and gestures found in game-songs and in various forms of recorded music suggest a dialectical relationship: between the culture of children and adults, between so-called folk music or music of the everyday and recorded songs, and between the popular music of local performances and mass-mediated music. (Gaunt, 2006, p. 103)

This dialectical relationship or interactivity between the media and children's musical play can be explored by examining several examples of different forms of musical play in various field locations. The first example, a clapping game, appeared in slightly varying guises at Springfield (Sydney), Bysiden (Stavanger), and Strandli (Ryfylke, Norway). It was called "Michael Jackson" by its seven- and eight-year-old performers at Springfield and demonstrates what Bishop and Curtis term "onomastic allusion" (2006, p. 3), the reference to proper names, such as those of actors, singers, characters, or brand names from popular culture, in the texts of children's play.[8]

Text	Movements
My name is	Hands in prayer formation. Flip back and forward on beat.
Michael Jackson,	C/O centre, C/R above, C/O centre, C/R below
Girlfriend Madonna	C/O centre, C/R above, C/O centre, C/R below
Kissing in the garden	C/O centre, C/R above, C/O centre, C/R below
(kiss) (kiss) (ugh) (ugh)	Kissing action with RH on L arm, LH on R arm, pelvic thrust x 2
Out comes the baby, out comes the boy	Triple clap
All the girls "Boo hoo" sexy!	Triple clap, rub eyes ("Boo hoo"), lift up skirts ("sexy")

This practice of textual inclusion of icons of popular culture in games is well known (Opie and Opie, 1959, 1988; Turner, Factor, and Lowenstein, 1982; Riddell, 1990; Harwood, 1994). In this instance, however, the references to U.S. singers Michael Jackson and Madonna were accompanied by sexually explicit movements of kissing, pelvic thrusts, and lifting of skirts to display underwear, emulating the popular singers' overtly sexualized performance styles.

The Bysiden version of this game (recorded in 2002) was also performed in English. While retaining the vertical clapping pattern of the first section, it was much less sexually charged in its movements. This was possibly because the referent, U.S. singer Elvis Presley, though equally given to overt sexual display in his performances, was no longer regularly seen by children in contemporary film or television performances:

Text	Movements
My name is	Hands in prayer formation. Flip back and forward on beat.
Elvis Presley	C/O centre, C/R above, C/O centre, C/R below
Come from a wesly	C/O centre, C/R above, C/O centre, C/R below
Kissin' in the morning	C/O centre, C/R above, C/O centre, C/R below
(Kiss) (kiss) sexy.	Kiss own RH then LH, point R then L thumb over shoulder

Instead of the thrusting and underwear display, this version's mimetic movements were confined to the throwing of a kiss on the relevant word, with "sexy" not being depicted in any graphic form. A similar version (with "kiss me" replacing "kissin'") was performed at Strandli. When I shared the lyrics of the "Michael Jackson" version with Charlotte, a confident fifth-grade performer at Bysiden, she looked slightly shocked at the articulation of "ugh, ugh" and told me that it was "a little bit more crazy" than the local variant, citing "ugh ugh" as the "more crazy" part.

However, at Bysiden, the Elvis Presley game was usually paired with another game, which also contained a large proportion of English text:

Text	Movements
My name is	Hands in prayer formation. Flip back and forward on beat.
Six baby, six baby	C/O centre, C/R above, C/O centre, C/R below
Shugga shugga boom boom	Close & open both hands x 2, C/P C/P
Charlie Chicken Chicken Charlie	C/O C/R C/O C/L
I love you.	RH on L arm, LH on R arm, gesture toward partner, arms crossed

(See transcription in appendix 5.)

The text of the third line could be interpreted as having a sexual meaning, although the movements accompanying these words (quick opening and shutting of hands to the rhythm of the text on "shugga shugga" and clapping both partner's hands on "boom boom") did not illustrate the sexual connotations and the girls did not seem aware of them, as they clearly were of the meaning of the English word "sexy." Charlotte told me that "Michael Jackson and Charlie Chicken is [*sic*] two popular stars" but did not identify who "Charlie Chicken" might be.[9] Again there appeared to be no direct performative models from the media for the Norwegian children to emulate.

As is evident in the two Norwegian examples above, these references to figures from popular culture have the capacity to cross language barriers and often outlive the original focus of popular attention. This was also the case with "Åli Åli Ei," another clapping game performed primarily in English at Bysiden:

Åli åli ei
Hei, minni minni mei
Makaroni fifty five
Fifty five five five
Oh my lei lei lei
Oh my happy happy happy
Oh my steppy steppy steppy
Oh my house house house
Mickey Mouse Mouse Mouse

(See transcription in appendix 4.)
Figures from the media assume a new and different identity within children's playlore and are retained as personifications of the adult world that the children parody, long after media saturation with the source material has disappeared. The continuing presence of characters such as Mickey Mouse in the playground is due more to the maintenance of this oral tradition than to their reappearance on television.

In another example, "One Day You're Gunna Get Caught," a group of twelve-year-old boys and girls at Springfield created a game from an advertisement for underpants, nursery rhymes, and a parody (involving yet another advertisement) of traditional cartoon figures. This exercise involved the creative manipulation of these elements, the aim being to ridicule the adult-transmitted sources of this material:

One day you're gunna get caught
One day you're gunna get caught
One day you're gunna get caught
With your pants down.

Come boys, show us your BMs
Come boys, show us your BMs
Come boys, show us your BMs
Make us girls go wild.

[Texts of various nursery rhymes (for example "Twinkle Twinkle"
    and "Humpty Dumpty") follow.]

Jingle bells, Batman smells
Robin flew away.

Wonderwoman lost her bosom
Flying TAA.[10]

These parody songs and related parodic movements aptly represent children's subversion of adult culture in their play. The creation of parallel texts allows children to ridicule adult concerns, reducing "adult order to humorous disorder" (Factor, 1988, p. 153), thus enacting an "antithetical reaction to the institutional and everyday hegemonies of the life about them" (Sutton-Smith et al., 1999, p. 6). In fact, Mitchell and Reid-Walsh (2002) see popular culture itself as a cultural space in which children can more readily assert themselves against adult authority, a "space of resistance" against adult-regulated high culture (p. 16).

Michael Jackson made an appearance in two other examples of musical play at Springfield. One of these examples, also entitled "Michael Jackson," was improvised by a group of Year 2 girls in 1993. In this play sequence the performers collaborated to create something entirely new using textual, melodic, and movement formulae from the media. They told me that their sources included a TV advertisement, the U.S. films *Grease* and *My Girl*, and the Michael Jackson song "Black or White." This rendition of an extended sequence playing out popular performance styles incorporated not only textual allusions to the song "Black or White" and other popular song material but also mimed guitar playing and Michael Jackson's sexualized movements seen in the video clip of the song.

In her discussion of similar references to popular singers and associated dance movements in the games of African American girls, Gaunt (2006) notes that the girls are embodying and being socialized into a popular discourse that encompasses black musical practices from the playground as well as mass-mediated forms of performance:

the girls dramatized a salient feature of these figures' personas, or image, through kinetic orality. One could assert that the girls were performing the communal discourse, as well as a musical grapevine of blackness, through the body and their in-body formulas . . . . The expressive interplay, the intertextuality of musical sound and motion, and their dramatic or theatrical embodied musical play, mirror popular culture, music television, and the composition of popular songs that tap into a community of listeners and a body of black vernacular traditions. (Gaunt, 2006, p. 74)

For the Australian performers of the Michael Jackson games at Springfield, there was less direct connection with a "musical grapevine of blackness" (Gaunt, 2006, p.74), although the influence of black American musical styles is continually promulgated by an ever-present global media stream. In their naming and imitation of the performative style of popular music icons there was, instead, interplay between parody and emulation of adults. In taking on the characteristics of the media icons, but subverting them through reinvention and subjection to their own musical idiom, children can be seen to take control of the mediated world of adults and refashion it for their own purposes. Thus children reverse the power relationship with what superficially appears to be an adult-generated hegemony of popular culture.

At times the seizing of control steers away from emulation into outright rejection. This was amply illustrated by a 2002 performance of the clapping game "Down Down Baby" by a group of ten-year-old girls at St Augustine's in Keighley in which pop star Britney Spears was soundly ridiculed:

> The train goes
> Down down baby down by the riverside
> Sweet sweet baby never let it go again
> Shimmy shimmy coconut shimmy shimmy ah
> Shimmy shimmy coconut shimmy shimmy ah
> I hate coffee, I love tea
> I hate Britney, she's never [indistinct] me
> Down by the fire peelin' potatoes
> Britney Spears is so crap.

(VIDEO SAMPLE: See video example *St. Aug DDB* and full transcription in appendix 6.)

"Down Down Baby" was a game that appeared in many forms in nearly all of my field locations, except in Korea.[11] Multiple variants of this game have also been documented in many European countries by Segler (1992). Its widespread appeal, at least in Australian schools, demonstrates the importance of the media both to the transmission and the maintenance of tradition of playground games. Originally a game devised and played by African-American girls in the United States (Gaunt, 2006), it appeared as the most popular singing game in the Springfield playground in the early 1990s, where most children had reportedly learned it from the American children's program *Sesame Street*, which was broadcast regularly on the national Australian television network (Australian Broadcasting Corporation, or ABC). The continual rescreening of this game on the program ensured that its popularity was maintained over a lengthy period of time, as discussed by a group of eleven- and twelve-year-old girls reflecting on their practice in 1994:

THUY: We learnt "Granma Granma" from *Sesame Street*.

K: Oh. That's how you learnt it, was it?

CLARA: Yeah. They had some black American girls and they were all play-ing it really fast and they were [indicates frenzied movement].

THUY: Yeah. Going in together and. . . .

TARA: Yeah.

K: So that's how you learnt that rather than from each other?

TARA: Yeah.

K: Uh huh. Do you think that's why so many people know it, that one?

ALL: Yes.

CLARA: And just *Sesame Street*—they do repeats.

JOANNE: And everyone used to watch *Sesame Street.*

CLARA: Yeah. Everybody used to watch *Sesame Street.* Lots of people still do, so. . . .

K: Do you think that might be a reason why it's still played, that game?

[Clara nods]

A decade later, another truncated version of the game was also learnt from *Sesame Street* by girls of varying ages at Telford Spring in central Australia. In this version the *Sesame Street* character Elmo had a more direct role:

Down down baby Elmo does karate
Down down baby Elmo phones his mummy
Down down baby Elmo eats salami
Down down baby Elmo shakes his body
Down down baby oops Elmo's sorry.

(⬤ VIDEO SAMPLE: See video example *Telford DDB 1.*)
    Despite the isolation of Telford Spring, which was more than 500 kilo-meters from the nearest city, television was a source of this game and others. However, the transmission process was more variable, as discussed by a group of Year 4 girls in 2002:

K: "Down down baby, Elmo shakes his body"—something like that. Where did that one come from?

ALL: *Sesame Street.*

K: That came from *Sesame Street?* And did you learn it off the TV or did you sort of teach each other?

MARY ANN: Elmo said it. He went "Elmo shakes his. . . ."

K: Oh, Elmo said it.

GEORGIE: Elmo said it and then she [indicating Mary Ann] passed it on to Mia. She taught me. . . .

[Several girls talk simultaneously, indicating different friends who had watched and taught it.]

K: So some of you watched it and then you taught it to each other.

JESSICA: Yeah.

Television programs were the direct source of several games in Telford Spring and the even more remote Bradford Well School. Telford Spring children reported that they had learned a popular clapping game, "Apple on a Stick" from the *Saddle Club* television show broadcast regularly on the ABC. Janey, an Aboriginal teacher and mother of one of the children who showed me games at Bradford Well, told me that games were "pulled up" from the *Playschool* program (a daily television program designed for young children) on the ABC.

Children in other field sites described similar televisual sources of games that were transferred into the playground. At Summerglen in Bedford, U.K., the mimetic "Teddy Bear" had been learned by some children from an unspecified television program for young children. The children at Ellington (Keighley) cited the *Tweenies* program (and a spinoff video which could be watched repeatedly in order to learn the game) as the source of a very popular clapping game, "My Sailor." At the two Busan schools a counting-out game that was popular with both boys and girls, "Sam Yuk Gu" (three six nine), along with a less frequently played memory game, "If I Go Some Place," was said to have been learned from an adult weekend television program translated as "Super TV Happy Sundays."

Films were another source of games and cheers. The American cheerleading film *Bring It On* was the nominated source of the cheer "I'm Sexy," which girls at Telford Spring were modifying to use when barracking for their team at the annual school sports carnival. Another popular cheer, "Brick Wall Waterfall," played by many children at Birch Vale School in Seattle, had been learned from a child character in the film *Dickey Roberts: Former Child Star.* (● **VIDEO SAMPLE:** See video example *BirchV Brick wall* and notated example in appendix 7.)

Bishop and Curtis (2006) report similar instances of games being learned from television and films, citing the English television soap opera *Eastenders*, the cartoon series *Recess*, and the U.S. film *The Hot Chick* as sources of games learned by children in several Yorkshire primary schools in 2003. McIntosh (2006) also describes how Balinese children's songs have been collected and released in both written and televised forms by an adult composer, teacher, and entrepreneur who has the power to modify the songs and games in the process of dissemination. Children learn these songs from the television, written publications, and classes held in the composer's studio, from which sources they are subsequently popularized.

Children's powers of invention are rapidly brought to bear on other material acquired from mediated sources. In several schools, children created clapping games or dance routines to accompany popular songs, reflecting the global influences on their auditory environments. A favorite source for girls at Ellington School was the Bollywood (Indian) movie industry.[12] On our first day at Ellington, a group of eight- and nine-year-old girls were playing a clapping game to the song "Bole Chudyan," from the movie *Khabi Khushi Kabhie Gham.* This game was performed in a circle both with a duple clap (C/O, C/P) and the endemic triple-clapping pattern. The first section of both versions ended with the performers turning around in an individual circle, their game incorporating part of the choreography that was an integral element of the movie performance. (● **VIDEO SAMPLE:** See video example *Ellington Bole ch 1 and 2.*)

Afterward, the girls discussed the song's source:

K: Do you do that very much? Do you sort of get songs off the movies?

ALL: Yes.

SAMARA: Then we learn it. . . . We learn them. Then we sing them. We know all of them.

K: Are they sort of favorite songs that you really like?

SAMARA: Yes.

K: Can you get those on CD as well or do you just mainly get them on video?

MARJANA: Video.

NADIA: And cassettes.

K: And cassettes too.

SAMARA: And Sky digital – 4BU.

SHANARA: Yes, 4BU.

K: Oh, Sky digital. So that's on the TV?

SAMARA: Yes.

I saw the song "Bole Chudyan" being performed several times by different groups of girls in the Ellington playground, more usually just in song form. However, it was given a very fluent performance by Halima, a talented Anglo Bengali ten-year-old and her Anglo Punjabi friend, Osma. Both girls reenacted the song and dance sequence from the film very accurately, with Halima displaying considerable vocal and kinesthetic talent. A few minutes before, the two girls had demonstrated a clapping game to the song "Like a Prayer," by U.S. singer Madonna, with Halima again emulating the idiomatic vocal inflections of the popular singer extremely well. What was especially interesting was the way in which the two girls were capable of performative code-switching with relative ease, moving seamlessly from the performance idiom of one tradition to that of another. (VIDEO SAMPLE: See video examples *Ellington Bole ch 3* and *Ellington LIM.*)

The appropriation of performance styles derived from popular music reflects the eclectic nature of the children's musical preferences. At Ellington, a group of nine and ten year-old girls, including the prolific game performers Halima and Farah, listed as favorites songs from *Khabi Khushi Kabhie Gham* (and other "Indian songs"), Madonna, English pop star Gareth Gates (whose single version of "Unchained Melody" was at the top of the charts at the time), English pop bands S Club 6 and Steps, girl group Atomic Kitten, and U.S. pop singer Britney Spears, in addition to the song "Dilemma," a duet between the rapper Nelly and Destiny's Child's Kelly Rowland, also topping the charts in 2002. Many of the songs were watched on television on shows such as *Top of the Pops*, and videos, cassettes, and CDs were purchased for repeated listening, watching, and learning. However, one of the girls also professed a liking for 1960s popular songs, which were not so obviously a part of the intensively marketed contemporary popular music specifically targeted at children and teenagers.

There was a similar diversity of musical preferences at other schools. For example at Birch Vale in Seattle, African American, Latino, and Anglo American children of both sexes professed a liking for rap and hip hop, but musical favorites of individual children also included the Nelly and Kelly Rowland duet, and songs by Barry Manilow and Canadian pop-rock singer Avril Lavigne. Another source of songs that were performed in the playground was the Disney Channel, from which the songs "Cinderella" and "Girl Power" were learned from the Cheetah Girls, a girl group created to perform on a series of branded movies on this channel. Children's preferences were developed from both child-focused sources, such as the Disney channel, and adult and teen-oriented rap and hip hop performances. Television, radio, CDs and the Internet were all conduits for the learning of songs that made an appearance in this playground.

Despite the lack of radio access and the geographical remoteness of Auston, in central Australia, childrens' and teenagers' musical preferences were developed through watching *Rage*, a weekly late-night music program on ABC television, and through reading the magazine *TV Hits*. Rap artists Niggers with Attitude and Eminem figured prominently in the Aboriginal teenagers' preferences, along with indigenous band Saltwater Music (playing a mix of traditional Aboriginal songs and reggae-influenced styles). Children also displayed their musical preferences at the discos that were coincidentally held during both of my field visits to the school in 2001 and 2002. Several songs gained major responses on the dance floor. "Cotton Eye Joe," by the manufactured Swedish country-techno band Rednex, was obviously well known by the children, who spontaneously sang along with the opening chorus. "Who Let the Dogs Out," an upbeat song by Bahamian Junkanoo group Baha Men, was more favored by younger children, especially girls, while "Freestyler," a hit song by Finnish rap-electro group Bomfunk MC's, was popular with everyone, energizing the dance floor and resulting in some virtuosic displays of break-dancing by boys from primary school age upward.

These musical preferences did not obviously filter into playground behavior at Auston, where there were very few overt displays of musical play. However, they formed a background to children's musical lives there, and the boys' prowess with break-dancing indicated that this was a musical activity that had been developed through frequent exposure to performance models, albeit accessed only through the limited available media, and through practice over time. Most remarkable was the seemingly limitless reach of globalized popular music into this very remote location, and its effect in shaping the musical lives of children in this community. While there was some identification with contemporary popular Aboriginal music, some of which encompassed traditional Aboriginal musical forms, the musical identity of children and teenagers at this settlement seemed, rather, to link in with a more global "musical grapevine of blackness" (Gaunt, 2006, p.74), as represented particularly by rap, hip-hop and, to a lesser extent, reggae. They appeared to have chosen more globalized signifiers of musical blackness (even if performed by the white Eminem) over localized forms that were generally less readily accessed or marketed through the media.

The appeal of rap and hip hop was not defined along racially determined boundaries in other locations. At Birch Vale, Zach, an eight-year-old Anglo American boy, was very keen to show me lengthy dance sequences that he had developed with the help of his teenage brother. The final demonstration was performed to a rap by the hip-hop artist Xzibit (🎧 **VIDEO SAMPLE:** see video example *BirchV rapdance*).

Zach discussed with me how he planned to add break-dancing to the repertoire of movements for this performance. In the same school, Charlotte, a Samoan American girl in grade 3, and her cousin Vera Lynn demonstrated a "rap" that was delivered with the declamatory style of the genre:

I woke up in the morning and I smell your breath
Oo ah oo ah need some Alka Fresh.
Wait. Come back. I found a Tic Tac
Don't mean to be mean but you need some Listerine.
Not a sip, not a drop but the whole d*** bot[tle].
I went to McDonalds to get a Big Mac
I took a bite an' she took it back.
I asked the lady what's the deal.
She slapped me in the face with a Happy Meal.

(See appendix 7 for a complete musical transcription.)
After Charlotte had performed this for me, I discussed its provenance with her.

K: OK, so does that one have a name? Is it a chant or a cheer?

CHARLOTTE: It's just a rap.

K: It's a rap is it? OK. And where did you get that rap from?

CHARLOTTE: I made it up.

K: You made that rap up did you? So did you make it up so that there's bits of ads in there or something?

CHARLOTTE: My cousin told us like half of it so we made the rest up.

K: Oh. And when you make up stuff how do you do it?

CHARLOTTE: You take some from other songs.

K: You take some from other songs and, what, you just put them together do you?

CHARLOTTE: Yes.

K: OK. And how do you know whether they fit together?

CHARLOTTE: Because my cousin . . . He listens to rap all the time so he knows if it's right or wrong.

K: Oh, OK. So you show it to him and then. . . .

CHARLOTTE: And he corrects us if we have one.

Charlotte's description accurately depicts the process of formulaic construction of this "rap" and the rap itself demonstrates the intertextuality that is involved. Several lines of Charlotte's text (those relating to Listerine) are found in multiple entries in a list of schoolyard taunts on "Cocojams," a website devoted to African American folk cultural forms (http://www.cocojams .com/index.htm). They are clearly textual formulae that are in wide circulation but Charlotte's claim to have "made up" the rap was not misplaced. Charlotte, with her older cousin's assistance, had put together a range of formulae "from other songs." In performing them with the highly syncopated delivery and declamatory stance of rap, Charlotte had appropriated this form for playground use.

Material derived from the media was appropriated and refashioned in various ways in different locations. For example, at Pada School, the "Digimon" game discussed in chapter 6 had been generated by adding a clapping pattern to the theme song of a Japanese children's television program. The clapping pattern appeared to be either the same as, or derived from, that of another traditional game, "Agi Yeomso" (baby goat). The grade-6 girls who had devised this game had also created a game to accompany the pop song "Neo" (You) by the Korean dance-techno singer and actress Jung Hyon Lee. The girls told us that they had made up the movements with friends the previous year and that they did not come from television performances. They consisted of a 16-beat sequence incorporating both standard clapping-game movements and movements that seemed to be more dance-related, as shown in table 7.3.

As can be seen in the table (and video example *Pada Neo*), the game began with the standard initiating formula, "sse, sse, sse" that immediately framed the performance as a game rather than a dance. This contrasted with other performances that reenacted televised dance sequences to popular songs, which girls were seen practicing inside the large hall at San school, also in Busan. ● **VIDEO SAMPLE**

In the Bedford playground, a large group of eight- and nine-year-old girls were also observed over a period of more than forty minutes creating a set of dance routines to various popular songs. The routines were mainly derived from those of the girl group Atomic Kitten, that they had regularly viewed on television, but each of the routines was developed beyond the dance steps on the televised videoclips, although one or two specific movements were incorporated. Dances were devised to "My Heart Will Go On" (Celine Dion's theme song to the film *Titanic*); "The Tide Is High," a hit song released in 2002 by Atomic Kitten; and another song topping the charts, "Automatic High," performed by the teenage band S Club 8 (also known as S Club Juniors). Dance steps were collaboratively suggested by various members of the group, usually just by demonstration, and then were either integrated into the performance or abandoned. Two girls, Zoey and Kirstie, seemed to be the leaders in this decision-making process, acting as arbiters of taste for the whole group. The dances were being created for an assembly performance later in the week and several members of this friendship group had been excluded from the routines. They observed at the edge of the group, periodically intruding to parody various dance steps that were being practiced. There was therefore an internal power play being enacted, with one group of girls gaining power

Table 7.3. Initial Text and Movements of Neo Game, Pada School, Busan

Text	Movement Sequence
Sse sse sse	Initial formula: hands shaken up and down with the 3 words
Neoman-el neomu sarang hasseo-sseo (I loved you so much)	4 sets of 3 movements First two movements in each set are 1 beat duration and third movement is 2 beats' duration.
Graeseo nae modeun-geol jungeo-ya (So I gave you my everything)	There are 8 beats in the first two text lines. The 3rd text line consists of 9 beats plus a 7-beat rest.
Whae gass'eo whae gass'eo narul dugo whae dd'onagass'o (Why? Why? Why did you leave me?)	1.1 Clap own hands (C/O) 1.2 Clap partners' hands down up (D/U) 1.3 Scissors paper rock movement (SPR) (two beats)
(Text continues on for 12 extra lines, omitting the middle section and repeated refrain of the original song.)	2.1 Clap own hands (C/O) 2.2 Clap partners' hands down up (D/U) 2.3 Pass hands over head of 1 girl who ducks down 3.1 (C/O) 3.2 (D/U) 3.3 SPR (two beats) 4.1 C/O 4.2 D/U 4.3 Each performer twirls around (two beats)
	Pattern repeated till end of song

through emulation of adult objects of media success, while another group of the disenfranchised acquired power through parody. (🔊 **VIDEO SAMPLE:** See video example *SummerG dance.*)

The dance sequences performed by this group of girls on this occasion included a re-enactment of the routine accompanying "Asereje" (also known as the "Ketchup Song"), a song with multiple versions in a mixture of Spanish, English, and nonsense syllables by the Spanish girl group Las Ketchup, who at that time appeared regularly on television music shows in England. On a previous day in the Summerglen playground I had seen two six-year-old girls also emulating the quirkily choreographed dance movements of this song, albeit with considerably less facility. (🔊 **VIDEO SAMPLE:** See video example *SummerG Ketchup.*)

In the musical play of these girls there was a synthesis of musical experiences derived from English television and from children's activities at a holiday venue in Spain, as I discovered when I questioned them about the dance that they had demonstrated:

K: Alana, what were you doing then?

ALANA: A dance from Spain.

K: It's a song from Spain is it? Where did you learn that one?

ALANA: I went to Spain with my Mum and my Dad and my brother. I went there on the summer holidays and I can still remember it.

K: Oh. Was it on the TV or did you learn it. . . ?

ALANA: We learned it, 'cause every night when we've had our dinner people came out and there was children's dance and we did that; we did dances. Like we run up and jump, like children's dances.

K: Oh and you still remember that one?

[They show me the dance again in response to my request].

K: And so Melissa, did you learn that from Alana?

MELISSA: Well once when I was round my aunty's house I saw it on TV and I learned it there.

K: Oh OK, so you know it as well.

ALANA: But she forgot it and I told her.

In this case the song and dance routine had been brought into the children's domain both by mediated mass marketing and by the capturing and re-branding of the song and associated movements as an activity suitable for children. That this occurs in more than one dimension is indicated by the ready availability of a VCD version of the song, labeled "video kids version" (Las Ketchup, 2002), in which children, members of Las Ketchup, and two large "tomatoes" demonstrate the dance movements with the text displayed on screen to help children to learn it. The catchy refrain of "Asereje" itself is a parody of an earlier hip hop song ("Rapper's Delight") recorded by the Sugarhill Gang, so the children's play version is only one point in a cycle of appropriation in which the echoes of multiple mediated "voices" are heard.

Moreover, children's dialectical relationship with the media results in cycles of appropriation and reappropriation whereby material derived from the media is appropriated for play purposes by children, reappropriated in this play form by the media, then reappropriated and regenerated in modified form by children. Such a cycle is signaled by the following discussion by a group of Year 4 girls following their performance of "Down Down Baby" at Springfield in 1993:

K: OK, now some of you knew some extra words.

ELLA: Yeah. We put them in.

K: How come you knew those ones?

ELLA: Well that's how, that's how, see, there's this thing on. . . .

ALICIA: *Sesame Street.*

ELLA: No, not *Sesame Street, Big.* There's this movie called *Big* and they sing it, they sing that, except you don't get to hear all of it and they sing "down the roller coaster" like that and then it goes "Gimme gimme Cocoa Pops, chimmy chimmy pow," and then you just hear the beginning of what we were doing and so I thought, well, it must be that, so I learnt that and then taught some other people.

K: So you connected those two together, did you?

ELLA: Yeah, and it works.

K: How does it work? I mean how do you know whether it works or not?

ANNETTE: Because of the rhythm and the beat. They fit together.

In the case of this game, it is not entirely clear whether African American children initially appropriated part of the text from a popular song, "Shimmy Shimmy Ko Ko Bop," written in 1959 by Bob Smith and recorded by the doo-wop group Little Anthony and the Imperials in 1960 (Riddell, 1990), or whether the text of this song was derived from the game. This issue has recently prompted further consideration (Gaunt, 2006; Marsh, 2006). Gaunt appears to favor the girls as the originators of this material: "it once again raised the chicken-or-egg question: which came first? I wondered if there might be something to say about girls' games influencing popular songs by male artists, particularly those involving popular dances like the Shimmy. . . . Some kind of musical as well as oral and kinetic dialogue and exchange are at work" (2006, p. 98).

Certainly both the doo-wop song and the children's game seemed to have also tapped into an older African American performative tradition, the shimmy dance, which was popularized in the 1920s. The text of the doo-wop song is almost entirely devoted to a description of a dance (presumably this is "Shimmy Shimmy Ko-Ko Bop," though it takes place in a "native hut") and the singing game in many instances includes in its text an invitation to move in a particular sequence of steps, as shown in the example below documenting a performance by twelve-year-old girls and boys at Springfield in 1990. (See full transcription in appendix 4.)

Down down baby, down down the roller coaster
Sweet sweet baby I'll never let you go.
Shimmy shimmy coco pops shimmy shimmy pow [punch fist].
Shimmy shimmy coco pops shimmy shimmy pow [punch fist].

Granma, granma sick in bed.
She called the doctor and the doctor said,
Let's get the rhythm of the head, ding dong [shake head].
Let's get the rhythm of the head, ding dong [shake head].
Let's get the rhythm of the hands [clap, clap].
Let's get the rhythm of the hands [clap, clap].
Let's get the rhythm of the feet [stamp, stamp].
Let's get the rhythm of the feet [stamp, stamp].
Let's get the rhythm of the hot dog [swivel hips].
Let's get the rhythm of the hot dog [swivel hips].
Put 'em all together and what do you get?
Ding dong [clap, clap, stamp, stamp] hot dog.
Put 'em all backwards and what do you get?
Dog hot [stamp, stamp, clap, clap] doing ding.

Multiple versions of the game proliferated in playgrounds across the United States (see, for example, Fulton & Smith, 1978, and Kenny, 1975). The version that was repeatedly broadcast on *Sesame Street* was constantly reappropriated by children in different locations for their own new variants of the game.[13] Another version of the game was also appropriated for use in the American film *Big* and was reappropriated in 1993 by members of the Springfield group who created their game ostensibly by amalgamating aspects of two media-derived versions. There have been further appropriations, including a rap by the hip hop artist Nelly, as discussed further below.

The doo-wop song and the game have only two text lines in common, both of which have an identical rhythm. Because of the semantic indeterminacy of the text of these lines, they vary considerably from one performance to another, but the rhythm of this textual link between the two genres remains relatively stable through many performances, as seen in table 7.4.

Although many other textual and rhythmic formulae in the song vary widely from group to group, variants of this "shimmy" couplet seem to remain in most versions of the game as a remnant of its original identity, whether this "original" was the game itself or the 1950s doo-wop song, and despite children's lack of knowledge of its derivation.

As can be seen in table 7.4, this shimmy couplet with the idiosyncratic text rhythm of the 1950s song has also been retained in a much more recent appropriation of the game by the hip hop artist Nelly in his song "Country Grammar," recorded in 2000 in the album of the same name. It is evident from Nelly's own words that this is a conscious borrowing and reworking: "What's old is new again: The 'Country Grammar' hook is a rhyme borrowed from a children's song; see also: Little Anthony and the Imperials' Shimmy Shimmy

Table 7.4. Textual and Rhythmic Variants of Shimmy Shimmy Line, *Down Down Baby*

Text of doo-wop Song	Text Rhythm
Shimmy Shimmy Ko-ko Bop Shimmy Shimmy bop!	
Shimmy Shimmy Ko-ko Bop Shimmy Shimmy bop! (Doo-wop song, Smith, 1981)	

Text of *Down down baby* Game Variants	
Shimmy shimmy coco pops shimmy shimmy pow	
Shimmy shimmy coco pops shimmy shimmy pow (Springfield, Sydney, 1990)	
Gimme gimme coco pop gimme gimme pow	
Gimme gimme coco pop gimme gimme pow (Springfield, Sydney, 1993)	
Cushy cushy coco pop cushy cushy bang	
Cushy cushy coco pop cushy cushy bang (Springfield, Sydney, 1994)	
Cherry cherry cherry go to the bow	
Cherry cherry cherry go to the bow (Telford Spring, Australia, 2001)	
Shimmy shimmy rocka rocka shimmy shimmy rock	
Shimmy shimmy rocka rocka shimmy shimmy rock (Summerglen, Bedford, U.K., 2002)	
Shimmy shimmy coconut shimmy shimmy ah	
Shimmy shimmy coconut shimmy shimmy ah (St. Augustine's, Keighley, U.K., 2002	
Chimmy chimmy coco pop chimmy chimmy shy	
Chimmy chimmy coco pop don' make me cry (Birch Vale, Seattle, 2004)	
Shimmy shimmy coco pop shimmy shimmy rah	
Shimmy shimmy coco pop shimmy shimmy rah (Nora Conn, Los Angeles, 2004)	
Shimmy shimmy coco what listen to it pound	
Light it up and take a puff pass it to me now (Nelly, *Country Grammar*, 2000)	

Ko-Ko Bop (1959)" (membersb.blackplanet.com/Nelly_Nellı/:2, accessed on 7 January 2006).

In "Country Grammar" Nelly has adopted a vernacular fused from the play language of African American children ("down down baby" and "shimmy shimmy coco what"), the "grammar" of the street, and the streetwise rapping of adolescents and adults to affirm a localized identity and way of life, revealed in frequent references within the song to street life and drug use (http://www .nellyhq.com/lyricsong4.html accessed on 19 December 2006).

In a similar way girls at Telford Spring in 2001 have personalized or localized their renditions of "Down Down Baby," including their own names or localities in the text, for example:

Down down baby Alana does karate
Down down baby Estella phones her mummy

I'm goin' down down baby go [Au]stralia baby
Boom boom baby got no rhythm though

(VIDEO SAMPLE: See video example *Telford DDB 2.*)

In adopting and adapting the lyrics and musical attributes of the 1950s song and the African American children's game, Nelly is adhering to the standard intertextuality of rap, an intertextuality that occurs just as frequently in the traditions of children's musical play.[14] There is a fluid interchange of musical, textual, and movement material between playground and mediated sources. In the case of "Down Down Baby," the interactive relationship between children's play and the media in this instance might be characterized as a cycle of appropriation between fixed and fluid forms, as shown in figure 7.1.

The cycle illustrated by figure 7.1 seems to support Mechling's view that, just as the media influences children, children also influence the media (Mechling, 1986, cited in Harwood, 1994). Gaunt adds to this view with her observation that there is a "dialogic relationship" between black girl's games and popular music genres "in which both spheres are creating and refashioning new musical ideas, based on pre-existing material from the other realm" (2006, p. 107).

Written Sources and the Internet

A similar cycle of appropriation and reappropriation can be found in the written media. In Australia, collections of children's playlore texts have been published in a highly accessible format for children (for example, Durkin and Ferguson, 1990; Factor, 1983, 1985, 1986; Factor and Marshall, 1992; Russell, 1990). Other collections with an intended child readership have been published in

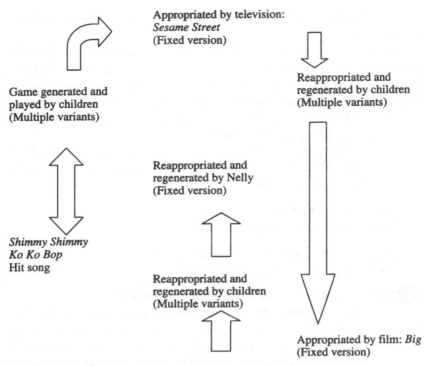

Appropriated by television:
Sesame Street
(Fixed version)

Reappropriated and
regenerated by children
(Multiple variants)

Game generated and
played by children
(Multiple variants)

Reappropriated and
regenerated by Nelly
(Fixed version)

*Shimmy Shimmy
Ko Ko Bop*
Hit song

Reappropriated and
regenerated by children
(Multiple variants)

Appropriated by film: *Big*
(Fixed version)

Figure 7.1 Cycles of Appropriation and Reappropriation in *Down Down Baby*

England and the United States (for example, Corbett, MacLean and MacLean, 1993; Martin, 1995). These collections are widely read by children; two of Factor's books were rated among the most popular books for primary aged readers in the Kid's Own Australian Literature Awards in 1991.[15]

In the Springfield playground, these game texts were frequently used as sources of material for recreating clapping games, as cited by two girls of differing ages in 1990 and 1993:

JULIE: . . . the kids usually, you know, read them from books or see them on TV. . . .

K: Where did you learn that or did you make that up?

ALICIA: We've got this book called *Far Out Brussel Sprout* and it's got all sorts of poems in it and that was in it.

As only the texts or brief movement instructions are reproduced in most of these publications, re-creation is a creative act resulting in considerable variation, a process outlined by Alicia and her friends:

SHEILA: . . . as we got older . . . we thought, we've got nothing to do. We may as well play them games that we've done when we were little kids and then we thought, hang on, how did them games go? And you'd go to them books—like, there's a couple of hand-clapping books out now. And you'd go to them and you'd try to pick up the rhythm, but all they've got is some pictures of a hand moving and you still can't pick them up from the book. So . . .

ALICIA: So you just have to dig hard in your memory.

ANNETTE: You really have to create your own game to, like, be able to remember it. You can't just look in a book or, like this is how you do it.

The appropriation cycle in this case results in transmission through an oral-literate continuum, with children regaining control of their own games through variation of published material. (A detailed example of this re-creation process is discussed in chapter 8.)

The Internet is a similar source of oral-literate material for musical play. Children can either download lyrics of songs to learn or can repeatedly listen to sound files that are also downloadable and transferable onto computers, or portable sound devices such as MP3 players, and mobile phones. At Birch Vale School in Seattle, I witnessed a group of eight-year-old girls and boys walking around the playground sharing downloaded song lyrics from an Eminem song from which they performed snippets. The printed lyrics were being used for learning purposes, particularly to refresh individual memories of more extended sections of the text. Many of the families in this school community were economically disadvantaged, so children were dependent on their more affluent friends to share Internet-derived material for self-regulated collaborative learning and elaboration within a play environment.

This process was explained by a group of nine- and ten-year-old girls who had generated a song and dance routine from a humorous parody song that had been downloaded from a Seattle radio Internet site:

CHELSEA: . . . it's just a little joke.

K: It's kind of like a joke thing is it? And did you learn that one or did you make that one up?

CHELSEA: From the Internet.

K: Oh. You got it from the Internet?

ASHLEY: It's KZOK Twisted Tunes.

K: KC. . . ?

ASHLEY: KZOK. It's a radio station and they, like, make up words to different songs but they put funny words in.

K: They put funny words in instead.

Romina and CHELSEA: Yeah.

K: And what—you download that from the Internet do you?

ASHLEY: Yeah.

K: And just listen to it?

ASHLEY: Yeah.

K: Do you learn it that way? . . . Do you then have it sort of on your computer and you listen to it a few times, or. . . ?

ASHLEY: I have it downloaded on my computer but—

CHELSEA: I don't.

ROMINA: I don't.

K: So how do you learn it then?

ASHLEY: You just . . . I just play it over and over and over again and then I just learned it— [laughter] from singing along to it so much.

Such practices were not just local, as a parent at San School in Busan confirmed in describing her children's learning of popular songs from Internet downloads. Song material from Internet sources is subject to similar creative responses from children as that derived from other mediated sources. The Seattle children's creative use of this resource is discussed in chapter 8.

Influences of the Classroom

Formal classroom activities can be another source of textual, melodic, and movement material for children's musical play. In the simplest instances of this, Christmas songs taught in the classroom at Springfield[16] were appropriated for playground use, where they were usually accompanied by well-known movement formulae, in particular the three-beat clapping pattern. These performances, where classroom teaching results in the generation of new game genres, can also be seen as examples of Lipsitz's (1994) capture of the colonizer, the adult colonizer being the teacher. By appropriating these adult-generated songs for game use, children claim them as their own, shifting ownership and control of adult material into their own domain.

Similar examples of appropriation of classroom material for use in the playground were observed in other locations. As discussed in chapter 5, the song "The Twelve Days of Christmas," modified by the Aboriginal "language ladies" with the substitution of Mudburra words for local birds and animals, was transformed into a clapping game played by a group of sisters at Auston school in central Australia. In another remote central Australian school, Maringa, to support the Aboriginal children's English literacy development the teacher had made big books of nursery rhymes that children could study at any given time. Two of these nursery rhymes, "Jack and Jill" and "Humpty Dumpty," had been used as the basis for clapping games that the children had devised. An equivalent transformation had taken place at Birch Vale in Seattle, where the Spanish-speaking children in the English Language Learners class played a clapping game to the song "There Was an Old Lady Who Swallowed a Fly," which they had learned from the music teacher (video example *BirchV Old lady*). It was interesting that this was the only clapping game that they played in English; the rest of their clapping game repertoire was performed entirely in Spanish. (🔊 **VIDEO SAMPLE**)

More complex transmission processes were also found at Springfield. One such example was the game "My Granma," performed in multi-age groups by Year 2, Year 3, and Year 5 girls in 1990. When some of the performers viewed the field recordings of this game in 1994, they reported that they had viewed the text and melody on several media sources but that they had derived some of the movements from drama lessons at school:

MATU: That was actually a song. . . .

K: It was a song? Where did the song come from?

TARA: [Sings a few bars] It was on *K-9*. At the end.

[Tara and Matu continue to have two separate conversations, Tara about the movie source and Matu about the videoclip source.]

MATU: It was on. . . .

K: It was on what?

MATU: A videoclip, a videoclip.

TARA: *K-9*.

MATU: It was a long time ago.

K: *K-9*?

MATU: A long time ago. This woman sang it.[17]

TARA: The ending. You know how they were driving the car down the road.

K: What's *K-9*?

TARA: It's a movie about this dog, a police dog.

K: Uh huh.

TARA: A comedy.

K: And it was on that?

TARA: At the end. Just the ending, you know, while all the words are going up the screen.

K: Uh huh. OK [to Matu] and you said a woman sang it?

MATU: Yeah

K: On a videoclip?

MATU: Yeah.

K: [To others] So you remember it too, do you? [Others indicate assent.]

SEVERAL: Ages ago.

K: Ages ago.

TARA: Yeah. It was pretty popular.

K: OK. So was that just something that people picked up from the video clip and put clapping to, or . . . how do you think. . . ?

TARA: I think we made it up in drama. I think we got one and then we made. . . . [indicates movements]

CLARA: I think it was when we were playing games and statues. Our drama teacher put it on.

TARA: Yeah, probably. And we did the actions [performs some of the movements].

CLARA: Yeah, and we were doing that [movements as for Tara].

K: So who was that?

SEVERAL: Mr. Young [drama teacher].

K: Mr. Young. OK, so do you. . . .

TARA: See, he used to play music and we had to copy him dancing.

CLARA: And when he stopped the music you'd have to freeze.

TARA: We probably got our ideas from him.

K: Right. So you sort of got the idea of using that music, maybe.

TARA: Yeah.

K: Would he have given you the actions or did you just make them up?

TARA: See, he just makes actions and we follow him.

CLARA: Or sometimes we'd just dance our own and we probably got our stuff from there.

K: So you can't remember what the case was there, whether you made up the actions or whether they were Mr. Young's?

TARA: I think they were a mixture.

The cycle of appropriation and reappropriation also took place with the classroom teaching of playground games at Springfield. Several playground games were taught by classroom teachers or by the music specialist teachers in the school. For example, the game "Da Da Dexi," also recorded by multi-age groups in 1990, was reportedly taught by a classroom teacher:

TARA: We learnt it from our. . . . We had a teacher, Miss Stillianos. She was Greek.

K: Uh huh.

CLARA: And she taught us that.

It is possible that this game received short-term validation in the playground through being taught in the classroom. However, it was no longer regularly played in 1993 when I resumed field recording at Springfield. The teaching of playground games by the music specialist teachers at Springfield had a much greater impact on the playground repertoire and on the longevity of games in the repertoire. The two major examples of this were "Miss Mary Mac" and "Sar Macka Dora," both of which were relatively popular in the playground. The classroom teaching of "Miss Mary Mac" resulted not only in its continued performance but also in the embellishment of the movement formulae used in the playground in relation to this game.

In the case of "Sar Macka Dora," the teachers at Springfield acquired the game through in-service and teaching publications, and one specialist music teacher taught it mainly to children from a variety of school grades from 1989 to 1991 (see chapter 9). Her successor usually taught the game to children who were new to the school. Thus, children entering kindergarten and the opportunity classes for gifted students were taught the game each year and then it was used with some regularity as a "fill-in" activity in the music classroom.

As a result, "Sar Macka Dora" was recorded by children from every age group during the major period of fieldwork at Springfield from 1990 to 1995. It was also consistently nominated as one of the few games that were still played by children in Year 5 and 6, when game performance usually diminished. The reason for its continued classroom transmission and its impact on variability in performance of this genre is examined in detail in chapter 9.

The teaching or endorsement of playground game practices on an ongoing basis also resulted in their proliferation in other playgrounds. For example, the singing game "Hop Old Squirrel," that was a favorite in the music classes of grade 3 children at Birch Vale School, made the transition into the playground where it formed part of the repertoire of several girls, and "Waddly Archer" underwent a similar transition from music classroom to playground at St. Augustine's in Keighley. As discussed in chapter 5, at Bysiden School the principal and her deputy, as well as several other staff members, strongly encouraged the playing of traditional games in the playground—teaching the games during class time, assisting with rope turning and chanting, demonstrating and inviting children to play games during recess times, and providing game materials such as skipping ropes. All of these practices not only encouraged game playing, but ensured that older games such as "Ein-å-Tyve" which had fallen out of the playground repertoire were reintroduced. A similar practice at Pada School in Busan resulted in new enthusiasm for older traditional games, such as "Nol Ttwigi," the jumping seesaws.

However, it was notable that the teaching of games by teachers was sometimes less effective than that by peers. For example, at Pada, some teachers had taught the clapping game "P'urun Hanŭl Ŭnhasu" to boys in preparation for my visit. The boys who I saw demonstrating this game during the staged play time on the first day of my visit generally had considerable difficulty performing it, yet the group of boys who learnt the much more complex "Digimon" game from their female classmates acquired the new game with ease.

Nevertheless, classroom and school practices could be seen to have both fleeting and enduring effects on children's musical play in the playground. In addition to repertoire, the provision of occasions for musical performance created extra purposes for play. The development of dance routines for a school assembly at Summerglen is one instance of this, as was practicing a movement routine with ribbon wands in preparation for an assembly performance by grade-4 girls at Pada School in Busan. Girls at Ellington School also recounted practicing dance routines for the school disco. It is therefore of concern that, in the majority of schools, there was little classroom recognition of the musical play taking place in the playground and the direct relationship it might have to both classroom musical influences and more general ones.

Other Influences

Incidental reference has been made in previous chapters to transmission from other sources outside of the playground. These include friends at afterschool care centers, ballet classes and sports teams, neighbors and relatives. Some mention has also been made of new games, such as "One Two Three" or game variants, such as "Black and White TV," being introduced by new students who had come from other schools or other countries.

In addition, children named school camps they had attended as a source of game material. It may have been transmission from camp sources, in fact, that explained the continued performance of games on a relatively large scale by Year 6 children at Springfield in 1990:

> JULIE: We learnt some when we were in kindergarten and we learnt some of them when we went to camps and when some people went this year to camp they learnt more songs. So, like, they share the songs. . . . Like, everyone sort of that went to camp from, like, 6KZ and 6SB,[18] all of them, they showed all of us and we started playing it for fun.
>
> K: And they showed them to you in the playground, did they?
>
> JULIE: Yeah.

Camp was also nominated as a source of a textual variant of one game by an older girl at Birch Vale School in Seattle. My Norwegian research collaborator also considered that "O Han Ola," a game played by Bysiden children, had been learnt at a summer camp. Given the durability and vibrancy of musical practices at both school camps and summer camps (Seeger & Seeger, 2006), their function as repositories of song and game material—appropriate for organized leisure activities and which children can easily use in their own play—is not surprising.

Another source of games and cheers was the Girl Guide movement in its different manifestations, known variously as guides (Telford Spring), Brownies (Seattle and Bedford) and Girl Scouts (also Seattle). As with camps, games were taught by adult or teenage leaders to younger children and then brought back to school and shared with friends.

At Birch Vale, some cheers, including the call and response chant "The Little Frog," were learned at softball games, where they were used as team motivators and as taunts for the opposing team. Some girls learned similar cheers at out-of-school cheerleading classes. The popular "Brick Wall Waterfall" and "Bang Bang Choo Choo Train" were reinforced in this manner, although they had been acquired by some children from the films *Bring It On* and *Dickey Roberts, Former Child Star*, as previously discussed. Once they entered the playground, they were embellished and used both for amusement only or for taunting and, occasionally, cheering.

In Australia, cheers are not a standard part of playground repertoire. At Telford Spring, however, there were some interesting exceptions to this. My last day at the school in 2001 coincided with the annual sports carnival, and

the four different sports teams into which the school was divided had been pre-
paring for the day by practicing various motivational chants. On the day of the
carnival, I saw two six-year-old girls at recess performing clapping games that
they had devised to two of these cheers. The text of the second cheer (performed
to the standard three-beat clapping pattern) gave some idea of its origin:

Sitting on the dunny [toilet]
Pull the chain
There goes _____ [name of opposing team] down the drain
Singing we will we will rock you.

There was a clear allusion, in the text, text rhythm, and melody of the last
line, to the well-known rock song by Queen. However, it appeared to have
come into the playground by a circuitous route. The art teacher at the school
was in the habit of playing popular songs, including "We Will Rock You," as
an accompaniment to art classes. The song was thus well known and had been
used to good effect in the formulaic composition of the sports cheer. In turn,
the six-year-old girls had added a clapping formula to the cheer to turn it into
a playground game. Although I did not see this game on my visit to the school
the following year, I did see the other cheer, "Coca Cola Pepsi Cola," still performed as a clapping game by another pair of girls.

It can be seen that material from all of these sources forms only one link
in the complex transmission process, as is evident in the discussion by some
Year 2 boys at Springfield about learning "Sor Macka Dora":

SAM: Yeah. We done it with our whole class, with Miss Fallwood.

K: Oh, you've been doing it with Miss Fallwood have you? What about,
Owen, but you didn't learn it from Miss Fallwood? Is that right?

OWEN: No.

K: Who did you learn it from?

LIAM: Fiona brought it to the school.

K: Who brought it to the school?

LIAM: Fiona.

OWEN: No. Before that—before Fiona came it was at. . . wasn't it?

LIAM: Someone would've brought it to the school, that's for sure.

OWEN: Kids would've brought it.

It is clear that multiple game sources result in the presence of multiple traditions rather than there being a single tradition of playground games at any

school. The role of borrowings from these external sources is further explored in the following chapter on variability in performance.

Transmission and Variability

It can be seen from the foregoing discussion of transmission processes in school playgrounds in many locations, that transmission and variability are inseparably linked. Children are certainly conscious of this relationship, as is clear from a discussion by ten-year-old girls at Springfield in 1994:

> HONG-SOO: But when . . . you learn a new version of something that you already know, like "See See My Playmate" like we've already seen, you sort of let go of what was and then catch hold of what is so you can't remember the one before it.

> K: So you can't remember the previous one. It just goes out of your mind? . . .

> SHEILA: You can remember the actions but you can't remember the song or you can remember the song but you can't remember the actions.

> ALICIA: Yeah. What usually happens—how different versions often spread, and this is what happened to me—what happens is, I learn something off Sadie and then I might have one movement which I think is right but isn't quite right. Then I'll teach Hong-Soo that and she'll probably catch on to what I had. And then she'll probably get one movement wrong and so different versions will just spread all over the school. And if you catch on every version of the person before you then, like, you've taught one that's been gradually changed through so many people teaching [it].

> HONG-SOO: Until gradually every single movement has been changed.

Although Alicia's summary gives the impression that these processes are accidental, and, in the words of Abrahams and Foss (1968, p. 35), "disastrously decadent," resulting in a "contamination" of the tradition, it is clear that many of the processes of variation are, rather, "wonderfully creative" (p. 35) and are the result of deliberate decisions made on the part of the performers. The many influences on the transmission and performance of playground games can be seen as regenerative rather than degenerative. In the following section, the processes involved in generation and regeneration will be further examined.

IV

COMPOSITION IN PERFORMANCE

✦ CHAPTER 8 ✦

Composition in the Playground

T he foregoing chapters have explored the interrelationship of transmission
   and generative practices in children's musical play within its social context. While some variation is inadvertent, it is clear that children also use deliberate processes of innovation to vary game material for a range of different
social and aesthetic purposes, in some cases creating entirely new compositions, as one group of ten-year-old girls at Springfield school attested:

> ALICIA: What happened was, we were singing these normal ones that
> everyone sings and then I started singing ones that no one had ever heard
> of, and we said "Let's make up another one," and we just kept on going
> and going and going.

> ELLA: No. Something happened. You said, "I wonder if there's any that we
> don't know about," and then we started singing and clapping and just
> doing [demonstrates clapping pattern]. . . .

> HONG-SOO: So sometimes it's an accident when you make up some. So I
> guess you don't really want to do it but then . . .

> ALICIA: It just happens.

> HONG-SOO: It just happens. It's a mystery.

In this chapter, I endeavor to further unravel the "mystery" of children's
playground composition in performance by considering children's statements regarding their innovation and by examining the compositional techniques used
by a particular group of Springfield children both to create a new version of a

game from a published game text and to vary their performances of the game "See See My Playmate" over a period of a year. In so doing, I challenge a number of adult paradigms of children's composition, which were initially outlined in chapter 2, and question adult preconceptions concerning the degree of innovative skill which children apply to composition in playground performance.[1]

Such preconceptions are articulated in Opie's (1994) reflection on British children's invention within this genre: "They do not invent major new games, all they ever do is slightly alter the established ones or amalgamate several traditional elements. What they do originate are a multitude of 'clever wheezes', hopeful experiments, and minor games which last no more than a day, or at the most a few weeks" (p. 12).

Children's Composition in Performance

It is undoubtedly true that children utilize known formulae from other sources, both traditional and related to other aspects of their auditory environment as many of the instances of "borrowing" described in previous chapters and children's statements of practice illustrate. For example, Aboriginal children at the remote Maringa School in central Australia told me that clapping patterns for newly made-up games were "copied from the other styles." At Strandli School in rural Norway children said that they used the same patterns, but with different songs.

However, formulaic construction is not a thoughtless process but rather a purposeful one, as some nine-year-old girls at Ellington School in Keighley who had just demonstrated variants of "Zig Zag Zoo" explained:

K: When you make it up, Farah, tell me how you do it.

FARAH: You just go upstairs and concentrate and, you know, make a list of games.

K: Yeah?

AMREEN: And take some words out of that and see if they make sense. And then add some of your own words.

K: Oh, so you use some of the words that you know from other games?

AMREEN: Yes.

K: And then you add some extra ones in, some new ones in do you?

AMREEN: Yes.

K: And what about the movements that you do? How do you decide what you're going to do with that?

AMREEN: Miss, we usually copied it a bit from the Punjabi version and then we took it from all these [others].

K: OK. So again you take some of the things that you know already.

AMREEN: Yes

K: And you add some new ones in. Do you do that very often?

FARAH and AMREEN: Yes.

K: Why do you do that? Why do you make up new ones?

FARAH: Because all the others are boring.

AMREEN: If you've known them for such a long time you're always doing them and you get to half of them and you're like "oh you don't want to do this now" and then you decide to make your own up.

K: Oh, right. So you do it quite a lot.

FARAH and AMREEN: Yes.

Changes to games may be immediate and fleeting, as in the same Ellington girls' improvisations on the counting-out games "Akkar Bakkar," "Scooby Dooby Doo," and "Tu Khota" mentioned in the previous chapter. Conversely, novel versions can also gain a lengthy tenure in the playground. While the experimental nature of children's innovation is evident in playgrounds in all of the field locations, it is necessary to question Opie's (1994) criterion of preservation as an indication of innovation. In their study of musical development in children's composition, Swanwick and Tillman (1986) include "the briefest utterances as well as more worked out and sustained invention" (p. 311) in their definition of composition: "Composition takes place when there is freedom to choose the ordering of music, without notational or other forms of detailed performance instruction" (p. 311).

Because the process of composition is inextricably linked with performance in playground singing games, innovation in one performance element, such as text, may lead to a corresponding innovation in another element, for example movement, as is evident from the words of some eight-year-old girls at Summerglen School in Bedford who had just demonstrated a game made of textual formulae from two others, "My Mother Told Me" and "Three Six Nine":

K: When you put them together, what do you do?

ZOEY: You just think of something.

BETHANY: Yeah we think of something. And we have to . . . We think of some words and we have to sing it out as we're doing it so then other people . . . [Bethany is interrupted by intrusive playing]. Yeah and then we just do handclaps [demonstrates clapping]. And say someone hears us, they go in this playground and then everyone remembers it.

It is clear from this statement that the performative element is integral to composition in the playground. It is part of the process of thinking out and sounding out that characterizes generative practices in musical play in this context. This cycle of composition and performance is ongoing. At no stage is there a clearly identifiable, unchanging product to be preserved.

As co-construction is a principal feature of composition in this genre, the notion that the cycle of composition and performance is a group process, rather than an individual one, is also of significance, as outlined by some eight- and nine-year-old girls at St. Augustine's school in Keighley:

JASMINE: Yeah, well it's easier if someone's helping you 'cause if you make it up on your own it's really difficult. . . . You don't usually make it up on your own. You usually make it up with a group so they know it.

HARRIET: 'Cause then all of the people can have like ideas to put in it and then you get more things to use in it.

JASMINE: It's really hard if you make it up on your own.

HARRIET: 'Cause you can't really think for yourself as much as in a group.

The group compositional process can clearly be seen in the following transcript in which the same group of Springfield Year 4 girls whose discussion of innovation began this chapter compose "Teacher Teacher," a rhythmic and movement setting of a text derived from popular publications of children's folklore (Factor and Marshall, 1992; Russell, 1990):

ALICIA: There's this one. There's this saying that people say a lot. Well, it's in a lot of funny books and stuff. I've heard a lot of boys say it. It's just this one about:

Music Example 8.1

Teacherteacher don't be dumb gi... dumb Givemebackmy bub-ble-gum

Teacherteacher don't be mean Gimmeacoinforthe cof-fee ma-chine

Music Example 8.1 *(continued)*

Tea-cher tea-cher   I   de-clare   Tar-zan's lost his   un-der-wear

We could probably do that to a handclapping rhythm.

HONG-SOO: And also there's one that goes. . . .

ELLA and ANNETTE: Teacher teacher [Ella and Annette try some clapping patterns: Ella the three-beat clap, Annette a syncopated four-beat pattern[2]].

HONG-SOO: I've got an idea:

Music Example 8.2

Tea - cher   tea - cher   you   no   fair

ALICIA: No. That's not how it goes.

HONG-SOO: Teacher teacher you are dumb.

ALICIA: OK.

[Performance of "Teacher Teacher" proceeds immediately:]

Music Example 8.3

Tea cher tea cher   don't be dumb   Give me back my   bub-ble-gum

Music Example 8.3 *(continued)*

Teacher teacher don't be mean   Give me a coin for the cof-fee ma-chine

HONG-SOO: How about going like that? ... [Demonstrates mimetic movement].

ALICIA: OK.

SADIE: Coffee machine [laughs].

[Hong-Soo and Alicia continue:]

Music Example 8.4

Tea - cher   tea-cher   I   de-clare   Tar-zan lost his un-der-wear

HONG-SOO: That's how we sometimes make it up.

K: OK. Well, do you want to do that one again . . . no, the one that you just made up? Can you do that one more time?

HONG-SOO: OK.

ALICIA: Yeah. Fine. OK

[Final performance of "Teacher Teacher" proceeds immediately:]

Music Example 8.5

These children's strategies involve an initial setting of the text with a metrically ambivalent rhythm, which fluctuates between a duple and triple subdivision of the beat, although phrase length is already constant. This is followed by a period of exploration of a variety of clapping patterns and textual variants. The latter are discarded in favor of the original text which, when combined with the chosen four-beat clapping pattern, attains a greater rhythmic regularity, although lack of synchronization of the clapping pattern between performers continues to be reflected in augmentation of the text rhythm. Further changes are made to the movement patterns as the text setting unfolds. The final rendition, recorded at the request of the researcher, exhibits a highly regular duple meter, in which the fourth phrase has, for the first time, a regular duple subdivision of the beat, the more natural speech rhythm of the first performance having eventually been formalized by the superimposition of the strictly metrical movement pattern. A constant phrase length is maintained throughout the process.

Composition in Performance and "Universal" Models of Children's Composition

How, then, does this correspond with theories of children's compositional processes? As outlined in chapter 2, Swanwick and Tillman's (1986) model of children's composition is represented as a spiral of development, in which children move through four successive levels, each encompassing two developmental modes. At the Materials level, children are engaged in Sensory exploration of sound sources, followed by the acquisition of manipulative skills in relation to these sound sources. The Expression level involves personal expression, where conscious expressive devices are used with little structural control, followed by engagement with the Vernacular, characterized by melodic and rhythmic patterning, repetition, and regular phrase structure. At this level, "What they do is predictable and they have clearly absorbed into their musical vocabulary much from their musical experience both inside and outside of school" (p. 333). Within the third level, form, children move into a Speculative phase, where there is "imaginative deviation" from, and a temporary lapse in control of, the vernacular, and then into the idiomatic mode, where the element of surprise is integrated into a specific style and "technical, expressive and structural control" is firmly established (p. 333). The final level, Value, contains symbolic and systematic modes, in which meta-cognitive reflection on compositional processes and products is prominent.

If this model is accepted, the processes of composition found in children's playground singing games appear to fall most readily within the Vernacular mode of development. This is not surprising, given the social context of children's playground composition. Playground singing games involve at least two, and often several performers. Although some of the performers state that they have "made up" their games or game variants individually at home, variants are more frequently produced collaboratively by performers during or immediately following a performance. The composer-performers, therefore, must work within the framework of a musical, movement, and textual vernacular, which is understood and able to be manipulated and performed by all members of the group.

Also inherent in the Swanwick and Tillman model is the assumption that these processes are developmental and that this development is age-related to some extent (Swanwick and Tillman, 1986; Swanwick, 1988, 1991). Yet in the compositional sequence documented above, the children would appear to be collaboratively working through a number of different developmental modes within a period of several minutes. The first recitation of the text exhibits features of the Speculative mode, followed by a period in which they are developing Manipulative control of movement materials, after which successive performances appear to be related to first Vernacular then Idiomatic modes.

Swanwick provides a possible explanation for this behavior: "each one of these stages or perhaps better, transformations, is swept up into the succeeding developmental thrust. We do not merely pass through one of these modes but carry them forward with us into the next. . . . It is important to be clear that these transformations are both cumulative and cyclical" (1988, pp. 63–64, and 1996, p. 26). Given that these children are ten years old, they would therefore have passed through and have at their disposal sensory, manipulative, personal expression, and vernacular compositional modes and, according to the model, would possibly be entering the Speculative mode. However, this statement cannot explain the upward thrust of these children's compositional skills, particularly those relating to the meta-cognitive domain that Swanwick (1988) equates with the compositional behaviors of much older children. This will be discussed further following the elaboration of the techniques used by this Springfield group to vary performances of "See See My Playmate."

Although devoid of a developmental paradigm, Kratus' (1994) model of compositional processes, discussed in chapter 2, also postulates a linear framework in which exploration is followed by a period of development, where ideas are revised and extended. The process culminates with a period of repetition, in which musical ideas are restated exactly, before the presentation of a replicable final product. In fact, Kratus defines composition as a product, "a fixed, replicable series of sounds or a set of directions for creating sounds" (1994, p. 129). Central to his argument is a distinction between composition as product and composition as process: "The process of composition as something separated in time from the performance of the product is one of the primary distinctions between composition and improvisation" (p. 129). This distinction, however, does not appear to operate with composition in the playground.

In the example "Teacher Teacher" above, the children would appear to have reached a product, a satisfactory end point of their compositional endeavors. However, this end point was circumstantial only, since the discussion and demonstration moved on to other game genres at the time. The more usual ongoing nature of creative activity in playground games can be demonstrated by a sequence of performances of "See See My Playmate" by the same group of children recorded in 1993 and 1994. An examination of this sequence reveals that children, during successive performances of a game, may collaboratively work through a succession of developmental compositional modes, composing a series of game variants that become more refined with each performance.

For example, the two performers of the first example, "See See My Play-mate" (SS 93 5) appear to be operating within the Speculative mode as they perform the vernacular triple-movement pattern with a new text derived from another published book of children's playlore texts (Factor and Marshall, 1992). As in the initial performance of "Teacher Teacher," the resultant textual rhythm is metrically ambivalent before assuming a regular duple meter (see full transcription in appendix 4).

The next variant, "Say Say My Playmate" (SS 93 6) was performed immediately following the first game by another pair of ten-year-old children from the same group (see full transcription in appendix 4). These performers seem to have moved into the Idiomatic mode, where the dissonant elements of triple-clapping pattern and duple textual rhythm have been integrated into a variant characterized by carefully regularized textual rhythmic patterns and consistent phrase lengths. There are still, however, some discrepancies between the two performers' vocal lines (particularly in relation to pitch). Performance practice appears to require that the triple-movement pattern be completed, even though it extends beyond the end of the textual and musical phrase. There has also been some modification of the movement rhythm at the beginning, to accommodate the duple meter of the text line. In this variant, the text is characterized by a reiterated symmetrical rhythmic figure:

Music Example 8.6

In the following performance (SS 93 7; see full transcription in appendix 4) three of the performers collaborate to substitute a new four-beat movement pattern which, because of the louder dynamic of the "clap own hands" movement, creates a syncopated relationship with the text rhythm:

Music Example 8.7

In addition, the melodic contour of the second, third, and fourth phrases is flattened out, developing the stepwise movement of the two final phrase endings of the previous version so that the symmetrical rhythm of these lines is now mirrored by a symmetrical melody:

Music Example 8.8

Once again, the control and regularity of rhythmic, melodic, and movement elements of this variant places its composer-performers within the Idiomatic developmental mode. It is therefore somewhat surprising to find that, on the same day, the final 1993 performance of this game by Ella, Annette, Hong-Soo, and Alicia (SS 93 8) displays less control of these elements, the destabilizing factor apparently being Hong-Soo's unfamiliarity with the full text and Ella's inability to perform simultaneously the full text and movement pattern.

In the following year, further changes had been made, the melody having been embellished by the addition of a leap of a third and a returning fifth. The substitution of a new seven-beat clapping pattern also created a different poly-metric relationship with the rhythm of the text (SS 94 3):

Music Example 8.9

It seems, then, that the compositional processes found in the production of playground singing games and game variants do not neatly fit the developmental model proposed by Swanwick and Tillman. It is more likely that the composer-performers of these game variants are, like the children in Davies's (1986, 1994) study of children's song composition, working simultaneously in a number of compositional modes. They appear to work through a cycle of experimentation, regularization and control, progressively introducing into the vernacular new elements that may be invented or come from a variety of sources (including written and audiovisual media, peers, and the classroom). Each new element has the potential to destabilize the performance before a new level of control is attained. The new elements may then be retained, reworked, or discarded, with experimentation continuing at virtually all stages of the process.

Continuing experimentation is therefore inherent in this form of composition. Kratus' emphasis on a fixed product as an implied indication of compositional craftsmanship and understanding seems misplaced. These children have a very highly developed understanding of what they are doing. The assumption that composition and improvisation are separate processes, with improvisation involving "inferior" levels of thought must also be questioned when the strategies used in developing and refining "Teacher Teacher" and "Say Say My Playmate" are considered. This assumption is outlined by Sloboda:

> Here, then, is the fundamental difference between improvisation and composition. The composer rejects possible solutions until he finds one which seems to be best for his purposes. The improviser must accept the first solution that comes to hand. . . . In composition . . . it is much more important to keep long-term structural goals in sight and to unify present material with what has gone before. (1985, p. 149)

What is also demonstrated by both the setting of "Teacher Teacher" and the set of variants of "Say Say My Playmate" is that these children have no difficulty in "keeping long-term structural goals in sight" and "unify[ing] present material with what has gone before" (Sloboda, 1985, p. 149). In fact, they appear to have the characteristic that Sloboda attributes to composers: a "superordinate plan" (1985, p. 103) or overall design for their compositions. This design includes an understanding of the interaction of formulaic elements, which are deployed with a high degree of musical complexity. This can be seen in the following discussion by these composer-performers in 1993:

ANNETTE: All clapping games are all the same.

ELLA: Like:

Music Example 8.10

My boy - friend gave me an ap - ple

My mo - ther works in the ba - ke - ry

ALICIA: See; they just keep on going up and down and up and down.

ELLA: Yeah:

Music Example 8.11

Da da da da da da da da da

K: OK, so it's just all the same kind of tune.

ANNETTE: Yeah. "Sar Macka Dora"'s different, but, because it's from another country.

ELLA: It's like every time you hit the hand it goes down:

Music Example 8.12

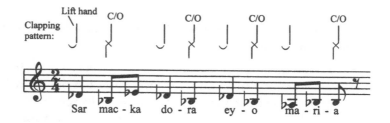

Sar mac - ka do - ra ey - o ma - ri - a

It goes down every time.

K: What goes down?

ELLA: The voice, the voice, the tune. The tune goes down.

What is evident from this transcript is that at least some children at Springfield not only had a clear conception of the formulaic construction of these games, but also a highly developed understanding of the structural relationship between the music and movement formulae used in the games. Their recognition of the melodic contours of the music formulae and the interplay between the melodic contour and the rhythmic accents provided by the clapping pattern is quite remarkable.

That this is not an isolated occurrence is illustrated by the explanations of several other children in different schools when discussing the parameters that must be considered in the generative process. For example, at Birch Vale in Seattle, nine-year-old Zach, who, prior to being recorded, had just demonstrated a rap and discussed how he had made it up, elaborated on the processes involved:

> K: Can you tell me again how you work out whether something fits with the rap or not? You were talking about rhyming or something.
>
> ZACH: Yeah. Like on that one rap I did, I did "everywhere" . . . and then "people on the stage just don't care." Everywhere and "just don't care" rhyme. If it's another word—if it's like "everywhere" and then something else and it doesn't rhyme they don't work.
>
> K: OK. And you said, you know, you were listening to the beats.
>
> ZACH: Yeah.
>
> K: So what do you mean by that?
>
> ZACH: I write songs on my own and I do the beats and there's one beat. Like how you do beats, you got to think of it and stuff in your mind and then you can play it out with your hands or your mouth.
>
> K: Yeah? And the beats—are they kind of in the words do you think . . . or is it something that's kind of behind the words? Can you explain it to me?
>
> ZACH: It's like behind the words but when you say the words it has to go like with the beat and stuff.

Zach was clearly aware not only of the textual requirements of rap, including the intricate forms of internal rhyme and word play, but also understood the way in which a rap must flow in relation to the underlying beats, referring both to "beat" in the more conventional sense, and "beats," in the sense of layers of sampled rhythmic and musical patterns that form a foundation on which the rhymes are built. Although his composition appeared to be an individual process, in reality it had a collaborative dimension. Zach explained that he checked his raps by performing them for his eighteen-year-old brother for endorsement and further refining. Charlotte, from the same school, also reported a similar process of consultation and refinement of her rap compositions.

In the more usual group approach to playground composition, eleven-year-old girls at Pada School in Busan displayed an equal grasp of musical requirements. They had initially made up the complex set of movements later applied to the "Digimon" game (see chapter 7) after trying out a wide range of movements. The movement sequence was originally devised to go with a classroom song, "Agi Yomso" (baby goat), and was worked out, as they told me, "according to the meter." In demonstrating how such movement formulae might be applied to other songs, they rejected a certain popular song because its meter was different from that of the movement formulae.

Because of the collaborative approach to composition, and the interdependence of composition and performance, this notion of design is dependent on a shared knowledge of the vernacular between group members. The presence of this design also indicates that some of the meta-cognitive processes found in the Symbolic stage of Swanwick and Tillman's model, seen by these authors to be characteristic of children from age 15 on (Swanwick and Tillman, 1986; Swanwick, 1988, 1991), can be found in the composition of much younger children.

The distinction between composition and improvisation may reflect a prevailing view of Western art music but is much less appropriate for music that is part of an oral tradition, as is the case with playground singing games. Nettl states that "music in oral tradition is normally composed by improvisation of a sort: the audible rendition of pieces . . . whose components may then be altered and recombined" (Nettl, in Randel, 1986, p. 392). Perhaps the definition of composition provided by Randel as "the activity of creating a musical work" (p. 182) is a more all-encompassing one, reflecting more directly the derivation of the word from the Latin *componere*, "to put together" (Randel, p. 182).

The assumed dichotomy between composition and improvisation may also derive partly from the consideration of a single improvisational event rather than the evolving cycle of composition and performance that characterizes this and many other orally transmitted genres. Multiple performances enable children to select and reject possible solutions rather than "accept the first solution that comes to hand" (Sloboda, 1985, p. 149). Webster's (1995, 2003) cyclical model of the creative process in music from which a final product may or may not emerge (as outlined in chapter 2) appears to integrate improvisation and composition in a way that more directly applies to children's techniques of innovation in this context. Similarly, Schafer's (1965, p. 37) admonition that "the form of the [improvisatory] work must be considered nothing less than the total sum of the work's transformations" may provide a more ac-

curate framework for assessing genres that exemplify composition in performance as a generative mode.

Such transformational processes were eloquently encapsulated by Charlotte, a ten-year-old girl from Bysiden School in Stavanger as she described the
way in which she and some friends had composed a game in celebration of my
presence in the school through initially singing it into being then through
adding formulae, reworking, and refining.

K: When you made that one up, how did you do that?

CHARLOTTE: I think I will have a song with you. And so I just begin
and sing. And so I sing and sing and sing. And I made it. I find up a song
for you.

INE: With clapping.

CHARLOTTE: With clapping.

K: OK. So you just sang it until it all came together, did you?

CHARLOTTE: Yes . . . and so I came to the song's melody. And so I found
up a melody from another song and so I sing it.

K: OK. So that melody comes from another song?

CHARLOTTE: Yes, from an English CD.

K: Oh, that's one you listen to on CD?

CHARLOTTE: Yes.

K: Yeah? What's the name of that song?

CHARLOTTE: I don't know. . . .

K: Do you hear it on the radio?

CHARLOTTE: Yeah, but I don't know.

K: You don't know the name of it. So you just got that melody from
the CD.

CHARLOTTE: Yeah. And so I think I can take that melody. And so I found
up "Kathryn Kathryn Kathryn Kathryn" and "we love you here in the
school" but . . . today I found up the whole song with another. She's name
Hege but I found it up and she help me. And so I have shown it to she
and we waiting there to the others. And so we can come in and show you.

K: Oh, well I'm very glad that you waited. So you made this up and Hege
helped you?

CHARLOTTE: Yes.

K: And then you taught it to Ine.

CHARLOTTE: Yeah.

K: Yes. OK, to show me. And how did you work out the clapping?

CHARLOTTE: I think of some other clapping game. And so I take some from that and some from that.

K: OK. So you took different clapping patterns from different games?

CHARLOTTE: Yeah.

K: Yeah? Where does "tra la la la la," where does that come from?

CHARLOTTE: That I found up.

K: You made that up?

CHARLOTTE: Yeah.

K: OK. And you made this [tries crossed arm clapping pattern] . . . Oh I can't do it.

CHARLOTTE: [Demonstrates clapping pattern] That?

K: Yes, that.

CHARLOTTE: No, that is "Åli Åli Ei."

K: So that one comes from "Åli Åli Ei"?

CHARLOTTE: Yeah.

K: Well it's made a very nice song for me, putting all these things together.

Although Charlotte's terminology is related to the fact that English is not her first language, in many ways her term "found up," is expressive of multiple features of the generative process. It combines the idea of "thought up" with that of finding and selecting appropriate material from already existing formulae or from the internalized palette of musical, textual, or kinesthetic materials that are brought up to consciousness and refined through performance with, and critical contributions of, collaborative friends.

Processes of Innovation in Children's Playground Singing Games in Field Schools

In considering the forms of compositional transformation that occur in children's playground singing games, it is perhaps more useful to draw on models of innovative processes used in other oral song traditions than on models of children's composition developed within an experimental research paradigm. Such processes include the re-organization of formulae; elaboration through the addition of new material or expansion of known material; condensation through omission or contraction of formulae and recasting of material (Barwick, 1994; Merrill-Mirsky, 1988). Table 8.1 gives examples of each of these processes as they apply to the three integral elements of text, music, and movement in playground singing games as observed at Springfield and other schools. It should be noted that this model represents techniques used by children in their musical play as observed in the field schools and does not purport to be a model of compositional activity for all children. Nevertheless, it gives an indication of the range of strategies in use by these children in their play.

From this table it can be seen that the children in these schools employ a vast range of techniques to vary their performances of playground singing games and other forms of musical play. This battery of innovative techniques conveys a sense of mastery and compositional skill much greater than that implied by Opie's (1994) statement quoted earlier: while any single technique might be considered a "minor wheeze" (Opie, 1994, p. 12), the use of multiple techniques to consciously change game material lends weight to the view that even young children are capable of complex compositional behaviors.

Although some of these techniques may be chance occurrences, we have seen that many children are conscious of the techniques used for variation. Variety is a highly desirable aspect of game performance practice in this playground. Reasons given for this include the avoidance of boredom, the promotion of further challenges, and the inclusion of group members, as attested by a group of Year 4 girls at Springfield in 1995. They were discussing their formulation of a new version of the game "Slide." This game had no text but was rhythmically complex, involving an initial seven-beat clapping formula that was gradually expanded using additive meters over ten consecutive iterations. Because of its complexity, it was usually played in pair formation. The variant devised by these girls was played by four or six performers in ring formation and involved switching between ring and pair clapping using higher or lower spatial levels at different points in the clapping pattern (⬤ VIDEO SAMPLE: video example *SpringF Slide*):

> K: And Clarissa, when you learnt it, did you learn it just with two people or did you. . . ?

> CLARISSA: Yes. Just with two people. And then we made up here the one. . . .

> K: Oh. So you've made up the doing it all together?

Table 8.1. Innovative Processes in Children's Playground Singing Games in Field Schools

Text	Music	Movement
Re-organization of Formulae		
Synthesis of textual formulae derived from several sources	Synthesis of melodic formulae derived from several sources	Synthesis of movement formulae derived from several sources
Re-ordering of formulae	Re-ordering of formulae	Re-ordering of formulae
Elaboration through Addition of New Material or Expansion of Known Material		
Addition of new text: —individual words —individual lines —stanzas —additive closing formulae	Additive meters resulting from cumulative addition of movement components	Cumulative addition of movement components
Addition of words or phrases to ensure consistency of phrase lengths of stanzas		
Addition of "scat" syllables to denote movement or extra-performance elements		
Condensation through Omission or Contraction of Formulae		
Truncation of line endings		Omission of movements
Extraction of textual formulae from larger constructions	Extraction of melodic formulae from larger constructions	Extraction of movement formulae from larger constructions
Truncation of closing formulae	Truncation of closing formulae	Truncation of closing formulae
Recasting of Material		
Word substitution, including localization and rationalization of text		
Translation of text from one language to another		
Variation in relationship of text and music to movement	Variation in relationship of text and music to movement	Variation in relationship of text and music to movement
Substitution of movement for text		Substitution of movement for text
Addition of movement formulae to texts or music derived from adult sources (e.g. written, audiovisual, teacher)	Addition of movement formulae to texts or music derived from adult sources (e.g. written, audiovisual, teacher)	Addition of movement formulae to texts or music derived from adult sources (e.g. written, audiovisual, teacher)

(continued)

Table 8.1. *(continued)*

Text	Music	Movement
Recasting of Material (continued)		
Addition of movement formulae to newly created texts	Addition of movement formulae to newly created melodies	Addition of movement formulae to newly created texts or melodies
		Substitution of different movements
		Use of different body parts
		Exaggeration of movements
		Changes to spatial relationship of performers
		Changes to spatial direction of movements
		Changes to grouping of performers
		Change of movement genre (e.g. from clapping game to dance sequence)
Hocketing of text and melody	Hocketing of text and melody	
	Changes to melodic contour	
	Alignment of melodic contour with rhythmic pattern (e.g. symmetrical melody aligned with symmetrical text rhythm)	

CLARISSA: Yeah

K: Who made it . . . so you can do it with either six or with four?

CLARISSA: Yeah

K: And who made that up?

ANDREA: Clarissa and Glenna.

GLENNA: We all sort of . . . I think it was me, Clarissa, Miranda, and Elsa that did the four one.

ANDREA: It wasn't me.

CLARISSA: Yeah, and then I kind of made up the six one.

GLENNA: Yeah, with Mirelle, Andrea, and all of us.

K: OK. Why did you decide to do that?

[Several talk at once; indistinct]

ANDREA: To make it more interesting.

MIRANDA: Yeah, it gets boring. . . .

CLARISSA: Yes. Like, 'cause we were getting a bit bored of doing it with just two people so we wanted to [indistinct] do something else.

GLENNA: So we tried to make it harder and. . . .

ANDREA: And to build up our skills. . . . Like if somebody makes mistakes then you help them.

GLENNA: Like if we do two and Miranda and Elsa want to do it as well, but they want to do it with us, like, it's easier just to. . . .

MIRANDA: Have four or six.

GLENNA: Yeah. Just have a four or a six.

K: So it's to, what, to include all of the group is it?

SEVERAL: Yeah.

GLENNA: Like, if there was only four of us there and then the other two didn't know how to do it and something, or we just wanted to do it, like, we didn't want to do it just with two, we wanted to do it with the whole group.

Children's consciousness of the strategies used in variation and reasons for varying was demonstrated through similar discussions on many occasions in different locations with performers from the ages of six onward. Such consciousness of variation, in addition to the complexity of innovative strategies illustrated in table 8.1, appears to transcend the expectations of compositional behaviors of children aged five to twelve years as extrapolated from experimentally derived models of composition. It is no coincidence that sophisticated levels of compositional skill are seen to emerge in other naturalistic environments where children are given the time and freedom to explore compositional activities either by themselves or collaboratively with others, as reported by Barrett, 1996, 2003; Borstad, 1990; Burnard, 1999, 2002, 2006; Christensen, 1992; Davies, 1986, 1994; DeLorenzo, 1989; Glover, 2000; Kanellopoulos, 1999; Loane, 1984; Pond, 1980/1992; Stauffer, 2001, 2002; Sundin, 1998; Wiggins, 1994, 1999, 2003; and Young, 2003).

In the following chapter, children's processes of variation are examined further through musicological analysis of one playground game genre, "Sar Macka Dora," which was found in nearly all field schools over the period from 1990 to 2004. The chapter provides a detailed account of the way in which this game is varied in each location and the influences that are brought to bear on children's variation processes in these different contexts.

CHAPTER 9

Variations on a Theme

"Sar Macka Dora"

The game genre "Sar Macka Dora" (SM game type), which I have called by the first name known to me, has been chosen for detailed analysis for a number of reasons. The first is my fascination with the high level of textual variability between performances of the game and its definition by the performers in terms of movement characteristics rather than text. Usually children will call a game by the first few words of the text. However, in this game genre, children consistently identified versions of the game with different texts as "the same game," even if the texts were newly composed or derived from another genre and bore no evident relationship to the prevailing text types.

This was particularly the case with children entering Springfield Primary School from other schools, who recognized and identified this game with the highly variant traditions found in the playgrounds of their previous schools. It was also the case with children whom I interviewed in Canberra in 1989 after I had introduced a version of the game to them at a children's music summer school (see chapter 1). All attested that they knew "this game but with different words" and proceeded to demonstrate a range of differing texts.

In adopting the classification system of the performers, I have therefore defined this genre in terms of its movements rather than its text, thus departing from the basis of the definition of other genres.[1] The game is an "elimination game" which, if played by more than two performers, involves multiple renditions of the text and associated movements, usually with the elimination, by counting out, of one performer at the culmination of each rendition or iteration. (See video example *Bysiden Slaa makaroni*.) Once the number of performers is reduced to two, the movements necessarily alter for the final performance. (🔺 **VIDEO SAMPLE**)

A second reason for selecting this genre is that it was the most frequently occurring game that I recorded over the complete fieldwork period. It was found in nine field schools in Sydney, central Australia, Norway, the southeast and north of England, and in Seattle and Los Angeles in the United States. I have recorded 144 performances of it, as shown in table 9.1.

During my first collection period at Springfield School in the 1990s, I discovered that this was an extremely popular game in this playground. This was apparent not only from the frequency of its performance (it was the third most frequently performed game in the recorded Springfield sample) but also by its nomination as a popular game by many of the children in the school. This was also the case at Bysiden, Ellington, Birch Vale, and Telford Spring schools almost a decade later and Segler's (1992) collection of children's games documents its appearance in many European locations. It is clear that this genre is part of a flourishing game tradition internationally.

Another characteristic that initially drew my attention to this genre was the mode of its transmission at Springfield school. Unlike many other game genres, SM was transmitted both by children in the playground and by teachers in the classroom, as attested by two Year 4 girls recorded in 1993:

K: Where did you learn that one?

ELLA: Kindergarten . . . [we've known that] for ages.

ANNETTE: We used to sit round in a circle in the classroom and then we sort of like just did it.

ELLA: I learnt it from her [pointing to Annette].

K: [To Annette] So did you learn that from the teacher?

ANNETTE: Yeah. One teacher taught us in kindergarten.

K: Right. [To Ella] But you're saying that you learnt it from other kids did you? You didn't learn it in the classroom?

ELLA: Yeah.

This dual mode of transmission in this school was partly the result of my own publication of a version of this game (in written and audio-recorded form) in a music-teaching kit for primary school teachers (Marsh, 1988). I had transcribed the published version of the game in the early 1980s from a version recorded by a teacher from another Sydney school. This version was disseminated through the kit to teachers in many schools throughout New South Wales, including Springfield. The specialist music teachers at the school had regularly taught this published version of the game to children entering the

Table 9.1. Samples of *Sar Macka Dora* Collected from 1990 to 2004

School	SM examples	Location	Year
Springfield Primary School	39	Sydney, Australia	1990, 1991, 1993, 1994, 1995
Telford Spring Primary School	14	Northern Territory, Australia	2001, 2002
Bysiden Skole	18	Stavanger, Norway	2002
Strandli Skole	2	Ryfylke, Norway	2002
Summerglen Lower School	5	Bedford, southeast England	2002
Ellington Primary School	31	Keighley, West Yorkshire, England	2002
St. Augustine's Primary School	8	Keighley, West Yorkshire, England	2002
Birch Vale Elementary School	17	Seattle, Washington, U.S.A.	2004
Nora Conn School	10	Los Angeles, California, U.S.A.	2004

school, either in kindergarten, or in the two Year 5 classes for gifted children. (See appendix 4 for a transcription of this version as taught in the classroom at Springfield.)

As with the *Sesame Street* version of "Down Down Baby," the published and teacher-disseminated version of SM created a consistently reiterated "template" of the game from which children in this school could derive their performances. It is possible, too, that another version of the game may also have entered the playground after being disseminated by a teacher at an earlier date, as I had used a version with a different text collected at another Sydney school (Arncliffe Primary School) at training courses for teachers in previous years. However, it is clear from the above statements of Annette and Ella, that playground transmission was equally important and often concurrent.

At Springfield School the game was also influenced by transmission between children that occurred outside of school, as discussed in chapter 7. For example, a seven-year-old girl explained that she had learnt two different versions of the game, one from a friend while waiting at ballet classes and another from an American teenager visiting her family. Both of these versions had, in turn, been transmitted to members of her friendship group. At other field schools, transmission was more usually reported as being from child to child at school, particularly within friendship groups. At Springfield the game was played by children from kindergarten to Year 6 and by both girls and boys, probably because it had been endorsed in the classroom, as discussed in chapter 5.

As a starting point in the analytical discussion that follows, I provide a detailed musicological analysis of attributes and forms of variation in the Springfield children's performances of this game genre. From this central "theme" of the chapter, shorter analyses of the performances of this game genre in other schools ensue, appearing almost as variations upon the main theme within the chapter. Although I conducted a complete analysis of all collected versions of this game, in this chapter, for reasons of brevity, I compare examples from selected schools, choosing one from Norway, one from the United Kingdom, and one from the United States.

As this chapter is musicological in intent, the language differs to some extent from that of the predominantly ethnographic descriptions of previous chapters, although the analyses are framed within the conditions that affect transmission and composition in performance within each individual school. I analyze the three elements of game performance: text, music, and movement, and focus on identifying attributes that are of some significance to the assumptions regarding characteristics of musical play that underlie music pedagogies, as discussed in chapter 1. Thus characteristics such as rhythm, range and tessitura, tonality, and melodic contour and intervals are closely examined. Short examples of text, music, and movement are provided to support particular points. Full musical transcriptions of selected performances that are discussed can be found in appendix 4.

Individual performances are designated by a code that indicates the location, the game genre (SM), the year it was recorded, and the chronological sequence in which it was recorded. For example, the code NC SM 04 8 indicates the eighth performance of the SM genre recorded in 2004 at Nora Conn School. It should be noted that, as pseudonyms have been used for all schools, the school code differs slightly from the pseudonym (for example, HV is the code used for the pseudonym "Birch Vale"). Because all recordings from 1990 to 1995 were made at Springfield Primary School, performances from this period do not include the location code in the text. As the defining element of this game is movement, rather than text, movement characteristics will be discussed first in this chapter.

Analysis of "Sar Macka Dora" Performances at Springfield Primary School (1990–1995)

As previously described, SM is an elimination or counting-out game, in which each of the performers is progressively eliminated by counting out at the end of each iteration of the text.[2] In the majority of performances at Springfield, the game was initially performed in a circle by three or more players who were gradually reduced to a pair through elimination. In the remaining performances, a single pair of performers played.

Movement Patterns

In the prevailing movement pattern, type 1, the movements are essentially the same for performers either in a circle or in pairs, although in a circle each performer will only be involved in clapping when the handclap reaches her/him in the circle, while in pairs, each performer will be involved in clapping on every beat. This movement type and its variations are described below in more detail.

Movement type 1 is found in twenty-seven performances: children sit either in a circle or in a pair facing each other; hands are horizontal and touch the hand of the performer on either side, with palms upturned and right hands on top of left hands. The clapping is initiated by one performer who claps with her/his right hand onto the left neighboring (or, in pairs, opposite) partner's right hand on the beat. (VIDEO SAMPLE: See video example *SpringF Son macaron*.) In this way the handclap is passed progressively in a clockwise direction around the circle on the beat. When the reiterated text "ch ch ch" or "tap tap tap" is recited, the performer clapping at that point claps the text rhythm (two quavers and a crotchet) instead of the beat. At the recitation of the final numeral, the child who is about to receive the handclap tries to withdraw his/her hand. If s/he avoids being clapped, s/he remains in the game and the person delivering the handclap is eliminated. If the delivery of the clap is successful, the person receiving the handclap is "out." The delivery of this final handclap is frequently subject to a great deal of feinting (tricking movements) with a number of associated rules. These rules, however, tend to be idiosyncratic to particular performing groups.

A second movement type operates in some of the ring performances of a group of Year 6 children of both sexes. It is essentially the same as movement type 1 but differs in that performers clap their own left hand first before passing the handclap on to the performer on their left. If a performer claps his/her own left hand on the final numeral, he or she is not eliminated from the game but, instead, the hand is eliminated and put behind the performer's back.

Two different movement types (types 3 and 4) are related to a limited number of pair rather than group performances. It is notable that movement type 3 had apparently been introduced to a Year 5 group by a new member, Sunni, who came into the class for gifted children from another school, and was introduced to a Year 1 group by Celia who had learnt it from her American friend. Once again this movement type is rhythmically identical to movement type 1 but involves a different hand placement and hand movements.

Hands are held facing and alternating with partner's hands, either vertically or horizontally. The clap by one player connects with the palm of the other player's hand, pushing the back of the partner's hand onto the other palm of the clapper. The final movement in the vertical hand version involves the hand of one player being withdrawn then feinting upward, the other player trying to catch it between both hands.

The fourth movement type was also introduced by children who entered the gifted class from other schools. Again this type is rhythmically identical to movement type 1 but the hand movements differ. These involve the gripping of right hand by partner's right hand and the rotation of the hands from right to left on the beat or relevant text rhythm. As with movement type 3, there are differences between the two performance groups in the elimination movements.

The dominance of movement type 1 is evident from its appearance in the performances of all groups except those who had only recently entered the school population. Some groups adopted several different movement types in their performances. It is possible that movement type 3 represents another tradition that was developing in the school, as it is found in the repertoire of the much younger groups. Given that the members of one group were also drawn from a wide variety of schools, movement type 2 may also have been imported into this playground from another, or it may have been a variant that developed within this class group.

Text

As discussed above, this genre is characterized by a high level of textual variability. In this school, two distinct text types are prevalent, with two additional text types being identified. A feature of almost all the texts within this genre is the use of vocables in varying proportions and of numerals to facilitate counting out in the final line. On several occasions children discussed the text's lack of meaning, attributing it to a supposed origin in another culture. For example, as described in chapter 5, the text was nominated in 1994 as "Italian" by one group and "Aboriginal" by another. There are three discernible categories of texts with shared characteristics within this genre and an additional category of related texts. All are characterized by assonance, alliteration, and internal repetition.

The first text type is usually a five-line text with internal repetition of lines (lines 3 and 4) and individual syllables. Given that this is the text type of the published version taught in the classroom, it is not surprising that it is found in the majority of performances recorded in this school (twenty-one performances in all). The published text, as taught by the music teacher in 1995, is outlined in table 9.2.[3]

Table 9.2. Text Type I, SM Performances at Springfield

Line		Text	Rhyme	Syllables
1.	Sar macka dora	a	a	5
2.	Eyo maria I maria	b	a	8
3.	Eyo eyo ch ch ch	c	b	7
4.	Eyo eyo ch ch ch	c	b	7
5.	One two three	d	c	3

In eleven performances the counting out in line 5 is extended to ten. In this text type, the numerals in line 5 constitute the only section of the text that is meaningful to the performers. The three repeated vocables at the end of lines 3 and 4, characteristic of this text type, are cues for a change in the movement pattern at these points.

The second text type, found in five performances (video example *SpringF Son macaron*), is clearly related structurally to text type 1 and again usually consists of five lines, with internal repetition of the vocables in lines 1 to 4 and repetition between lines 3 and 4. This text type, shown in table 9.3, also features the reiterated movement cues in lines 3 and 4. (🅐 **VIDEO SAMPLE**)

In its most usual form (for example in SM 93 1), this text type closely resembles the text of the game collected at Arncliffe Public School in 1982 (see previous discussion of this genre's transmission). Although it was recorded by two performance groups in 1990, with one exception it had apparently been maintained in its original or transitional form by only one recorded friendship group over a four-year period of recording to 1994. It would seem, then, that this text type was the vestige of a previous performance tradition that had gradually lost popularity and been supplanted by the new teacher-transmitted text type 1. It is curious, then, that an expanded variant form of this text type, with markedly different patterns of repetition, is found in two performances of a much younger performance group in 1994, as shown in table 9.4. A visiting

Table 9.3. Text Type II, SM Performances at Springfield

Line		Text	Rhyme	Syllables
1.	Son macaron	a	a	4
2.	Son ferio ferio ferio	b	b	10
3.	Leya leya tap tap tap	c	c	7
4.	Leya leya tap tap tap	c	c	7
5.	One two three	d	d	3

Table 9.4. Expanded Text Type II, SM Performances at Springfield

Line		Text	Rhyme	Syllables
1.	Sor macaron	a	a	4
2.	Son ferio ferio ferio	b	b	10
3.	Son ferio	b1	b	4
4.	Sor macaron	a	a	4
5.	Son ferio	b1	b	4
6.	1 2 3 4 5 6 7 8 9 10 11 12 13 14 15 16 17 18 19 20	c	c	32

American friend had reportedly taught this version of the text to one member of the group (Celia).

A third text type is derived from the text of another game genre, "Down by the Banks" (DBB), but has, in common with text types I and II, counting out, either numerically or alphabetically, in the final line. It is found in a single performance of one Year 6 group in 1990 and in the performances in 1993 of two Year 2 groups with members in common. The performances by these groups have a five-line structure, as for text types I and II. The text is outlined in table 9.5.

This text type has been reported in conjunction with this game genre in Los Angeles by Merrill-Mirsky (1988, pp. 162–63) and Riddell (personal communication, 1995) and was the most common text type in the examples that I collected in Canberra in 1989 (see chapter 1) and later at Ellington School in West Yorkshire and Nora Conn School in Los Angeles. It was, however, a much less dominant text type at Springfield.

A number of other texts were performed within this movement-defined genre but were otherwise unrelated to each other. For example, one performance, described in chapter 7, was improvised by a large Year 6 group, using preexisting texts derived from a variety of sources, including a television adver-

Table 9.5. Text Type III, SM Performances at Springfield

Line		Text	Rhyme	Syllables
1.	Down by the banks of the hanky panky	a	a	10
2.	Where the bullfrogs jump from bank to bank	b	a1	9
3.	With a hip hop lollipop	c	b	7
4.	With a hip hop belly flop	c1	b	7
5.	One two three	d	c	3

tisement for underpants, several nursery rhymes, and a popular published playlore text.

The close relationship between text types I and II seems to facilitate the textual elision of the two forms in a number of performances. For example, "tap tap tap" (from text type II, lines 3 and 4) is often substituted for "ch ch ch" in the same location in performances of text type I. In some performances, however, elements of the two text types are more evenly distributed. This may result in transitional texts where the superimposition of the two text types creates new syllable relationships, as in the example shown in table 9.6, performed by two girls who had entered the gifted class from a neighboring school.

As can be seen from a number of examples above, the lack of semantically identifiable content in the majority of texts in this genre would seem to account for the high degree of phonetic substitution in the text. Thus, the initial syllable in text type I occurs as "sar," "sor," "sun," "sa," and "san" in this playground. This may also account, to some extent, for the development of the two distinct text types, I and II, within the wider interschool community, in addition to other text forms such as that exemplified by SM 95 3 imported from the nearby school.

The lack of semantic content of the majority of the text in text types I and II also explains another form of textual variation, the expansion or contraction of lines by the addition or deletion of vocables, seemingly at will. Variation by expansion is more common, for example:

Sor macka dora
Ayu ayu maria maria maria

Some older children in this playground are certainly conscious of this form of variability, as elaborated by a Year 5 girl in 1994:

ALICIA: I was just thinking, "Sar Macka Dora" has changed a tiny bit because when I was little we used to go:

Sar macka dora
Eyo mario mario mario
[some intervening discussion]
Eyo eyo tap tap tap
Eyo eyo one two

And we'd like leave out, we'd only do one tap tap tap but we'd put in three marios and two eyos before it. We used to go:

Eyo eyo mario mario mario

and then it is like slightly, same words and everything but slightly different amounts of each word which could make the song not make sense.

Table 9.6. Transitional Text Example, SM Performances at Springfield

Line	SM 95 4	Text	Rhyme	Syllables
1.	Sar macka do	a	a	4
2.	Oh stedio macka do macka do	b	a	10
3.	Leyo leyo tap tap tap	c	b	7
4.	Leyo leyo tap tap tap	c	b	7
5.	One two three	d	c	3

Line 2 is the site of the greatest amount of variation of this kind. The breaking of line 2 into two phrases by the school music teacher in her teaching of the game may contribute to the children's view of the text of line 2 as having additive properties. However, line 5 in text types I and II is also subject to expansion (by increasing numerals, as previously discussed) or contraction, by substituting movements for the final numeral.

Text Setting

In this genre at Springfield, text setting is entirely syllabic. The one exception to this utilizes the text and melody of a television advertisement and cannot be said to be representative of the genre as a whole. In two text type III performances the text was performed as a hocket, with individual words being delivered by each performer in turn around the circle.

Text Rhythm

With the exception of two text type III performances, all items within this genre are consistently duple metrically. However, difficulties with negotiating changes to clapping patterns, which occur at three main points in this game, may add rhythmic value to a line of text. The addition of numerals to the final line of text types I and II also results in the addition of rhythmic value to this line, as do the frequent feinting and evasive movements associated with the recitation of the final numeral which determines who will be eliminated from the game in most text types.

Categories of text rhythm in this genre closely parallel the text types discussed previously. Thus, there are four categories of text rhythm that can be identified in this genre. Text rhythm type I corresponds exactly with text type I. Type I text rhythms consist of two two-beat motifs using crotchets and paired quavers in lines 1, 3, and 4, with an expanded line usually comprising six beats in line 2 and an expanded or contracted line 5, depending on the number of numerals recited:

Music Example 9.1

The expansion of text is almost always accommodated by additive rhythms while retaining the duple meter, for example:

Music Example 9.2

The second rhythmic type was performed with text type II. In most performances it is identical to text type I from lines 3 to 5. However, it differs from text type I in regard to the displacement of the first syllable of line 2 as an anacrusis. Thus, the most commonly occurring form of text rhythm type II is: SM 93 I (fourth iteration):

Music Example 9.3

However, the interruption of the anacrusic pattern at the end of line 2, in order to begin line 3 on a stressed beat, is the cause of considerable rhythmic variation at this point. The rhythm of line 2 may be curtailed by the omission or truncation of the rest at the end of the line, sometimes creating disparities between the rhythms of different iterations within a single performance.

The third rhythmic type (type IIIA) was more usually associated with another game genre (DBB). It consists of two compound duple phrases in lines 1 and 2, the first nonsyncopated and the second involving both syncopation and anacrusis:

Music Example 9.4

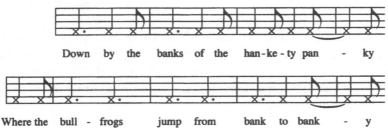

Line 3 consists of single-beat syllables with an anacrusis, the line length being determined by the duration of the feinting and evasion before the final clap:

Music Example 9.5

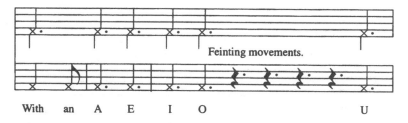

However, another text rhythm (type IIIB) occurs in two performances of this text (DBB 93 4 and 11) by members of one friendship group. It is ametric, consisting almost entirely of unstressed crotchet beats corresponding with hand movements and punctuated by crotchet rests from lines 3 to 5. Lengths of intervening rests vary because the movement conditions of these particular performances create an inherent instability. The markedly different rhythm seems to be derived from the performance practice of DBB 93 11, which is performed as a hocket, with each word being recited by each performer in turn as they either receive and/or pass the handclap around the circle. This practice results in an augmentation of the rhythmic values that are more usually associated with performances of this text (see text rhythm type IIIA): DBB 93 11. Letters above the manuscript indicate the name of the performer who is reciting the syllable.

Music Example 9.6

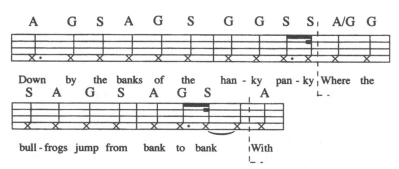

The intervening rests in lines 3 to 5 are linked to the usual rendition of this text, DBB, associated with different movements in this playground. This rhythmic feature is also found in the Los Angeles form of this game that I collected at Nora Conn School, although the duration of the rests in some performances is also affected by variation in the duration of the clapping movements:

Music Example 9.7

Relationship of Text Rhythm and Movement Pattern

Variation of the text rhythm is closely linked with the nature of the idiosyncratic movements of this game genre. The most obvious point of movement-influenced variation is in the final line of the texts, particularly in the majority of text types that involve counting out using numerals. The level of variation that may result from the practice of feinting can be clearly seen in a comparison of the final lines of two iterations of SM 94 7:

Music Example 9.8

First iteration:

One   two   three

Fourth iteration:

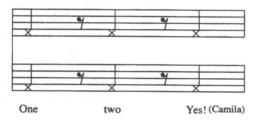

One   two   Yes! (Camila)

The relationship between the text and movement rhythms at the ends of lines 3 and 4 of text types I and II is quite clear:

Music Example 9.9

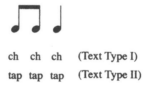

ch ch ch   (Text Type I)

tap tap tap   (Text Type II)

Melody

Melodic range varies between a perfect fourth and a minor seventh, with a perfect fifth being the most common range. Tessitura for the genre at Springfield lies between G below middle C and B♭ above middle C:

Music Example 9.10

In the majority of performances, however, the range lies between B♭ below middle C and G above. Interestingly, the most common tessitura for individual performances lies between middle C and the G above, which is the pitch of the published version, both as notated and as taught by the specialist music teacher at the school. Range is otherwise linked to melodic type, as discussed below. Five items were performed at completely indefinite pitch.

This genre is characterized by melodic contours[4] that are cyclical only for two of the five text lines in the two prevailing melodic types. Three of the other melodic types have no cyclical melodic contours. One of the musical characteristics that emerged in my study of other genres of children's playground games at Springfield (Marsh, 1997) was the idiosyncratic tonality, whereby the initial tone of the melody became its tonal center. Within this SM genre the initial pitch functions as a tonal center but its pre-eminence is achieved not only by frequency of occurrence but in a variety of other ways, depending on melodic type. These will be discussed in relation to each of the melodic categories below.

The first melodic type, corresponding with text type I, is the melodic form of the published example of this game taught by the music teacher. It is, not surprisingly, found in the majority of performances of this genre. It is built up of a falling minor third and conjunct major seconds at either end of the melodic range, with one bridging interval of a perfect fourth and interpolated text of indefinite pitch at the end of lines 3 and 4. The culminating line is of indefinite pitch. Melodic range in this type is a perfect fifth:

Line

1	g - e - a - g - e
2	g - e - d - e - d - e
3	g - e - g - e - ind
4	g - e - g - e – ind
5	Indefinite

In this melodic type, the initial pitch is not the most frequently occurring, but it maintains its status as a tonal center through its reiteration at the beginning of every text line (with the exception of the indefinitely pitched final line).[5]

The second melodic type (video example *SpringF Son macaron*) consists predominantly of conjunct major and minor seconds, melodic movement therefore always being stepwise, with the exception of a falling minor third at the beginning of line 1. (▲ VIDEO SAMPLE) As in type I melodies, the final line is at indefinite pitch. However, in this melodic type, the three reiterated words at the end of lines 3 and 4 are set to a stepwise melody, instead of indefinite pitch. Melodic range in this type is a perfect fourth:

Line

1	g - e - f - g
2	a - g - f - e - f - g - e - f - g
3	g - a - g - f - e - f - g
4	g - a - g - f - e - f - g
5	indefinite

In this melodic type, the initial note is the most frequently occurring and recurs on the first accented syllable of each line, as well as the last syllable of each line, thus maintaining a tonal dominance.

The third melodic type is performed at completely indefinite pitch throughout. It is found in conjunction with all performances of text type III. A range of other variant melodies is found in performances of other variant texts. Perhaps the most unusual is in the performance by girls originally from a nearby school (SM 95 4). It is characterized by the use of melodic sequences and differs from all other types through its more frequent use of large melodic leaps, including a perfect fourth, perfect fifth, and augmented fourth. Consequently the melodic range is greater than that of other melodic types, stretching to a minor seventh:

Line

1	g - e - f - g
2	c' - c' - a - d - e - f - d - e - f
3	b - a - g
4	b - a - g
5	indefinite

As in melodic type II, the initial note is the most frequently occurring.

Transition from one melodic type to another can occur when the melodic characteristics of type II melodies are juxtaposed with those of type I, usually at the end of the second line. This contributes to the level of melodic variety found in this genre at Springfield.

Summary of Springfield Analysis

It can be seen that transmission practices were influential in determining the degree and forms of variation in performances of this genre at Springfield. The continued transmission of this game through classroom teaching led to the increasing dominance of one text and melodic type over a period of time. At the same time, the idiosyncratic movement characteristics of the game ensured that variation within designated textual and melodic forms has continued through playground transmission. In this genre, the relative stability and simplicity of the movement type, in addition to the text's lack of semantic content, seems to allow for greater textual variation and melodic complexity. External sources of melodic, textual, and movement material also continue to exert influences of change on the performance practices of this game. However, the version taught in the classroom is a stabilizing influence.

Features of melody, range, and tonality will now be further explored as performances of the genre at other field locations are examined. As the size of the sample and characteristics of performances at different locations varied, several sites have been selected for more detailed analytical attention. Text types from all field localities are included in a comparative table in appendix 3.

Variation 1: "Sar Macka Dora" Genre at Bysiden

Both the movements and the text in the 18 performances of this game at Bysiden placed it securely within the parameters of the SM genre. Although performances by pairs were more prominent than those by groups in a circle, the movements were identifiably those of this genre and are discussed later in this section. A group performance can be seen in the video example *Bysiden Slaa Makaroni.* (⬤ VIDEO SAMPLE). See appendix 4 for a transcription of the first iteration of this performance.)

In almost all instances, the game was performed with a five-line text characterized by internal repetition of lines (lines 3 to 5) and of individual syllables. Wordplay was evident in the patterns of rhyme, assonance, and alliteration that abounded in the text, illustrated in table 9.7. English translations of the Norwegian text are shown in brackets.

The text of all performances of the game at Bysiden corresponds most directly with Springfield text type I (although there is one less syllable in line 2). However, there are elements of text type II in the first line ("macaron" at Springfield and "makaroni" at Bysiden). Text setting in all performances of this genre is entirely syllabic, as was found at Springfield.

Text Rhythm

As for Springfield, this text type has two two-beat motifs utilizing crotchets and paired quavers in lines 1, 3, and 4 (though lines 3 and 4 generally end in a clipped syllable notated as a quaver). The second line is usually expanded to six beats and there is an expanded or contracted line 5, depending on the num-

Table 9.7. Text of SM Performances at Bysiden

Line		Text	Rhyme	Syllables
1.	Slå makaroni [Slap macaroni]	a	a	5
2.	Tiam basta marasta	b	b	7
3.	Tiam tiam bass bass bass	c	c	7
4.	Tiam tiam bass bass bass	c	c	7
5.	Ein to tri [One two three]	d	d	3

ber of numerals recited and the space between their recitation. While the usual number of numerals is three, in a significant proportion of performances the final elimination clap is substituted for the recitation of "tri" (three). The standard form of the text rhythm is illustrated below.

Music Example 9.11

Variations in this text rhythm tend to occur either as a result of deliberate changes to the text or because of difficulties with the performance. For example, the second iteration of B SM 02 4 has an additional paired quaver "tiam" at the beginning of line 3 due to one player's memory lapse.

In B SM 02 5 an additional formula "oh baby," "oh baby baby," or "baby" is found in 8 of the 12 iterations. Though most frequently consisting of a crotchet and a pair of quavers, this formula is highly rhythmically variable:

Music Example 9.12

A more conscious form of rhythmic variation can be observed in one of four iterations of B SM 02 7, where "tiam" in the third and fourth lines is elided to form a crotchet rather than two quavers:

Music Example 9.13

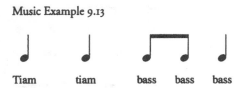

Although there is a slight modification of the second line with a resultant change to the text rhythm in B SM 02 8 (performed by Charlotte and Ine from class 5), the line maintains its six-beat length:

Music Example 9.14

This performance also has an unusual clapping pattern, vacillating between a triple and four-beat pattern. This group is known for innovation, and their performances involve several variants. There also appear to be age-related performance traditions.

Tessitura and Melodic Range

The tessitura and melodic range appropriate to children's songs has been a focus of some conjecture within pedagogical literature; other research into children's playground games has indicated that there may be considerable discrepancy between the tessitura of published songs for children and those performed by children within their own milieu (Campbell, 1991). For this reason, I have analyzed this aspect of SM performances. At Bysiden, there was a considerable variation in range between iterations, as well as between performances, so I have included these variations in the analysis, as shown in table 9.8.

As can be seen from both tables 9.8 and 9.9, performances (or iterations) of this game at Bysiden most frequently begin on B or B♭ below middle C with an upward range of major or minor 7. This range is generally greater than that

Table 9.8. Melodic Range and Tessitura of SM Performances at Bysiden

Performance	Range (Multiple Iterations)	Intervallic Range
B SM 02 1	c-b	maj 7
B SM 02 2	c-c#; c-d; e♭-e; c#-b♭; d-c#	min 9, maj 9, min 9, maj 6, maj 7
B SM 02 3	d-c#; d-d	maj 7, 8ve
B SM 02 4	b-a; b♭-a♭	min 7
B SM 02 5	b♭-c; c-a; b-g#; b-a; b-a#; a-g; b-g#; b♭-a; b♭-b; b♭-a (g#-e♭); b-a (g#-d); c-b	maj 7, maj 6, maj 6, min 7, maj 7, maj 7, maj 7, min 9, maj 7, (per 5), min 7 (aug 4), maj 7
B SM 02 6	b-a	min 7
B SM 02 7	b-g; b-a♭; b-g; a-e	min 6, maj 6, min 6, per 5
B SM 02 8	g-f	min 7
B SM 02 9	b♭-a	maj 7
B SM 02 10	b-b♭; a#-g#; b-a; b♭-g	maj 7, min 7, maj 6
B SM 02 11	c#-a	min 6
B SM 02 12	b-b♭	maj 7
B SM 02 13	c#-a	min 6
B SM 02 14	b-b♭	maj 7
B SM 02 15	Not transcribed	
B SM 02 16	c-b♭; b-a; b-g#; b-a♭; b-a	min 7, maj 6, maj 7, min 7

Table 9.9. Frequency of Range of SM
Performances at Bysiden (Notated Examples)

Interval	Frequency of Occurrence
Maj 7	13
Min 7	8
Maj 6	7
Min 6	4
Min 9	3
Per 5	2
8ve	1
Maj 9	1
Aug 4	1

of Springfield performances of the genre, where the most frequent range was a perfect fifth. This is in keeping with the larger melodic range of the majority of Bysiden games.

Tonal Frequency and Tonal Shift

As previously stated, a characteristic of several game genres that emerged in my study of children's playground games at Springfield (Marsh, 1997) was the unique tonality, whereby the initial tone of the melody became its tonal center, either because it was the most frequently occurring tone, or because it was reiterated at line beginnings or points of rhythmic or textual emphasis. [6] This characteristic was therefore specifically explored in subsequent analyses of the SM genre in its various international locations.

As the games from the 2002 and 2004 field collections were being transcribed, another tonal characteristic became evident. This was the apparent proclivity of children to shift the tonal focus from one tone to another at a change of text line or textual/melodic formula. This typically occurred in the form of a gradual downward displacement of pitch, generally by degrees of a semitone or tone.[7] An investigation of this tonal characteristic was therefore also incorporated into melodic analysis of the games collected in Norway, the United Kingdom, and the United States.

In ten of the fifteen notated performances at Bysiden the initial tone functions as the tonal center of the song by virtue of its frequency of occurrence. In the majority of performances, this tone is also emphasized by occurring at line beginnings or on accented notes in at least two text lines. However, there is also a sense in most performances that the tonal focus of each separate formula shifts, most frequently at the beginning of the third and/or fourth text lines. Generally this shift is by a tone or semitone, with the initial note of line 4 usually dropping a tone or semitone from that of line 3 (an identical textual formula).

Melody

The melody of the initial line is the most stable, being found in eight of the fifteen performances. The melody for line 2 is identical for six performances. Melodic contours of these lines are shown in table 9.10.[8] Of the five performances with a textual variant in line 2, two have the same melodic contour (shown in table 9.10).

The remaining performances have melodies consisting of intervals of major and minor seconds and thirds that adhere to the shape of the melodic contours shown (that is, in terms of upward or downward melodic movement) but vary in relation to the actual intervals used at any one point.

Lines 3 and 4 are textually identical. The melodic formula employed for this textual formula consists of two alternating notes (most frequently a falling minor third but sometimes a major second or major third) followed by an upward melodic leap of anything between a third and a sixth, this note being reiterated three times. As with the preceding lines, there is a high level of variability in the actual intervals, but stability of melodic shape. The level of variability of lines 3 and 4 can be seen in table 9.11.[9]

Intervals vary both between performances and between performers. Some performative variation, for example the hocketing of text in B SM 02 9, appears to influence the relative "accuracy" of the pitches. However, it would appear that maintaining melodic contours, rather than exact pitch accuracy, is most important to the performers of this genre in this school. As in the majority of performances of this genre, the final line (line 5 at Bysiden) is at an indefinite pitch for all performances, presumably to facilitate concentration on the counting-out aspect of the movement at this point.

Table 9.10. Melodic Contours of Bysiden SM Performances, Lines 1–2

Line	Melodic contour	Performances
1	g e f g c¹	B SM 02 1, 2, 3, 4, 5, 10, 12, 16
2	g e f d e f d	B SM 02 1, 2, 4, 5, 10, 16
2 text var	g e f g e f g e	B SM 02 11, 12

Table 9.11. Melodic Contours of Bysiden SM Performances,
Lines 3–4

Line	Melodic contour	Performances
3	g e g e b♭	B SM 02 1
3	g e g e b	B SM 02 2, 4, 8, 13
3	g f g f c b♭	B SM 02 3
3	g d g d a	B SM 02 5, 11
3	g e g e c	B SM 02 6
3	g f g f b♭	B SM 02 7
3	g f g f b	B SM 02 9
3	g f g f a	B SM 02 10
3	g e g e g#	B SM 02 12, 16
4	g e g e c#	B SM 02 1
4	g e g e b d# c#	B SM 02 2
4	g e g e b	B SM 02 3, 4
4	g e g e c# c b	B SM 02 5
4	g e g e c	B SM 02 6
4	g e g e g#	B SM 02 7
4	g e g e a	B SM 02 8, 11, 12, 16
4	g e g e ‖ c d e♭	B SM 02 9 (hocketed 2 performers)
4	g f g f g	B SM 02 10
4	g e g e a#	B SM 02 13
4	g e♭ g e♭ a♭	B SM 02 14

Movement

Except for two performances, the standard passing clap of the SM genre (Springfield movement type 1) is utilized, with the clap on the beat. At Bysiden, where pair performances predominated, only six instances of the larger group circle formation were observed, and members of these larger groups sometimes initiated game playing in pairs. The usual two-person form at Bysiden is that of the right hand gripping the partner's hand and moving it alternately from right to left on the beat, correlating with the Springfield movement type 4. In one performance the two players move thumbs instead of whole hands, and in another the clapping pattern appears to be a variant of the triple clap with an additional single handclap inserted.

The rhythm of movements for the final line is generally three crotchets, or three crotchets alternating with crotchet rests. These movements coincide with the articulation of the text "ein, to, tri." As with other performances of this genre, however, the regularity of the rhythm (particularly the final elimination clap) is disturbed by feinting movements that may augment the length of the final line.

Other Forms of Variation

As found in the Springfield sample, the lack of semantically identifiable content in the text leads to a range of slight textual variations, for example "pasta" or "pass pass pass" and "mapasta." Unusually, these forms of variation were not evident in performances of this game at St. Augustine's, due to the meaningful nature of the texts of this genre at the school.

Variation 2: "Sar Macka Dora" Genre at St. Augustine's

I have chosen to discuss SM genre at this English school because the prevailing form of the game there is different from any others that I recorded, with quite idiosyncratic movements. Although the school was located only a mile away from Ellington, the performance practices of this game were quite disparate in many ways, though there were also similarities.

There are two distinct text types for this genre as performed at St. Augustine's. The first type, known by its performers as "Down in the Jungle," begins with the same initial word as that of one form of this game from Ellington but diverges completely from this point. There were six recorded performances of this text type at St. Augustine's and it seemed to be the most generally known form of the game in the school. Performances of this text type were notable for the large groups that played them, several performances having nine or more performers. In addition, there was an idiosyncratic rendition of the movements, with individual body parts (two hands then head) being eliminated in turn. This meant that these performances had multiple iterations, many more than were usual in performances of this genre in other schools. As performers' hands were eliminated, the movements became more exaggerated, with performers trying to pass the beat with their heads or upper bodies and performances of this version of the game often became increasingly ebullient. (● **VIDEO SAMPLE:** See video example *St Aug Down in jungle*.) The text of this form of the game is shown in table 9.12.

Line 1 uses an identical text formula to a game recorded by Opie and Opie (1988) in Dundee, Scotland in 1975 (though melodically there is no similarity). There are two minor textual variants. The most frequently occurring is the ad-

Table 9.12. Text Type 1, SM Performances at St. Augustine's

Line		Text	Rhyme	Syllables
1.	Down in the jungle where nobody goes	a	a	10
2.	There's a big fat gorilla, pickin' his nose	b	a	11
3.	He picks it and he flicks it to see how far it goes	c	a	13
4.	Who's gonna get that, who's gonna get that	c	b	10
5.	Who's gonna get that slimy snot?	d	c	8

dition of "and" to the beginning of text line 3, thereby augmenting the line by one syllable:

And he picks it and he flicks it to see how far it goes.

The other variant is the elision of "he picks" and/or "to see" into single syllables, for example:

H'picks it to flicks it t'see how far it goes

Unusually for this game genre, there are no vocables in the text. This, in addition to the subversive content, probably contributes to the relative stability of the text.

A second text type was also performed at Ellington. It consists of a recitation of the alphabet from A to Z, with the final elimination clap on Z. There were two performances of this text type recorded at St. Augustine's, both performed by a grade-4 group of girls of predominantly Pakistani descent. The texts of both text types are completely syllabically set. There is no hocketing (alternation of text between players) in any performances.

Text Rhythm

As for other examples of this genre, text rhythms correspond with text types. Text type 1 is stable in terms of the length of the text line, which remains within an eight-beat basic line structure throughout all performances. However, there is considerable disparity between the subdivision of beats both between performances and between iterations within performances. The first two lines are relatively stable in that they adhere almost exclusively to a triple subdivision of the beat. The final two lines are least stable in that beats are subdivided into triplet, paired quavers, and dotted quaver–semi-quaver pairs. Line 3 also exhibits instability in accommodating the textual variants listed above.

The most internally stable performance between iterations is ST SM 02 7, somewhat surprisingly given the rather chaotic rendition toward the end of the performance (where a large group of girls who have been eliminated congregate in the middle of the circle performing mimetic movements, as discussed further below). (See appendix 4 for a transcription of one iteration of this performance.)

Music Example 9.15 Text rhythm ST SM 02 7 (Iteration 7)

As can be seen, there is a high level of syncopation in the second half of lines 1 and 2 and an anacrusis at the beginning of line 3, though this varies in length with the addition or elision of text. Variation occurs mainly through the substitution of paired quavers for crotchet–quaver triplets, for example:

Music Example 9.16 ST SM 02 2 Iteration 6 Line 2

There's   a   big   fat   go-rill - a   pick - in   his   nose.

Music Example 9.17 ST SM 02 4 Iteration 1 Line 3

And   he   picks it and he flicks it   to   see how far it goes.

Similarly, crotchet-quaver triplets or dotted quaver-semiquaver pairs can be substituted for paired quavers in the final two lines. Interestingly, the length and regularity of the final line in which the elimination occurs is quite stable in all of the notated performances, with no hesitations or movement intrusions.

The text rhythm of text type 2 is similar to the ametrical performances of this text type at Ellington (and to hocketed performances of the genre at Springfield). Each syllable of the alphabet (except W) is recited with the approximate duration of a crotchet. However, the duration between each syllable is of irregular length that was virtually impossible to notate. A system of proportional notation was devised to indicate the relative lengths of each syllable, with the total length of the performance indicated in seconds. For example, ST SM 02 5 appears as:

Music Example 9.18

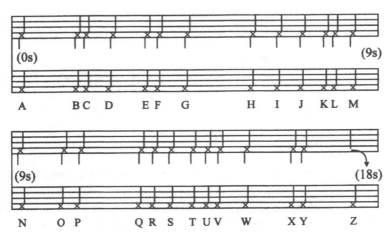

Tessitura and Melodic Range

There is only one melodic type found in this school, as text type 2 is at an indefinite pitch throughout. Performances of text type 1 most frequently begin on B, B♭, middle C, or middle C#. However, as can be seen in table 9.13, the tessitura of each performance often went just below this starting note, the most frequently occurring tessitura being from A below middle C to F or G above. The most common range was a perfect fifth, though ranges of a seventh or sixth were not uncommon, as shown in table 9.14.

Tonal Frequency and Tonal Shift

It was frequently difficult to transcribe pitches of performances of "Down in the Jungle" accurately, both because of the large number of performers and the level of excitement, which resulted in wide discrepancies in pitch both between performers and between iterations. For this reason, the first or clearest iterations were selected for analysis. Because some notes were difficult to differentiate in performance, they were "normalized" for purposes of analysis.

In the notated performances of text type 1 the initial tone does not function as the tonal center of the song by virtue of its frequency of occurrence. In some performances of text type 1, this tone is emphasized by its occurrence at line beginnings in at least two text lines. In the majority of the performances the tonal focus of each separate formula shifts, most frequently at the beginning of the third and/or fourth text lines. Generally this shift is by a tone or semitone.

Melody

Performances of the "Down in the Jungle" text type were pitched. Discrepancies between the pitches sung by different members of the group in a number of performances made it impossible to analyze melodically, though sometimes the melodic line of a dominant voice was used for purposes of analysis.

Table 9.13. Melodic Range and Tessitura of Text Type 1 Performances at St. Augustine's

Performance	Range (Multiple Iterations)	Intervallic Range
ST SM 02 1	e♭-b♭	Per 5
ST SM 02 2	a-g♭x 2; a-g; a-f#	Maj 6 x 3; min 7
ST SM 02 3	a♭-f#; g-e; a♭-e	Min 7; maj 6; min 6
ST SM 02 4	a-f; a-e x 2; b♭-a♭-f#; b-c	Min 6; per 5 x 3; min 7; min 9
ST SM 02 7	b-f# x 3; b♭-f#; c#-a, b-a#; c#-b	Per 5 x 3; aug 4; min 6; maj 7; min 7

Table 9.14. Frequency of Range of Text Type 1 Performances at St. Augustine's (Notated Examples)

Interval	Frequency of Occurrence
Per 5	7
Min 7	4
Maj 6	4
Min 6	3
Min 9	1
Maj 7	1
Aug 4	1

In its archetypal form, most evident in ST SM 02 7, the melody is characterized by a rising contour with successive intervals of a major third, minor second, and major second. The melody of the first three lines of this genre is thus a reiterated rising motif outlining four notes, equating to G B C D. It is possible that the melody of text type 1 performances of this game was originally derived from the popular song "Three Little Fishies," composed by Saxie Dowell and Lucy Bender Sokole, which was a hit song performed by Kay Kayser and his orchestra in 1939. The first three lines of this song have the same melody as lines 1 to 3 of text type 1. Given that the first line of the popular song is "Down in the meadow in a little bitty pool," it appears that parts of the song may have been appropriated in this rendition of the game. Whether the performances of this text and melodic type at St. Augustine's are the result of a long-standing tradition or derive from more recent renditions of this popular song in the classroom or in audiovisual media can only be conjectured. It is interesting, though, that the melody of the more popular form of the genre at Ellington also had these characteristics.

Rhythmic variation of text lines is usually incorporated within this melodic contour, but occasionally additional passing notes are used for particular syllables. The melodic contour is stable, but there is variability in the actual intervals, most often a flattening of intervals as the melody rises during each text line, as can be seen in table 9.15.[10]

The fourth text line is primarily performed on a single note that is repeated for the first four beats of the final line. This final line culminates in a falling melodic leap of approximately a fourth, followed by two rising intervals of a third and a second (though not necessarily in that order). All melodic lines are subject to a certain level of instability, again because of the tendency for in-

Table 9.15. Melodic Contours of St. Augustine's SM Performances Melodic Type 1

Performance	Contour By Text Line	Intervals
ST SM 02 1	g b♭ c d	min 3, maj 2, maj 2
	g b	maj 3
	g# a# indefinite	maj 2 [+unclear]
	Indefinite (multiple pitches)	[Unclear]
ST SM 02 2	g b c d	maj 3, min 2, maj 2
Iteration 5	g a b c d	maj 2 x 2, min 2, maj 2
	a b c d	maj 2, min 2, maj 2
	e♭ e e♭	min 2 x 2
	d g a b	per 5, maj 2 x 2
ST SM 02 3	g b♭ c	min 3, maj 2
Iteration 4	g b♭ c	min 3, maj 2
	g b♭ c#	min 3 x 2
	c b	min 2
	b f g b♭	aug 4, maj 2, min 3
ST SM 02 4	g b c# d d#	maj 3, maj 2, min 2 x 2
Iteration 16	a g# c d d#	min 2, maj 3, maj 2, min 2
	a c e♭	min 3 x 2
	e♭	monotone
	e♭ b♭ b c	per 4, min 2 x 2
ST SM 02 7	g b c d	maj 3, min 2, maj 2
	g b c d	maj 3, min 2, maj 2
	g b c d	maj 3, min 2, maj 2
	d	monotone
	d g b♭ c	per 5, min 3, maj 2

tervallic uncertainty and slight change to the tonal center. The second text type is performed at indefinite pitch throughout. This is similar to the performance of the lesser-known text type at Ellington.

Movement

The rendition of the movements in St. Augustine's performances of the SM genre were unique, involving the elimination of first one, then two hands, then the head of each player. Passing of the beat began with the standard SM clapping movement but became progressively less regular as the game progressed, because the passing movement involved a greater stretch from either a right hand to the next performer's left hand or to her head. Even more dislocation of rhythmic regularity of movements occurred when a player was required to pass the beat using her head. This occurred in all performances of text type 1. The progressive change in regularity can be seen, for example in a comparison of the movement rhythms of iterations 1 and 4 of ST SM 02 3, lines 1–2. In iteration 1 the passing clap is regularly on the beat. By iteration 4, it is irregular and less frequent[11]:

Music Example 9.19

Iteration 1

Iteration 4

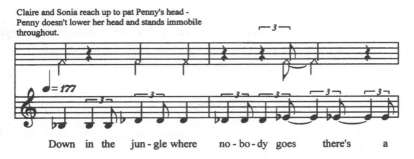

As discussed earlier, the rhythm of text type 2 is quite irregular. Claps in this form coincide exactly with the delivery of the text and are similarly of irregular duration. In one performance players eliminate hands and use their elbows to pass and receive the beat, a movement variation that contributes to the irregularity of the rhythm.

Other Forms of Variation

In two performances of text type 1, ST SM 02 4 and 7 (involving two different friendship groups) the girls formed an internal group as they were progressively eliminated. This group congregated within the external circle and its enlarging presence made the passing of the beat even more difficult because the remaining few players in the outer circle had to pass the beat around the large group in the middle. The movements of the internal group varied. In ST SM 02 4, the girls swayed from side to side and nodded (their movements not in time with the beat). In ST SM 02 7, the large group, contained within a small room, had a very cramped space in which to perform. This seemed to contribute to the increasingly anarchic actions of the internal group. Initially they formed a circle sitting down and continued to pass the beat in a standard clapping manner, though not synchronized with the outer circle. When the internal group became too big to fit in a circle, they stood up and began to make mimetic movements illustrating the song text with increasing stridency. The more colorful aspects of the text ("gorilla" and "picking his nose") were favorites. These movements became more subversive, thus creating a form of parody of the game itself.

Variation 3: "Sar Macka Dora" Genre at Birch Vale

Although there was less open subversion in performances of this genre at Birch Vale in Seattle, there was considerable performative variation nevertheless. There were seventeen performances of this game recorded at Birch Vale, making it one of the most popular games recorded in this school. A total of thirteen performances were transcribed for analysis. There was only one text type for this genre as performed at Birch Vale. This text type, known by its performers as "Quack Diddely Oso" or "Quack Diddy Oso," corresponds to some extent with one form of this game ("Sella Ella Oola") from Ellington. (◉ **VIDEO SAMPLE**) See comparative table of texts in appendix 3. See also video example *Birch V Quack diddely* and appendix 4 for a transcription of one performance at Birch Vale.)

As can be seen from table 9.16, there are a number of textual variants that occur in approximately half of the notated performances. The second word of

Table 9.16. Text of SM Performances at Birch Vale

Line		Text	Rhyme	Syllables
1.	Quack didd(el)y oso quack quack quack	a	a	8/9
2.	(Say/Go) san Marico rico rico rico	b	b	10/11
3.	Flora flora flora flora flora	c	c	10
4.	One two three (four)	d	d	3/4

the text is either "diddely" or shortened to "diddy." Some performances contain both forms in successive iterations. In two performances there is an elision of syllables in the following word so that the overall effect is that of syllable maintenance:

Quack diddy lyoso

Another form of textual variation also involves elision. In approximately half of the performances, "flora" has been rationalized to "Florida." However, in most instances, the extra syllable is elided ("Flor(i)da") so that the syllable count remains the same. One performance contains both versions within the text line and additionally shortens two words to "Flor":

Flor(i)da Florida Flor Flor Flor(i)da

Several other performances also truncate "Flora" to Flor in the second half of line 3. This line may thus appear as:

Flora flora flor flor flora

or

Flora flora flora flora flora

As is evident in the above examples, performers may change the text in different iterations of a single performance. Particular performers may favor one form of the text, but this may be changed with increasing tempo of rendition. The other main textual variant is the inclusion of "Say" or "Go" at the beginning of line 2. The final line may count out numerals to three or four. Characteristically for this genre, the texts of all performances are syllabically set. Two performances are partially hocketed.

Text Rhythm

As could be anticipated, the text rhythm reflects the textual variants. The first line usually consists of seven beats (crotchets and one set of paired quavers or triplet quavers). Line 2 most frequently has an initial anacrusis (on "say" or "go") with an idiosyncratic dotted crotchet-quaver pair at the beginning of the line. The remaining parts of line 2 and line 3 usually consist of crotchets and paired quavers. In performances where there is no anacrusis at the beginning of line 2, line 1 is extended by a crotchet rest. The final line may be delivered as single crotchets or alternating crotchets and crotchet rests. There is a certain amount of rhythmic variability in the final line because of variation in the elimination movements and because of the differing number of recited numerals (three or four). The following rhythmic outline of HV SM 04 1 represents one basic form of this text type at Birch Vale.

Music Example 9.20

A number of rhythmic variants equating with textual variants for each line are outlined in table 9.17

Tessitura and Melodic Range

There is only one melodic form, corresponding with the single textual entity of this genre at Birch Vale. This genre is sung at a fairly low tessitura in this school. Performances most frequently begin on D, E♭, or E above middle C but could begin on notes as low as A below middle C. The tessitura of each performance always dipped below the starting note, the most frequently occurring tessitura being from G, A, or B♭ below middle C to C# or E above. Sev-

Table 9.17. Variants in Text Rhythm of SM Performances at Birch Vale

Text Line	Rhythmic Variant	Performance
Line 1	Quack did-de-ly o - so quack quack quack	HV SM 04 1 (Iteration 2)
Line 1	Quack did - dy lyo - so quack quack quack	HV SM 04 6
Line 1	Quack did - dy lyo - so quack quack	HV SM 04 4
Line 2	San Ma - ri - co ri - co ri - co ri - co	HV SM 04 4
Line 3	Flo - ra flo - ra flo flo flo - ra	HV SM 04 9
Line 3	Flo - ri - da Flo - ri - da Flor(i) - da Flor(i) - da Flor(i) - da	HV SM 04 3
Line 3	Flor(i) - da Flo - ri - da Flor Flor Flor(i) - da	HV SM 04 5
Line 4	One two three	HV SM 04 5
Line 4	One two three four	HV SM 04 9 (Iteration 1)
Line 4	One two three four	HV SM 04 9 (Iteration 2)
Line 4	One two three four out	HV SM 04 9 (Iteration 3)
Line 4	One two three	HV SM 04 11
Line 4	One two three four	HV SM 04 12

eral performers, particularly the older girls, sang in a very low tessitura. For example, Melinda and Savannah (grade 5) had a range from E below middle C to middle C, and Ashley and her friends generally sang from G below middle C to D above. Some performances were closer to heightened speech than to pure melody. As seen in table 9.18, ranges of a major and minor sixth and major third were relatively common within the notated sample.

Tonal Frequency

In all but one notated performance the initial tone does not function as the tonal center of the song by virtue of its frequency of occurrence. In the majority of performances this tone is emphasized by occurring at line beginnings or on accented notes in text lines 1 and 2. In most performances, the tonal focus of each separate formula shifts, most frequently at the beginning of or during the second or third text lines. Generally this shift is by a tone or semitone within text lines, but the shift is often greater in the third line. The melodic variation between performers makes the level of tonal shift difficult to determine in many instances.

Melody

There is such a high level of intervallic instability between performances and iterations of this genre at Birch Vale that it is difficult to decipher an archetype. However, the archetype is most probably found in Iteration 1 of HV SM 04 11. (See appendix 4 for transcription.) Similar melodic aspects occur in several other performances, but they are often disguised by discrepancies between the pitches of multiple performers or change at some point in the performance. Melodic accuracy changes according to performers' individual competence

Table 9.18. Frequency of Range of SM
Performances at Birch Vale (Notated Examples)

Interval	Frequency of Occurrence
Maj 6	6
Min 6	4
Maj 3	3
Per 4	2
Min 7	2
Min 3	2
Aug 4	1

and also with tempo. Many performances are at a fast tempo, and the tempo frequently increases with subsequent iterations. Some performances are more like heightened speech and therefore have a small melodic range and highly variable intervallic relationships. Nevertheless, the shape of the melodic contour is generally maintained throughout the sample. Melodic contours and intervallic relationships within notated performances are outlined in table 9.19.

Again, it is difficult to analyze group performances when there are pitch discrepancies between different performers singing simultaneously; in instances when it is difficult to determine exact pitches, some level of normalization has been adopted. The "archetype" of this melody is characterized by melodic leaps of a fourth at the beginning of lines 1 and 2 and the end of line 1. The exact interval of this melodic leap varies in different performances and can be as small as a minor second. Line 2 can vary both intervalically and in the location of the first note that, as in other performances of this genre, may have a shift in tonal focus. Line 4 is at indefinite pitch in all performances. What is most characteristic of this melodic type is the pairing of intervals, so that perfect fourths, major and minor thirds, and major seconds often appear twice or more in immediate succession, usually with one rising followed by one falling interval. There is thus a form of internal melodic symmetry apparent. A similar melodic characteristic was found in performances of one version of the genre at Ellington.

Movement

The group performance practice at Birch Vale involves the standard passing clap and elimination movement for this genre. The elimination clap for two performers varies. Some performers favor the standard two-person gripping of right hands and shaking backward and forward. Others grip right hands and swing them alternately right and left to slap the palm of their left hands.

The ideal movement rhythm seems to be a clap on every beat. However, the regularity of this clap is highly variable, especially in performances by younger children. This appears to be related to the relative difficulty that these performers have negotiating the movements of this game. Older girls (grades 4 and 5) perform the claps on the beat with relative stability. The final elimination line is also quite rhythmically variable in younger girls' performances, but more regular in the older girls' performances.

Other Forms of Variation

One group of girls at Birch Vale was consistently creative in their approach to games. As at St. Augustine's, they found alternative ways to remain engaged

Table 9.19. Melodic Contours of Birch Vale SM Performances

Performance	Contour By Text Line	Intervals
HV SM 04 1	g e f# e♭ d f# f ind	Min 3, maj 2, min 3, min 2, maj 3, min 2
	g f g f g f g f g ind	Maj 2 x 8
	e♭ g♭ e♭ f e f e♭ ind	Min 3 x 2, maj 2, min 2 x 2, maj 2
	Indefinite	
HV SM 04 2	g e f# e d# f	Min 3, maj 2 x 2, min 2, min 3
(Iteration 2)	g e f# e g# f f# e f# e	Min 3, maj 2 x 2, maj 3, min 3, min 2, maj 2 x 3
	d# f# d# f# e f# e f# e	Min 3x 3, maj 2 x 5
	Indefinite	
HV SM 04 3	Heightened speech	
HV SM 04 4	g f g e f#	Maj 2 x 2, min 3, maj 2
	g e g e d	Min 3 x 2, maj 2
	d# e (unclear)	Min 2
	Indefinite	
HV SM 04 5	g e♭ e e♭ e g	Maj 3, min 2x 3, min 3
	Unclear f# e	Maj 2
	e f# e f# e f#	Maj 2x 5
	Indefinite	
HV SM 04 6	g e♭ f e♭ e f# g	Maj 3, maj 2 x 2, min 2, maj 2, min 2
	f# e♭ e e♭ g e f# e f e♭	Min 3, min 2 x 2, maj 3, min 3, maj 2 x 2, min 2, maj 2
	e♭ f e f e ind	Maj 2, min 2x 3
	Indefinite	
HV SM 02 7	g f g♭ f e f# g	Maj 2, min 2 x 3, maj 2, min 2
	g f# g f g ind	Min2 x 2, maj 2 x 2
	f g f# g f# g	Maj 2, min 2 x 4
	Indefinite	
HV SM 04 8	g d e d g	Per 4, maj 2 x 2, per 4
	g e f# d# f# d# f e f e	Min 3, maj 2, min 3x3, maj 2, min 2 x 3
	d e d e d e	Maj 2 x 5
	Indefinite	
HV SM 04 9	g d e d b d	Per 4, maj 2 x 2, min 3 x 2
Iteration 2	g d e d e d e d	Per 4, maj 2 x 8
	b d b d b	Min 3 x 4
	Indefinite	
HV SM 04 11	g d e d b d	Per 4, maj 2 x 2, min 3 x 2
(Archetype)	g d e d e d e d	Per 4, maj 2 x 8
	b d b d ind	Min 3 x 3
	Indefinite	
HV SM 04 12	g d e♭ d b d d♭	Per 4, min 2 x 2, min 3 x 3
Iteration 2	e c# d# c# b♭ c# d# c#	Min 3, maj 2 x 2, min 3 x 2, maj 2 x 2
	c d c d e♭ ind	Maj 2 x 3, min 2
	Indefinite	
HV SM 04 13	g d e d♭ b♭ d♭	Per 4, maj 2, min 3 x 3
	g e♭ e d♭ e d♭ e d♭ e d♭	Maj 3, min 2, min 3 x 7
	b d# b d# ind	Maj 3 x 3
	Indefinite	
HV SM 04 14	g d e d b d d# Ind	Per 4, maj 2 x 2, min 3 x 2, min 2
Iteration 2	g# d# f d# d d# f d#	Per 4, maj 2 x 2, min 2 x 2, maj 2 x 2
	c# d# c# d# ind	Maj 2 x 3
	Indefinite	

once they had been eliminated from the main circle in performances of the SM genre. In one performance of the game (HV 04 6), this group moved into additional playing pairs as soon as two girls were eliminated, so that two groups were playing in parallel with each other. When the main game had finished, one pair continued to improvise a dance to the song, moving quite formally backward and forward, and experimenting with different arm positions, until they became aware of my scrutiny and stopped in embarrassment. (🔺VIDEO SAMPLE: See video example *BirchV Quack diddely.*)

Conclusion

Although there is considerable variation in performances of this game genre, and multiple traditions develop both within and between school playgrounds in different localities, there are a number of characteristics that remain relatively constant. One of these is the wordplay involving assonance and alliteration within the text, in addition to a large proportion of vocables in many of the texts. The lack of semantic content leads to considerable textual variation and, consequently, to variable text rhythms.

Rhythmic variation in the SM genre is effected within metric boundaries. Textual variation is, however, characterized by additive rhythms. Syncopation is also found in the text rhythm of this game genre in several localities. Where changes in the movement pattern occur, for example in the final counting-out line of the text, a greater degree of ametricality results. Metrical delivery also appears to be of less importance in performances where children are concerned with complex forms of variation such as hocketing of the text to match the movement pattern.

It appears that melodic contours are relatively stable but that there is intervallic instability in many game performances. In other words, the melodic shape seems to be more important to the singers than the actual intervals. Melodic leaps have a greater level of intervallic variability, but stepwise melodic movement is also subject to variation in the intervals used.

Although the falling minor third is found in many performances, stepwise movement is also prevalent. The preponderance of both minor and major seconds in this genre, in addition to intervals of a perfect fourth, perfect fifth, and augmented fourth, is evidence that an anhemitonic pentatonic scale is not a universal basis of children's musical play. Additionally, the initial tone functions as the tonal center of many of the pitched performances. Tonal dominance is achieved either through frequency of iteration or through reiteration at points of emphasis, such as line beginnings, accented notes, or notes of longest duration. Another significant tonal feature is that of tonal shift, most usually by a downward movement of a tone or semitone at the beginning of text lines, or by a flattening of the melodic line as a text line proceeds. This is more apparent toward the end of an iteration, and may be affected by increasing levels of excitement as the game proceeds. In fact, increasing tempo and excitement appear to have an effect on forms of variation in melody, text, and movement rhythms.

The interrelatedness of text, movement, melody, and rhythm is evident in game performances in all locations, as is children's willingness to innovate and to draw on influences both within and external to the playground for material with which to generate new play ideas. The range of textual, movement, and musical ideas represented in the sample of games that have been analyzed in this chapter contributes to an evolving view of complexity in children's musical play. Further stylistic features and culturally idiosyncratic forms of play found in different field locations are discussed in the following chapter.

CHAPTER 10

Style and Cultural Idiosyncrasy
in Musical Play

A s can be seen from the previous chapter's analysis of one genre of play-ground singing games in all its cross-cultural manifestations, a number of musical, textual and movement characteristics appear to transcend cultural boundaries. In this chapter I first discuss features of children's musical play that have been found in multiple field locations and therefore could be seen to be more generally occurring, then turn to an examination of some of the differences between play in different localities and relate this to the contexts in which they are found.

Style

"Playing Around": Improvisatory Skill

As is clearly evident from the discussion of children's creative proclivities in chapters 8 and 9, one major stylistic feature of children's musical play is their disposition to "play around with" the texts, movements, melodies, and rhythms of games in a constant effort to create something new, to increase the level of amusement and stamp their own imprimatur on the games they play. This improvisatory capacity was enacted in playgrounds in all field locations, resulting in multiple variants of some game genres, such as "Sar Macka Dora," both within and between playgrounds and across cultural boundaries.

This improvisatory skill can be further demonstrated by performances of "When Sue Was a Baby" recorded at the after-school care program at Nora

Conn School in Los Angeles in 2004. This is a well-known game genre found in many locations (Arleo, 2001), but the children at Nora Conn played a very idiosyncratic version. In these performances by a group of boys and girls, a single child, "Miss Sue" or "Mr. Sue," crouched down between the two hand-clappers and improvised both text and mimetic movements to exemplify each stage in Sue's life cycle signaled by the textual formula: "When Miss/Mr. Sue was a (baby, toddler and so on) s/he went like this." The Nora Conn version of this game culminated in the Sue figure jumping up and chasing the other performers, eventually catching a new Sue to restart the game cycle. The extent of the solo improvisation by two different Sues can be seen in two successive iterations of this game by the same group of children; their improvised texts and mimetic movements differed significantly, as illustrated in table 10.1.

(⊙ **VIDEO SAMPLE:** See video example *NoraC Susie*.)

It is notable that, in a subsequent performance of this game by members of this group, individual children's improvisations differed again (as shown in the excerpt from this game in chapter 5). While the group or pair sections of the performance remained within strict formulaic and metrical parameters, the solo improvisations were quite free (though they sometimes bore some formulaic resemblance to each other, as in the kinesthetic depiction of sore backs or wings of the protagonists). Such practices diverge considerably from performances of this game genre observed in other locations, both by myself and other researchers (Arleo, 2001) and entail the ability of a solo performer to improvise at some length over an extended sequence.

Disjuncture

The Nora Conn performances of "When Sue Was a Baby" demonstrate another stylistic characteristic of many games: that of flow and disjuncture for humorous or surprise effect. A large number of games create a feeling of heightened expectation by maintaining a regular pattern of movements, cyclic rhythms, and reiterated melodic phrases or segments that are interrupted by sudden textual, rhythmic, or kinesthetic rifts in the pattern.

Such rifts are caused in a number of ways. One of the most frequently occurring of these is the intrusion of mimetic movements illustrating text (often in an exaggerated or amusing way) into reiterated melodic and movement patterns. For example, in the Nora Conn performances of "When Sue Was a Baby," a repetitive word sequence and cyclic three-beat clapping pattern performed by a pair or group is interrupted by contrasting humorous and emphatic text accompanied by ametric mimetic movements performed by the solo "Sue" at the end of each verse. This mimetic verse ending is also found in

Iteration 1: NC S 04 1 Performers: Pam, Khryslynn, Patrick, Keenan Improviser: Pam	Iteration 2: NC S 04 1 Performers: Pam, Khryslynn, Patrick, Improviser: Patrick
When Mr. Sue was a baby a baby a baby When Mr. Sue was a baby He went [Pam corrects: She] like this: Pam: Ahaah Hah! [*Puts up head and cries*]	When Mr. Sue was a baby a baby a baby When Mr. Sue was a baby He went like this: Patrick: Whah! I want to change my diaper! [*Flaps fists backward and forward*]

When Miss Sue was a toddler a toddler a
   toddler
When Miss Sue was a toddler
She went like this:
Pam: Mummy I can see up your nose
[*Points to Khryslynn's nose*]
	When Miss Sue was a toddler a toddler a
	   toddler
	When Miss Sue was a toddler
	He went like this:
	Patrick: I want a toy!
	[*Shrugs arms emphatically*]

When Miss Sue was a teenager a teenager a
   teenager
When Miss Sue was a teenager
She went like this:
Pam: Oh I left my bra in my boyfriend's car.
[*Crosses hands over chest*]
	When Miss Sue was a teenager a teenager a
	   teenager
	When Miss Sue was a teenager
	He went like this:
	Patrick: Where's my portrait? I can't find it!
	[*Flings arms around and stamps*]

When Miss Sue was a mother a mother a mother When Miss Sue was a Momma She went like this: Pam: Kids go to your room! [*Points emphatically at Khryslynn*]	When Miss Sue was a Daddy a Daddy a Daddy When Miss Sue was a Daddy He went like this: Patrick: I can buy you everything you want. [*Gestures with one hand*]
When Miss Sue was a granma a granma a granma When Miss Sue was a granma She went like this: Pam: Oh, I fell and broke my back! Help me! [*Clutches at Khryslynn*]	When Miss Sue was a granpa a granpa a granpa When Miss Sue was a granpa He went like this: Patrick: Oh, my aching back. Where's my cane? [*Bends over and puts hand on back*]
When Miss Sue was an angel an angel an angel When Miss Sue was an angel (She) went like this: Pam: I'm afraid, afraid of heights! [*Flutters arms quickly like wings*]	When Miss Sue was an angel an angel an angel When Miss Sue was an angel He went like this: Patrick: Oh, I can see my house from here. [*Flaps "wings" and looks down*]
When Miss Sue was a devil a devil a devil When Miss Sue was a devil She went like this. [*Pam jumps up and chases the others*]	When Mr. Sue was a devil a devil a devil When Mr. Sue was a devil He went . . . [*Ends in shrieks as Patrick jumps up and chases the girls*]

other versions of this game, though more usually performed to a predetermined text by a pair. Most frequently in English-language versions the text and movements remain within the same meter as the rest of the verse, but they are more freely performed in French versions (Arleo, 2001).

Other examples of this phenomenon are found in the play of children in varied locations. In the game "Cuando el Reloj" (when the clock), played by newly arrived Latino children at Birch Vale, the text of the intrusion was a regularly occurring onomatopoeic refrain, but the mimetic movements of the refrain varied conspicuously, breaking into the cyclical clapping pattern accompanying the verse, in this instance a duple pattern of C/O C/R C/O C/L. The first three verses of "Cuando el Reloj" are shown below.

Spanish	*English Translation*
Cuando el reloj marca las uno	When the clock strikes one
Las calaveras salen de su tumba	The skeletons leave their tombs
Chumba ka chumba	Chumba ka chumba
Chumba chumba ta	Chumba chumba ta
	[Hands in prayer formation move up and down]
Cuando el reloj marca las dos	When the clock strikes two
Las calaveras comen arroz	The skeletons eat rice
Tumbaka tumba	Tumbaka tumba
Tumba tumba tumba	Tumba tumba tumba
Tumba ka tumba	Tumba ka tumba
Tumba tumba ta	Tumba tumba ta
	[Rhythmic spooning motions with hands]
Cuando el reloj marca las tres	When the clock strikes three
Las calaveras juegan ajedrez	The skeletons play chess
Tumbaka tumba	Tumbaka tumba
Tumba tumba tumba	Tumba tumba tumba
Tumba ka tumba	Tumba ka tumba
Tumba tumba ta	Tumba tumba ta
	[Join hands and swing around in a circle]
	(HV CR 04 3 V Recorded Birch Vale 2004)

(🅐 **VIDEO SAMPLE:** See video example *BirchV Cuando* and appendix 7 for a musical transcription.)

Another example of this practice of disjuncture through mimetic intrusion can be found in "Down Down Baby," a game genre recorded by Segler (1992) in many European countries and recorded in almost all British, Australian, and American field locations in my study (see discussion in chapter 7). In this game the reiterated text and regular clapping on the beat at the beginning of text lines is interrupted by mimetic movements at the ends of text lines, for example:

Text:	Down	down	ba-	by,	down	by	the roller coaster
Movement:	*Clap*	*clap*	*clap*	*clap*	*clap*	*clap*	*move hand up and down*

	Sweet	sweet	ba-	by,	I don't wanna let you go
	Clap	*clap*	*clap*	*clap*	*hold arms in hugging motion*

(DDB 94 1 AV Recorded Sydney 1994)

In the *Sesame Street* and Springfield versions of the game recorded in the 1990s the regular down up clapping pattern was used for line beginnings, with the intervening mimetic movements sometimes accommodated within the standard eight-beat line but in some performances distorting the regular text and movement rhythms at line ends. This was particularly the case when there were exaggerated movements such as a suggestive swivelling of hips that accompanied the words "hot dog," as can be seen in the full transcription of DDB 90 1 AV recorded at Springfield school in 1990 (appendix 4).

The down up clapping pattern was maintained in performances by two Aboriginal girls at Auston in central Australia, but the text was more cyclical, with mimetic movements at line endings and the emphatic declamation of a departure from the textual cycle at the end of the performance, as seen below and in the full transcription in appendix 9:

Text:	Down	down	ba-	by,	rock yourself a baby
Movement:	*Clap*	*clap*	*clap*	*clap*	*cradling movement*

	Down	down	ba-	by,	rock yourself a baby
	Clap	*clap*	*clap*	*clap*	*cradling movement*

	Down	down	ba-	by,	rock yourself a baby
	Clap	*clap*	*clap*	*clap*	*cradling movement*

	Ready		seddy	go	
	Clap	*clap*	*clap*	*clap*	*clap*

(E DDB 01 2 AV Recorded Auston 1994)

At St. Augustine's there was a range of both text types and regular movement patterns used in *Down down baby* performances, from a clutching and interweaving hand movement to twirling of index fingers, though the prevailing pattern was the three-beat clap. All of these were typically interrupted at line endings, for example:

Text:	Down	down	ba-	by,	down	by	the	river-	side
Movement:	*Clutch*	*weave*	*clutch*	*weave*	*clutch*	*weave*		*tickle*	*tickle*

	Sweet	sweet	ba-	by,	no	place	to	go	
	Clutch	*weave*	*clutch*	*weave*	*point*	*point*	*point*	*point*	

(ST DDB 02 13 AV Recorded Keighley 2002)

Text:	I	hate	cof-	fee	I	love	tea	
Movement:	*Clap*	*clap*	*clap*	*clap*	*clap*	*clap*	*clap*	*clap*

	I	hate	Brit-	ney she never (unclear) me				
	Clap	*clap*	*clap*	*clap*	*point*	*point*	*point*	*point*

	Down	by the	fire		peel-	in' po-	ta-	toes
	Clap	*clap*	*clap*	*clap*	*chop*	*chop*	*chop*	*chop*

	Britney Spears	is so	crap.
	RH on partners' shoulders	*LH on partners' shoulders*	*Arms in air*

(ST DDB 02 1 V Recorded Keighley 2002)

(The extent of the interruptions to the regular flow by mimetic intrusions can be seen in the complete transcription of these two performances in appendices 10 and 6 respectively.) A full discussion of the phenomenon of flow and disjuncture with reference to the "Down Down Baby" genre can be found in Marsh (2006).

A similar performance strategy is found in "My Father Is a Garbage Man," recorded in 2002 in Norway and the United Kingdom, in which each verse, accompanied by a regular three-beat clap, culminates in rhythmically varying onomatopoeic text with illustrative movements which gradually accumulate over the course of the game, as demonstrated in the first few verses:

Norwegian	*English Translation*
Min far han er en søppelmann,	My father is a garbage man
En søppelmann, en søppelmann	A garbage man, a garbage man
Min far han er en søppelmann	My father is a garbage man
Og vet du hva han sa?	Do you know what he said?
Æsj æsj	Yuk yuk
Holder seg for nesen med tommel og pekefinger	*Pinch their noses between thumb and forefinger.*
Min mor hun er en baker	My mother is a baker
En baker, en baker.	A baker, a baker

Min mor hun er en baker
Og vet du hva hun sa?
Æsj æsj Nam-nam
Holder seg for nesen med tommel og
   pekefinger, gnir seg på magen

My mother is a baker
Do you know what she said?
Yuk yuk Yum yum
Pinch their noses between thumb and
   forefinger, rub their stomachs

Min søster er ei jåle
Ei jåle, ei jåle
Min søster er ei jåle
Og vet du hva hun sa?
Æsj æsj Nam nam Krølle krølle
Holder seg for nesen med tommel og
   pekefinger, gnir seg på magen, krøller
   håret med pekefingen

My sister is a show-off
A show off, a show-off
My sister is a show-off
Do you know what she said?
Yuk yuk Yum yum Curl curl
Pinch their noses between thumb and
   forefinger, rub their bellies with circular
   movements, curl hair with forefingers

Min bror han er en cowboy
En cowboy, en cowboy
Min bror han er en cowboy
Og vet du hva han sa?
Æsj æsj Nam nam Krølle krølle Pang pang
Holder seg for nesen med tommel og
   pekefinger, gnir seg på magen, krøller
   håret med pekefingen, skyter med pistol
   over skuldrene

My brother is a cowboy
A cowboy, a cowboy
My brother is a cowboy
Do you know what he said?
Yuk yuk Yum yum Curl curl Bang bang
Pinch their noses between thumb and
   forefinger, rub their bellies with circular
   movements, curl hair with forefingers,
   fire guns over shoulders

Min tante er en turner
En turner, en turner
Min tante er en turner
Og vet du hva hun sa?
Æsj æsj Nam nam Krølle krølle Pang pang
   Hopp hopp
Holder seg for nesen med tommel og
   pekefinger, gnir seg på magen, krøller
   håret med pekefingen, skyter med pistol
   over skuldrene, hopper to ganger

My aunt is a gymnast
A gymnast, a gymnast
My aunt is a gymnast
Do you know what she said?
Yuk yuk Yum yum Curl curl Bang bang
   Jump jump
Pinch their noses between thumb and
   forefinger, rub their bellies with circular
   movements, curl hair with forefinger, fire
   guns over shoulders, jump twice

Min onkel er en fotballspiller,
En fotballspiller, en fotballspiller
Min onkel er en fotballspiller
Og vet du hva han sa?
Æsj æsj Nam nam Krølle krølle Pang
   pang Hopp hopp Mål
Holder seg for nesen med tommel og
   pekefinger, gnir seg på magen, krøller

My uncle is a football player
A football player, a football player
My uncle is a football player
Do you know what he said?
Yuk yuk Yum yum Curl curl Bang
   bang Jump jump Goal
Pinch their noses between thumb and
   forefinger, rub their bellies with circular

håret med pekefingen, skyter med pistol
over skuldrene, hopper to ganger, sparker
til en imaginær ball

Min andre tante er sexy
Er sexy er sexy
Min andre tante er sexy
Og vet du hva hun sa?
Æsj æsj Nam nam Krølle krølle Pang
  pang Hopp hopp Mål Vu hu!
Holder seg for nesen med tommel og
  pekefinger, gnir seg på magen, krøller
  håret med pekefingen, skyter med pistol
  over skuldrene, hopper to ganger, løfter
  brystene

movements, curl hair with forefingers,
fire guns over shoulders, jump twice, kick
an imaginary ball

My other aunt is sexy
Is sexy is sexy
My other aunt is sexy
Do you know what she said?
Yuk yuk Yum yum Curl curl Bang
  bang Jump jump Goal! Whaow!
Pinch their noses between thumb and
  forefinger, rub their bellies with circular
  movements, curl hair with forefingers,
  fire guns over shoulders, jump twice, kick
  an imaginary ball, lift their breasts
(B MFI 02 3 Recorded Stavanger 2002)

In all of these examples, the interruptions to the established flow of the game defeat expectations and overturn adult poetic and performative norms. In this way children perform small acts of subversion and resistance to the "acceptable" adult world. In "Min Far Han Er en Søppelmann" the level of subversion is gradually intensified by the inclusion of increasingly transgressive text and exaggerated movements. The subversive effect is emphasized by the cumulative nature of the performance, with constant reiteration and a building up of these elements to effectively create a crescendo of rebellion.

Challenge

The cumulative form of "Min Far Han Er en Søppelmann" can also be seen to exemplify another facet of children's musical play: the creation and fulfilment of self-imposed challenge. In many games children invent challenges for themselves, striving to master cumulative text or movements, increasing tempi, altered clapping patterns or the substitution of head or whole body movements for hand movements. In meeting the verbal, kinesthetic, and cognitive challenges of games, children triumph over seemingly impossible conditions to acquire a feeling of mastery. This contributes to their sense of power in a world where they are otherwise relatively powerless.

Some games appear to be predicated completely on the notion of challenge. Games such as "Slide," usually played by a pair of children, require total cooperation between the players in order to progress. "Slide" (named after a sliding hands movement that sometimes initiates the main part of the game) consists of a seven-beat clapping pattern, divided into three sections of two plus two plus three hand movements: C/O C/R‖ C/O C/L‖ C/O B/B C/P. The object of the game is to complete ten clapping cycles. With each cycle an extra set of claps is added to each section. For example, the clapping pattern for the second cycle would be: C/O C/R‖ C/O C/R‖ C/O C/L‖ C/O C/L‖ C/O B/B C/P ‖ C/O B/B C/P. The ensuing clapping pattern thus has an additive meter with a seven-beat core, as shown in music example 10.1.

Music Example 10.1 Rhythm of "Slide" Clapping Game

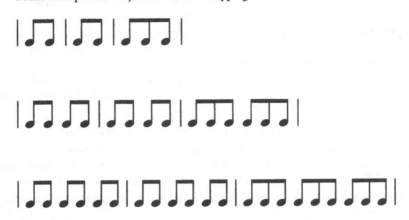

This game was found in field schools in Sydney, Telford Spring, Seattle, and Los Angeles, and a variant form, "Ujeong Test" (friendship test) was played in the two schools in Busan. In most instances, the game was textless, presumably to avoid distraction from the intricate clapping pattern that demanded complete attention. However, children in many performances counted the number of the cycle at the beginning of each section to help co-ordinate the number of claps. One example, performed by Charlotte and Hali at Birch Vale, had an initial formula: "Slide baby one baby two baby I love you baby." "Ujeong Test" also had an opening formula in all performances:

Sse sse sse (standard opening vocables for clapping games)
Ujeong test, jjan! (friendship test, exclamation of surprise)

This formula indicates the seemingly contradictory dispositions both to collaborate and compete in many of the games involving intense challenge. One highly collaborative variant of "Slide" at Springfield was devised to include multiple members of a friendship group, one of whom had a broken leg. The game was played in a square formation, and the children clapped at two different levels to accommodate the injured girl, who performed kneeling

(🔊 **VIDEO SAMPLE:** see discussion of this variant in chapter 8 and video example *SpringF Slide*). This variant made it possible for everyone in the group to play but simultaneously increased the level of difficulty, as the players recognized. The performance of "Slide" is also underscored by the knowledge that one player may not be as adept as another player and will be responsible for the game breaking down before the desired tenth cycle, indeed a test of friendship or of the power of co-operation.

The competitive aspect of challenge is more evident in games where less adept players are eliminated. One game of this kind, known variously as "My Aunt Biano," "My Aunty Anna," and "Mrs. Biano Had a Piano" was played at Bysiden (Stavanger), Bradford Well (central Australia), and Summerglen (Bedford). All versions (even in Norway) involved the recitation of an English text accompanied by a regular three-beat clap until the final line, where players would jump their feet apart, for example:

Text:	My	aunt	Bia-	no	plays	the	pia-	no
Movement:	D/U	C/P	C/O	D/U	C/P	C/O	D/U	C/P

	Twenty	four	hours	in the	day	
	C/O	D/U	C/P	C/O	D/U	C/P

Step!
Jump

(B MAB 02 3 Recorded Stavanger 2002)

With each iteration of the game the players' feet moved further apart (in "splits" formation) until they could no longer remain upright and fell over, at which point they were eliminated from the game. The last player "standing" won the game.

A similar game, "Mailman", was extremely popular at Birch Vale and was also played at Nora Conn. Again the major part of the text was accompanied by the three-beat clap, but on the final line the players (usually a pair) slid their feet outward in four successive movements, the outcome being the same as for "My Aunt Biano":

Text:	Mail-	man	mail-	man	do	your	du-	ty
Movement:	D/U	C/P	C/O	D/U	C/P	C/O	D/U	C/P

	Here	comes the	lady	with the	Afri-	can	boo-	ty
	C/O	D/U	C/P	C/O	D/U	C/P	C/O	D/U

	She can do the	pom	pom	she can do the twist	
	C/P	C/O	D/U	C/P	C/O	D/U	C/P	C/O

Most	of		all	she can	kiss	kiss	kiss	
D/U	C/P		C/O	D/U	C/P	C/O	D/U	C/P
K			I		S		S	
Slide feet			Slide feet		Slide feet		Slide feet	

(HV MLM 04 2 V Recorded Birch Vale 2004)

(See appendix 7 for full transcription.)

The challenge of a game may be physical or be more cognitively oriented. More pronounced forms of kinesthetic challenge were found in jump rope games such as Double Dutch, observed at Nora Conn, where players had to negotiate jumping over two ropes that were moving simultaneously (see Beresin, 1999, and Gaunt, 2006, for a detailed discussion of this game genre). At Bysiden various games of elastics also demanded considerable kinesthetic skill. Performers were required to jump rhythmically for a designated number of times over, around, and inside long elastic bands, in a variety of formations, supported by players' legs or surrounding pillars. The "elastics" were regularly raised so that the action of jumping became increasingly difficult. Another Bysiden game, "ABC Stå På Same Sted" (ABC stay at the same place) began as a ring game, with players walking around the circle on the beat to a chant, but rapidly changed to a physical battle as players tried to jump onto the foot of the adjacent person to eliminate her or him from the game. The difficulty was increased for the final pair who folded their arms and tried to knock each other over while hopping on one foot.

Perhaps the most extreme physical challenge was found in the "Nol Ttwiggi" (Jumping seesaw) game at Pada School in Busan. This game, popular with both boys and girls, required one player to stand on one end of a short wooden seesaw while the other jumped onto the other end, catapulting his or her counterpart into the air from where he or she landed back on the seesaw, initiating a corresponding catapult. Balance and accuracy were required in equal measure. Forms of kinesthetic challenge (such as "splits" or trying to push a partner off balance) or cognitive challenge, where rapid movement or textual shifts were demanded of the players, were especially characteristic of Korean games and are discussed in more detail in the second section of this chapter.

Stylistic Characteristics

Melody, Tonality, Tessitura, and the Acoustic Environment

Each of the characteristics examined in the analysis of the "Sar Macka Dora" genre in chapter 9 merits further discussion with reference to a wider range of musical play repertoire. Perhaps the most interesting of these features in terms of adult preconceptions is that of melody.

What is evident from observing children at play in all of the field contexts is that melody seems to be of secondary significance in game performance practice. Children playing a game may correct each other's movements or words but they never, in my experience, correct the melody. "Messing up," (the American children's term for making a mistake), is not ascribed to melodic inaccuracy. It may be that this lack of significance can be attributed to the function of various elements in maintaining a game performance. For example, if the movements in a clapping game are not synchronized it will be difficult for the players to bring a performance to a successful conclusion, though differences in movements and text are frequently accommodated within performances, as outlined in chapter 6. On the other hand, lack of melodic synchronization between players does not affect their capacity to continue a game.

Children appear to be aware of melodic shape; usually all of the performers maintain the melodic contours. However, the actual intervals vary between performances, and there are frequent pitch discrepancies between players within most performances. It is as if what is important in game performance is a signification of any given melody rather than an actualization of it. As the extent to which this occurs varies in different locations, it is further delineated in discussions of cultural idiosyncrasy later in the chapter. It is notable, however, that Blacking (1973) drew attention to a similar phenomenon in Venda children's songs, stating that "[t]he pattern of intervals is considered more important than their exact pitch" (p. 69), albeit in the context of performance of a tonal language.

Pitch discrepancies seem to be further exacerbated by issues to do with vocal range. Age appears to be one factor in determining the range players use. For example, older girls in the field schools often had more developed, lower voices and they also seemed embarrassed to sing in a higher register. In contrast, younger children tended to sing in a higher tessitura but in many cases appeared to have less control over their vocal pitching. This had different observable results. Sometimes when older and younger players were singing together, they sang at a different tessitura at the same time, so that the performance had parallel melodies with similar pitch contours but different pitches, up to a fifth apart. An example of this can be found in a performance of "Slå Makaroni" at Bysiden in 2002, where a group of nine- and ten-year-olds consistently sang at two different pitches throughout several iterations.

However, a predilection for a particular range was sometimes found in the performances of particular individuals, who would consistently sing in a different tessitura from that of other performers. Thus two nine-year-old girls at

St Augustine's sang virtually a whole performance of "That's the Way I Like It" at parallel pitches (see full transcription of ST TTW 02 6 V in appendix 6).

Music Example 10.2

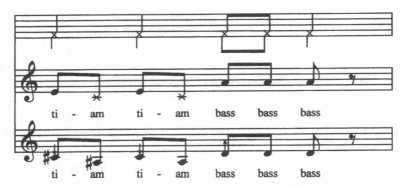

On the whole, older children demonstrated a greater degree of pitch stability in their performances, though individual proficiency and other factors such as increasing difficulty of movements or greater excitement also influenced this aspect of pitch.

The sonic environment and its acoustic properties also seemed to affect children's pitch, in particular the tessitura used in play. From listening to a range of recorded games it was evident that the average pitch center of children's games outside in the playground was approximately F above middle C, while performances recorded inside on average had a tonal center a fourth or fifth lower. In the noisy playground environment, children had to sing and chant loudly in order to be heard above the background sound. In addition, children were often more confident in the playground, which was their domain and in which they had the freedom to be loud in voice and expansive in movements. Increased volume appeared to be matched by a higher pitch, and frequent use of a calling register that was different from the more self-conscious murmured chest register that many children used in performances inside buildings. This self-consciousness could, of course be partially attributed to the circumstances in which internal recordings took place. Often they were elicited recordings inside a classroom more usually associated with teacher-directed activity, and the presence of a video camera and an observing adult was much more obtrusive.

However, nervousness, whether in response to performing for a camera or in front of other children with whom the performers were less comfortable, almost invariably led to singing in a lower tessitura, often centering on A below middle C. This nervousness also had the effect in some performances of compressing the intervals used, so that pitch contours were flattened. In some internal recording situations, initially shy children gained in confidence or lost self-consciousness as the game developed and the group dynamics prevailed. As a result the pitch of game performances gradually crept higher. This was most noticeable in the increasingly anarchic performances of "Down in the Jungle" at St. Augustine's (discussed in chapter 9), in which each subsequent iteration tended to be sung up to a semitone higher than its predecessor as the performers became more animated. Blacking (1973) reported similar pitch changes in Venda children's performances as excitement increased.

As outlined in chapter 9, the tonality of children's games was also different from functional tonality in many instances, although some games are originally derived from functionally tonal models. Two characteristics predominate in performances of children's games. The first is the functioning of the initial tone as the tonal center of the melody. This characteristic may be ameliorated by the second feature of children's performances, which relates to tonal shift in the melody, either at the beginning of text lines or through intervallic variation (most frequently flattening) as text lines proceed. Again these features may both be affected by excitement or nervousness. It would seem that, while playground games are conceptualized as a whole, with children always starting a game at the beginning and singing it right through, the tonality of a game is not conceptualized by children as a complete entity, or even conceptualized at all.

Rhythm and Meter: Syncopation and the Three-Beat Clap

As intimated in the description of "Slide," children's games are often rhythmically complex. The additive meter of "Slide" is only one of many forms of rhythmic complexity. Another prevailing feature might be termed polymetricality, though more accurately it could be seen as contrasting rhythmic cycles that co-exist in the text and movement domains of game performance. This most frequently occurs in the pairing of a duple text rhythm with a triple hand-clapping pattern. The standard three-beat clap that has been alluded to in various examples in earlier chapters consists of a cycle of three sequential hand movements on three beats: the down up clap (D/U), followed by clapping both partner's hands (C/P) and finally clapping own hands together (C/O). This cycle is repeated without pause, creating a metrically triple accompaniment to many games. Although it has been attributed to the African American game tradition (Merrill-Mirsky, 1988), it was the most frequently encountered clapping pattern in all field locations (with the exception of Busan) and is seen by children as applicable to most game texts. When combined with texts that are more usually in duple or quadruple meters (again with the exception of some Korean games), they create a sonic polymeter, as can be seen in the following example, "See See My Playmate," performed by two Year 2 girls at Springfield in 1993: SS 93 2 AV Lines 1 & 2.

Music Example 10.3

See see my play - mate I can - not play with you

My sis - ter's on the loo since eight - een nine - ty two

This example also demonstrates the additional element of syncopation in text rhythms, again widely occurring in games in all field locations. Syncopated text rhythms might also be ascribed to origins in African American traditions of playground games and popular music. This is clearly the case in the invariably syncopated performances of "Down Down Baby," shown by table 10.2, which delineates text rhythm variants in the first line of 50 performances of "Down Down Baby" at Springfield from 1990 to 1996.

Table 10.2. Text Rhythm of Line 1 of "Down down baby" Performances, Springfield

However, games such as "See See My Playmate" originally had a nonsyncopated model (Opie and Opie, 1988; Marsh, 1997; Riddell, 1990) that has developed syncopated characteristics in the playground. Its Norwegian counterpart, "Si Si Kom Plei Me" (recorded in 2002), also had a syncopated initial text line, though it reverted to a rhythm closer to the original model in subsequent lines.

Examples in chapters 8 and 9 also illustrate other forms of rhythmic complexity. These include ametricality and "elastic" meters (as in the final line of the "Sar Macka Dora" performances discussed in chapter 9) and asymmetrical meters, as in the seven-beat clapping cycle that accompanied one of the performances of "See See My Playmate" recorded at Springfield in 1994 (chapter 8).

Although there were many characteristics that were common to children's play in all locations, each playground had its own performative attributes, which I will now discuss in relation to each location and the context in which they occur.

Cultural Idiosyncrasy

Musical Play at Springfield (Sydney) and in Central Australian Schools

The games of Australian children in all field schools had notably "flattened" melodic contours. While some game melodies may have had their genesis in popular songs or songs learnt in the classroom, in the playground these melodies underwent a transformation whereby some of the intervals were typically narrowed from a fifth or fourth to a third, resulting in melodic compression.

In the Springfield games, melodies usually had a range limited to a fifth and rarely in excess of an octave. Melodic ranges were even more restricted in central Australian schools, particularly in the performances of Aboriginal children, especially those recorded in more remote Aboriginal communities. It was not unusual for Aboriginal children (nearly all girls) recorded in these locations to sing in a very low tessitura and for their songs to be focussed on a low monotone, around G below middle C, with little melodic movement. Tessitura of the analyzed game sample at Springfield was also relatively low, falling between F# below middle C and B above middle C. Head voice was used rarely by children performing games in any of the Australian field schools.

Games in all Australian locations were formally quite variable, though repetitive and cyclical to some extent. Movement patterns were usually cyclical, but frequently punctuated by mimetic movements at points of textual emphasis or surprise, as discussed earlier. There were no examples of canon, rondo, echo, or call and response forms in any of the sample (488 recorded items in Springfield, 209 items at Telford Spring, 47 items at Auston, 22 items at Maringa, and 17 items at Bradford Well).

What is particularly important to note is that the kinds of clapping games played by Aboriginal children in the central Australian schools were not traditional Aboriginal games. Traditional games did not appear to be played by children in the field school contexts, although other games involving text and movement were traditionally played in previous generations and some genres are still played in non-school settings in other communities. One example of this is the genre of sand stories, or milpatjunanyi (translated literally as "putting the stick"), found in Anangu Pitjantjatjara Yankunytjatjara Lands in central Australia (southwest of my field collection areas). This is a form of rhythmic storytelling where a bent "story wire" is tapped rhythmically into the sand to accompany the performance of stories, whose images are also drawn in the sand. This form of stylized play is also known as "mani mani" or "muni muni" and in previous generations entailed the use of a stick or leaves for the rhythmic accompaniment (Eickelkamp, 2008; Haagen, 1994).

In Telford Spring, three older Warumungu women informants recounted traditional forms of musical play from the surrounding area. One of these forms was a taunting song to the moon, in which girls jumped rhythmically while chanting to the "brother" or "sister" moon:

Kapurlu arni kumppu (Big sister I am big)
Angi manjun (You are little)
(Source: R. N. Plummer and D. N. Dawson, June 2001)

Angi paparti parlkarr (You are the short brother)
Arni paparti junmarn (I am the tall brother)
(Source: K. F. Nappanangka, June 2001. See full transcription of
    Moon Song in appendix 9.)

The meaning of the song was that the children were bigger and more important than the moon, despite appearances to the contrary. Again this was a form of assertion of power by children who were socially without power. This game song had been learnt when the older women were children, living either at the Telegraph Station to the north of Telford Spring or at the Aboriginal community of Alekarenge to the south, traditionally part of Alyawarre lands. A similar boys' game of dancing and singing to the moon, learnt in the vicinity of Alekarenge was also recounted by a Kaytetye elder on a recent video recording designed for Kaytetye language maintenance (Warlpiri Media, 2001), though the game is no longer played.

Another traditional girls' game reported by Warumungu elder K. F. Nappanangka was a form of counting out, where the names of totemic animals from the Dreaming were successively chanted, accompanied by a finger play culminating in tickling. Again it appeared that such games were not in the contemporary play repertoire of Warumungu children at Telford Spring.

By contrast, musical games currently played in schools at Telford Spring, Bradford Well, Auston, and Maringa were invariably performed in English and clearly derived from non-Aboriginal traditions. Nevertheless, there were interesting performative practices that were evident in the musical play of Aboriginal children in these contexts.

The usage of English language forms within performances of games, for example, was very idiosyncratic. For example, word stress patterns were often different from those used by standard English speakers. A clear example of this was found in the performance of "My Aunty Anna" (NW MAB 02 1 AV) by two Aboriginal girls, aged nine and eleven, at Bradford Well. In this performance, the word "hours" was split into two syllables, and the natural stress that would normally occur on "day" was displaced to the preceding word "a" (stresses are shown by underlining below):

My Aunty Anna plays the piana
Thirty four hou-urs a day.

As can be seen in the transcription of this performance in appendix 10, the clapping pattern of C/O C/R C/O C/L emphasized the standard stress pattern of the text, as the C/O (clap own hands) clap is sonically louder than the intervening claps. When the stressed word was displaced, the new stress was reinforced by the C/O clap coinciding with "a." In this school the same two performers also truncated the text of another game, leading to the abbreviation rather than extension of the text rhythm, in this case by two beats in the initial line:

I went to sea sea sea
To see what I could see see see
And all what I could see see see
Was the bottom of the deep blue sea sea sea.

What was particularly interesting in this performance was the adjustment of the clapping pattern to match the truncated text. Text lines 2, 3, and 4 were accompanied by four movements of the triple-clap pattern followed by three C/P (clap partner) claps coinciding with the repeated words at line endings. The C/O (clap own hands) movement which completes the three-beat cycle `was then performed with the anacrusis that begins the following line, prior to the commencement of the whole cycle again:

To	see	what	I	could	see	see	see
C/O	D/U	C/P	C/O	D/U	C/P	C/P	C/P

And	all	that	I	could	see	see	see
C/O	D/U	C/P	C/O	D/U	C/P	C/P	C/P

Was the	bottom of the deep		blue	sea	sea	sea
C/O	D/U	C/P	C/O	D/U	C/P	C/P	C/P

However, as the first line was curtailed, the clapping pattern was also adjusted to accommodate this:

I	went	to	sea	sea	sea
D/U	C/P	C/O	D/U	C/P	C/P

The performers did this almost automatically, without hesitation or interruption of the rhythmic flow, as can be seen in the full transcription (NW AS 02 4 AV) in appendix 10.

Although performing in English, Aboriginal children demonstrated other departures from standard English usage, particularly in regard to word endings, in addition to localizing the text to reflect their own experience in a number of games. Thus a newly created clapping game by two sisters at Auston referred to another game played with accessible materials:

Three tins three
Three tin we play
Three tin we play
All the way
(E TTN 01 1 AV. See another transcription in appendix 9.)

At Bradford Well, a popular game using the three-beat clap appeared to refer to the natural watercourse nearby, again with nonstandard English usage:

Down by the billabong, down by the sea
(Tasha) broke the bottle and blame it on me
I told Ma, Ma told Pa
(Tasha) got a hiding with a ha ha ha.
(NW DBI 02 3 AV)

Maringa versions of games, many learnt through association with relatives at Telford Spring or Alekarenge, tended to be truncated and included reversals of usual word order, for example in "My mother your mother":

Your mother my mother live down the street
Eighteen nineteen Marble Street
Every night they had a fight
And this is what they say say say.
(M MM 02 1 V)

In this version the first two pairs of words were reversed from the usual form and the performance terminated before the standard extended taunting, which represents what the mothers "say." It was as if the girls had copied the form but were insufficiently aware of the semantic content to complete it meaningfully.

The children performing these games at Maringa came from four different Aboriginal language groups (Warlpiri, Warumungu, Alyawarre, and Kaytetye) and spoke Kriol as a lingua franca for ordinary discourse among themselves. English was thus their third language. These children, and children in the other predominantly Aboriginal field schools, have learnt and adopted these forms of play in English without having the opportunity to learn the semantic, syntactic, and rhythmic verbal conventions of the genre. They are therefore performing outside the linguistic constraints outlined by Rubin (1995). This especially appears to be the case where the games have been learnt orally (as in almost all cases) or created without recourse to models (as in the Auston game "Three tins," which defies metrical conventions although it is delivered rhythmically). Where a written model has been adapted, as in the nursery rhyme clapping games at Maringa, the linguistic conventions of the original are maintained in the new play form.

The teacher at the Maringa school commented that there was evidence of Kriolisation in the children's use of English in the games. The children at Maringa also demonstrated considerable facility with code switching. Clapping games were played in English, the language in which they had been transmitted, but the Maringa children switched effortlessly between English game performance and Kriol game instructions and discussion. Such exchanges aptly encapsulate ways in which "the standard dialect is associated with front stage [public] behavior, [while] the local dialect symbolizes in-group solidarity" (Boztepe, n.d., p. 11).

Games at Maringa were learnt through kinship ties or adapted from classroom sources (such as songs taught in the classroom, or books of nursery rhymes displayed there). Kinship provided the main form of transmission for Aboriginal children in all the central Australian field schools, though Aboriginal and non-Aboriginal children frequently played together at Telford Spring and games traversed large distances, through the travel patterns of both Aboriginal and non-Aboriginal children, as discussed in chapter 7.

Musical Play at Bysiden and Strandli, Norway

Modes of transmission were quite different at Bysiden and bore a much closer resemblance to forms of transmission encountered at Springfield School. Perhaps the most obvious difference in game performance at Bysiden was a greater emphasis on diatonic singing and pitch accuracy. There tended to be less divergence in pitch between performers and less disparity in melody as a result. Playground songs generally had a wider vocal range than songs in other locations, with ranges up to a minor ninth. Wider intervallic leaps of a fifth or sixth were also characteristic of games, particularly at Bysiden. Children at Bysiden were more likely to use a "head voice" in their vocal production than children at other field schools. However, the disposition of older children both to flatten melodic contours and to sing in a lower tessitura than younger children was also observed in these playgrounds.

It is difficult to ascertain whether these characteristics are derived from musical antecedents within the culture. Bjørkvold (1989/1992), in his study of young children's spontaneous musical play, maintained that only 20 percent of young children's standard play song repertoire in Norway was directly obtained from the media and that the major part of this repertoire emanated from "a living song tradition extending from our own time back through many, many generations" (p. 80), though whether this is a child or adult song tradition is not explicitly stated. Certainly the melodies of some folk songs recorded in Rogaland, the county of Norway in which Stavanger and Strandli are both situated, have frequent melodic leaps of a fifth or sixth, and ranges of at least an octave are common (Bakka, Moen, & Sørstrønen, 1989; Walderhaug, Moen, Nilsen, & Haga, 1987).

However, Norwegian folklorist Ruth Ann Moen states that contemporary Norwegian children's singing games have little in common with older forms of traditional children's songs. Although some Norwegian vocal traditions are characterized by wide vocal ranges and large melodic intervals, use of head voice is not typical in traditional Norwegian folk song. Moen attributes the use of head voice and wider vocal range to the influence of educational experiences particularly at Bysiden, where there is a greater emphasis on singing in the classroom and better access to other forms of choral music (R. A. Moen, personal communication, April 20, 2007). Certainly in-tune singing cannot be said to be a general characteristic of children's song performance in Norway. Rather, it varies considerably between schools, depending on the amount and types of singing activity provided for the children (M. Espeland, personal communication, April 9, 2007). At Bysiden the presence of a trained music teacher ensured that children had regular school music activities, including singing, although the focus was more on music theater than on choral work (T. G. Norås, personal communication, April 18, 2007). In contrast, there was less educational emphasis on singing at Strandli School and vocal ranges of playground songs were more frequently limited to a sixth, with less use of head voice.

The emphasis in Bysiden School on traditional forms of play almost undoubtedly contributed to the diversity and frequency of game performance there. As previously discussed, the musical play of children at Bysiden in 2002 also contained many media influences. That children's vocal production and play in Norway is affected by the media on a global level is endorsed by experts in the fields of folklore (Moen and Norås) and music education (Espeland) (see personal communications above).

Although playground games at Bysiden incorporated many of the standard movement patterns found elsewhere, such as the three-beat clap, the Stavanger games were notable for complex clapping patterns and other idiosyncratic movement sequences. A number of clapping patterns incorporated crossed arms alternating with claps, for example, in the games "Kan du Huske den Gang" (can you remember that time), "Åli Åli Ei," and "O Han Ola" (oh Ola, a name). Back to back (B/B) handclaps were also prevalent in some games, such as "Her Polinesse" (a name).

Game configurations and use of space were also different from those encountered in Australian field locations. The game "Vet du Hva Som Hente Meg i Går" (do you know what happened yesterday, sung to the melody of the American song "She'll Be Comin' Round the Mountain") entailed a static line of children singing to accompany another performer who, facing the line, skipped sideways to the left then back to the right. Toward the end of each verse, the solo skipper picked two other players from the line who joined her skipping sideways during the "yi yi yippee" refrain. At this point in the game there were thus two lines perpendicular to each other, one stationary and the other in motion. A similar game structure was exemplified by the game "Det Kom to Piker Fra Berget det Blå" (there come two girls from the blue mountain) where two girls walked backward and forward toward and away from the singing line of performers, each choosing a partner at the culmination of the verse. During the chorus the two pairs of girls joined first right, then left elbows, swinging around each other and clapping at the point at which they changed directions.

Several ring games were also recorded at Bysiden, including "Vil du Ride" (will you ride). In this game children walked singing in unison around a single child in the middle, asking her or him whether he or she would ride with a named child of the opposite sex as a life partner. The child in the middle then responded with a solo answer, either agreeing to or disagreeing with this proposition, before picking another child to take the place in the middle. This game was therefore in call and response mode, though the call and response were musically identical and punctuated by whispered conferring in the center by members of the circle about the name of the chosen partner for the next soloist. (● **VIDEO SAMPLE:** See video example *Bysiden Vil du ride.*)

A call and response game was also found in the play of the three pairs of sisters of Eritrean, Somalian, and Ghanaian backgrounds who attended Bysiden School. The game (B EGB 02 2), learned by the two Eritrean sisters on a visit to Eritrea, contained a question and answer section between two players, followed by a boisterous refrain by all players at a faster tempo. The call–response section went as follows:

> What's your name?
> (Name)
> What time are you going to school?
> Three o'clock
> What are you gonna do now?
> I'm gonna buy chocolate/caramel.

It was sung while players walked sedately around the circle with hands joined. However the culminating section involved fast sideways skipping around the circle, punctuated by jumps at the line endings. Although this game was said to be in an Eritrean language (Tigrigna), the refrain appeared to be at least partly in Italian ("Maria ciao, ciao"), reflecting the colonial linguistic legacy of Eritrea and neighboring Ethiopia.

As mentioned in chapter 7, this group of friends also performed another Eritrean[1] ring game with a binary structure (ABB) and tempo change. The syncopated first section entailed the girls crouching down with bowed heads and crossed arms. At the beginning of the second section all performers sprang up and rhythmically pointed to their heads with one hand and their hip with the other, regularly reversing this movement which became faster and faster as the tempo increased. The final Eritrean game was also very syncopated but was performed only by the Eritrean sisters to a fast three-beat clap. (● **VIDEO SAMPLE:** See video example *Bysiden Eritrean games.*) Both this and the first game also incorporated regular metrical changes as the text unfolded. It appeared that these games were shared within the friendship group but that their performance did not extend into the general school community. Full transcriptions of several game melodies recorded in the Bysiden playground, including the Eritrean games, can be found in appendices 5 and 10.

It was at Bysiden that the only example of a canon found in the entire collection of games was encountered. This game, "Jeg Gikk en tur På Stien" (I walked along the path) used a well-known round about a cuckoo, equivalent forms of which are found in a number of European languages. The two seven-year-old performers had almost certainly learned this song in the classroom, but they had adapted it to game form in the playground by adding the ubiquitous three-beat clap. It was notable that the players had difficulty maintaining the canon; one of the girls adjusted her melody to match her partner's pitch while singing the words of a contrasting phrase. Another group of players who performed this game sang it in unison throughout and it was clear that the canon form was not usually represented in the playground.

The visit to Strandli was relatively brief and therefore did not provide a large number of games for discussion. Nearly all of the games recorded at Strandli were also found at Bysiden. The main difference in their performance was that the game texts were truncated, for example that of "Slå Makaroni." Musical play flourished in this playground, too, and was the province of both girls and boys, though the children stated that girls learned the games first and then passed them on to the boys. Perhaps because of the presence of the boys, many games were quite energetic, particularly "Slå På Ringen" (also found at Bysiden), a ring game in which two players raced around the perimeter of the circle in opposite directions, each trying to reach the spare place in the circle before the other, entailing several collisions and near misses.

Game sources here, as at Bysiden, were both ancient and modern. One elimination game, "Third Man in the Wind," was reported by my collaborator Thor Norås to have been described in the twelfth century. Another, "My Name Is Elvis Presley," bore a strong resemblance to the "Michael Jackson" game I had recorded at Springfield in 1990, complete with "kiss, kiss" and "sexy" verbal formulae, as described in chapter 7. Clearly multiple influences were at work in this playground, in spite of its location deep in the Norwegian countryside.

Musical Play at Summerglen, Ellington, and St. Augustine's, United Kingdom

Summerglen, Ellington, and St. Augustine's schools were much less isolated but, despite many similarities, play in each school still had its own particularities. Perhaps the most striking aspect of musical play at Summerglen was its relative exuberance. There was a high level of excitement and a high vocal dynamic level in game chants, especially when children were in groups of four or more.

Some games were quite subversive in their content and delivery. One of these was "Cat's Got the Measles," in which girls crossed and uncrossed their legs with a jumping movement to the following text, shouted out with enormous energy:

Cat's got the measles
Dog's got the fleas

Chicken's got the chicken pox
So have we.

Any player with uncrossed legs on the final word was required to remove an item of clothing, first of all one shoe, then another, then a sweater, and so on. The girls explained to me that this was played more in summer because of the need to remove clothing, although modesty could be preserved by removing small items such as hair clips. Not surprisingly, this game, with its steadily growing pile of clothes and unshod children as evidence of its performance, attracted the disapproval of teachers and thus had the added cachet of illicitness for the performers who played it regardless (and perhaps because of) adult ire. Although this game was also found at Ellington and St. Augustine's, it was not performed in such a vehement fashion elsewhere.

Another Summerglen game, which was apparently less controversial but quite anarchic in its performance, was "Orange Balls," a game not found in any other field location but known to exist in other schools in the Bedford area.[2] Similar to the Norwegian ring game "Vil du Ride" in intent, it was also performed in a circle to variants of the following text accompanied by mimetic movements:

Orange balls, orange balls
(Walk around circle)

The last one to sit down has a boyfriend
(Sit down quickly—last one to sit down moves out of the circle)

[Whispered conferring together to determine a "boyfriend's" name
    then the person who is out returns to the center of the circle]

(Name) says he loves you, (Name) says he loves you
(Walk around player in center of circle)

Clap your hands if you like him, orange balls
(Walk around player in center of circle, clapping own hands on
    beat)

Stamp your feet if you hate him
(Walk around player in center of circle, stamping feet on beat)

Stamp your feet if you hate him
Stamp your feet if you hate him, orange balls

Stick your hands out if you want to marry him, orange balls.

The final lines were often not articulated, but movements were substituted, with knowledge of the text assumed. Some performances were terminated after the first four lines by frenzied tickling of the victim in the center of the circle and, in one case, removal of her shoes. When the complete text was chanted, the game finished with the remainder of the players descending in a pile on the hapless child in the middle and trying to pull her arms outward to demonstrate her desire to marry the named "boyfriend." Usually this activity became quite violent but seemed to stop short of any actual physical harm. It appeared to me that such excessive levels of physicality and subversion were related to the high degree of adult control that was exerted in the playground. It seemed that greater control resulted in a greater level of resistance demonstrated through play.

Another very popular energetic game that I recorded only in the Summerglen playground was "I Found a Box of Matches." Like the Norwegian game "Vet du Hva Som Hente Meg i Går" this game adopted the refrain from the song "She'll Be Comin' Round the Mountain When She Comes," with some bizarre formulaic additions, as demonstrated by this version performed by two eight-year-old Anglo Indian girls:

> I found a box of matches
> Behind the kitchen door door door
> And when I wasn't looking
> They dropped them on the floor floor floor
> Singing I yi yippee yippee yi, Captain's pie
> Singing I yi yippee yippee yi, Captain's pie
> Singing I yi yippee, dancing like a hippie
> I yi yippee yippee yi, Captain's pie

(⬤ **VIDEO SAMPLE:** SP IFB 02 15, see full transcription in appendix 6. A video example of another performance can be seen in *SummerG I found.*)

As with "I Went to Sea Sea Sea" at Bradford Well in central Australia, the first section of this game was accompanied by a three-beat clap that was interrupted in order to perform C/P (clap partner) claps with the repeated words at the ends of lines 2 and 4. At the refrain, the girls linked right arms and swung each other around (as at Bysiden), but this movement was punctuated by a clap above then below the knee on "Captain's pie" and fingers placed close to the head and waved forward and back on "dancing like a hippie," delivered with a cheeky insouciance. The meaning of this game was never explained but it was always performed with great verve and humor.

There was also a strong assertion of children's identity in the game "That's the Way I Like It," which was recorded in all of the English field schools and, in a contrasting form, at Bysiden. The text of this game was appropriated from the hit disco song of the same name, recorded in 1975 by the American group KC and the Sunshine Band and found in numerous re-releases, advertisements, and film soundtracks since then. Whereas the Ellington and Bysiden versions of the game were limited to an articulation of the iconic song text "That's the way, uh huh uh huh, I like it, uh huh uh huh" (with the addition of scat syllables at Bysiden), the versions at Summerglen and St. Augustine's interpolated individual markers of identity and power within the appropriated song text. For example, Teela and Shaneeka, two eight-year-old Anglo Caribbean girls at Summerglen performed the following text to the standard upward and downward weaving hand movements used in this game (previously described in chapter 6):

BOTH: A B C hit it

That's the way (uh huh uh huh) I like it (uh huh uh huh)

That's the way (uh huh uh huh) I like it (uh huh uh huh)

TEELA: Teela is my name and basketball's my game.

BOTH: That's the way (uh huh uh huh) I like it (uh huh uh huh) . . .

SHANEEKA: Shaneeka's my name and basketball's my game

BOTH: So that's the way (uh huh uh huh) I like it (uh huh uh huh)

(SP TTW 02 4 AV)

As can be seen in this example, performers typically took turns to outline their names, preferences, and other markers of identity as solos then received affirmation of this by a combined rendition of the chorus by their partner or group. There was thus a structural reinforcement of these identity markers within the game performance.

At St. Augustine's the flouting of school-based conventions was a focus of the interpolated text, as in the version sung throughout by two nine-year-old girls:

BOTH: One two three hit it

That's the way (uh huh uh huh) I like it (uh huh uh huh)

That's the way (uh huh uh huh) I like it (uh huh uh huh)

My name's Jordan. I'm really really cool

And when I'm out shopping my friends are still at school

So that's the way (uh huh uh huh) I like it (uh huh uh huh)

That's the way (uh huh uh huh) I like it (uh huh uh huh)

(ST TTW 02 6 V. See full transcription in appendix 6.)

It seemed that these games, played in the schools where playgrounds were more regulated, functioned as ways in which the children (in this case, all girls) could reassert their individual power and identity.

At Ellington School, games were distinguished by markers of ethnic identity rather than individual identity. The most obvious feature of musical play in this school was the relatively large proportion of games of Punjabi or Bengali origin within the general play repertoire of children, reflecting the children's cultural and linguistic backgrounds. Of the 196 game items recorded at Ellington, there were 37 Punjabi game items and three Bengali. In addition, there were eight examples of musical play involving Bollywood songs, either emulating the singing and dancing sequences of the films or converting the songs to games. There was also active sharing of these games between different groups in the playground. When asked whether it was difficult to bridge the language gap between Punjabi and Bengali games, one nine-year-old girl told me that this was not a problem because "they were all Muslim" and would understand a Punjabi game even if they were Bangla-speaking. Another Bengali girl stated that both groups understood Urdu and could therefore understand Punjabi games. Certainly the proportion of Punjabi games reflected the dominant ethnic group in the school.

All of the Punjabi and Bengali games with text recorded at Ellington were recited rhythmically at indefinite pitch. There were no sung games emanating from these cultural sources other than those that were based on Bollywood songs. Movements for these games were most frequently of a counting-out variety, pointing at or tapping on or between individual fingers of all players until a finger was eliminated at the end of an iteration. Because of the number of fingers of multiple players, each game involved many iterations before coming to an end. Often the texts of the Punjabi counting-out games were quite scatological, as discussed in chapter 7, and play became increasingly raucous as the number of scatological references increased during the course of a game.

The Punjabi clapping game "Zig zag zoo," also discussed in chapter 7, was more salubrious in semantic content but ended with a punch or jab at the other player, the requisite skill for players being to punch their partners first. Like "Grandpa's Waking Up," "Zig Zag Zoo" was a clapping game, the first with claps at different vertical levels, the second with a triple clap punctuated by three C/O (clap own hands) claps of two quavers and a crotchet after each phrase in the middle section of the game. While "Zig zag zoo" culminates in a punch, "Grandpa's Waking Up" ends with one player pointing at the other. The first player to point then "punishes" the other player by hitting her on the back ten times. Elimination, surprise, or punishment in some form was thus a feature of many of the games observed.

The majority of the Punjabi games had simple duple meters, with rhythmic elements consisting largely of quavers and crotchets, though rhythms could be extended by additional phrases, sometimes added at the end of the game for emphasis. The Bengali counting-out game *Mas mas amar mas* contained divisive rhythms. Many of the games accelerated toward the end as excitement mounted. Transcriptions of "Zig Zag Zoo," "Grandpa's Waking Up," and "Mas Mas Amar Mas" can be found in appendices 4 and 6. (● **VIDEO SAMPLE:** See video examples *Ellington ZZZ 1 and 2*, and *Ellington Mas mas*.)

It is interesting that Punjabi and Bengali games have been maintained in this community, in direct contrast to the situation in the central Australian schools where traditional Aboriginal games were not in evidence. It would seem that many years of assimilationist policies, particularly in regard to Aboriginal languages, have contributed to the loss of Aboriginal games, just as the languages themselves are in decline. It is only in recent decades that strategies for maintaining the languages have begun to be employed within schools and other organizations in these central Australian communities. It is within more remote communities with less culture contact that some traditional play forms such as *milpatjunanyi* appear to have survived. Although there was clearly a disposition for cultural maintenance within the Asian communities in Keighley through familial transmission and return visits to the country of origin, there was less overt performance of Punjabi games at St Augustine's, for reasons outlined in chapters 5 and 7. It would appear that both school and community endorsement is required for game traditions to continue publicly.

There were other musically related differences between the games recorded in English field schools and those recorded in Australia. In the analyzed sample, the vocal range of the English songs tended to be greater, particularly at Summerglen and St. Augustine's, where ranges of a major or minor seventh were common and even ranges of a major or minor ninth were found. This occurred less frequently at Ellington, where ranges were more likely to be a fifth or sixth and rendition at indefinite pitch was more common. Once again, tessitura was relatively low, from A below middle C to F or G above. The tessitura was, however, higher than that found in the Australian schools and use of head voice was more evident.

Musical Play at Birch Vale (Seattle) and Nora Conn (Los Angeles), United States

Playground games in the U.S. field locations differed from the English games in a similar way. The recorded American children tended to use chest register more than children in the English or Norwegian field schools, even when singing higher notes within playground songs. Melodic intervals within songs were generally compressed so that the intervallic range was not large. Ranges of a sixth were most common, although there were occasional exceptions to this, such as one example of the "Sar Macka Dora" genre at Nora Conn that had a range of a minor ninth. Tessitura was also generally low, extending from A below middle C to G above. The performances of some older girls at Birch Vale were even lower in tessitura, extending downward from middle C to E below. Tonal shift within and between text lines was in evidence in musical play forms at both Birch Vale and Nora Conn. It was notable that, even in call–response forms, such as "The Little Frog" (where call and response phrases of the original model were identical in pitch), the response often varied in tonality from the call.

Many of the games of the recently arrived Latino immigrant children at Birch Vale were rendered at indefinite pitch or had very labile melodies with frequent pronounced shifts in tonality. As in the English games, this was particularly the case when games involved high levels of excitement. Thus the melody of the very active and suspenseful game "Lobo" (wolf) constantly vacillated between pitched melody and heightened speech. In this call and response game, widely known throughout South America, children of both sexes danced in a circle, singing out to the 'wolf' about her whereabouts.[3] The "wolf" responded that she was doing a range of activities to ready herself to emerge from the tree (or "house") where she was hiding. She gradually revealed herself, and then, at the words "Estoy abriendome la puerta" (I am opening the door), leapt out to catch the children, an activity accompanied by much animated chasing, screaming, and violent "eating" of victims. Children could only escape this fate by reaching another tree that represented a point of safety, calling out "close the door" when the safe area was secured. Once caught, the victims joined the wolf in the tree and the process started again. One interesting aspect of the game in this playground was the multiple versions of the call. Because the players had each brought their own version from their place of origin, the performance reflected regional differences. As shown in the text below, different variants were dominant in different iterations of the game, depending on who remained in the circle and who was singing more loudly. Similarly, the wolf's responses varied according to who occupied the role, with one wolf responding with an imaginative variant in English.

Spanish	*English Translation*
Group Calls (Variants):	Group Calls (Variants):
Juguemos en el bosque	We play in the forest
Cuando el lobo no esta aquí	When the wolf isn't here
¿Lobo, lobo estas aquí?	Wolf, wolf, are you here?

Buscaremos en el bosque	We look in the forest
Preguntamos al lobo si esta aquí	And ask the wolf if he is here
¿Lobo, lobo estas aquí?	Wolf, wolf, are you here?
Jugaremos en el bosque	We play in the forest
Mientras el lobo no esta aquí	While the Wolf isn't here
¿Lobo, lobo estas aquí?	Wolf, Wolf, are you here?
Lobo answers:	Wolf answers:
Estoy poniendo me . . .	I am putting on . . .
. . . los zapatos	. . . my shoes
. . . mis pantalones	. . . my pants
. . . la camisa	. . . my shirt
. . . los calzones	. . . my underwear
. . . los guantes	. . . my gloves
. . .hairy armpits	. . .hairy armpits
Estoy bañiando me	I am bathing myself
Estoy abriendo me la puerta!!!!!!!	I am opening the door!!!!!!!

(HV WT 04 1 V Recorded Birch Vale 2004. See video example *BirchV Lobo.*)
🔊 VIDEO SAMPLE

Another game with antecedents in many parts of the Americas was "Melon y Sandia" (melon and watermelon). Although this was sung throughout, the melody shifted tonality between text lines. This game was kinesthetically identical to the English game "Oranges and Lemons,"[4] with children passing in a line under an arch formed by the uplifted arms of two players until at the culminating text line the arch descended to catch one child. The caught player then decided whether she would become a melon or watermelon, and joined on behind the corresponding side of the arch.

However, the first part of the game text in this performance varied from the usual forms found in the second half of the song. The new text reflected these children's (or others') recent experiences of immigration, with travel and border-crossing figuring prominently in the first few lines:

Spanish	*English Translation*
A la piporo piporo	(Vocables used as a count in)
De la mar, de la mar	From the sea, from the sea
Por aquí por el pasar	From here to pass the time
Lo delante corre mucho	The ones at the front run fast
Lo de atrás se quedaran	The ones behind get left behind
Tras tras tras	Behind, behind, behind

Una mexicana con blusa bonita	A Mexican girl with a pretty blouse
Se fue a trabajar	Went to work
¿Melón o sandia?	Melon or watermelon
Verbena, verbena	Street party, street party
La vieja gatena	The old woman with cat's eye
La. . . . . . cae arena	Sand. . . . . falls on her.
Campanita de oro deja me pasar	Golden bell let me pass
Junto a mis hijos	Together with my children
Menos los de atrás	But without those behind
Dame los otro día,	Give them to me another day
Otro día, Otro día, día, día,	Another day, another day, day, day
día, día	day, day
¿Melón o sandia?	Melon or watermelon?

(HV OL 04 1 V Recorded Birch Vale 2004)

The reference to the Mexican girl going to work probably denotes the expectation that work will be found in the United States. It is possible that the request "golden bell let me pass" may refer to a U.S. or border landmark known by Mexicans, although the latter part of the song is commonly found throughout the Americas, in Venezuela the landmark being a river, and in other places a bridge (C. Derwent, personal communication, 31 January 2005).[5] The fracturing of families that may also occur during the process of immigration is another theme explored in the final lines.

It is notable that similar textual formulae referring to difficulties encountered in immigration were found in another clapping game that these children played at Birch Vale, "Frankenstein", in which the lifestyle California offered was typically the object of both longing and ridicule:

Spanish	*English Translation*
Frankenstein	Frankenstein
Fue a ver	Went to see
Al Castillo	To the castle
Del vampiro	Of the vampire
Se asusto	He was frightened
Y grito:	And he shouted:
A la ver, a ver, a ver	To see, to see, to see
De la mar, de la mar	To the sea, to the sea
Por la culpa de pasar	For the fault of passing here
Lo' de delante corre mucho	Those at the front run fast
Lo' de atrás se quedaran, tras,	Those behind, will stay behind,
tras, tras	behind, behind

California, California	California, California
Estados Unidos	U.S.A.
Viajes presumidos	Trips cancelled
California, California	California, California
Blanco chúpate un mango	White (man) suck a mango
Se callo de la silla (OW!)	He fell from the seat (OW!)

(HV FR 04 1 Recorded Birch Vale 2004)

As discussed in chapter 7, these games in Spanish were very much the province of the children attending the English Language Learning classes and were not transmitted to other children in the Birch Vale playground. They included clapping games, ring games, and chasing games, but the jump rope games that they had learnt from English-speaking peers in the Birch Vale playground were all performed in English.

The English language games that were more prevalent at Birch Vale were frequently syncopated, reflecting the influences of African American games and popular music forms, as discussed in chapter 7. The effect of cheerleading was evident in certain genres of musical play that were found only in the schools in the United States. Cheers, such as "Brick Wall Waterfall" and "The Little Frog" were often rendered with an aggressive body stance and vocal delivery. On some occasions they were performed by a single group while on others they formed the locus of a verbal 'battle' between two or more performers. (◉ VIDEO SAMPLE: See video example *BirchV Brick wall*.)

Perhaps the most memorable example of this was the extended improvised oral "battle" (based on the cheer "The Little Frog") between a prolific group of grade-4 girls and their African American male recreation co-ordinator, which I witnessed on my first day at the school without the benefit of recording equipment. The girls referred to this as a "competition" between themselves and the popular coordinator.

It was clear that such exchanges, with their derisive overtones, were learnt from external sources before becoming standard fare in the playground. Many girls at Birch Vale heard cheers at baseball games (either as spectators or while waiting to play) and others attended cheerleader classes held outside school hours, where these routines were mastered before becoming raw material for musical play in the playground. Cheers were also learned from peers, more frequently by emulation but, on one occasion, by memorizing the text from a written source playmates had provided. The original function of these cheers, to support or deride a sports team, was retained in the playground at times. In one instance of this I saw two African American girls emphatically calling out "Brick Wall Waterfall" to a group of boys who were playing football in a corner of the Birch Vale playground.

There appears to be considerable overlap in definitions of play genres termed "cheers," "stepping" (or "steps"), "drill teams," and "routines." Harwood (1998b) describes "genres known variously as cheers, drill teams, and routines" as activities in which "individuals improvise and then practice to refine an extended set of movements to the accompaniment of a traditional cheer text or a contemporary rap or pop song" (p. 117). Gaunt (2006) defines cheers as forms of musical play involving synchronized "performances of percussive choreography–based on a more polyrhythmic and multi-limbed sequence of handclapping gestures, thigh-slapping, and foot-stomping" (p. 76). At Birch Vale, cheers performed by predominantly white groups were more verbal and were termed chants, though the group described above in a verbal competition with the recreation coordinator frequently devised movement routines to other chants and songs. Groups that had several African American members incorporated the choreographed movements more frequently in their performances, though when one group was in the process of learning a cheer, they were told by a knowledgeable member to "just say it" and to make up the movements later, in response to another girl's concern that she did not "know the moves." The syncopated "I Woke up in the Morning," described by its Samoan American performer as a "rap" (see chapter 7) was accompanied only by minimal shifting from one foot to another on the beat, though it had been made up in collaboration with the performer's older cousin, who was a cheerleader. (See appendix 7 for transcription.)

At Nora Conn School, the cheer form as defined by Gaunt (2006) was more clearly in evidence in performances of "H-E-L-L-O," previously described in chapter 5. With its heavily percussive movements involving stomping and slapping of thighs and calves, "H-E-L-L-O" perhaps more closely resembled the antecedent form of "stepping," "a complex multilayered dance genre created by black American Greek-letter fraternities and sororities," featuring "synchronized, precise, sharp, and complex rhythmical body movements combined with singing, chanting and verbal play" (Malone, 1996, p. 188). In fact, as Gaunt indicates, there is regional variation in terminology, and Chagall, more familiar with children's play on the West Coast of the United States, identifies this form as "stepping" (I. Chagall, personal communication, 2 April, 2007). The performances observed at Nora Conn were clearly in keeping with Malone's description of stepping, in which, "through clapping, foot stamping, and intricate slapping of the hands against various body parts, multiple rhythms are produced" (1996, p. 191). The children themselves termed "H-E-L-L-O" a "rhythm" and demonstrated how this rhythm could be varied by starting the stomping on either the left or right foot, the synchronization of this being prearranged by the performers. (⬤ VIDEO SAMPLE: See video example *NoraC HELLO*.) Although jump rope was popular in both Birch Vale and Nora Conn playgrounds, the playing of Double Dutch jump rope, using two ropes, was only observed at Nora Conn. Again this may have been due to the larger proportion of African American children both at the school and attending the after-school arts activities. However, as with other forms of musical play found at Nora Conn, Double Dutch jump rope was transmitted across gender and ethnic boundaries.

Musical Play at Pada and San (Busan, Korea)

As the two schools in Busan were ethnically homogeneous in population, there was little evidence of cross-cultural transmission between children in the playground. However, it was clear that cross-cultural transmission has occurred in the past and continues in some forms today. There are corollaries between a number of game genres found in Busan and Japanese children's games (T. Murao, personal communication, 11 July 2006). This is not surprising, given the extensive period of colonization of the Korean peninsula by Japan well into the twentieth century, the current omnipresence of Japanese media in Korea, and the geographical proximity of the two nations. As Busan is a port city located in the southeast corner of Korea closest to Japan, it has frequently been the site of intercultural contact both with Japan and other trading nations for centuries. Strong historical links with China have also resulted in cultural borrowings in both directions. It appears that some games recorded in Korea have an extensive lineage, though their genesis is uncertain. One such game is "Yongsimi" (a girl's name), played in both of the Busan field schools. Variants of this game have also been reported in Taiwan and Singapore (C. H. Lum, personal communication, 19 November 2006).

"Yongsimi" exemplified the high levels of both kinesthetic and cognitive skill that distinguished the musical play of Korean children. As previously stated, one feature of the musical play recorded in Busan was the interpolation of the scissors-paper-rock (or "gawi bawi bo"—scissors-rock-cloth) formula into many games. This often entailed split-second changes of movement and text within a game, requiring rapid cognitive shifts. In "Yongsimi," played by two performers, two claps on the beat were followed by a scissors-paper-rock movement on the next beat. Depending on the outcome of this movement, the players had to immediately respond with appropriate text selected from several alternatives, the winner calling *merong* (a teasing word) and the loser *silsu* (mistake) or else both chanting *jjak jjak maja* (perfect). Each verbal response was accompanied by a corresponding different movement. In recorded performances this sequence was maintained repeatedly within the game at a very fast tempo, as can be seen in the video example *Pada Yongsimi* and in the full transcription (appendix 8). (🔊 VIDEO SAMPLE)

Similar feats of cognitive and kinesthetic skill were displayed in other games. For example, in "P'ong Dang" (onomatopoeic words representing the sound of stones hitting water) the left hands of the two players remained clasped throughout the game but on every alternate beat there was a scissors-paper-rock movement with right hands. On the other alternating beat the winner of each scissors-paper-rock contest hit the back of the loser's clasped left hand with the palm of her right hand. If there was no winner, both players hit the back of each other's hands. Athough this was in a much slower duple meter than "Yongsimi," it still required a considerable level of competence to maintain the pattern. It is notable that this was achieved without any hesitation or irregularity of meter.

The most frequently recorded game in the Busan schools was "P'urŭn Hanŭl Ŭnhasu" (blue sky, Milky Way) which, though not incorporating scissors paper rock, still contained very complex movement sequences (⏵ **VIDEO SAMPLE:** see video example *Pada P'urun*). This game was in 6/8, the clapping pattern consisting of 12 discrete movements over a 12 quaver cycle, preceded by the standard shaking of joined hands on the initial formula "Sse sse sse," as shown in table 10.3.

Immediately following the performance transcribed above, the two grade-6 players spontaneously performed a variant in which the second half of the movement cycle was replaced by interweaving climbing hands movements (as in "That's the Way I Like It," discussed in chapter 6), creating a new cycle of equal virtuosity. (See appendix 8 for a complete transcription of K PH 04 23.)

The mastery of such complex sequences seems to be culturally specific, requiring culturally determined schemata for successful performance. While the Anglo Australian children I observed learning games from Korean Australian friends in Sydney were able to master a simpler Korean game ("Ach'im Baram") because of their familiarity with the scissors-paper-rock formula, they had much greater difficulty with the intricate clapping pattern of "P'urŭn Hanŭl Ŭnhasu," which contained movement patterns outside the scope of their previous experience. The fast sequences of multiple movements and clapping movements at different levels that are characteristic of Korean games seemed to cause particular difficulty.

As might be evident from the description of "P'urŭn Hanŭl Ŭnhasu" above, the games recorded in the Busan field schools also tended to be more metrically regular than many games recorded elsewhere. Although the majority of the games were in simple duple meter, the triple subdivision of the beat in "P'urŭn Hanŭl Ŭnhasu" reflects the triple meter typically found in traditional Korean folk music. Perhaps because of the general level of kinesthetic dexterity, there were fewer deviations from standard duple (either simple or compound) meters caused by the insertion of mimetic movements or elimina-

Table 10.3. Text and Movements of "P'urŭn Hanŭl Ŭnhasu," Pada School, Busan

Text	Movement Sequence
Sse sse sse	Initial formula: hands shaken up and down with the three words.
P'urŭn Hanŭl Ŭnhasu (In the blue sky, in the Milky Way)	12-beat movement cycle, each movement one quaver duration. Each text line is twelve quavers' duration:
Hayan jjokbae-ae (In a white boat)	1 Clap own hands (C/O) 2 Clap backs of right hands together (B/BR) 3 Clap right hands together (R/R)
Gyesu-namu han gru (There is a great laurel tree)	4 Clap own hands (C/O) 5 Clap backs of left hands together (B/BL) 6 Clap left hands together (L/L)
Toggi han mari (And one rabbit)	7 Clap own hands (C/O) 8 Down up clap (D/U) 9 Clap partner's hands (C/P)
Dotdae-do ani dalgo (Without any stick)	10 Clap own hands (C/O), one player above the other 11 Modified D/U, one player both palms up, other player both palms down.
Satdae-do opsi (Or any pole)	12 Clap partner's hands (C/P)
Gagido jaldo ganda (Goes well)	
Seojjok nara-ro (To a land to the west)	

(K PH 04 23 Recorded Busan 2004)

tion movements than were found in games in other locations. However, there were exceptions to this rule. Additive meter was utilised in the game "Ujeong Test," discussed earlier. (See appendix 8 for a complete transcription of this game.)

Additionally, in one performance of "P'ong dang" recorded in the Pada playground the movement sequence varied, with either one or two scissors-paper-rock movements alternating with the clap around closed fists. The resultant movement meter vacillated between duple and triple, though the text rhythm remained duple throughout.

Another difference between the musical play of the children recorded in Busan and that of children in other localities was a generally wider vocal range within melodies, with some genres such as "P'ong Dang" and "P'urŭn Hanŭl Ŭnhasu" having ranges of a major or minor ninth. The wide vocal range of the "Digimon" game (also a minor ninth) and "Saeukkang" (an octave) might be attributed to their genesis in adult-generated media songs (*Digimon* being a television theme song and "Saeukkang" a television advertisement for shrimp crackers). The text and melody of "P'urŭn Hanŭl Ŭnhasu" also originated from an adult source, "Bandal "(half moon) a very popular song composed for children by Geuk Yeong Yun in 1924, during the period of Japanese occupation (J. Song, personal communication, 28 March 2005). Other game songs, such as "Yongsimi," "Yennal Yecch'oge" (long ago), and "Ppon Deggi" (Pupa) had ranges of a major or minor sixth. In contrast, "Ujeong Test," which was pitched only in the initial formula, had a limited range of a major third. It is interesting that "P'urŭn Hanŭl Ŭnhasu" has retained its wide range despite many years of playground performance, as distinct from games such as "See See My Playmate" in Sydney where the melodic contour has been flattened through playground use. (See appendices 8 and 10 for full transcriptions of "Digimon" game, "Saeukkang," "Yongsimi," "Yennal Yecch'oge," "Ujeong Test," and "P'urŭn Hanŭl Ŭnhasu.")

Like all song games found in the field playgrounds, the games at Busan were also subject to tonal shifts in performance and therefore could not be said to be pentatonic in their rendition. Nevertheless there was an intact sense of pentatonicism within short phrases, denoted by typically gapped melodies with combinations of major and minor seconds and thirds. However, these forms of tonality were more likely to be related to the antecedent Korean scale forms of *p'yongjo* and *kyemonjo* than to any notion of a "universal" pentatonic scale (Kim, 1998). Large melodic leaps of a minor seventh, minor sixth and perfect fifths and fourths were found in performances of the adult-derived "Saeukkang" and "P'urŭn Hanŭl Ŭnhasu." Once again this reflects a different practice from that found in the Australian playgrounds where melodic leaps were flattened in performance.

In form, many of the games were repetitive, with reiterated phrases interspersed with changing numbers, letters, or movements (such as scissors-paper-rock, splits, pushing off balance, or punching). A particular favorite of the boys at San School was a game called "Cchanggu Mokku" (Cchanggu eats) in which the exploits of an animated character, Cchanggu, from a Korean children's television show were mimed between clapping movements which culminated in a punch on the word "pow." Other highly physical forms of play popular with both sexes included call and response games such as "Uri Jip-ae Whae Wanni" (why did you come to our house) and the competitive counting-out games "Hana Tul Set" (one two three) and "Sam Yuk Gu" (three six nine) described in chapter 5. (⬤ **VIDEO SAMPLE:** See video examples *Pada Uri jipe* and *San Hana tul set.*)

The "punishments" of flicking, hitting, and pounding children's arms, hands, necks and backs were relatively idiosyncratic to Korean games when compared with games in other field schools. While some clapping games such as "P'urun Hanŭl Ŭnhasu" were typically only played by girls, many games were played by both boys and girls, because of the confines of time and space imposed by the Korean school day on children's leisure time at school.

Conclusion

What emerges from ethnographic study of children's musical play across several continents is a view of musical play as cognitively, linguistically, and kinesthetically challenging. As can be seen in the foregoing examples, children draw on performative stimuli from their environment both to emulate them and to spontaneously improvise multiple variants of their own devising. Play involves constant improvisatory evolution, constant self-imposed challenge, and constant resistance to adult-imposed norms, expressed through performative and structural features. The musical outcomes of these characteristics negate notions of structural simplicity in children's musical play. A summary of the characteristics of musical play occurring in school playgrounds and the implications of this for music pedagogy occurring in school classrooms follows in the culminating chapter.

Conclusions and Pedagogical Implications

CHAPTER II

Conclusions and Pedagogical Implications

In the opening chapter I outlined assumptions regarding children's musical play that have led to the global adoption of certain pedagogical practices in music education. These assumptions, based on observations and patterns of thought linked to particular cultural and historical contexts, have been reinforced by findings of children's playlore studies that are also historically and culturally bound. In attempting to create "universals" from decontextualized data, music educators and researchers into children's musical play traditions in the first half of the twentieth century created mythologized versions of these traditions which have direct implications for classroom practice. More recent studies (for example, Addo, 1995; Campbell, 1991, 1998; Harwood, 1996; Marsh, 1997; Merrill-Mirsky, 1988, and Riddell, 1990) have challenged this mythology. My international observations of children's musical play in many school playgrounds over fifteen years support the view that performance practices and processes of transmission and generation used by children in their play demonstrate a complexity that is often discounted in educational settings.

Children's Musical Play: Theories and Practices

As discussed in chapter 1, the "playlike" features attributed to children's musical play include spontaneous movement as an embodiment of enjoyment, and simplicity of form, rhythm, and melody. "Playlikeness" in pedagogical terms incorporates movement to assist in the development of musical understanding. In addition, "playlike" pedagogy, especially in the early years of school, is also characterized by the use of simple reiterative structures, in particular, ostinato, canon, rondo, echo, and call-response forms; materials focused rhythmically on the precedence of duple meter, with simple two and four-beat rhythmic units predominating; and melodic materials based on the falling minor third, building to anhemitonic melodies using from three to five tones, with the pentatonic scale prevailing. What is deemed to be "fitting for children" is a collection of materials and activities that are simple enough to fit the perceived "pre-intellectual" (Orff, 1963/1990, p. 142) needs of children.

Critiques of this pedagogy have focused on the lack of congruence between the overly limited musical materials of the classroom and the musical environment provided both by the music of the playground and music widely disseminated by the media. Attention has been drawn to the rhythmic complexity and melodic and tonal variety of children's singing games, partly as a result of the direct influence of media-disseminated music on stylistic characteristics of the games.

The analysis of playground singing games collected globally supports these pedagogical critiques. Rhythmically, playground singing games are much more complex than their pedagogical counterparts. While the texts of the majority of games exhibit a duple meter for part of their rendition, there is frequently a polymetric relationship between text rhythm and movement pattern. This is particularly the case when texts are combined with the three-beat clapping pattern that is deemed by the children to be universal in its application to a variety of texts and which was the most frequently observed clapping pattern in many playgrounds.

Although a developmental sequence in the learning and performance of clapping patterns was observed and articulated by the children, with a duple clapping pattern being said to precede the acquisition of the triple pattern, the three-beat pattern was generally acquired and ably demonstrated (in conjunction with duple texts) by children from the age of six years. Eight-year-olds were observed performing games with seven-beat and thirteen-beat clapping patterns and additive meters.

In addition, the expansion and contraction of text rhythms resulting from the interaction with movement formulae result in partially ametric renditions of singing games. While some examples of ametricality might be viewed as accidental, in many instances there was consistent ametricality in the performance of particular text and movement formulae, especially when these formulae involved "counting out" or elimination of players, as in the game genre "Sar Macka Dora." When text rhythm and movement are considered in combination, then, neither duple meter nor the "universal" binary rhythms postulated by Brailoiu can be seen to dominate playground singing game performance. Rhythmic complexity in children's musical play is also influenced by the adoption of syncopation from popular music disseminated by the media.

Melodically, there is a similar lack of congruence between the assumed characteristics of playground games and those observed in the field schools. Although singing games exhibit less complexity melodically than rhythmically, the melodic simplicities do not conform to those specified in classroom practice. The falling minor third was found in many performances of singing games, but was just as often absent from many performances. The most frequently occurring intervals throughout the collection of children's playground games and other forms of musical play were both major and minor seconds. The incidence of minor seconds would indicate that children's musical play does not currently fit the anhemitonic pentatonic model espoused by prominent classroom methodologies.

A much more important melodic structural feature of singing games in some playgrounds is the functioning of the initial tone as the tonal center of each game and the presence of movable or flexible tonality within and between text lines. This has particular implications for teaching practices that have functional tonality (where "doh" equals the tonic) as a core premise. Clearly, tonality in these children's singing games operates in a different way from pentatonic, major, minor, or modal tonalities. Tonal melodies do, of course, form part of children's wider musical environment and are adopted and adapted for performance in a playground context. When held within the repertoire of a performing group for a protracted period of time, however, what may have originated as a tonal melody is frequently transformed into something quite different.

The use of tonic solfa in the teaching of play-based materials in the classroom is thus problematic. Similarly, the common practice of pairing song material derived from playground games with pentatonic accompaniments in which the tonic and fifth are reiterated as drones demonstrates a complete mismatch between the tonality of playground games and the tonality into which it is subsumed in the classroom.

Other melodic features of playground singing games that have pedagogical implications are those of range and tessitura. The melodic range of individual games in analyzed performances varied widely between different schools. Ranges of up to a ninth were found in some games in Norway, England, and Korea, though some of the games with wide vocal ranges had been derived from adult sources. In the American and Australian locations and in one English school, ranges of songs performed in the playground rarely exceeded a sixth. It is therefore difficult to generalize in this regard, with significant local and cultural differences being evident. Nevertheless, within given cultural contexts there may be a mismatch between ranges of song material provided in the classroom and that of the playground. For example, my observations in U.S. playgrounds support those of Campbell (1991), who found that the melodic range of American songs published for use with children in the classroom was usually much wider than that found in playground songs *by* children.

Tessitura of games was also much lower than that commonly found in published classroom material.[1] The tessitura of the analyzed game sample fell between E below middle C and C above middle C, with a concentration of performances in the middle to lower end of the tessitura. A probable explanation for the low tessitura of the games is the common performance practice of moving from pitched song to unpitched speech. As the tonal center of the children's speech appears to be fairly low, the melodies with which the speech is interwoven are also low in pitch. In some cases, (for example, in some performances of "Down Down Baby") melodic renditions can arise directly from exaggerated speech inflections.

An appropriate tessitura for classroom songs has been the focus of considerable debate in recent years. Some music educators expound the theory that a higher tessitura is required for children to "find their singing voice," that is, to sing rather than chant using nonspecific pitches (Bridges, 1994; Phillips, 1992). Others have held to the view that children (especially in the early years of schooling) sing more comfortably and learn songs more easily when a small range and low tessitura (a - a') are employed (McDonald and Simons, 1989, pp. 92–93). The material recorded in school playgrounds supports the latter view. Moreover, the children appeared to have relatively little difficulty in moving between a "singing" and "speaking" voice, although it may be that renditions exhibiting inflected speech patterns may sometimes have been intended as pitched renditions.

It was also the case in many performances that pitches and intervals did not always conform to pitches within a Western twelve-tone scale. The use of nonstandard pitches has been equated with nonacquisition of a "singing voice" by some music educators (Rutkowski, 1996). Such a view, however, must be considered both Eurocentric and "adultocentric" in the context of children's musical play. Addo (1995) has commented on the necessity to view the pitch of children's songs within the culture from which they are drawn. She also suggests that a less Eurocentric notion of pitch is necessary for analyzing Ghanaian games.

These games have their own authenticity of tonality and timbre in performance that, as Harwood (1996) has stated, should not be regulated for classroom consumption. Nevertheless, their relative tunefulness, or lack of it, appears to bear some relationship to exposure to singing in other contexts. It is difficult to make generalizations regarding this issue. While the singing of the children at Bysiden and Springfield seemed to be more in tune as a result of regular formal singing experience within the school, there was no similar correlation at Birch Vale, where singing was also regularly undertaken with the school music specialist. Indeed, the notion of singing in tune did not appear to be part of the game aesthetic in any location. Children's indoor and outdoor singing behavior was affected by situational factors such as confidence and the need to project. Developing an understanding of these factors may be more important in engendering desired singing behaviors in the classroom than trying to "harness" children's play singing.

One interesting characteristic of playground performances of the "Sar Macka Dora" genre that was repeatedly transmitted through classroom teaching at Springfield was that the most commonly performed tessitura (c' - g') was the same as that of the published version taught in the classroom.[2] Similarly, although several melodic traditions were evident in playground performances of this genre at this school, the most frequently performed melodic type was that taught in the classroom, with the dominance of the classroom type increasing over the collection period. It may be that providing a strong and repeated singing model over a lengthy period of time in the classroom assists children's development of accurate pitch.

It can be seen, then, that classroom practice has the capacity to change playground practice. In view of Basic's (1986) critique of the oversimplification of playground materials for use in the classroom, it would seem that an over-dependence on simple rhythmic, melodic, and formal elements in classroom programs might well lead to the "systematic impoverishment" (Basic, 1986, p. 131) of playground traditions. This influence, however, is certainly countered, to some extent, by children's attraction to novel forms of the games and their proclivity to vary material.

This variability can also be seen in musical form, rhythm, melody, text, and movement. The text, rhythm, and melody of analyzed game genres were reiterative and sometimes aggregative and cyclical. However, there were exceptions to most generalizations. For example, while the melodies and rhythms of "Down Down Baby" were cyclical at the text line or phrase level, those of the "Sar Macka Dora" genre were not, for the larger part of their rendition. The process of formulaic construction results in augmentation or diminution of text lines and phrases and the juxtaposition of newly acquired or invented textual, rhythmic, or melodic phrases into a known form, as discussed in chapter 8. Game genres therefore exhibit a certain "plasticity" of form.

The structural features of these playground singing games can be seen to adhere in some ways to the general features of orally transmitted forms delineated by Ong (1982). They are, to varying extents, additive, aggregative, and repetitious. However, these structural characteristics are deployed in quite different ways in different genres and performances and cannot be seen to constitute evidence of a particular oral "mentality." The inclusion of adult-derived materials disseminated by oral and literate means in the playground repertoire further precludes the possibility of making generalizations of this kind.

The ostinato, which has prevailed as a pedagogical tool in Orff-Schulwerk, can certainly be identified in the frequently cyclical movement patterns of playground singing games. Once again, however, there are exceptions to any generalization. In performances of many game genres, mimetic movements and textual intrusions intervened to interrupt and vary any cyclical pattern that was established, as outlined in chapter 10. There was no evidence of Orff's rondo forms in any of the game repertoire at any school and only one instance of canon, an example that was derived from classroom performance in that school.

The incidence of other formal categories varied in different contexts. At Springfield, echo and call-response forms might be seen to be implicit in the reiteration of paired lines, for example, in the "Down Down Baby" genre. However, with the exception of the hocketed rendition of several performances of the "Sar Macka Dora" genre by particular friendship groups, all performances of playground singing games at Springfield and other Australian schools were performed monophonically and non-antiphonally. Echo and call-response therefore did not constitute part of performance practice of the games in these schools as they are seen to do in pedagogical lore. It is clear, though, that cultural factors affected this in other locations. The typical call-response form of sports cheers was transferred into the playground in the U.S. schools. The African American traditions of musical play also utilized this form, as exemplified by the game "Jigalo," recorded at Nora Conn School in Los Angeles and discussed at length by Gaunt (1997, 2006). A number of traditional games such as the Spanish "Lobo," Norwegian "Vil du Ride," and Korean "Uri Jip-ae Whae Wanni" also demonstrated call and response in their performance. In the English schools call-response form was adapted from examples occurring in the media, as in "That's the Way I Like It," though, as with Australian games, this form was not prevalent in the U.K. field schools. Addo (1995) identifies call-response forms in Ghanaian children's playground games but contextualizes them within the general characteristics of Ghanaian music.

What is important to acknowledge, then, is the contextual nature of many characteristics of children's musical play, though some generalizations can be made. It is also evident that there is a dichotomy between many of the stylistic characteristics of children's playground games as observed in the field schools and the assumptions about children's musical play which have guided pedagogical provision of repertoire and practices considered "fitting for children" (Orff, 1963/1990, p. 142). However, Orff's observations of children's performance practice of these games as "never music alone, but music connected with movement, dance and speech—not to be listened to, meaningful only in active participation" (1963/1990, p. 142) appear to hold true in children's musical play globally. Such performance practices also influence transmission processes that, in turn, have implications for teaching and learning processes in the classroom.

Teaching and Learning: Lessons from the Playground

"Active participation" in musical play in the playground occurs in the context of a friendship group that provides the psychological safety within which children can accommodate both aesthetic and socio-cultural differences. Performance practice of the games within social groups in some playgrounds is therefore inclusive and tolerant of variation. Indeed, constant variation and striving for novelty is part of the game aesthetic. However, as with musical characteristics, the extent to which this occurs varies significantly in different contexts. Inclusiveness of performative difference appeared to flourish more readily in contexts where cooperative behavior was fostered and where children were allowed a greater degree of responsibility and freedom. The personalities of individual children also affected their willingness to countenance experimentation or variation in performance practice.

Participation in game performance confirms group solidarity and appears to help children attain individual popularity, or at least acceptance. At Springfield this was particularly important for children who had language backgrounds other than English, or who had migrated into the playground either from other schools or other countries. The school practice of deliberately integrating children of different ages (in composite classes) and different ethnicities (in classroom activities) appeared to facilitate the transmission of games across age and ethnic boundaries, by creating classroom friendship groupings that continued to function in the playground.

Policies that endorse the pairing of children from older and younger classroom cohorts for various activities seem to encourage a disposition on the part of older children to help younger friends, acquaintances, or siblings. This was certainly the case with the children at the Nora Conn after-school center, where children of different ages were constantly engaged in planned experiences together and extended this inter-age bonding to their unplanned play activities in the playground. In addition, inter-age familial and kinship bonds were particularly significant in the transmission practices of the Aboriginal children in central Australian schools and the Punjabi and Bengali children in West Yorkshire.

As reported by Harwood (1992), games are usually transmitted between age peers and from older to younger children. In a number of field locations, however, it was also evident that children were engaged in careful tuition of novice players. Children were aware of developmental differences in playing abilities, particularly in the performance of movement patterns, and accommodated these differences, supporting learners' progress by modeling behaviors slightly beyond their present level of competence. In so doing they were enacting a process that strongly resembled the educational notion of "scaffolding" propounded by Wood, Bruner, and Ross (1976).

In the playground, proficiency was increased by observing and participating in modeled performance. Learning was constantly facilitated by physical proximity to, and physical contact with, other performers. Like the children in Harwood's (1992, 1998a) study, children in all field locations might practice new games or performance skills in pairs, at times moving away from a larger group to do so. In all forms of playground teaching and learning of games, the whole game was observed and attempted by adept players and novices alike. Skills were never isolated from a game to be taught in individual developmental segments but were taught within the holistic framework of the complete game. Song acquisition therefore occurred through aggregative "catching" of musical, textual, and movement formulae during repeated renditions of a musical whole.

Moreover, children did not have a linear requirement for mastery of one skill or performance genre before moving on to a new one. Instead, they created constant challenges for themselves by devising or incorporating new movements, words, or music into their play. The resulting variants might then be circulated within the playground by being performed with other players in slightly different friendship configurations or being imitated by observers who watched the performance and "caught" the game.

Clearly, these characteristics have important implications for teaching and learning procedures in the music classroom. My observations support Harwood's (1987, 1992, 1993a, 1993b, 1994a, 1994b, 1996, 1998a), Riddell's (1990), and Wiggins' (2001) recommendations that children may engage more productively in classroom musical activities in small groups or pairs. Modeling and observation of more skilled child practitioners may assist a learning process that is largely participatory in nature. Children's practice of skills is also likely to be facilitated by small group work, rather than the large group drill that frequently occurs in classrooms, and by providing sufficient room and opportunity for physical movement and discussion through which ideas might be demonstrated and exchanged (see also Campbell's 1998 discussion of the benefits of opportunities for small group work and movement in the classroom).

The common practice of segmenting songs into phrases for teaching in the classroom also needs to be reconsidered. As Harwood's (1987, 1992, 1998a) research also indicates, children in the playground learn through repeated observation and gradual participation in a whole song. In the classroom, children's song acquisition can be facilitated by repeated renditions of the whole song with varied listening, performance, and creative responses to maintain children's interest and involvement while familiarity with the song is increased.

Although musical development is clearly evident in children's playground teaching and learning, as Basic (1986) and Campbell (1998) suggest, it does not conform to adult notions of increasing musical difficulty. For example, six-year-olds have frequently mastered polymetric performance practice in their playground performances, a practice that is far beyond what is expected of them in the classroom. Similarly, at any given time, children are often engaged in the simultaneous development of several skills associated with different game genres and are creating constant challenges for themselves by devising variants.

Teachers, therefore, need to look beyond a prescribed adult conception of increasing difficulty, to the skill levels that children demonstrate in their playground performances. If children are allowed to generate their own variants of classroom activities they can, with teacher assistance, increase the level of difficulty at their own pace and introduce and follow different musical directions. Teachers can take on a scaffolding rather than directive role, providing new materials for performance, listening, and composition which acknowledge children's observed current musical skills and take them further. The advantages Kodály perceived of linking classroom content with play so that children could practice classroom materials in the playground might be more productive if the process were to operate in a two-directional way, so that the "musical richness and dynamism of open forms" (Basic, 1986, p. 131) of playground materials were incorporated into classroom programs.

Creativity in Children's Musical Play

As I have undertaken a detailed discussion of children's innovative strategies in the playground in chapter 8, my comments here will focus on implications for the classroom. What is clear from the analysis of children's composition in performance is their high level of innovative skill. As children are engaged in a continuing cycle of creation and variation both within and between multiple performances, this process can be seen as a synthesis of improvisational and compositional strategies. These strategies can be grouped according to patterns of formulaic construction, as demonstrated in some other oral performance traditions, rather than adhering to any "universal" models of children's composition or improvisation. Individual strategies, however, are linked to the specific characteristics of the playground traditions in different contexts. Thus the table of innovative strategies that children use in their play (see chapter

313

8) does not constitute a generalized model either of formulaic construction or of children's composition.

Nevertheless, this table demonstrates the wide variety of compositional strategies in use in these playgrounds, an array that far surpasses the usual compositional devices available for classroom use in the primary or elementary school. While children in the playground are capable of manipulating complex musical materials using a vast range of techniques, in the classroom the limitation of musical materials for composition is compounded by the limited techniques available for use, and the teachers' limited expectations, especially of younger children.

If teachers increase both the complexity and diversity of materials and techniques available for classroom composition and improvisation, it is likely that compositional outcomes will improve and that children will be able to demonstrate their potential to the full, an approach Glover (2000) recommends. Children, for example, might devise pieces involving polymeters or additive meters. They might manipulate the melodic contours of a piece, augment or diminish the length of phrases, or rearrange a series of rhythmic, melodic, or textual formulae, rather than creating yet another ostinato accompaniment, a canon, or a rondo. Once again, their observed behaviors can provide a guide to possible classroom techniques that will improve rather than hinder their compositional progress.

A sufficient illustration of the progressive "deskilling" of children in an educational environment can be taken from a 1994 conversation with the girls whose innovations in performances of "Teacher Teacher" and "See See My Playmate" were discussed in chapter 8. Despite the fact that they had effortlessly negotiated polymeters and syncopation in their performances in 1993 and, to a lesser extent, in 1994, they told me that they now knew, through their music education, that it was inappropriate to put the three-beat clap with the duple meter that was found in most popular music. It was instructive, and slightly distressing, to observe that their game performances in 1994 tended to be less rhythmically proficient than their 1993 performances and their compositional strategies less diverse.

Another important implication is that teachers need to allow for collaborative compositional activity to take place in the classroom as well as the playground. The usefulness of group interaction in generating creative activity has been attested by DeLorenzo (1989), Borstadt (1990), Davidson (1990), Wiggins (1994, 1999, 2003), Kaschub (1997), and Burnard (2002), and the ability to work collaboratively as well as independently is seen by Gardner (1993) as constituting one aspect of observable creative processes. Many curriculum documents advocate collaborative work to some extent. Yet many teachers seem unable to trust children to work independently and to make their own decisions as small groups or individuals.

Of equal importance is the need to allow children time to revisit and refine material that is being explored, as advocated by Davidson (1990), Webster (2003), and Wiggins (2003). While school timetables and curricula impose inevitable time limits on creative endeavors, compositions in the classroom might perhaps be viewed more frequently as works in progress, with children being the arbiters of the time required to produce what they judge to be a product. The recursive and constant nature of variation in the playground might then have a more readily identified corollary in the classroom, and children would have the opportunity to develop their holistic compositional plans (Davies, 1994; Wiggins, 1994, 2003) to the full. As teachers, we need to focus less on a perceived dichotomy between process and product in composition and give children the time, diversity of materials, and trust which will enable them to reach in the classroom the potential that they so confidently display in the playground.

A Changing Tradition

The recursive processes inherent in the maintenance and change of an orally transmitted musical tradition can clearly be seen to operate within school playgrounds on a global basis. For the children in many schools, diversity was a feature of their social and auditory environment that was not only accommodated, but used to creative advantage. Material for musical play was acquired from a variety of sources, then combined and manipulated using a multiplicity of strategies.

Interethnic transmission of games and game formulae appeared to be facilitated by a number of factors: the multiethnic constitution of friendship groups; a high level of ethnic diversity, so that "difference" was a norm; the psychological safety provided by the friendship group; the confidence and popularity of individual children; the interest in novelty; and the recognition of known formulae in new manifestations. The lack of importance of the texts' semantic content also contributed to the ease with which children from other language backgrounds could participate in games in the dominant language and game formulae from traditions utilizing other languages could be adopted into the canon of games in the playground for varying periods of time. However, the extent to which this occurred varied among schools, often depending on an established climate of acceptance to flourish. Limited exposure to ethnic difference, as in the Busan schools, naturally also limited interethnic exchange, though traditions had often been influenced by interethnic borrowings over an extended period of time.

Formulae were also frequently derived from audiovisual and written media. This was evident not only in the texts, but in the adoption of rhythmic and movement formulae from popular songs on television, videos, movies, CDs, and the Internet. In addition, the cycle of maintenance and change was extended through the appropriation and dissemination of game material in books, television shows, and movies intended for the child market. The media is thus seen to contribute to the continued performance of musical play, rather than to its decline.

In view of children's continual use of media-disseminated music as a source of creative materials, it would seem that music that is "fitting for children" (Orff, 1963/1990, p. 142) must be defined more broadly and that the improvisation and creative activity that are integral to Orff-Schulwerk practice should operate in relation to an expanded musical repertoire that takes account of children's real musical worlds. Classroom methods have acknowledged the importance of allowing children to engage in musical play, to explore and create music and movement in the classroom but they have tended not to acknowledge in a similar way the real complexity of children's compositional and performance skills.

It is time to move away from unnecessary limits on children's classroom activities. In providing classroom music materials teachers should therefore include music that is already part of children's creative repertoire, rather than insisting on the exclusive classroom use of music "of unquestioned quality" (Kodály, cited in Choksy, 1981, p. 8), a value judgment which, it must be conceded, is subjective. While it will always be the role of the teacher to extend children's musical horizons beyond their current repertoire, it can be done in conjunction with children's own preferences and in line with their own proclivity for novelty.

Does this mean that every aspect of musical play demonstrated in the playground must be adopted in the classroom? Clearly this is not entirely advantageous, as different aims are "in play" in different environments. There are times when limiting musical parameters may be helpful in achieving certain aims, such as learning standard forms of notation, an important skill focus of Kodály method. However, to generalize these limitations to all forms of classroom activity is not the most appropriate approach for fully developing children's performative and creative potential. It may be that different strands of classroom musical activity can be planned that accommodate these differing needs in various ways.

As noted by Kodály so many years ago, the classroom is also a source of material for children's performance and creative manipulation in the playground. Songs that are enjoyed in the classroom also enter the playground canon and the teaching of playground games in the classroom helps to perpetuate the tradition. It is possible that the endorsement of playground singing games in the classroom may contribute to an increased incidence in the playing of these games by boys. Although the classroom appropriation of musical material owned by children might be cause for some ethical concern, it is evident that appropriation of adult material is a standard feature of the playground tradition and that children's constant variation of materials helps to invalidate any form of adult ownership.

Teachers are thus in a position to show an acceptance of children's musical traditions and the varied sources on which they draw. From this position of acceptance, they can then broaden children's musical perspectives by providing a wide range of music for performance, listening and as a basis for creation. New repertoire and classroom approaches to music can then be utilized, at will, by children in the playground. Classroom musical activities can thus contribute to, rather than be antithetical to, the continued flourishing of multiple traditions of children's musical play.

The Challenge of Children's Musical Play

Self-imposed challenge is a characteristic of children's musical play. Perhaps a challenge may also be thrown out to music educators and interested adults alike: that is, to acknowledge children's musical play in all its variety and complexity. The adoption of "universal" models and orthodoxies can assist music educators and musicologists to order and make sense of musical materials in their aural and social environment, but the adherence to these models can blind us to situated realities. Such models and underlying assumptions must be seen to be neither universally applicable nor immutable. I have endeavored to demonstrate that music educators, musicologists, and other adults have much to learn from the detailed and contextualized observation and analysis of the operant processes and characteristics of children's musical play. Yet, in almost every school I visited I was told by adults that children did not engage in that sort of play any more. My observation of more than two thousand play performances would indicate that this was a problem of adult perception, an opacity of view, rather than a reality.

Musical play is all around us and it is no longer possible to ignore its existence in and outside of school without ignoring its essential importance in the lives of children. During my time in Korea I visited the Bulguksa Buddhist temple in the ancient city of Gyeongju on the occasion of Buddha's birthday. A large group of girls and boys, clothed in traditional dress, sat in orderly rows waiting to participate in the day's ceremonies. As they waited, one or two began to play clapping and flicking games, accompanied by chants. Gradually the numbers playing increased until the whole group was involved in an irrepressible outbreak of play. I have seen these outbreaks in many different communities worldwide. To disregard them is to lose a vital opportunity to enrich our pedagogical conceptions. To allow an outbreak of play to permeate pedagogy is to infuse it with exciting possibilities.

It is time for adults to peer out through the windows of the classroom and *notice* children's musical play. By incorporating observed manifestations of this play into the classroom, it is possible to develop a "playful" rather than "playlike" pedagogy, one that takes account of the cultural nuances and realities of children's musical capabilities and preferences, providing cognitive, performative, creative, and kinesthetic challenge. In so doing, music educators may lessen the dichotomy between the playground and the classroom. Harnessing the combined resources and efforts of teachers and collaborative classmates to transcend previously imposed educational boundaries can remove tensions created by these strictures, providing an outcome that brings satisfaction to all. In the words of a group of girls performing a clapping game in an English playground:

BONITA: My name's Bonita. I'm really in a stress

Got my friends, my teachers, to help me 'n' never end

ALL: So that's the way (uh huh uh huh) I like it (uh huh uh huh)

That's the way (uh huh uh huh) I like it (uh huh uh huh)

Index of Playground Singing Game Genres from International Field Sites, 1990–2004

Code	Title/Type	Location	1990	1991	1993	1994	1995	1996	2001	2002	2004	Total
A	Skipping counting out alphabet	Bysiden								3		3
A		Strandli								2		2
A	(total for A):	All schools										5
AA	Áli áli ei	Bysiden								19		19
AAO	The big ship sailed on the alley alley o	St Augustine's								2		2
AB	ABC (Barbie/Michael Jackson version)	Springfield				2						2
ABC	ABC	Springfield			9	2						11
ABCD	ABCD...	Telford Spring							1			1
ABCDE	ABCD	Nora Conn									2	2
AC	ABC	Bysiden								3		3
AF	ABC (feet)	Ellington								3		3
AHO	À han Ola	Bysiden								1		1
AIB	Ach'im baram	San									6	6
AIB		Pada									1	1
AIB		Springfield				4						4
AIB	(total for AIB):	All schools										11
AIM	Angel in the moonlight	San									1	1
AIT	All in together girls	Nora Conn									2	2
AK	Akkar Bakkar	Ellington								6		6
AL	Anne Liane	Bysiden								21		21
AL		Auston							3			3
AL		Strandli								3		3
AL		St Augustine's								4		4
AL	(total for AL):	All schools										31
ALC	Alison's camel	Maringa								2		2
ALR	A la rueda	Birch Vale									2	2
AOS	Apple on a stick	Bradford Well								1		1
AOS		Telford Spring							13	2		15
AOS	(total for AOS):	All schools										16

Code	Title	School	No.
AS	A sailor went to sea sea sea	Bysiden	17
AS		Ellington	20
AS		Birch Vale	2
AS		Bradford Well	5
AS		Strandli	1
AS		Summerglen	4
AS		Springfield	1
AS		St Augustine's	5
AS		Telford Spring	2
AS	(total for AS):	All schools	57
AY	Agi yomso	Pada	3
B	Bluebirds through the window	Bysiden	1
BB	Baa baa black sheep	Springfield	5
BBC	Bluebells cockle shells (jumprope)	Nora Conn	4
BBS	Bo bo see at m tat	Birch Vale	2
BBY	Baby baby, can you come with me	Birch Vale	2
BC	Bole chudyan	Ellington	5
BD	Dance to Blue Danube (sung)	Birch Vale	1
BG	Bosnian Game	Bysiden	1
BHG	Boys' hand game (Year 1)	Springfield	1
BM	Big Mac	Nora Conn	3
BNG	B I N G O	St Augustine's	1
BS	Boom shakalaka	Telford Spring	3
BW	Black and white	Springfield	9
BWT	Black and white TV	Springfield	3
BWW	Brick wall waterfall	Birch Vale	28
C	Cinderella	Birch Vale	1
C		Nora Conn	1
C		Springfield	8
C	(total for C):	All schools	10
CC	Chinese checkers	Springfield	4

(continued)

Code	Title/Type	Location	1990	1991	1993	1994	1995	1996	2001	2002	2004	Total
CCC	Ching Chong/King Kong Chinaman	Auston							3			3
CCK	Chocolate Cake	Auston							4	2		6
CCL	Coca cola	Summerglen								8		8
CCL	Coca cola	St Augustine's								5		5
CCL	(total for CCL):	All schools										13
CCR	Cat's cradle	St Augustine's								2		2
CG	Chinese girls are very funny	Ellington								22		22
CG		Auston							2			2
CG		Birch Vale									4	4
CG		Maringa								4		4
CG		Summerglen								2		2
CG		Springfield	1									3
CG	(total for CG):	All schools						1				37
CGA	Counting game	Springfield										1
CGM	Cat's got the measles	Ellington					1			7		7
CGM		Summerglen								2		2
CGM		St Augustine's								3		3
CGM	(total for CGM):	All schools										12
CH	Cheater's handshake	Birch Vale									3	3
CHK	Che che koolay	Ellington								1		1
CI	Cinderella [Disney]	Birch Vale									2	2
CIN	Cinderella [Korea]	San									1	1
CJ	Chinese Japanese	Springfield			1							1
CJM	Cowboy Joe from Mexico	Ellington								1		1
CK	Cuckoo [Jeg gikk en tur på stien]	Bysiden								5		5
CL	Clap clap click click	St Augustine's								1		1
CM	Cchanggu mokku mokku	San									5	5
CO	Concentration	Springfield					1					1
CP	Coca cola pepsi cola	Telford Spring							2	4		6

Code	Item	School					Total
CR	Cuando el reloj	Birch Vale				3	3
CS	Claire's song	Summerglen			1		1
CSF	Concentration Sixty-Four	Birch Vale				3	3
CSH	Chagi sogae hagi	San				2	2
CW	Chinese whispers	Ellington			1		1
D	Dilemma	Ellington			1		1
DA	Dolphins are	St Augustine's			1		1
DB	Debajo del puente	Birch Vale				1	1
DBB	Down by the banks	Springfield	7	19	8	1	35
DBB		Bradford Well			2		2
DBB		Nora Conn				14	14
DBB		Telford Spring			10	1	11
DBB	(total for DBB):	All schools					62
DBI	Down by the billabong	Auston				6	6
DBI		Bradford Well				4	4
DBI		Telford Spring				2	2
DBI	(total for DBI):	All schools					12
DBV	Down by the valley	Birch Vale				3	3
DBZ	Don Butz	Birch Vale				1	1
DD	Double Dutch (jumprope)	Birch Vale			1		1
DD		Nora Conn				7	7
DD	(total for DD):	All schools					8
DDB	Down down baby	Auston			4		4
DDB		Birch Vale				7	7
DDB		Maringa			2		2
DDB		Bradford Well			2		2
DDB		Nora Conn				6	6
DDB		Summerglen			3		3
DDB		Springfield	6	1	23	20	50
DDB		St Augustine's				15	15
DDB		Telford Spring	19			9	28

(continued)

Code	Title/Type	Location	1990	1991	1993	1994	1995	1996	2001	2002	2004	Total
DDB	(total for DDB):	All schools										117
DDG	Duck duck goose	Ellington								1		1
DDG		Summerglen								1		1
DDG		St Augustine's								1		1
DDG		Telford Spring								1		1
DDG	(total for DDG):	All schools										4
DG	Digimon game	Pada									7	7
DH	Deck the halls with kerosene	Springfield				1						1
DI	Drop in the ocean	Ellington								1		1
DIS	Disco	Birch Vale									4	4
DK	Dr Knickerbocker	Springfield	1		3							4
DKT	Der kom to piker fra berget det blå	Bysiden								2		2
DM	Don't mess	Birch Vale									1	1
DP	Don Pancho y su Barriga	Birch Vale									2	2
DR	Dance routine with chant	Bysiden								1		1
DS	Dari segi (Counting legs)	San									2	2
DT	Do do this this	Birch Vale									9	9
DT		St Augustine's								11		11
DT		Springfield			1							1
DT	(total for DT):	All schools										22
DUK	Du, kota / Tu khota	Ellington								2		2
DX	Da da dexi	Springfield	3		5	1						9
DYE	Do you ever think	Birch Vale									1	1
E	Everyday	Springfield			1							1
EAT	Ein-å-tyve	Bysiden								1		1
EB	Eggs bacon chips or cheese	Springfield				2						2
EC	Emma the camel	Summerglen								4		4
ECC	Eni ci ci ci	Bysiden								1		1
EE	Eli Eli (I went to a Chinese restaurant)	Ellington								1		1

Code	Game	School	Total
EE		Birch Vale	10
EE		St Augustine's	6
EE		Summerglen	10
EE		Springfield	22
EE	(total for EE):	All schools	49
EGA	Eritrean game 1	Bysiden	2
EGB	Eritrean game 2	Bysiden	3
EGC	Eritrean game 3	Bysiden	2
EGH	Eg va på Grand Hotell	Bysiden	6
EGH		Strandli	2
EGH	(total for EGH):	All schools	8
EL	Elastics game	Bysiden	1
EL		Pada	6
EL	(total for EL):	All schools	7
ELV	Elevator game	San	1
EM	Eeny meeny [NB: crossnumbered with AK]	Ellington	4
EMD	Eeni meeni desameeni	Bysiden	2
EP	Elvis Presley	Springfield	3
ER	Everything's ready it's time to bake	Springfield	1
ET	Stå på samme sted	Bysiden	3
ETT	En ten tini	Bysiden	8
EX	Extra extra	Telford Spring	1
F	Fly	Springfield	1
FC	Firecracker	Springfield	12
FDC	On the first day of Christmas	Auston	1
FJ	Frère Jacques	Ellington	1
FO	Flip over	Springfield	1
FPT	Four person textless	Telford Spring	1
FR	Frankenstein	Birch Vale	1
FS	Fruit Salad	Ellington	2
FST	Five Stones	Ellington	1

(continued)

Code	Title/Type	Location	1990	1991	1993	1994	1995	1996	2001	2002	2004	Total
G	Gatekeeper	Pada									1	1
GIW	Girls in white dresses	Springfield				2						2
GP	Girl power	Birch Vale									2	2
GS	Goodbye song	Bysiden								1		1
GWU	Grandpa's waking up	Ellington								4		4
H	I want a hippopotamus for Christmas	Springfield				1						1
HB	Happy Birthday	Springfield	1									1
HBO	Honica Bonica	Ellington								3		3
HBR	Harbour Bridge	Springfield				1						1
HCB	Hot cross buns	Telford Spring							1			1
HD	Humpty Dumpty	Maringa								1		1
HE	Helicopter game	Nora Conn									1	1
HL	High low jolly peppers	Springfield			1							1
HLO	H E L L O	Nora Conn									10	10
HLP	Help	Nora Conn									3	3
HOP	Hopscotch	Pada									1	1
HOS	Hop old squirrel	Birch Vale									1	1
HP	Her Polinesse	Bysiden								4		4
HP		Strandli								3		3
HP	(total for HP):	All schools								7		7
HS	Heads and shoulders knees and toes	Ellington								1		1
HS		Summerglen								2		2
HS	(total for HS):	All schools								3		3
HTS	Hana tul set ABCD	San									3	3
HTS		Pada									1	1
HTS	(total for HTS):	All schools									4	4
HVH	Birch Vale Hornets	Birch Vale									2	2
HWG	Here we go loop de loop	Nora Conn									1	1
HYE	Have you ever ever ever	St Augustine's								2		2

Code	Title	School				
I	Improvised game 1	Bysiden				2
IAN	I'm a nut	Telford Spring		2	2	2
IC	Icecream icecream cherry on the top	Birch Vale			3	3
ICL	I can't live it	Birch Vale			1	1
ICS	Icecream soda	Nora Conn			6	6
IFB	I found a box of matches	Summerglen			26	26
IG	Improvised game 2	Bysiden			1	1
IIG	If I go someplace	San				1
IIG		Pada			1	1
IIG	(total for IIG):	All schools				2
IKL	I know a little Chinese girl	St Augustine's			6	6
ILD	I am a little Dutch girl	Springfield				4
ILD		Telford Spring	1	3		12
ILD	(total for ILD):	All schools		10	2	16
ILT	I'm a little teapot	Maringa			2	2
IMS	I'm sexy	Telford Spring			1	1
IO	Ickle ockle bluebottle	St Augustine's			1	1
IP	Ip dip dogshit	Ellington			1	1
IP		Summerglen			2	2
IP	(total for IP):	All schools				3
IPP	Inky pinky ponky	Ellington			1	1
IPP		Telford Spring		1		1
IPP	(total for IPP):	All schools				2
IS	Indian song (unidentified)	Ellington			1	1
IWS	Incy wincy spider	St Augustine's			1	1
IWU	I woke up in the morning	Birch Vale			5	5
J	Jigalo	Nora Conn			4	4
JB	Jingle Bells	Ellington			3	3
JB		Springfield		3	2	5
JB	(total for JB):	All schools			3	8
JJ	Jack and Jill	Maringa			5	5

(continued)

Code	Title/Type	Location	1990	1991	1993	1994	1995	1996	2001	2002	2004	Total
JNY	Johnny on one foot	Nora Conn									1	1
JPL	Jjok pal lyeo	San									7	7
JW	Joy to the world	Springfield				1						1
K	Korean clapping song (93 type)	Springfield			3							3
KB	Kookaburra	Ellington								1		1
KD	Kan du huske den gang	Bysiden								14		14
KFC	Kentucky Fried Chicken and Pizza Hut	Summerglen								1		1
KG	Korean game (textless, Joseph)	Springfield				1						1
KHG	Korean hand game (textless, learnt in bus)	Springfield				1						1
KK	To Kathryn from Charlotte	Bysiden								4		4
KN	Konggi nori	San									2	2
KP	Kom palppadak so palppadak	Pada									3	3
KS	Ketchup song	Ellington								1		1
KS	Ketchup song	Summerglen								6		6
KS	Ketchup song	St Augustine's								2		2
KS	(total for KS):	All schools										9
KSN	Kamja e ssagi naso	San									3	3
KSN	Kamja e ssagi naso	Pada									4	4
KSN	(total for KSN):	All schools										7
KT	Korean textless clapping game (94 Year 5 type)	Springfield				1						1
KTK	Kitty Kat	Nora Conn								1		1
KWO	Kaeguri wa olch'aengi	Pada									4	4
L	Litter	Springfield			2							2
LAD	Ladders	Ellington								1		1
LB	London Bridge	Summerglen								1		1
LBM	La Bomba	Birch Vale									1	1
LCG	Leg crossing game	Springfield				1						1
LEM	Lemonade	Birch Vale									4	4
LEM	Lemonade	Nora Conn									8	8

(continued)

Code	Title	School	n
LEM	(total for LEM):	All schools	12
LF	Little Froggy	Birch Vale	3
LG	Ladies and gentlemen	Springfield	4
LIM	Life is a mystery	Ellington	3
LMP	Little Miss Piggy	Springfield	1
LO	Lollipop	St Augustine's	1
LOB	Gom dari (Legs of the bear)	San	6
LS	Las señoras que caminan en el puente	Birch Vale	1
M	Michael and Madonna	Springfield	3
MA	My auntie's sick in bed	Springfield	1
MAB	My aunt Biano	Bysiden	5
MAB		Bradford Well	2
MAB		Summerglen	7
MAB	(total for MAB):	All schools	14
MAC	Macarena	St Augustine's	4
MB	My boyfriend gave me an apple	Ellington	11
MB		Auston	3
MB		Summerglen	11
MB		St Augustine's	10
MB		Springfield	28
MB		Telford Spring	26
MB	(total for MB):	All schools	89
MBI	My boyfriend (improvised)	Telford Spring	1
MBL	Mabel Mabel set the table	Nora Conn	2
MBR	Miss Brown	Auston	2
MBR		Birch Vale	11
MBR		Nora Conn	2
MBR		Summerglen	8
MBR		Springfield	8
MBR		Telford Spring	2
MBR	(total for MBR):	All schools	33

Code	Title/Type	Location	1990	1991	1993	1994	1995	1996	2001	2002	2004	Total
MCB	Me cal de un balcón	Birch Vale									2	2
MCK	Mickey mouse	Summerglen								2		2
MD	My dog is a good dog	St Augustine's								1		1
MDS	Mary Mary do the splits	Ellington								2		2
MEX	Mexico Mexico (jumprope)	Birch Vale									1	1
MF	My father	Springfield			2							2
MFI	My father is a garbage man	Bysiden								10		10
MFI		Ellington								10		10
MFI		Summerglen								12		12
MFI	(total for MFI):	All schools										32
MG	My granma [Iko Iko]	Springfield	3		1							4
MGN	Mugunghwa ggochi pieossm-nida	Pada									1	1
MHB	Mama's havin a baby	Nora Conn									2	2
MIK	Mama's in the kitchen	Birch Vale									1	1
MIW	Third man in the wind	Strandli								1		1
MJK	Michael Jackson (93 type)	Springfield			3	1						4
MJN	Michael Jackson (90 type)	Springfield	1			4						5
ML	Meter lang makaroni	Bysiden								4		4
ML		Strandli								5		5
ML	(total for ML):	All schools										9
MLM	Mailman	Birch Vale									24	24
MLM		Nora Conn									4	4
MLM	(total for MLM):	All schools										28
MM	My mother (your mother)	Auston							12	4		16
MM		Maringa								3		3
MM		Bradford Well								1		1
MM		Springfield	8	1	20	13	2					44
MM		Telford Spring							18	13		31
MM	(total for MM):	All schools										95

330

Code	Title	School							Total
MMA	Mas mas amar mas	Ellington					2		2
MMM	Miss Mary Mac	Birch Vale						1	1
MMM		Nora Conn						5	5
MMM		Springfield			18				30
MMM		Telford Spring				8			11
MMM	(total for MMM):	All schools			12	8	3		47
MMS	My mother said	St Augustine's					5		5
MN	My name is	Bysiden					9		9
MN		Strandli					1		1
MN		Summerglen					20		20
MN		St Augustine's					14		14
MN	(total for MN):	All schools							44
MSS	Miss Susie had a steamboat	Birch Vale						7	7
MSS		Nora Conn						2	2
MSS	(total for MSS):	All schools							9
MT	My mother told me	Summerglen					5		5
MW	Mrs White had a fright	Springfield							1
N	Nicky nacky nocky noo	Springfield		1					1
NC	Noisy classroom	Ellington					1		1
NEO	Neo (You)	Pada						2	2
NG	Name game	Springfield					1		1
NK	Nobody knows but Dinah	Birch Vale						1	1
NT	Nol ttwigi	Pada						6	6
OB	Orange Balls	Summerglen					12		12
OD	One day you're gunna get caught	Springfield	1						1
ODR	One day a rabbit	Springfield	1						1
ODW	Oh dear what can the matter be	Springfield		2					2
OL	Oranges and lemons	Birch Vale							1
OMD	Oh my darling	Ellington						1	1
OTT	One two three	Auston							3
OTT		Springfield	8					3	11

(continued)

Code	Title/Type	Location	1990	1991	1993	1994	1995	1996	2001	2002	2004	Total
OTT		Telford Spring							13	6		19
OTT	(total for OTT):	All schools										33
P	Patacake	Birch Vale									2	2
P		Springfield			1							1
P	(total for P):	All schools										3
PB	Peanut butter marmalade jam	Telford Spring							6			6
PBU	Peanut butter (jelly)	St Augustine's								1		1
PC	Pussy cat	Summerglen								1		1
PD	P'ong dang	San									12	12
PD		Pada									6	6
PD	(total for PD):	All schools										18
PDG	Ppon deggi	San									9	9
PDG		Pada									2	2
PDG	(total for PDG):	All schools										11
PG	Pushing game	San								1		1
PGU	Pigu (Dodgeball)	San								1		1
PH	Pu'rün hanül ünhasu	San									11	11
PH		Pada									28	28
PH	(total for PH):	All schools									39	39
PI	P'aeng I	Pada								1		1
PP	Peas in the pot	Springfield			1							1
PPP	Pica Pica Piedra	Birch Vale									1	1
PS	Popeye the sailor man	Springfield			2	2						4
R	Rudolph the rednosed reindeer	Springfield			2	2						2
RB	Ribena	Summerglen								1		1
RC	Racing car number nine	Ellington								1		1
RC		Springfield			2							2
RC	(total for RC):	All schools										3
RG	Raspberry gooseberry strawberry jam	Ellington								2		2

Code	Title	School				Total
RR	Rockin Robin	Nora Conn			5	5
RRR	Ringa ringa rosy	Summerglen		1		1
RU	Reach up for the stars	St Augustine's		2		2
S	When Susie was a baby	Birch Vale			4	4
S		Nora Conn			2	2
S		Summerglen		7		7
S		St Augustine's		4		4
S		Springfield	18		1	19
S	(total for S):	All schools	18	11	7	36
SAA	Saaba Saaba	Ellington		1		1
SAS	Silencio en la sala	Birch Vale			1	1
SD	Scooby dooby doo (Song and dance)	Birch Vale			1	1
SDD	Scooby dooby doo	Ellington		3		3
SF	Skorstein's feier'n	Bysiden		2		2
SG	Somalian game	Bysiden		1		1
SHA	Selena had a....	Bysiden		4		4
SHK	Shake it	Birch Vale			1	1
SIS	Sister sister	Summerglen		1		1
SK	Sisters in the kitchen	Maringa		3		3
SKK	Saeukkang	Pada			7	7
SL	Slide	San			2	2
SL		Birch Vale			23	23
SL		Pada			11	11
SL		Nora Conn			5	5
SL		Springfield	5			5
SL		Telford Spring		1		1
SL	(total for SL):	All schools	5	1	41	47
SLC	Subo a la campana	Birch Vale			1	1
SLG	Splits game	San			1	1
SLP	Slaps	St Augustine's		1		1
SLT	Subo a la torre	Birch Vale			2	2

(continued)

Code	Title/Type	Location	1990	1991	1993	1994	1995	1996	2001	2002	2004	Total
SM	Sar macka dora	Bysiden								18		18
SM		Ellington								31		31
SM		Birch Vale									17	17
SM		Nora Conn									10	10
SM		Strandli								2		2
SM		Summerglen								5		5
SM		St Augustine's								8		8
SM		Springfield	8		7	16						39
SM		Telford Spring					8		7	7		14
SM	(total for SM):	All schools										144
SN	Snakies	Birch Vale									1	1
SN		Nora Conn									1	1
SN		All schools										2
SNO	Sutccha nori	Pada									2	2
SP	Slå på ringen	Bysiden								2		2
SP		Strandli								1		1
SP	(total for SP):	All schools										3
SPA	Spanish song	St Augustine's								2		2
SPR	Scissors Paper Rock	San									3	3
SPR		Ellington								1		1
SPR		Springfield			4	9						13
SPR		Telford Spring							1			1
SPR	(total for SPR):	All schools										18
SPS	Salt, pepper, Scooby Doo	St Augustine's								1		1
SS	See see my playmate	Bysiden								3		3
SS		St Augustine's								2		2
SS		Springfield			8	7						15
SS		Telford Spring							2			2
SS	(total for SS):	All schools										22

ST	Shirley Temple	Springfield			1			1
STO	San t'okki	San					1	1
SVV	Sa vali vali (Samoan song)	Birch Vale					1	1
SYG	Sam yuk gu	San					7	7
SYG		Pada					4	4
SYG	(total for SYG):	All schools						11
T	Tennis	Birch Vale					1	1
TB	Teddy bear	Ellington				2		2
TB		Nora Conn					8	8
TB		Summerglen				8		8
TB		Springfield	1					1
TB	(total for TB):	All schools						19
TBT	There's a bear in there	Springfield		1				1
TF	24 robbers	Ellington			1			1
TFG	Train formation game	Bysiden			1			1
TFS	2 4 6 8 (elastics game)	Ellington			6			6
TG	Thumb game	Springfield	1					1
TGF	Tiger fans	Birch Vale					2	2
TH	Thinrath	St Augustine's		1				1
TL	Toodaloomalooma	Springfield		1				1
TM	Teenage mutant ninja turtles	Springfield	3	1				4
TO	This old man	Summerglen			1			1
TS	To stop the train	Ellington			1			1
TSN	Three six nine	Summerglen				4		4
TSN		Springfield	1					1
TSN	(total for TSN):	All schools						5
TT	Teacher teacher	Springfield	1					1
TTA	Tic tac toe	Birch Vale					17	17
TTA		Nora Conn					2	2
TTA	(total for TTA):	All schools						19
TTC	Twinkle twinkle chocolate bar	Summerglen				2		2

(continued)

Code	Title/Type	Location	1990	1991	1993	1994	1995	1996	2001	2002	2004	Total
TTN	Three tins	Auston							2			2
TTT	Tip tap toe	Springfield				1						1
TTW	That's the way I like it	Bysiden								6		6
TTW		Ellington								4		4
TTW		Summerglen								8		8
TTW		St Augustine's								9		9
TTW	(total for TTW):	All schools										27
TU	Tukkoba tukkoba	Pada									1	1
TW	There was an old lady who swallowed a fly	Birch Vale									1	1
TWR	Thumb wrestling game	Pada									1	1
UA	Under an apple tree	Springfield				1						1
UAT	Under the apple tree	Summerglen								13		13
UAT		St Augustine's								7		7
UAT	(total for UAT):	All schools										20
UD	Up and down and all around	Summerglen								2		2
UG	Urdu game	St Augustine's								1		1
UJ	Uri jip-ae whae wanni	Pada									2	2
UNG	Unidentified game 6	San									1	1
UT	Ujeong test (Slide variant)	San									2	2
UT		Pada									11	11
UT	(total for UT):	All schools										13
VDR	Vil du ride	Bysiden								6		6
VS	Vegetable song	Birch Vale									1	1
VV	Vera Vera Vap	Strandli								1		1
W	Wombat on a surfboard	Springfield				1						1
WA	Waddly Archer	St Augustine's								2		2
WAP	We are the pirates	Birch Vale									1	1
WB	Who's got a beard	Springfield			2							2
WCD	We can do anything	Ellington								1		1

336

WGU	We're going up	St Augustine's	7	
WGU		Telford Spring	1	
WGU	(total for WGU):	All schools		8
WK	We know you can do it	Birch Vale	3	3
WM	Welcome to McDonalds	Birch Vale	1	1
WS	Welsh song	St Augustine's	1	1
WST	Welsh song 2	St Augustine's	1	1
WT	What's the time Mr Wolf	Ellington	1	
WT		Birch Vale	1	
WT	(total for WT):	All schools		2
WTD	Wash the dishes	Telford Spring	5	5
WW	We will rock you	Telford Spring	2	2
YD	Yankee doodle	Ellington	1	
YD		Springfield	3	
YD	(total for YD):	All schools		4
YS	Yong simi	San	3	
YS		Pada	7	
YS	(total for YS):	All schools		10
YY	Yippee yi yi	Bysiden	3	3
YYO	Yennal yecch'oge	San	5	
YYO		Pada	6	
YYO	(total for YYO):	All schools		11
ZB	Zapatito blanco	Birch Vale	5	5
ZG	Zero game	Pada	1	1
ZZB	Zero zero 7 bang	San	3	3
ZZZ	Zig zag zoo	Ellington	18	
ZZZ		St Augustine's	12	
ZZZ	(total for ZZZ):	All schools		30

(continued)

Title/Type	Location	1990	1991	1993	1994	1995	1996	2001	2002	2004	Total
Total items recorded											
	San									102	102
	Bysiden								202		202
	Ellington								196		196
	Auston							35	12		47
	Birch Vale									254	254
	Pada									131	131
	Maringa								22		22
	Bradford Well								17		17
	Nora Conn									113	113
	Strandli								22		22
	Summerglen								203		203
	St Augustine's								166		166
	Springfield	48	4	221	175	24	16				488
	Telford Spring							146	63		209
	All schools	48	4	221	175	24	16	181	903	498	2172
Total game types recorded											
	San									28	28
	Bysiden								40		40
	Ellington								50		50
	Auston							10	4		12
	Birch Vale									66	66
	Pada									29	29
	Maringa								8		8
	Bradford Well								7		7
	Nora Conn									30	30
	Strandli								11		11
	Summerglen								36		36
	St Augustine's								41		41
	Springfield	18	3	46	48	7	6				84
	Telford Spring							24	16		29
	All schools	18	3	46	48	7	6	31	172	122	333

Performances crossnumbered between two genres: Springfield 93: 1 DBB/SM
Nora Conn: 1 TB/DD, 10 SM/DBB, Auston 02: 2 CCK/MBR, San: 1 STO/PD, 2 UT/SL, Pada: 11 UT/SL.
Ellington: 4 AK/EM

Transcription Methods and Notation and Documentation Conventions

In documenting the collected material, I have adopted the practice of the Springfield children of designating the games by using the first few words of the text. These designations usually delineate game genres, the exceptions being games with limited or no text (such as "Black and White TV" or "Slide"), or genres such as "Sar Macka Dora" in which movement patterns, rather than text, are the basis of classification. Textual variants in game titles nominated by children have been incorporated into their documentation, with, for example, "Sar Macka Dora," "Sor Macka Dora," and "Sor Macka Dino" designating different performances of the same game genre.

Each performance item of the games has also been labeled by a code denoting where it was recorded, in addition to an alphabetical code derived from the title of its genre (see Appendix 1 for a list of game genres and corresponding codes), and numerals which indicate the date of recording and the chronological order in which it was recorded during that year. For example, the second performance of "Sar Macka Dora" recorded in Ellington School in 2002 is labeled E SM 02 2. In the transcriptions of selected game genres (appendices 4–10) the performance code has an additional suffix to designate the mode of recording the performance. The initials AV, V, or A indicate, respectively, that the performance was recorded on both audio and video, video only, or audio only.

Musical Transcription Conventions

In transcribing each performance, I endeavored to "represent, precisely and in visually comprehensible form, musical factors essential to a piece" (Stockmann, cited in Ellingson, 1992, p. 142). All performances are transcribed at absolute pitch so that tessitura could be established. To assist comprehension of the transcriptions, melodic and rhythmic rendition of each performance is notated using a Western five-line stave and pitches from the twelve-note chromatic scale. Pitches which are less than a semitone higher than the transcribed pitch are indicated by ↑. Pitches which are less than a semitone lower than the transcribed pitch are indicated by ↓. Vocal glissandi are indicated by /. Frequency of pitch iteration for each performance is shown by a weighted scale table below each transcription.

The treble clef is used at the beginning of staves containing notes of definite pitch. Where a game is performed entirely at indefinite pitch, the text rhythm is notated by using a crossed notehead. Where a game performance fluctuates between definite and indefinite pitch, indefinite pitches are notated using a crossed notehead (see list of notational conventions at the end of this appendix).

To avoid the overuse of accidentals, the accidentals for melodies of each text line are sometimes placed in the key signature position at the beginning of each line. These indicate accidentals only and do not signify any notion of "key." They frequently vary from line to line, depending on the component notes in each line.

Although most performances exhibit metrical patterns, there are frequently ametrical sections and flexibility of meter in the rendition of games. I decided, therefore, not to impose unrepresentative notions of meter through the use of time signatures in the transcriptions. However, barlines are used at points of vocal stress in the text line so that metrical patterns are clearly apparent. In some transcriptions, bar lines are also placed at some points of vocal rest to delineate regular metrical patterns.

Each text line of a performance is notated on a separate stave. In order to clearly show rhythmic and structural variants in each performance there is synoptic alignment of each text line. Corresponding movements are also synoptically aligned on staves above each text line, so that the relationship between text rhythm and movement can be seen.

Transcription Modifications

The transcriptions document not only differences between performances but also discrepancies between performers within a given performance. These have been indicated in the music stave either by using an upward note stem for one performer and downward stem for the other performer (or performers) or by using split staves labeled with the performers' names. Movement differences are mostly recorded on the same stave, but not through use of note stem orientation, because this denotes the use of right or left, as discussed below under "Transcription of Movements." Discrepancies between performers' movements are indicated by labeling of relevant movement rhythms with performers' names and sometimes with descriptive annotations.

At times, differences between performers were difficult to determine and transcribe exactly, for example when multiple performers were simultaneously producing slightly different vocal pitches. The level of indeterminacy was increased by high levels of extraneous noise in outdoor performances. In these cases, the most clearly audible elements of the performance were transcribed and supplemented with descriptive comments.

Transcription of Movements

To transcribe movements with a level of rhythmic complexity I utilized a five-line stave, in which each line and space was assigned a particular movement, for example, "clap own hands" being distinguished from "clap partner's hands, hands horizontal" and "clap partner's hands, hands vertical." This basic rhythmic notation was supplemented by verbal descriptions of changes in movement patterns and occasional iconic representation. In addition, a range of different stave positions, noteheads, and additional signs have been used to denote the mimetic movements found in many genres. Notational conventions are listed at the end of this appendix.

Documentation of Transcriptions in Appendices 4–10

In addition to the name and performance code, each transcription is labeled with the names of the performers and the place and date of the recording, with pseudonyms being retained. Appendix 4 contains transcriptions related to specific analytical points made in the book. Appendices 5–9 include selected transcriptions from each field location, while additional transcriptions of interest are found in appendix 10. A list of notation conventions follows.

List of Musical Notation Conventions

Musical Notation Convention 1

Movement key

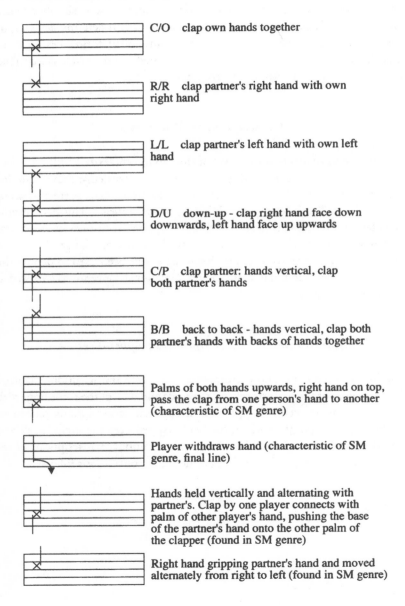

C/O   clap own hands together

R/R   clap partner's right hand with own right hand

L/L   clap partner's left hand with own left hand

D/U   down-up - clap right hand face down downwards, left hand face up upwards

C/P   clap partner: hands vertical, clap both partner's hands

B/B   back to back - hands vertical, clap both partner's hands with backs of hands together

Palms of both hands upwards, right hand on top, pass the clap from one person's hand to another (characteristic of SM genre)

Player withdraws hand (characteristic of SM genre, final line)

Hands held vertically and alternating with partner's. Clap by one player connects with palm of other player's hand, pushing the base of the partner's hand onto the other palm of the clapper (found in SM genre)

Right hand gripping partner's hand and moved alternately from right to left (found in SM genre)

Musical Notation Convention 2

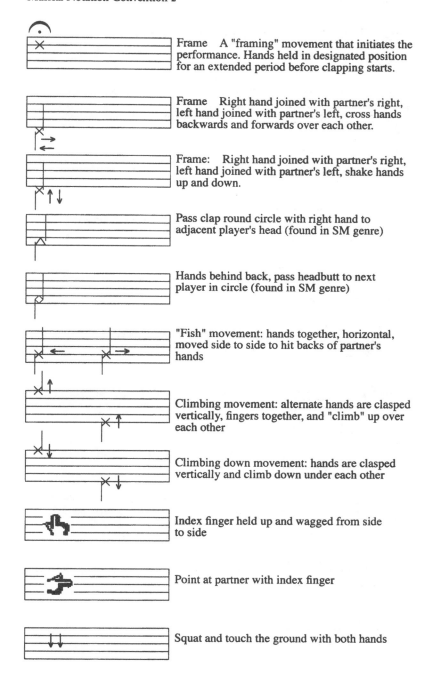

Frame   A "framing" movement that initiates the performance. Hands held in designated position for an extended period before clapping starts.

Frame   Right hand joined with partner's right, left hand joined with partner's left, cross hands backwards and forwards over each other.

Frame: Right hand joined with partner's right, left hand joined with partner's left, shake hands up and down.

Pass clap round circle with right hand to adjacent player's head (found in SM genre)

Hands behind back, pass headbutt to next player in circle (found in SM genre)

"Fish" movement: hands together, horizontal, moved side to side to hit backs of partner's hands

Climbing movement: alternate hands are clasped vertically, fingers together, and "climb" up over each other

Climbing down movement: hands are clasped vertically and climb down under each other

Index finger held up and wagged from side to side

Point at partner with index finger

Squat and touch the ground with both hands

Musical Notation Convention 3

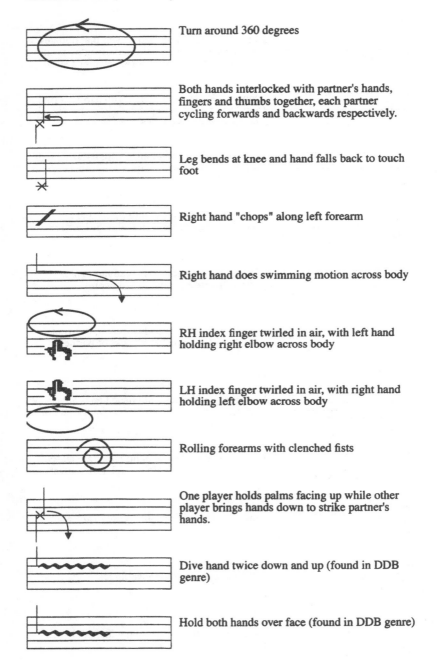

Turn around 360 degrees

Both hands interlocked with partner's hands, fingers and thumbs together, each partner cycling forwards and backwards respectively.

Leg bends at knee and hand falls back to touch foot

Right hand "chops" along left forearm

Right hand does swimming motion across body

RH index finger twirled in air, with left hand holding right elbow across body

LH index finger twirled in air, with right hand holding left elbow across body

Rolling forearms with clenched fists

One player holds palms facing up while other player brings hands down to strike partner's hands.

Dive hand twice down and up (found in DDB genre)

Hold both hands over face (found in DDB genre)

Musical Notation Convention 4

Hug own chest with both arms (found in DDB genre)

Jerk hand/s, thumb extended, over shoulder (DDB genre)

Hold imaginary telephone to ear, little finger and thumb outstretched (found in DDB genre)

Wind finger around close to ear in dialling motion (found in DDB genre)

Wind finger around ear plus hold an imaginary telephone next to other ear (found in DDB genre)

Bend head to one side and then the other (found in DDB genre)

Stamp foot

"Hot dog" movement (found in DDB genre): rotate hips then bring to a stop at final note value

Rotate hips (without bringing to a stop)

"Eat salami" mimetic movement (found in "Elmo" DDB variant): palms raised alternately to open mouth

Musical Notation Convention 5

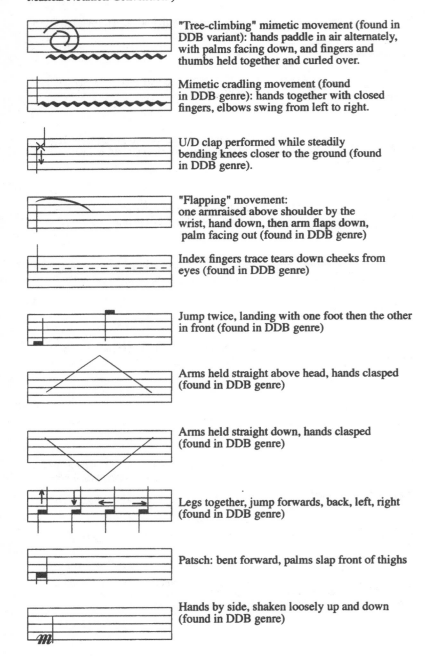

"Tree-climbing" mimetic movement (found in DDB variant): hands paddle in air alternately, with palms facing down, and fingers and thumbs held together and curled over.

Mimetic cradling movement (found in DDB genre): hands together with closed fingers, elbows swing from left to right.

U/D clap performed while steadily bending knees closer to the ground (found in DDB genre).

"Flapping" movement: one arm raised above shoulder by the wrist, hand down, then arm flaps down, palm facing out (found in DDB genre)

Index fingers trace tears down cheeks from eyes (found in DDB genre)

Jump twice, landing with one foot then the other in front (found in DDB genre)

Arms held straight above head, hands clasped (found in DDB genre)

Arms held straight down, hands clasped (found in DDB genre)

Legs together, jump forwards, back, left, right (found in DDB genre)

Patsch: bent forward, palms slap front of thighs

Hands by side, shaken loosely up and down (found in DDB genre)

Musical Notation Convention 6

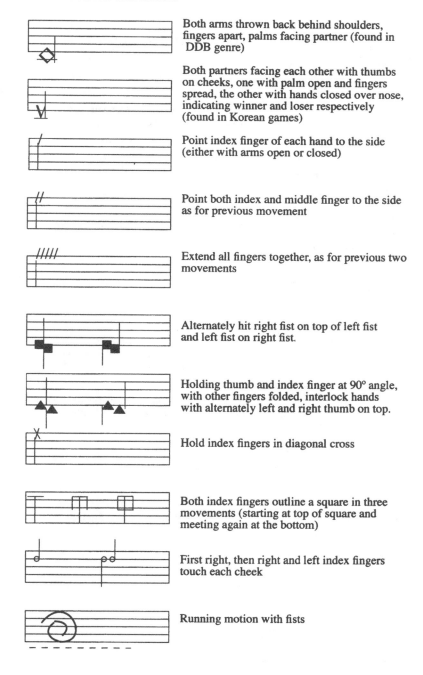

Both arms thrown back behind shoulders, fingers apart, palms facing partner (found in DDB genre)

Both partners facing each other with thumbs on cheeks, one with palm open and fingers spread, the other with hands closed over nose, indicating winner and loser respectively (found in Korean games)

Point index finger of each hand to the side (either with arms open or closed)

Point both index and middle finger to the side as for previous movement

Extend all fingers together, as for previous two movements

Alternately hit right fist on top of left fist and left fist on right fist.

Holding thumb and index finger at 90° angle, with other fingers folded, interlock hands with alternately left and right thumb on top.

Hold index fingers in diagonal cross

Both index fingers outline a square in three movements (starting at top of square and meeting again at the bottom)

First right, then right and left index fingers touch each cheek

Running motion with fists

Musical Notation Convention 7

Right hand held palm out, then joined
by left hand

Bow towards partner, with hands held
together in front of chest

Beat chest alternately with left and right
fist

"Dust" hands by brushing them together
up and down

Elbows flapped, with fists resting on chest

Hold hands together in prayer
position, move hands up and down while
slightly shaking them from side to side

Rhythmical "spooning" mimetic movement,
imitating spooning food into mouth

Jump and move feet further apart (splits).
Found in MAB genre.

Hold nose with forefinger and thumb

Rub tummy

Twirl fingers in circles behind ears

Musical Notation Convention 8

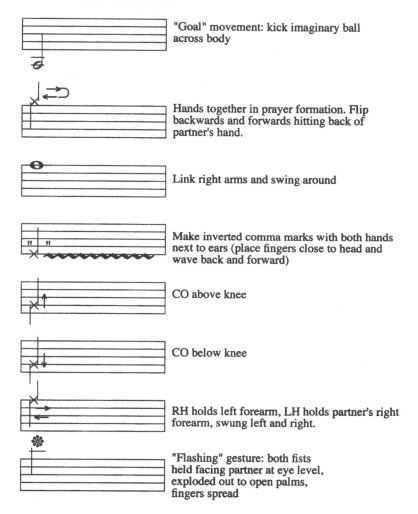

"Goal" movement: kick imaginary ball across body

Hands together in prayer formation. Flip backwards and forwards hitting back of partner's hand.

Link right arms and swing around

Make inverted comma marks with both hands next to ears (place fingers close to head and wave back and forward)

CO above knee

CO below knee

RH holds left forearm, LH holds partner's right forearm, swung left and right.

"Flashing" gesture: both fists held facing partner at eye level, exploded out to open palms, fingers spread

APPENDIX 3

Text Variants of the
"Sar Macka Dora" Game Genre

Springfield, Sydney, 1990–1995 (Text Type 1)

Line		Text	Rhyme	Syllables
1.	Sar macka dora	a	a	5
2.	Eyo maria maria	b	a	8
3.	Eyo eyo ch ch ch	c	b	7
4.	Eyo eyo ch ch ch	c	b	7
5.	One two three	d	c	3

Springfield, Sydney, 1990–1995 (Text Type 2)

Line		Text	Rhyme	Syllables
1.	Son macaron	a	a	4
2.	Son ferio ferio ferio	b	b	10
3.	Leya leya tap tap tap	c	c	7
4.	Leya leya tap tap tap	c	c	7
5.	One two three	d	d	3

Bysiden, Norway, 2002

Line		Text	Rhyme	Syllables
1.	Slå makaroni [*Slap macaroni*]	a	a	5
2.	Tiam basta marasta	b	b	7
3.	Tiam tiam bass bass bass	c	c	7
4.	Tiam tiam bass bass bass	c	c	7
5.	Ein to tri [*One two three*]	d	d	3

Telford Spring, Central Australia, 2001–2002

Line		Text	Rhyme	Syllables
1.	Sy mary on mary on mary on	a	a	10
2.	Laya laya tap tap tap	b	b	7
3.	Laya laya tap tap tap	b	b	7
4.	1 2 3 4 5 6 7 8 9 10	c	c	11

Springfield, Sydney, 1990–1995 (Text Type 3)

Line		Text	Rhyme	Syllables
1.	Down by the banks of the hanky panky	a	a	10
2.	Where the bullfrogs jump from bank to bank	b	a1	9
3.	With a hip hop lollipop	c	b	7
4.	With a hip hop belly flop	c1	b	7
5.	One two three	d	c	3

Ellington, Keighley, U.K., 2002 (Text Type 1)

Line		Text	Rhyme	Syllables
1.	Down by the river goes the hanky panky	a	a	11
2.	Where the two fat frogs go back to banky	b	a	10
3.	With a hip hop solo pop	c	c	7
4.	And this is where it stops	c	c1	6

St Augustine's, Keighley, U.K., 2002 (Text Type 1)

Line		Text	Rhyme	Syllables
1.	Down in the jungle where nobody goes	a	a	10
2.	There's a big fat gorilla, pickin' his nose	b	a	11
3.	He picks it and he flicks it to see how far it goes	c	a	13
4.	Who's gonna get that, who's gonna get that	c	b	10
5.	Who's gonna get that slimy snot?	d	c	8

Ellington, Keighley, U.K., 2002 (Text Type 2)

Line		Text	Rhyme	Syllables
1.	Sella ella oola quack quack quack	a	a	9
2.	Say yes chigga chigga challi chap chap	b	aI	10
3.	Say yes chigga chigga flo flo flo flo flo	c	b	11
4.	Say one two three four five	d	c	6

Birch Vale, Seattle, U.S., 2004

Line		Text	Rhyme	Syllables
1.	Quack didd(el)y oso quack quack quack	a	a	8/9
2.	(Say/Go) san Marico rico rico rico	b	b	10/11
3.	Flora/Florida flora flora flora flora	c	c	10
4.	One two three (four)	d	d	3/4

Summerglen, Bedford, U.K., 2002

Line		Text	Rhyme	Syllables
1.	Oma me(l/h)i (m)o	a	a	5
2.	Un deux trois [One two three]	b	b	3

Selected Musical Transcriptions of Games

Example A4.li

Zig Zag Zoo
(Punjabi)

EA ZZZ 02 5 AV
Performers: Salima, Kaneez
Recorded: Ellington, inside
6/11/02
Video: EA 02 2 (53:10)
Audio: EA 02 1.33

Movements are slightly unsynchronised,
so movement rhythms are approximate.

Hands together in prayer formation. Flip
backwards and forwards hitting back of
partner's hand.

Zig   Zag   Zoo

Ka - bhi oo - per, ka - bhi nee-chey,

Hesitation   Accelerating

Saima CP
Kaneez DU   Saima BB
              Kaneez CP

Ka-bhi see - tey, ka - bhi bhoo - key

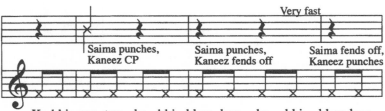

Very fast

Saima punches, Saima punches, Saima fends off,
Kaneez CP   Kaneez fends off Kaneez punches

Ka-bhi see - tey, ka - bhi bhoo-key, ka - bhi bhoo-key

Example A4.lii

EA ZZZ 02 5 AV continued

Zig Zag Zoo
Kabhi ooper, kabhi neechey
Kabhi seetey, kabhi bhookey
Kabhi seetey, kabhi bhookey, kabhi bhookey

Zig Zag Zoo
Sometimes on top, sometimes underneath
Sometimes comfortable, sometimes starving
Sometimes comfortable, sometimes starving, sometimes starving

Example A4.2i

Down down baby

SH DDB 09 1 AV

Performers: Tony, July, Rafael,
Amira, Jorge, Roland
Recorded: Primary playground
Springfield Public School, NSW
5/12/90, by Kathryn Marsh

♩ = 170

Down down ba - by down   down the rol - ler coas - ter

Sweet sweet ba - by   I'll ne - ver let you go

Shi-mmy shi-mmy co-co pops shi - mmy shi - mmy pow

Shi-mmy shi-mmy co-co pops shi - mmy shi - mmy pow

Example A4.2ii

SH DDB 90 1 AV continued

Gran-ma gran - ma   sick in   bed   she

called the doc - tor and the   doc - tor said

Let's get the rhy-thm of the   head   ding   dong

Let's get the rhy-thm of the   head   ding   dong   Let's

Example A4.2iii

SH DDB 90 1 AV continued

get the rhy - thm of the hands   Let's

get the rhy - thm of the hands

Let's get the rhy - thm of the feet

Let's get the rhy - thm of the feet

Example A4.2iv

SH DDB 90 1 AV continued

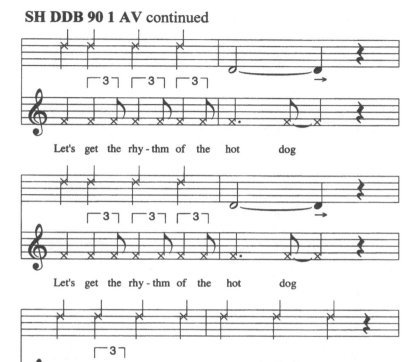

Let's get the rhy-thm of the hot dog

Let's get the rhy-thm of the hot dog

Put it all to-ge-ther and what do you get

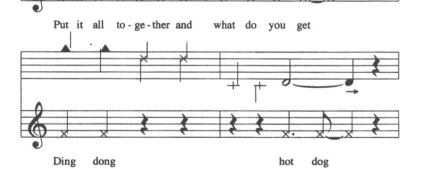

Ding dong hot dog

Example A4.2v

SH DDB 90 1 AV continued

Put em all back - wards and what do you get

Dog   hot   dong   ding

Example A4.3

See see my playmate

SH SS 93 5 AV

Performers: Ella, Sadie
Recorded: ESL Classroom,
Springfield Public School, 10/12/93

Example A4.4

Say say my playmate

Performers: Hong-Soo, Alicia
Recorded: ESL Classroom,
Springfield Public School, 10/12/93

Example A4.5

Say say my playmate

SH SS 93 7 AV

Performers:Ella, Annette (movement)
Hong-Soo (text)
Recorded: ESL Classroom,
Springfield Public School, 10/12/93

Say   say my   play - mate   I can - not   play with you.

My sis - ter's   got the flu   And Ger - man   meas - les too.

Example A4.6i

Åli Åli ei

B AA 02 9 AV
Performers: Tina, Benedicte
Recorded: Inside, lunch,
Bysiden School,
Norway, 23/8/02
Video: B 02 4 (15:48)
Audio: B 02 2.06

Example A4.6ii

B AA 02 9 AV continued

lei   lei   lei   oh   my

hap – py   hap – py   hap – py   oh   my

step – py   step – py   step – py   oh   my

house   house   house   Mic – key

Example A4.6iii

B AA 02 9 AV continued

Mouse Mouse Mouse Mouse

Example A4.7

Sar macka dora

SH SM 95 T1 AV

Performers: Sheryl Fallwood (music teacher)
teaching kindergarten class
Recorded: Music room, 10/4/95
Springfield Primary School, Australia

Example A4.8i

Son macaron

Iteration 4 of 5

SH SM 93 1 AV

Performers: Matu, Clara, Joanne,
Tara, Thuy, Carrie
Recorded: Playground, 30/11/93
Springfield Primary School, Australia
Video: SH 93 1 (1.28.43)
Audio: SH 93 3 Side 1

Example A4.8ii

SH SM 93 1 AV continued

One   two   three

Example A4.9i

Down in the jungle
1st iteration of 24

ST SM 02 7 AV
Performers: Claire, Lauren, Georgina,
Becky, Clarissa, Penny,
Francesca, Amy, Sofie
Recorded: Inside, lunchtime, 29/11/02
St Augustine's Primary School, UK
Audio: ST 02 2.26
Video: ST 02 4 (20:29)

Down in the jun-gle where no-bo-dy goes   there's   a

big fat go-rill-a   pick-in his nose.   He

picks it and he flicks it and he sees how far it goes.

Example A4.9ii

ST SM 02 7 AV iteration 1 of 24 continued

Who's go-nna get that, who's go-nna get that,

who's go-nna get that sli - my snot?

Example A4.10i

Quack diddely oso
Iteration 1 of 2

HV SM 04 11 AV
Performers: Ashley, Romina,
Chelsea
Recorded: Music room,
Birch Vale Elementary School,
Seattle, USA, 4/5/04
Video: HV 04 4 (10:10)
Audio: HV 04 2.07

Dominant voice notated

Example A4.10ii

HV SM 04 11 AV Iteration 1 of 2 continued

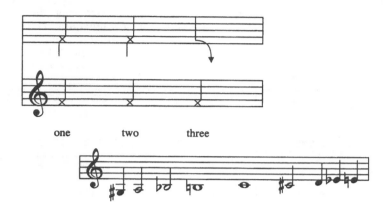

one   two   three

Example A4.11i

Sella ella oola

Iteration 1 of 7

EA SM 02 15 AV

Performers: Amreen, Aklima,
Farah A, Farah K, Halima, Rukhsana, Nasheen
Recorded: Inside, lunchtime,11/11/02
Ellington School, UK
Audio: EA 02 2.24
Video: EA 02 4 (52:45)

Se - lla e - lla oo - la   quack quack quack

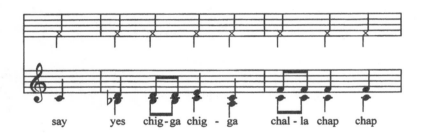

say   yes chig-ga chig - ga   chal - la chap   chap

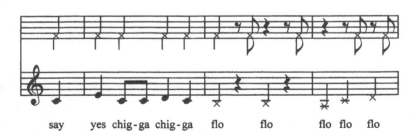

say   yes chig-ga chig-ga flo   flo   flo flo flo

Example A4.11ii

EA SM 02 15 AV iteration 1 of 7 continued

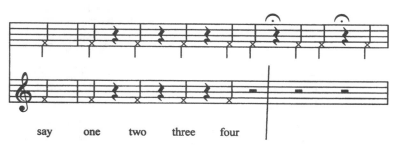

say   one   two   three   four

Aklima passes clap on and
Farah K. doesn't withdraw.
Halima says "you have to..."
and they pass the clap on two more
times around the circle. Halima
explains: "No she has to hit you
and then you're going to be out."
Aklima hits Farah's hand once
more without Farah withdrawing.
Nobody is decided to be out
and they start again.

Example A4.12i

Slå makaroni
1st of 6 iterations

B SM 02 10 V
Performers: Charlotte, Fayroz,
Nora, Mina, Marianne
Recorded: Playground, 26/8/02
Bysiden School, Norway
Video: B 02 5 (7:15)

Slå   ma - ka - ro - ni

ti - am bas - ta ma - ras - ta

ti - am ti - am bass bass bass

ti - am ti - am bass bass bass

Example A4.12ii

B SM 02 10 V Iteration 1 of 6 continued

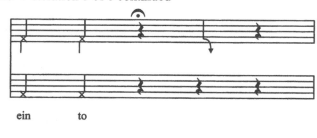

ein   to

Chapter 1

1. This assumption is derived from the work of Heinz Werner, published in 1917, on stages of musical development in young children (cited in Michel, 1976, and Nettl, 1956).

2. The pentatonic scale used in Orff-Schulwerk is in the configuration equivalent to CDEGA, usually with a tonal center of C, F, or G to avoid the use of accidentals.

3. Kodály's thoughts in this regard draw on contemporaneous theories of developmental psychology (Kraus, 1967/1990, p. 79).

4. These are rhythmic mnemonics originally devised by Aimé Paris in the 1830s and later used by Curwen in England (Bridges, 1984/1992).

5. For example, the *Music for Children: Orff-Schulwerk American Edition* (Regner, 1977, 1980, 1982) incorporates rhymes and songs from the English, Anglo-American, and African American traditions in addition to a number of songs reflecting the multicultural nature of American society. Similarly, the revised edition of the Kodály-based *A Developmental Music Program* (Hoermann and Bridges, 1987) is notable for its inclusion of songs contributed by Australians of varying ethnicity.

6. See, for example, the discussion of "contamination," or degenerative forces as opposed to regenerative forces, in Abrahams and Foss (1968), Barwick (1994), Bronson (1950), Coffin (1977), and McMillan (1964).

7. As Riddell (1990) and other authors have provided a comprehensive review of historical collections of playlore (such as those of Gomme, 1894/1964, and Newell, 1883/1963), it seems unnecessary to replicate it here.

Chapter 2

1. This does not preclude researchers who are working within quantitative paradigms from reaching similar conclusions. For example, Dowling's (1988) analysis of sponta-

neous songs of children aged two to six indicated that children engaged in repetitive patterning from the age of three.

2. *Guslars* are performers of epic tales in the former Yugoslavia who were accompanied by the *gusle*, a bowed string instrument.

Chapter 3

1. The reasons for the use of these dual technologies are discussed in the section "Recording of Multiple Performance Elements" later in this chapter.

2. Ellis (1985) describes the multiple levels of meaning of many Australian Aboriginal song texts that have a spiritually significant meaning known only to initiated men or women or by elders. The term "false front" (pp. 63–64) is used to describe the superficial meaning attributed to such Aboriginal song texts, which is given to children or other uninitiated members of the audience.

3. Video recording of children's musical play for musicological research has only been undertaken fairly recently (Addo, 1995; Campbell, 1998; Harwood, 1992, 1993; Merrill-Mirsky, 1988; Riddell, 1990). Addo discusses in some detail her use of video technology and the role of multimedia in her study. Beresin (1999) examines the role of video recording of children's play from a more anthropological perspective.

4. This number does not include the members of the Kindergarten and Year 5 classes (approximately sixty children) who were recorded learning the games from the music teacher in a classroom context in 1995.

5. Throughout the book I use terminology to designate age-related class groups that is appropriate for the setting. For example, in Sydney, Australia, school age levels are referred to as "Years," while in the United States they are called "grades." See chapter 4 for more details.

6. In transcripts of interview material, the children are designated by pseudonyms, and I am designated by my first initial, K.

7. Depending on the length of the field visit and the facilities available, it was sometimes possible to process video recordings and still photos and return copies to the children during the course of the fieldwork. When this was not possible, photos were sent to the school at a later date for sharing with children.

8. I was unable to obtain translations of the three Eritrean games recorded in Stavanger. Transcriptions of these games are therefore rendered phonetically.

9. My research assistant for the whole project from 2001 to 2007 was Corin Bone, whose work was invaluable.

Chapter 4

1. In referring to Springfield Public School the customary abbreviation Springfield PS will also be used.

2. The prevailing sunny climate in much of Australia has led to a high incidence of skin cancer in the Caucasian population. Because of this, most primary schools require children to wear hats when outdoors.

3. This is the Aboriginal Community Development Employment Program.

4. In Norway, all children begin learning English from the first year of school.

5. In the United Kingdom, the term "Asian" is used to denote people from the Indian subcontinent, including those originating in India, Pakistan, and Bangladesh.
6. All schools in the United Kingdom are subject to regular evaluation by a national body, OFSTED. This reviews teaching and management practices and learning outcomes based on mandated national standards.
7. As with all schools, pseudonyms have been used. "Pada" is translated as "beach" and "San" is translated as "mountain." "Hakkyo" means "school" and "ch'odung hakkyo" means elementary or primary school. Note that the orthography for romanisation of Korean language has been recently altered, so Korean words may appear in slightly differing Romanised forms.

Chapter 5

1. This pattern consists of three successive clapping movements performed on the beat: (1) right hand claps down while left hand claps up (hands horizontal); (2) clap partner's hands (hands vertical); (3) clap own hands together.
2. A similar use of the textless clapping routine of "Down by the Banks" by males in their early teens was reported to me by an adult Aboriginal teacher-education student in 1995, who showed me the clapping pattern he had played with his male friends at the local swimming pool in a western New South Wales town during the 1980s.
3. As the source named is American in origin, it seems to indicate the presence of this practice among American boys. Again, this is not reflected in much of the literature from the United States. Gaunt (2006) indicates that this movie has been involved in the dissemination of "Down Down Baby" but indicates that this is predominantly related to girls' game practice.
4. The interethnic transmission of the game "Son Macaron" (a variant of "Sar Macka Dora") at Arncliffe PS, another Sydney school, reportedly occurred under similar circumstances in the early 1980s. A Macedonian girl who had returned with the game from a holiday in her home country was on a ferry excursion with a large number of children from her school. During the course of the trip, as the children had no access to other play equipment, the new game was transmitted to the majority of children on board and then became a regular part of the playground repertoire (reported by Phil Nanlohy, a teacher at the school).

Chapter 6

1. My observations confirm that the game was not played at Springfield prior to 1995.
2. C/O C/P designates a duple clapping formula where a performer claps her own hands together then claps her partner's hands (hands vertical). These movements occur on alternate beats.
3. The clapping formula designated here is a six-beat cycle consisting of the following clapping movements: C/P = clap partner's hands (hands vertical); C/O = clap own hands; R/R = clap partner's right hand (hands vertical); L/L = clap partner's left hand (hands vertical). The pairing of a C/O movement with each contrasting clap means that this clapping pattern consists of three pairs of duple movement components.
4. Code switching is more usually defined as the alternation between two languages

within a conversation (or language exchange) between bilingual people (Boztepe, n.d., Crystal, 1987; Milroy and Mysken, 1995). It may involve considerable linguistic flexibility to enact quite frequent switches from one language to another. I have extended the use of the term to refer to the rapid alternation between more than one performative "code," or standard.

Chapter 7

1. In Russell's (1984) field notes for her study, published in 1986, she records "Black and White," alternatively entitled "Or Sam," "Sin Sam," Or "Si Sam," as having been played extensively in 1984 by children at Debney Meadows, a multicultural primary school in Melbourne. Although the game was played by children of different ethnicities, it had evidently been introduced into the school playground by Vietnamese, Lao, and Chinese children, many of whom reported having learnt the game in their country of origin.

2. Following Alicia's answer, all the children in the group demonstrated their knowledge of Italian, which they had gained from Italian language classes conducted in the early years of their schooling.

3. My Norwegian translator, Thor Gunnar Noraas, informed me that this text contains no standard Norwegian words.

4. Reiterated text formulae seem to invite word substitution. In 1995, a group of Year 4 girls at Springfield demonstrated several variants of this game in which names of different body parts, clothing, or letters of the alphabet were substituted for the reiterated text (e.g., "Mr. finger finger finger, Mr. knee knee knee. . . ").

5. I remember playing this game during my own primary school years in the early 1960s.

6. Although it is also possible to attribute this combination of formulae to the aggregation of two separate games, one Korean and one English, the game appears in this complete form, with full Korean text, in *Roots and Branches*, a book of multicultural songs and games compiled in the United States (Campbell, McCullough-Brabson, and Tucker, 1994). That this was a common form of the game as taught in Korea was endorsed by my recordings of the game in Korea in 2004.

7. This is the translation I have from the translator, but the text of this version seems slightly different. He seems to have translated a standardized version with only one variant.

8. This was the game performance viewed on video and reconstructed by the Year 6 girls discussed previously in chapter 6.

9. The most obvious candidate was Charlie Chaplin, the comedic star of silent movies in the early twentieth century.

10. TAA is the former name of an Australian airline. It is interesting to note that the name of this airline changed before these performers were born but has been retained in the oral tradition.

11. I did not record an example of "Down Down Baby" during my fieldwork in Norway. However, the principal of Bysiden School subsequently sent me a commercial video recording of playground games from Bysiden, recorded later in 2002, that included an example of the "Down Down Baby" genre, called "Dam Dam Deah." This must

have been part of the playground repertoire during the period of my fieldwork, but it was never observed or demonstrated during my time there.

12. Bollywood is the term used to describe the movie industry emanating from Mumbai, in India. With dialogue and lyrics in combinations of Hindi, Urdu, and, more recently, English, Bollywood films are characterized by lavishly choreographed song and dance sequences. Song recordings are often released separately before the movie as a marketing ploy. Bollywood movies are popular not only within the Indian subcontinent and Southeast Asia but with the Indian diaspora in the United Kingdom, Canada, Australia, and the United States.

13. The version recorded in Sydney in 1990 is almost identical both textually and rhythmically to the *Sesame Street* version.

14. For a more extended exposition of this argument and more detailed analysis of the relationship between the children's game and Nelly's rap version, see Marsh (2006) and Gaunt (2006).

15. Reported in "Bookworm," *The Sun Herald*, Sydney, 3 November 1991, p. 115.

16. The use of Christmas songs in the Springfield playground reflects the timing of my fieldwork, which was mostly conducted in November and December, when Christmas songs are usually taught in the classroom.

17. The song that forms the basis of this game is "Iko Iko." The videoclip to which Matu refers was either performed by Cyndi Lauper, who recorded the song on her album *True Colours*, or The Belle Stars, whose recording of the song appears on the soundtrack of the film *Rain Man*, released in 1989. The film to which Tara refers is *K-9*, released in the United States in 1989 by Universal Studios and Imagine films Entertainment. The performance of "Iko Iko" (attributed to Hawkins, Jones, Johnson, and Thomas in the credits) is by Amy Holland. It is possible that, like "Shimmy Shimmy Ko Ko Bop" (Riddell, 1990), the song itself may have originated in a playground game, as the text incorporates the vocables that are characteristic of many games.

18. These are the abbreviated names for two Year 6 classes at the school.

Chapter 8

1. Sections of this chapter, including the discussion of "Teacher Teacher," variants of "See See My Playmate," and the relationship of these to the Swanwick and Tillman model have previously been published in *Research Studies in Music Education*, number 4, June 1995 (Marsh, 1995) and are reproduced with permission.

2. The clapping patterns for this segment have all been discussed in the previous chapters. Mimetic movements are delineated at the right-hand side of the movement notation.

Chapter 9

1. This also means that a number of items listed in the index are subject to dual forms of classification, being listed according to text type but also, by reason of their idiosyncratic movement characteristics, being designated as belonging to this genre for the purposes of analysis. It follows, therefore, that some performances analyzed within this genre may be referred to using prefixes related to their text type (for example, DBB indicating "Down by the Banks") rather than by the SM prefix.

2. For the purposes of analysis of Springfield versions of the game, only one iteration within each performance was transcribed, unless significant differences were evident between iterations, as the volume of material precluded transcribing all iterations in all performances. Generally the iteration chosen for transcription was the most stable or displayed characteristics that seemed to be most significant. Differences between iterations, and the movement type adopted by the final two performers, were noted in transcriptions.

3. It is notable that the music teacher taught the song line by line, except for line 2, which she taught in two sections, the break between them indicated by the vertical line in the text. Possible implications of this for textual and rhythmic variability in this text type are discussed later. In the published text, the second and third words in line 2 are written as "mardia." However, the music teacher's recorded articulation of this word is indistinguishable from "maria."

4. In order to create melodic contours for the "Sar Macka Dora" genre at Springfield, all performances have been transposed so that the most frequently occurring intervals are placed on the following notes: minor third as g - e, major seconds in two positions: g - a and d - c and the minor second as e - f. As one melodic type in this genre is characterized by an interpolated text of indefinite pitch, this is indicated by "ind." The final line in this genre is almost always performed at indefinite pitch as indicated.

5. It should be noted that this version has been disseminated from an adult-transmitted version of the game (see discussion on in-service transmission of the game earlier in the chapter). It is therefore possible that the distinctive features of tonality found in playground renditions may have been ameliorated in the adult transmission of this game.

6. The first or clearest iteration was selected for analysis.

7. I am indebted to my research assistant, Corin Bone, for drawing this to my attention.

8. All melodic lines have been transposed so that the line begins on G. The contours therefore show intervallic relationships within lines but not between lines.

9. The melodic contours have been derived from the initial iteration or clearest iteration of each performance.

10. Melodies have been transposed so that the initial note of the performance begins on G. Intervallic relationships within *and* between lines are shown. For the purposes of this analysis, the notes of anacruses beginning text lines have been incorporated at the end of the previous line.

11. The diamond shaped notehead indicates movement of the head.

Chapter 10

1. Although this game was learnt in Eritrea, it did not appear to be in Tigrigna and the girls were unable to translate it.

2. Opie and Opie (1988) identify this game as having attained popularity in south England and the Midlands in the 1960s, but I did not encounter it in any location other than Summerglen. My research collaborator in Bedford, Elizabeth Grugeon, noted that the game was played in other schools in the area. The Opies also contend that this game has its origins in the courtship dances of young adults in earlier times.

3. This game also has an equivalent in English, "What's the Time Mr. Wolf?" It was recorded at Ellington in the United Kingdom and is found in Australian game collections (Factor, 1988; Turner, Factor, and Lowenstein, 1982), though it was not recorded at any of the Australian field schools. In the Australian version children stand in a line and gradually creep up toward the "wolf" who is facing in the opposite direction. The text, relating to time rather than activity, is spoken, not sung.

4. Descriptions of this game, its possible origins, and variants found in the United Kingdom, Australia, France, and the United States, can be found in Opie and Opie (1988) and Factor (1988).

5. I am indebted to my Spanish translator Clarita Derwent, who has lived for some years in Mexico and a number of South American countries, for her insights into common playground game practices, nuances of game performance by the ELL children at Birch Vale, and the interpretations of text and performance of these games.

Chapter 11

1. I have not undertaken a comparative analysis of classroom publications to support this statement. However, this conclusion is based on my exposure to and use of a wide range of music teaching materials over a period of more than 30 years as a teacher in early childhood, primary/elementary, and tertiary settings.

2. The music specialist teacher maintained the tessitura of the published source when observed teaching two different classes (kindergarten and Year 5) in 1995.

Abrahams, R. D., & Foss, G. (1968). "The cycle of oral transmission and composition."
In *Anglo-American folksong style* (pp. 12–36). Englewood Cliffs, N.J.: Prentice-Hall.

Abrahams, R. D. (1969). *Jump-rope rhymes: A dictionary.* Austin: University of Texas Press.

Adams, C. R. (1976). "Melodic contour typology." *Ethnomusicology 20*(2), 179–215.

Addison, R. (1988). "A new look at musical improvisation in education." *British Journal
of Music Education 5*(3), 255–67.

Addo, A. O. (1995). "Ghanaian children's music cultures: A video ethnography of selected
singing games" (Doctoral dissertation, University of British Columbia, Canada,
1995), *Dissertation Abstracts International 57/03*, AAC NN05909.

Aga, E. N., & Næss, H. E. (2001). *From runes to rigs: Cultural history treasure of the Stavanger region.* Trans. R. E. Gooderham. Stavanger: Kulturkonsult.

Arleo, A. (2001). "The saga of Susie: The dynamics of an international handclapping
game." In J. C Bishop & M. Curtis (Eds.), *Play today in the primary school playground* (pp. 80–97). Ballmoor, Buckingham: Open University Press.

Australian Bureau of Statistics. (1993). *Australia in profile: 1991 Census* (ABS Catalogue
No. 2821.0). Canberra: Australian Government Publishing Service.

Bakka, E., Moen, R. A., & Sørstrønen, B. (1989). *Songleiker frå Rogaland.* Sand, Norway:
Folkemusikkarkivet for Rogaland, Ryfylkemuseet.

Balkin, A. (1990). "What is creativity? What is it not?" *Music Educators Journal 76*(9),
29–32.

Barrett, M. (1996). "Children's aesthetic decision-making: An analysis of children's musical discourse as composers." *International Journal of Music Education 28*, 37–62.

——— (2003). "Freedoms and constraints: Constructing musical worlds through the dialogue of composition." In M. Hickey (Ed.), *Why and how to teach music composi-*

tion: A new horizon for music education (pp. 3–27). Reston, Va.: Music Educators National Conference.

Barwick, L. (1994). "Variation or 'contamination'?: Narrative instability in the Italian song tradition of Donna Lombarda, 1840–1980." In D. Stockman & A. Erler (Eds.), *Historische Volksmusikforschung. Studiengruppe zur Enforschung historischer Volksmusikquellen um ICTM. Bertrage der 10 Arbeitstagung in Göttingen 1991.* Göttingen: Editions RE.

Barz, G. (1997). "Chasing shadows in the field: An epilogue." In G. F. Barz & T. J. Cooley (Eds.) *Shadows in the field: New perspectives for fieldwork in ethnomusicology* (pp. 205–09). New York: Oxford University Press.

Basic, E. (1986). "Differences in the authenticity of children's expression and the viewing angle of the adults (II)." In I. Ivic & A. Marjanovic (Eds.), *Traditional games and children of today: Belgrade, OMEP Traditional Games Project* (pp. 129–34). Belgrade: OMEP.

Bauman, R. (1982). "Ethnography of children's folklore." In P. Gilmore & A. A. Glatthorn (Eds.), *Children in and out of school: Ethnography and education* (pp. 172–86). Washington D.C.: Center for Applied Linguistics and Harcourt Brace Jovanovich.

Beresin, A. R. (1999). "Double Dutch and double cameras: Studying the transmission of culture in an urban schoolyard." In B. Sutton-Smith, J. Mechling, T. W. Johnson, & F. McMahon (Eds.), *Children's folklore: A source book* (pp. 75–91). Logan, Utah: Utah State University Press.

Bishop, J. C., & Curtis, M. (2001). *Play today in the primary school playground.* Ballmoor, Buckingham: Open University Press.

——— (2006). "Participation, popular culture and playgrounds: Children's uses of media elements in peer play at school." Paper presented at "Childhood and Youth: Participation and Choice" conference, University of Sheffield.

Bjørkvold, J. (1992). *The muse within: Creativity and communication, song and play from childhood through maturity.* Trans. W. H. Halverson. New York: HarperCollins (originally published 1989).

Blacking, J. (1973). *How musical is man?* Seattle: University of Washington Press.

——— (1985). "Versus gradus novos ad parnassum musicum: exemplum Africanum." In *Becoming human through music: The Wesleyan Symposium on the Perspectives of Social Anthropology in the Teaching and Learning of Music* (pp. 43–52). Reston, Va.: Music Educators National Conference.

——— (1995). *Venda children's songs: A study in ethnomusicological analysis.* Chicago: University of Chicago Press (originally published 1967).

Borstad, J. L. (1990). "But I've been pouring sounds all day: An ethnographic study of music composition by young children." Unpublished master's thesis, Queen's University, Kingston, Ontario.

Boztepe, E. (n.d.). "Issues in code-switching: competing theories and models." Accessed on 30 October 2005. www.tc.columbia.edu/academic/tesol/Webjournal/Boztepe.pdf.

Brady, M. (1975). "This little lady's gonna boogaloo: Elements of socialization in the play of black girls." In R. Bauman (Ed.), *Black girls at play: Perspectives on child development* (pp. 1–51). Austin, Texas: Southwest Educational Development Laboratory.

Brady, M. K. (1974). "Gonna shimmy shimmy 'til the sun goes down: Aspects of verbal and nonverbal socialization in the play of black girls." *Folklore Annual,* 1–16.

Brailoiu, C. (1954). "The children's rhythm—liminal notions." In *Les Colloques de Wegmont* (pp. 1–21). Brussels: International d'Etude Ethnomusicolique.

Bredekamp, S. (1987). *Developmentally appropriate practice in early childhood programs serving children from birth through age 8.* Washington: NAEYC.

Bridges, D. (1992). "Integrity, integration, and eclecticism in the early stages of a developmental music program." In M. Comte (Ed.), *Doreen Bridges: Music educator* (pp. 118–22). Parkville, Victoria: Australian Society for Music Education (originally published 1984).

———— (1994). *Music, young children and you.* Sydney: Hale and Iremonger.

Bronson, B. H. (1950). "Some observations about melodic variation in British-American folk tunes." *Journal of the American Musicological Society 3*(2), 120–34.

Brunton, M. (1976). "The usage of musical patterns by primary school children." (Unpublished master's thesis, University of Adelaide.)

Burnard, P. (1999). "Bodily intention in children's improvisation and composition." *Psychology of Music 27,* 159–74.

Burnard, P. (2002). "Investigating children's meaning-making and the emergence of musical interaction in group improvisation." *British Journal of Music Education 19(2),* 157–72.

Burnard, P. (2006). "The individual and social worlds of children's musical creativity." In G. E. McPherson (Ed.), *The child as musician: A handbook of musical development* (pp. 353–74). New York: Oxford University Press.

Campbell, P. S. (1991). "The child-song genre: A comparison of songs by and for children." *International Journal of Music Education 17,* 14–23.

———— (1998). *Songs in their heads: Music and its meaning in children's lives.* New York: Oxford University Press.

Campbell, P. S., & Scott-Kassner, C. (1995). *Music in childhood.* New York: Schirmer.

Campbell, P. S., McCullough-Brabson, E., & Tucker, J. C. (1994). *Roots and branches: A legacy of multicultural music for children.* Danbury, Conn.: World Music Press.

Carder, P. (Ed.) (1990). *The eclectic curriculum in American music education,* rev. ed. Reston, Va.: Music Educators National Conference.

Choksy, L. (1981). *The Kodály context.* Englewood Cliffs, N. J.: Prentice-Hall.

Choksy, L., Abramson, R. M., Gillespie, A. E., & Woods, D. (1986). *Teaching music in the twentieth century.* Englewood Cliffs, N. J.: Prentice-Hall.

Christensen, C.B. (1992). "Music composition, invented notation and reflection: Tools for music learning and assessment." Unpublished doctoral dissertation, Rutgers University, New Brunswick, N.J..

Clifford, J. (1986). Introduction. In J. Clifford & G.E. Marcus (Eds.), *Writing culture: The poetics and politics of ethnography* (pp. 1–26). Berkeley and Los Angeles: University of California Press.

Clunies Ross, M., & Wild, S. A. (1984). "Formal performance: the relations of music, text and dance in Arnhem Land clan songs." *Ethnomusicology 28,* 209–35.

Coffin, T. P. (1977). "A description of variation in the traditional ballad of America." In

T. P. Coffin (Ed.), *The British traditional ballad in North America*, rev. ed. Austin: University of Texas Press.

Cohen, L., Manion, L., & Morrison, K. (2000). *Research methods in education*, 5th ed. London: Routledge Falmer.

Coleman, S. N. (1922). *Creative music for children*. New York: Knickerbocker Press.

Collins, J. (1991). *Migrant hands in a distant land*, 2nd ed. Leichhardt, NSW: Pluto Press.

Comenius 3 Network (2002). The profile for country: Norway. *MIR: Migration and Intercultural Relations, Comenius 3 network – 101605-CP-1-2002-1-NO-Comenius-C3.* Accessed 29 March 2006. http://www.migrationhistory.com/comenius.index.php?section=countries&id=1.

Commission for Racial Equality (2002). *A place for us all: Learning from Bradford, Oldham and Burnley.* London: Commission for Racial Equality.

Cooke, J. A. (1980). "Children's rhymes, songs and singing games in Birdsedge, West Yorkshire." Unpublished bachelor's dissertation, Institute of Dialect and Folklore Studies, University of Leeds.

Coplan, D. B. (1993). "Ethnomusicology and the meaning of tradition." In S. Blum, P. V. Bohlman, & D. M. Neuman (Eds.), *Ethnomusicology and modern music history* (pp. 35–48). Urbana: University of Illinois Press.

Corbett, P., MacLean, C., & MacLean, M. (1993). *Clapping rhymes and ball-bouncing games.* London: Kingfisher Books.

Cox, G. (2006). "Historical perspectives." In G. McPherson (Ed.), *The Child as Musician: A handbook of musical development* (pp. 397–413). Oxford: Oxford University Press.

Cruickshank, K. (1991). "A study on the playground lore of bilingual children." Unpublished master's thesis, University of Sydney, Sydney.

Crystal, D. (1987). *The Cambridge encyclopedia of language.* Cambridge: Cambridge University Press.

Curtis, M. (2000). "Zig Zag Zoo and other games: The oral tradition of children of Asian origin in Keighley, West Yorkshire." *Folklife, the Journal of Folk Life Studies 38*, 71–82.

Davey, L. (1982). *Children's play: A source of natural learning materials for music education.* Unpublished research project, NSW State Conservatorium of Music, Sydney.

Davidson, L. (1990). "Tools and environments for musical creativity." *Music Educators Journal 76*(9), 38–51.

Davies, C. (1986). "Say it till a song comes (reflections on songs invented by children 3–13)." *British Journal of Music Education 3*(3), 279–93.

———(1994). "The listening teacher: An approach to the collection and study of invented songs of children aged 5 to 7." In H. Lees (Ed.), *Musical connections: Tradition and change. Proceedings of the 21st World Conference of the International Society for Music Education* (pp. 120–28). Tampa, Fla.: ISME.

Delamont, S. (1992). *Fieldwork in educational settings: Methods, pitfalls and perspectives.* London: The Falmer Press.

DeLorenzo, L. C. (1989). "A field study of sixth-grade students' creative music problem-solving processes." *Journal of Research in Music Education 37*(3), 188–200.

Doekes, E. (1992a). "Music and movement in the children-streetculture (1)," *De Pyramide 46*(3), 46–48.

———— (1992b). "Music and movement in the children-streetculture (2)," *De Pyramide 46*(5), 94–98.

———— (1992c). "Music and movement in the children-streetculture (3)," *De Pyramide 46*(6), 118–23.

Doekes, E., & van Doorn-Last, F. (1993). "Music and movement in the children-street-culture (4)," *De Pyramide 47*(1), 11–12.

Dowling, W. J. (1988). "Tonal structure and children's early learning of music." In J. Sloboda (Ed.), *Generative processes in music*. Oxford: Clarendon Press.

Durkin, P., & Ferguson, V. (1990). *You beaut, juicy fruit!* Melbourne: Oxford University Press.

Eckhardt, R. (1975). "From handclap to line play." In R. Bauman (Ed.), *Black girls at play: Perspectives on child development* (pp. 57–99). Austin, Texas: Southwest Educational Development Laboratory.

Edwards, V., & Sienkewicz, T. J. (1990). *Oral cultures past and present: Rappin' and Homer*. Oxford: Basil Blackwell.

Eickelkamp, U. 2008. "'I don't talk story like that.' On the social meaning of children's sand stories at Ernabella." In J. Simpson & G. Wigglesworth (Eds.), *Children's Language and Multilingualism: Indigenous Language Use at Home and School*. London: Continuum International Press.

Ellingson, T. (1992). "Transcription." In H. Myers (Ed.), *Ethnomusicology: An introduction* (pp. 110–52). London: Macmillan.

Ellis, C. (1985). *Aboriginal music: Education for living*. St Lucia: University of Queensland Press.

Factor, J. (1980). "A forgotten pioneer: Dorothy Howard." *Educational Magazine 37*(6), 22–24.

———— (1983). *Far out, brussel sprout!* Melbourne: Oxford University Press.

———— (1984). "Drop dead, pizza head!: Racism in children's culture." *Meanjin 43*(3).

———— (1985). *All right, Vegemite*. Melbourne: Oxford University Press.

———— (1986a). *Unreal, banana peel!* Melbourne: Oxford University Press.

———— (1986b). *Children's folklore in Australia: An annotated bibliography*. Kew, Victoria: Australian Children's Folklore Publications.

———— (1988). *Captain cook chased a chook: Children's folklore in Australia*. Ringwood, Victoria: Penguin.

———— (2001). "Three myths about children's folklore." In J. C. Bishop & M. Curtis (Eds.), *Play today in the primary school playground: Life learning and creativity*. Ballmoor, Buckingham: Open University Press.

Factor, J., & Marshall, A. (1992). *Roll over Pavlova!* Rydalmere, NSW: Hodder and Stoughton.

Farkas, A. (1990). "Can Kodály help my teaching?" In P. Carder (Ed.), *The eclectic curriculum in American music education* (rev. ed.) (pp. 103–06). Reston, Va.: Music Educators National Conference.

Feld, S. (1986). "Orality and consciousness." In Y. Tokumaru & O. Yamaguti (Eds.), *The oral and the literate in music* (pp. 18–28). Tokyo: Academia Music.

———— (1994a). "Notes on 'World Beat.'" In C. Keil & S. Feld (Eds.), *Music grooves* (pp. 238–46). Chicago: University of Chicago Press.

———— (1994b). "From schizophonia to schismogenesis: On the discourses and commodification practices of 'World Music' and 'World Beat.'" In C. Keil & S. Feld (Eds.), *Music grooves* (pp. 257–89). Chicago: University of Chicago Press.

Fine, G. A. (1999). "Methodological problems of collecting folklore from children." In B. Sutton-Smith, J. Mechling, T. W. Johnson, & F. McMahon (Eds.), *Children's folklore: A source book* (pp. 121–39). Logan, Utah: Utah State University Press.

Finnegan, R. (1986). "The relation between composition and performance: three alternative modes." In Y. Tokumaru & O. Yamaguti (Eds.) *The oral and literate in music* (pp. 73–87). Tokyo: Academia Music.

Finnegan, R. (1992). "Oral poetry." In R. Bauman (Ed.), *Folklore, cultural performances, and popular entertainments* (pp. 119–27). New York: Oxford University Press.

Foley, J. M. (1995). *The singer of tales in performance*. Bloomington: Indiana University Press.

Folkestad, G. (1998). "Musical learning as cultural practices as exemplified in computer-based creative music-making." In B. Sundin, G. E. McPherson, & G. Folkestad (Eds.), *Children composing* (pp. 97–134). Malmö: Lund University.

Fujita, F. (1989). *Problems of language, culture and the appropriateness of musical expression in Japanese children's performance* (Ph.D dissertation, Queen's University, Belfast). Tokyo: Academia Music.

Fulton, E., & Smith, P. (1978). *Let's slice the ice*. St Louis: Magnamusic-Baton.

Galton, M., & Delamont, S. (1985). "Speaking with forked tongue? Two styles of observation in the ORACLE Project." In R. G. Burgess (Ed.), *Field methods in the study of education* (pp. 163–89). Barcombe, Sussex: The Falmer Press.

Gardner, H. (1993). *Multiple intelligences: The theory in practice*. New York: BasicBooks.

Gaunt, K. D. (1997). "The games black girls play: Music, body, and 'soul'" (Doctoral dissertation, University of Michigan, 1997). *Dissertation Abstracts International*, 9721980.

Gaunt, K. D. (2006). *The games black girls play: Learning the ropes from Double-Dutch to hip-hop*. New York: New York University Press.

Glover, J. (2000). *Children composing 4–14*. London: RoutledgeFalmer.

Gomme, A. B. (1964). *The traditional games of England, Scotland, and Ireland*, Vols. 1 and 2. New York: Dover (originally published 1894)

Grugeon, E. (1988). "Underground knowledge: What the Opies missed." *English in Education* 22(2), 9–17.

———— (1993). "Gender implications of children's playground culture." In P. Woods & M. Hammersley (Eds.), *Gender and ethnicity in schools*. Buckingham: Open University Press.

———— (2000). "Girls' playground language and lore: what sort of texts are these?" In E. Bearne & V. Watson (Eds.), *Where texts and children meet*. London: Routledge.

———— (2001). "'We like singing the Spice Girl songs and we like Tig and Stuck in the Mud': Girls' traditional games on two playgrounds." In J. C Bishop & M. Curtis

(Eds.), *Play today in the primary school playground* (pp. 98–114). Ballmoor, Bucking-ham: Open University Press.

———— (2005). "Listening to learning outside the classroom: Student teachers study playground literacies." *Literacy* (April), 3–9.

Haagen, C. (1994). *Bush toys: Aboriginal children at play.* Canberra: Aboriginal Studies Press.

Hall, G.S. (1920). *Youth.* New York: D. Appleton.

Hall, H. (1984). "A study of the relationship between speech and song in the playground rhymes of primary school children." Unpublished doctoral dissertation, Monash University, Melbourne.

Hammersley, M., & Atkinson, P. (1995). *Ethnography: Principles in practice* (2nd ed.). London: Routledge.

Harwood, E. (1987). "The memorized song repertoire of children in Grades 4 and 5 in Champaign, Illinois." Unpublished doctoral dissertation, University of Illinois, Cham-paign Urbana.

Harwood, E. (1992). "Girls' handclapping games: A study in oral transmission." *Bulletin of the International Kodály Society* *17*(1), 19–25.

———— (1993a). "Content and context in children's playground songs." *Update* (Fall/Winter), 4–8.

———— (1993b). "A study of apprenticeship learning in music." *General Music Today* *6*(3), 4–8.

———— (1994a). "Stalking the wildflower with multiple lenses. Exhibit One: Playground and chant research." *The Orff Echo* (Spring), 13–25.

———— (1994b). "Miss Lucy meets Dr Pepper: Mass media and children's traditional playground song and chant." In H. Lees (Ed.) *Musical connections: Tradition and change.* Proceedings of the 21st World Conference of the International Society for Music Education, Tampa, Florida, pp. 187–94.

———— (1996). "Listening to learn." *The Orff Echo* (Fall), 18–20.

———— (1998a). "Music learning in context: A playground tale." *Research Studies in Music Education* *11*, 52–60.

———— (1998b). "Go on girl! Improvisation in African-American girls' singing games." In B. Nettl & M. Russell (Eds.), *In the course of performance: Studies in the world of musical improvisation* (pp. 113–25). Chicago: University of Chicago Press.

Herzog, G. (1947). "Some primitive layers in European folk music." *Bulletin of the Amer-ican Musicological Society* *10/11*, 11–14.

Hickey, M. (Ed.) (2003). "Creative thinking in the context of music composition." In M. Hickey (Ed.), *Why and how to teach music composition: A new horizon for music ed-ucation* (pp. 31–53). Reston, Va.: Music Educators National Conference.

Hochschule für Musik und Darstellende Kunst Mozarteum in Salzburg (1972). *10 Jahre Orff-Institut: eine Dokumentation.* Salzburg: Hochschule für Musik.

Hoermann, D., & Bridges, D. (1987). "A developmental music program: Stage two." *Teacher's Manual* (rev. ed.). Brookvale, NSW: Educational Supplies.

Høibo, R., & Tjeltveit, N. (1992). *Kulturhistorisk vegbok Ryfylkevegen.* (*A historical and cul-tural guide through Ryfylke*) (English trans. B. & R. Vinsen). Sand: Ryfylke Museum.

Howard, D. (1955). "Folklore of Australian children." *Journal of Education* *2*(1), 30–35.

Howard, D. (1976a). "Ball bouncing customs and rhymes in Australia." In B. Sutton-Smith (Ed.), *A children's games anthology: Studies in folklore and anthropology.* New York: Arno Press. [Reprinted from *Midwest Folklore 9*(2), 77–87 (1959).]

Howard, D. (1976b). "Marble games of Australian children." In B. Sutton-Smith (Ed.), *A children's games anthology: Studies in folklore and anthropology.* New York: Arno Press. [Reprinted from *Folklore 71*, 165–79 (1960).]

Hughes, L. A. (1999). "Children's games and gaming." In B. Sutton-Smith, J. Mechling, T. W. Johnson, & F. McMahon (Eds.), *Children's folklore: A source book* (pp. 3–9). Logan, Utah: Utah State University Press.

Information Technology Directorate (1994). *In brief: Midyear Census 1994.* Sydney: Department of School Education.

Isenberg, J. P., & Jalongo, M. R. (1993). *Creative expression and play in the early childhood curriculum.* New York: Merrill.

Jones, B., & Hawes, B. L. (1987). *Step it down. Games, plays, songs & stories from the Afro-American heritage.* Athens, Georgia: University of Georgia Press (originally published 1972).

Kaeppler, A. (1972). "Method and theory in analysing dance structure with an analysis of Tongan Dance." *Ethnomusicology 16*(2), 173–217.

Kanellopoulos, P. A. (1999). "Children's conception and practice of musical improvisation." *Psychology of Music 27*, 175–91.

Kartomi, M. (1980). "Childlikeness in play songs—A case study among the Pitjantjara at Yalata, South Australia." *Miscellanea Musicologica 11*, 172–214.

———(1981). "Songs of some Aboriginal Australian children's play ceremonies." *Studies in Music 15*, 1–35.

Kaschub, M. (1997). "A comparison of two composer-guided large group composition projects." *Research Studies in Music Education 8*, 15–28.

Keetman, G. (1974). *Elementaria.* Trans. M. Murray. London: Schott.

Keller, W. (1970). "What is the Orff-Schulwerk—and what is not!" *Musart 22*(5).

Kenny, M. (1975). *Circle round the zero.* St. Louis: Magnamusic-Baton.

Kim, Y-Y. (1998). "Traditional Korean children's songs: Collection, analysis and application." Unpublished doctoral dissertation, University of Washington, Seattle.

Knapp, M., & Knapp, H. (1976). *One potato, two potato . . . : The folklore of American children.* New York: W.W. Norton.

Kratus, J. (1989). "A time analysis of the compositional processes used by children ages 7 to 11." *Journal of Research in Music Education 37*(1), 5–20.

——— (1991). "Growing with improvisation." *Music Educators Journal 78*(4), 35–40.

——— (1994). "The ways children compose." In H. Lees (Ed.) *Musical connections: Tradition and change. Proceedings of the 21st World Conference of the International Society for Music Education* (pp. 128–41). Tampa, Fla.: ISME.

Kraus, E. (1990). "Zoltan Kodály's legacy to music education." In P. Carder (Ed.), *The eclectic curriculum in American music education* (rev. ed.) (pp. 79–92). Reston, Va.: Music Educators National Conference. (Reprinted from *International Music Educator*, Fall 1967.)

Landis, B., & Carder, P. (1990). "The Kodály approach." In P. Carder (Ed.), *The eclectic curriculum in American music education* (rev. ed.) (pp. 55–74). Reston, Va.: Music Educators National Conference.

Landis, B., & Carder, P. (Eds.)(1972). *The eclectic curriculum in American music education: Contributions of Dalcroze, Kodály and Orff.* Washington: Music Educators National Conference.

Lave, J., & Wenger, E. (1991). *Situated learning: Legitimate peripheral participation.* Cambridge: Cambridge University Press.

Lea, John P. (1989). "Government and the community in Tennant Creek 1947–78." Monograph of the North Australia Research Unit. Casuarina, NT: Australian National University.

Lindsay, P. L., & Palmer, D. (1981). *Playground game characteristics of Brisbane primary school children* (ERDC Report No. 28). Canberra: Australian Government Publishing Service.

List, G. (1963). "The boundaries of speech and song." *Ethnomusicology 7,* 1–16.

Loane, B. (1984). "Thinking about children's compositions." *British Journal of Music Education 1*(3), 205–31.

Lord, A. B. (1960). *The singer of tales.* Cambridge, Mass.: Harvard University Press.

———— (1995). *The singer resumes the tale.* Ithaca, N.Y.: Cornell University Press.

MacDonald, R. A. R., & Miell, D. (2000). "Creativity and music education: The impact of social variables." *International Journal of Music Education 36,* 58–68.

Malone, J. (1996). *Steppin' on the Blues: The visible rhythms of African American dance.* Urbana: University of Illinois Press.

Marsh, K. (1974). "The origin and development of Orff-Schulwerk and its application in Australian schools." Unpublished bachelor's honours thesis, University of Sydney, Sydney.

————(1988). *Teaching music K–6: A multicultural perspective.* Sydney: NSW Department of School Education.

———— (1995). "Children's singing games: Composition in the playground?" *Research Studies in Music Education 4,* 2–11.

———— (1997). "Variation and transmission processes in children's singing games in an Australian playground." Unpublished doctoral thesis, University of Sydney, Sydney.

———— (1999). "Mediated orality: The role of popular music in the changing tradition of children's musical play." *Research Studies in Music Education 13,* 2–12.

———— (2001). "It's not all black or white: The influence of the media, the classroom and immigrant groups on children's playground singing games." In J. C Bishop & M. Curtis (Eds.), *Play today in the primary school playground* (pp. 80–97). Ballmoor, Buckingham: Open University Press.

———— (2003). "Across virtualities and realities: The role of audiovisual media in song acquisition and preservation in outback Australia." In E. Olsen (Ed.), *Samspel: Proceedings of the 25th Biennial World Conference of the International Society for Music Education,* Bergen, Norway, 11–16 August 2002. Bergen, Norway: Media Centre, Bergen University College.

———— (2006). "Cycles of appropriation in children's musical play: Orality in the age of reproduction." *The World of Music 48*(1), 8–23.

Martin, A. M. (1995). *Baby-sitters little sister jump rope rhymes.* New York: Scholastic.

McAllester, D.P. (1966). "Teaching the music teacher to use the music of his own culture." International Seminar on Teacher Education, Ann Arbor, August 1966.

McDonald, D. T., & Simons, G. M. (1989). *Musical growth and development: Birth through six.* New York: Schirmer.

McDowell, J. H. (1999). "The transmission of children's folklore." In B. Sutton-Smith, J. Mechling, T. W. Johnson, & F. McMahon (Eds.), *Children's folklore: A source book* (pp. 49–62). Logan, Utah: Utah State University Press.

McIntosh, J. A. (2006). "Moving through tradition: Children's practice and performance of dance, music and song in South-Central Bali." Unpublished doctoral dissertation, Queen's University, Belfast.

McMillan, D. J. (1964). "A survey of theories concerning the oral transmission of the traditional ballad." *Southern Folklore Quarterly 28,* 299–309.

Merrill-Mirsky, C. (1988). "Eeny meeny pepsadeeny: Ethnicity and gender in children's musical play." Unpublished doctoral dissertation, University of California, Los Angeles.

Michel, P. (1976). "The need for close interdisciplinary co-operation between music education and psychology." In *Challenges in music education: Proceedings of the XI International Conference of the International Society for Music Education* (pp. 98–105). Perth: International Society for Music Education, 1974.

Milroy, L., & Muysken, P. (1995). *One speaker two languages: Cross-disciplinary perspectives on code-switching.* New York: Cambridge University Press.

Mitchell, C., & Reid-Walsh, J. (2002). *Researching children's popular culture: The cultural spaces of childhood.* London: Routledge.

Nash, D. (1984). "The Warumungu's reserves 1892–1962: A case study in dispossession." *Australian Aboriginal Studies* 1984(1), 2–16.

Nettl, B. (1956). "Infant musical development and primitive music." *Southwestern Journal of Anthropology, 12*(1), 87–91.

——— (1992). "Recent directions in ethnomusicology." In H. Myers (Ed.) *Ethnomusicology: An introduction* (pp. 375–97). London: Macmillan.

Newell, W. W. (1963). *Games and songs of American children.* New York: Dover (originally published 1883).

Niles, J. D. (1999). *Homo narrans: The poetics and anthropology of oral literature.* Philadelphia: University of Pennsylvania Press.

Nyomi, S. (2001). "Heritage: The viewpoint of an African committed to intercultural exchanges." *International Journal of Music Education 37,* 64–66.

Ong, W. (1982). *Orality and literacy: The technologizing of the word.* London: Methuen.

Opie, I., & Opie, P. (1977). *The lore and language of schoolchildren.* Oxford: Oxford University Press

——— (1979). *Children's games in street and playground.* Oxford: Oxford University Press.

——— (1988). *The singing game.* Oxford: Oxford University Press (originally published 1985).

Opie, I. (1994). *The people in the playground.* Oxford: Oxford University Press.

Orff, C. (1990). "The Schulwerk—its origins and aims." In P. Carder (Ed.), *The eclectic curriculum in American music education* (rev. ed.) (pp. 137–44). Reston, Va.: Music Educators National Conference. (Reprinted from *Music Educators Journal* April/ May 1963.).

Orff, C., & Keetman, G. (n.d.). *Music for children.* English version adapted by M. Murray. Vols. 1–5. Mainz & London: Schott.

Paynter, J. (1972). *Hear and now.* London: Universal Edition.

———— (1978a). "The arts in school and society." *Schools Council Project: Music in the secondary school curriculum, Discussion Paper 3.* York: Schools Council.

———— (1978b). "The content of the school music curriculum." *Schools Council Project: Music in the secondary school curriculum, Discussion Paper 4.* York: Schools Council.

Paynter, J., & Aston, P. (1970). *Sound and silence.* Cambridge: Cambridge University Press.

Perkins, K., & Russell, H. (1993). "Let's play it again: Children participate in the redesign of their primary school play environment." In *Environments for play: Proceedings of the World Play Summit,* IPA and International Toy Library Association, Melbourne.

Phillips, K. H. (1992). "Research on the teaching of singing." In R. Colwell (Ed.), *Handbook of research on music teaching and learning* (pp. 568–76). New York: Schirmer.

Pond, D. (1992). "The young child's playful world of sound." In B. L Andress & L. M. Miller (Eds.), *Readings in early childhood music education* (pp. 39–42). Reston, Va.: Music Educators National Conference.

Pressing, J. (1988). "Improvisation: methods and models." In J. Sloboda (Ed.), *Generative processes in music.* Oxford: Clarendon Press.

Prim, F. M. (1989). "The importance of girls' singing games in music and motor education." *Canadian Journal of Research in Music Education 32,* 115–23.

Randel, D. M. (Ed.) (1986). *The new Harvard dictionary of music.* Cambridge, Mass.: Harvard University Press.

Regner, H. (Ed.) (1977–82). *Music for children: Orff-Schulwerk, American ed.* (Vols. 1–3). London: Schott.

Reyes Schramm, A. (1982). "Explorations in urban ethnomusicology: Hard lessons from the spectacularly ordinary." *Yearbook for Traditional Music 14,* 1–13.

Rice, T. (1994). *May it fill your soul: Experiencing Bulgarian music.* Chicago: University of Chicago Press.

Riddell, C. (1990). "Traditional singing games of elementary school children in Los Angeles." Unpublished doctoral dissertation, University of California, Los Angeles.

Rogers, C. R. (1970). "Towards a theory of creativity." In P. E. Vernon (Ed.), *Creativity* (pp. 137–51). Harmondsworth, U.K.: Penguin (originally published 1954).

Romet, C. (1980). "The play rhymes of children—a cross cultural source of natural learning materials for music education." *Australian Journal of Music Education 27* (October), 27–31.

Royal Ministry of Education, Research and Church Affairs (1999). *The curriculum for the 10-year compulsory school in Norway.* Oslo: Royal Ministry of Education, Research and Church Affairs.

Rubin, D. C. (1995). *Memory in oral traditions: The cognitive psychology of epic, ballads, and counting-out rhymes.* Oxford: Oxford University Press.

Rubin, K. H. (1982). "Early play theories revisited: Contributions to contemporary research and theory." In D. H. Pepler & K. H. Rubin (Eds.), *The play of children: Current theory and research* (pp. 4–14), Contributions to Human Development Series. Basel: S. Karger.

Russell, H. (1984). "Descriptions of games at Debney Meadows". Unpublished field notes, Children's Folkore Collection, University of Melbourne Archives.

——— (1986). *Play and friendships in a multicultural playground.* Melbourne: Australian Children's Folklore publications.

——— (1990). *Toodaloo kangaroo.* Sydney: Hodder and Stoughton.

Rutkowski, J. (1996). "The nature of children's singing voices: characteristics and assessment." In S. C. Woodward (Ed.), *Universal and particular elements of early childhood music education,* Proceedings of the 7th International Seminar of the Early Childhood Commission of the International Society for Music Education. Winchester, U.K.: International Society for Music Education.

Schafer, R. M. (1965). *The composer in the classroom.* Don Mills, Ontario: BMI Canada.

——— (1967). *Ear cleaning.* Don Mills, Ontario: BMI Canada.

——— (1969). *The new soundscape.* Don Mills, Ontario: BMI Canada.

——— (1975). *The rhinoceros in the classroom.* Canada: Universal Edition.

Seeger, A. (1991). "Styles of musical ethnography." In B. Nettl & P. V. Bohlman (Eds.), *Comparative musicology and anthropology of music* (pp. 342–55). Chicago: University of Chicago Press.

Seeger, A., & Seeger, K. (2006). "Beyond the embers of the campfire: The ways of music at a residential summer children's camp." *The World of Music 48*(1), 33–65

Segler, H. (1992). *Tänze der Kinder in Europa.* Hannover: Moeck Verlag.

Serafine, M. L. (1988). *Music as cognition: The development of thought in sound.* New York: Columbia University Press.

Shelemay, K. K. (1997). "The ethnomusicologist, ethnographic method, and the transmission of tradition." In G. F. Barz & T. J. Cooley (Eds.) *Shadows in the field: New perspectives for fieldwork in ethnomusicology* (pp. 189–204). New York: Oxford University Press.

Singh, R. (1994). Introduction. In *Bradford Heritage Recording Unit, Here to stay: Bradford's South Asian communities.* Bradford: City of Bradford Metropolitan Arts, Museums and Libraries Division.

Sloboda, J. (1985). *The musical mind: The cognitive psychology of music.* Oxford: Oxford University Press.

"Springfield" Public School (1995a). English as a Second Language records (Unpublished data).

——— (1995b). "School profile." (Unpublished).

——— (n.d.). "Student welfare policy." (Unpublished).

Statistics Norway (2004). *Figures on Stavanger Municipality.* Accessed 29 March 2006. http://www.ssb.no/english/municipalities/hoyre_side.cgi?region=1103.

Stauffer, S. (2001). "Composing with computers: Meg makes music." *Bulletin of the Council for Research in Music Education* 150, 1–20.

——— (2002). "Connections between the musical and life experiences of young composers and their compositions." *Journal of Research in Music Education* 50(4), 301–22.

Stoeltje, B. (1978). *Children's handclaps: Informal learning in play.* Austin, Texas: Southwest Educational Development Laboratory.

Sundin, B. (1998). "Musical creativity in the first six years: A research project in retrospect." In B. Sundin, G. E. McPherson, & G. Folkestad (Eds.), *Children composing* (pp. 35–56). Malmö: Lund University.

Sutton-Smith, B. (1970). "Psychology of childlore: The triviality barrier." *Western Folklore 29*, 1–8.

——— (Ed.). (1972). *The folkgames of children.* Austin: University of Texas Press.

——— (Ed.). (1976). *A children's games anthology: Studies in folklore and anthropology.* New York: Arno Press.

——— (Ed). (1980). *Play and learning.* New York: Halstead.

——— (1982). "Play theory of the rich and for the poor." In P. Gilmore & A.A. Glatthorn (Eds.), *Children in and out of school: Ethnography and education* (pp. 187–205). Washington D.C.: Center for Applied Linguistics and Harcourt Brace Jovanovich.

Sutton-Smith, B., Mechling, J., Johnson, T. W., & McMahon, F. (Eds.) (1999). *Children's folklore: A source book.* Logan, Utah: Utah State University Press.

Sutton-Smith, B., & Rosenberg, B. G. (1972). "Sixty years of historical change in the game preferences of American children." In B. Sutton-Smith (Ed.), *The folkgames of children.* Austin: University of Texas Press.

Swanwick, K. (1988). *Music, mind, and education.* London: Routledge.

——— (1991). "Further research on the musical development sequence." *Psychology of Music 19*(1), 22–32.

——— (1996). "Theory, data and educational relevance." *Research Studies in Music Education 6*, 18–26.

Swanwick, K., & Tillman, J. (1986). "The sequence of musical development: A study of children's composition." *British Journal of Music Education 3*(3), 305–39.

Takhvar, M. (1988). "Play and theories of play: A review of the literature." *Early Child Development and Care 39*, 221–44.

Treitler, L. (1974). "Homer and Gregory: the transmission of epic poetry and plainchant." *Musical Quarterly 60*(3), 333–72.

——— (1986). "Orality and literacy in the music of the European Middle Ages." In Y. Tokumaru & O. Yamaguti (Eds.) *The oral and literate in music* (pp. 38–56). Tokyo: Academia Music.

Turner, I. (1969). *Cinderella dressed in yella.* Melbourne: Heinemann.

Turner, I., Factor, J., & Lowenstein, W. (1978). *Cinderella dressed in yella,* rev. ed. Melbourne: Heinemann.

——— (1982). *Cinderella dressed in yella,* 2nd ed. Melbourne: Heinemann.

Volk, T. M. (1996). "Satis Coleman's 'creative music.'" *Music Educators Journal 82*(6), 31–47.

Walderhaug, M., Moen, R. A., Nilsen, J., & Haga, P. (1987). *Folkemusikk frå Rogaland.* Oslo: Victor-Trykk.

Walsh, M., & Yallop, C. (1993). *Language and culture in Aboriginal Australia.* Canberra: Aboriginal Studies Press.

Warlpiri Media (2001). *Arrkantele [For Fun].* Kaytetye language resource.

Waterman, C. A. (1993). "*Juju* history: Toward a theory of sociomusical practice." In S. Blum, P. V. Bohlman, & D. M. Neuman (Eds.), *Ethnomusicology and modern music history* (pp. 49–67). Urbana: University of Illinois Press.

Webster, P. R. (1995). "Creativity, composition and computers: Connections for the new century." In H. Lee & M. Barrett (Eds.), *Honing the craft: Proceedings of the 10th National Conference of the Australian Society for Music Education* (pp. 22–33). Hobart: Artemis Publishing.

——— (2003). " 'What do you mean, make my music different?': Encouraging revision and extensions in children's music composition." In M. Hickey (Ed.), *Why and how to teach music composition: A new horizon for music education* (pp. 55–65). Reston, Va.: Music Educators National Conference.

Wiggins, J. H. (1994). "Children's strategies for solving compositional problems with peers." *Journal of Research in Music Education 42*(3), 232–52.

——— (1999). "The nature of shared musical understanding and its role in empowering independent musical thinking." *Bulletin of the Council for Research in Music Education 143,* 65–90.

——— (2001). *Teaching for musical understanding.* New York: McGraw-Hill.

——— (2003). "A frame for understanding children's compositional processes." In M. Hickey (Ed.) *Why and how to teach music composition: A new horizon for music education* (pp. 141–65). Reston, Va.: Music Educators National Conference.

Wood, D., Bruner, J. C., & Ross, G. (1976). "The role of tutoring in problem solving." *Journal of Child Psychology and Psychiatry 17,* 89–100.

Young, S. (2003). Time-space structuring in spontaneous play on educational percussion instruments among three- and four-year-olds. *British Journal of Music Education 20*(1), 45–59.

Zumwalt, R. L. (1999). "The complexity of children's folklore." In B. Sutton-Smith, J. Mechling, T. W. Johnson, & F. McMahon (Eds.), *Children's folklore: A source book* (pp. 22–47). Logan, Utah: Utah State University Press.

Discography

Hargreaves, T. (1990). *Toodaloo Kangaroo.* Brunswick Recordings, BR12.

Las Ketchup. (2002). *The Ketchup Song (Asereje).* Sony Music Entertainment (Australia), 673209.9.

Filmography

Big (1988). CBS Fox Video.

Jackson, M. (n.d.). *Dangerous: The short films.* Sony Music Video Enterprises, 49164 2.

INDEX

ethics
  ethnomusicology in, 60
  fieldwork methodology of musical play
    investigation and, 21
ethnic diversity, and transmission be-
    tween ethnic groups, 128–29
ethnic groups. *See also* interethnic trans-
    mission; transmission between
    ethnic groups
  social boundary crossing between,
    128–35
  transmission of playground singing
    games between, 128–35
ethnicity, in cultural idiosyncrasy of chil-
    dren's musical play, 290, 291–92
ethnography, 43
ethnomusicological conceptions of chil-
    dren's musical play, 15–18
  music education conceptions and, 6
ethnomusicological methodologies
  children's musical play and, 15
  music education practices and, 15
ethnomusicological studies of children's
    musical play
  change, stability and continuity in,
    17–18
  children's playlore and, 17–18, 20
  cultural analysis in, 17–18
  enculturation in, 18
  evolutionary developmental paradigm
    and, 15
  implications of, 22
  musical genres in, 17
  rhymes in, 16
  rhythm in, 15–16
  societal contextualization of, 17
  universals in, 17
  variations of children's musical play in,
    17
ethnomusicology
  child as primitive ideology and, 8
  ethics in, 60
  innovation in children's musical play
    and, 6

marginality in, 61
performance of children's musical play
    and, 6
transmission of children's musical play
    and, 5, 6
evolutionary developmental paradigm.
    See also child as primitive ideology
  children's music making and, 15
  ethnomusicological studies of children's
    musical play and, 15
  contemporary children's musical envi-
    ronment and, 12–13, 15
  music education practices and, 14–15
  music pedagogies and, 15

Factor, J., 18, 19, 20, 44, 48, 185, 186
Feld, S., 37, 48, 59
field collection practices
  philosophical/ethical/practical issues
    in, 21
  in studies of children's musical play, 21
field collection/techniques, and fieldwork
    methodology of musical play investi-
    gation, 21, 43, 46–51, 57–68
field notes, and fieldwork methodology of
    musical play investigation, 65, 67
field sites. *See also* Aboriginal field sites;
    Australian field sites; English field
    sites, game sites; fieldwork schools in
    children's musical play investigation;
    Korean field sites; Los Angeles field
    sites; Norwegian field sites; Seattle
    field sites
  fieldwork methodology of musical play
    investigation and, 51–53, 54*t*–55*t*,
    60–66
  index of playground singing game gen-
    res from international, 319,
    320*t*–338*t*
fieldwork methodology of children's mu-
    sical play investigation. *See also*
    philosophical issues of children's
    musical play investigation; studies of
    children's musical play

410

Riddell, C., vii, 5, 13, 18, 19, 51, 53, 65, 97, 106, 113, 119, 136, 228, 278, 305, 312
ring games, 106
  in cultural idiosyncrasy of children's musical play, 285–86, 384*n*1
  Eritrean, 285, 384*n*1
Rubin, D. C., 37, 282
Russell, H., 19, 158

"Saeukkang," 300
San ch'odung hakkyo, 99–101, 115. *See also* Korean fieldwork schools
sand stories, 279
"Sar Macka Dora" game genre, 3, 108, 193, 381*n*4
  analysis overview of, 22, 221-61
  at Birch Vale Elementary School, 222
  at Bysiden Skole, 222
  classroom influence on, 191
  cultural idiosyncrasy of children's musical play in, 292
  as elimination game, 138, 139, 221, 224
  at Ellington Primary School, 222
  friendship groups and, 223
  movement in, 221
  participants, 223
  performances of, 223
  performers classification system, 221, 383*n*1
  playground singing games analysis of, 309, 310
  popularity of, 222
  publication of, 222
  samples of, 222, 223*t*
  at Springfield PS, 221, 222–23
  teaching and learning in playground of, 138–39, 191
  at Telford Spring Primary School, 222
  text variants, 130–31, 221, 350*t*–352*t*
  transmission between ethnic groups and, 130–31, 381*n*4
  transmission between genders and, 119–20
  transmission in classroom, 222–23

  transmission of playground singing games, 222, 223
  transmission outside school, 223
  variation in playground singing games and, 220, 224
  versions of, 222–23
  widespread use of, 222
"Sar Macka Dora" genre at Birch Vale, 253, 254*t*
  Ellington Primary School and, 253
  melodic range in, 255, 257*t*
  melody in, 255, 257*t*, 258, 259*t*
  movement in, 258
  other forms of variation in, 258, 260
  performance range frequency in, 257*t*
  tessitura in, 255, 257*t*
  text in, 253, 254*t*, 255*f*, 256*t*, 257*t*
  text rhythm in, 254, 255*f*, 256*t*, 257*t*
  text variants in, 253, 254, 255, 256*t*
  tonal frequency in, 257
"Sar Macka Dora" genre at Bysiden
  melodic range in, 241*t*, 242*t*
  melody in, 241*t*, 242*t*, 243*t*, 244*t*, 384*n*6, 384*nn*8–9
  movement in, 238, 244–45
  other forms of variation in, 245
  participants in, 238
  performance range frequency in, 242*f*
  Springfield PS and, 238, 242, 245
  tessitura in, 241*t*, 242*t*
  text in, 238, 239*t*, 240*f*, 241
  text rhythm in, 238, 239*t*, 240*f*, 241
  tonal frequency/tonal shift in, 242–43, 384*n*6
"Sar Macka Dora" genre at St. Augustine's, 245, 246*t*
  "Down in the Jungle" and, 245
  Ellington Primary School and, 245, 246, 248, 251
  melodic range in, 249*t*, 250*t*
  melody in, 249–50, 251*t*, 384*n*10
  movement in, 245, 251, 252*t*, 253, 384*n*11
  other forms of variation in, 253

Printed in the USA/Agawam, MA
May 11, 2021

774458.163